Praise for
Don't Shoot the Ice Cream Man

"A pithy and readable account of some extraordinary experiences."
— George P. Shultz,
former U.S. Secretary of State, Treasury, and Labor

"James Waste's memoir is a fascinating read by a lone operator whose vital great service to our nation contrasts with those of us in uniform or civilian life. It includes close calls, history we missed, and personal insights into the Cold War era and the new nations formed after the breakup of the Soviet Union. Particularly interesting is the author's early visit to the Chernobyl disaster."
— Harold A. Hyde, Brigadier General, AUS (Retired)

"This is a well-written first-hand story of a private citizen recruited by the CIA to become an undercover observer as the Soviet Empire was unraveling. A 'must read' adventure story."
— J.G. Knapp, former Assistant Secretary, USAF (I&L)

"As a former commanding officer, I'm struck by what the author did on his own initiative and under great stress. Waste seems ideally suited for the loner-type assignments of CIA special operations— and he certainly knew what to do about his midlife crisis."
— F. Stuart Kuhn, Captain, USN (Retired)

"The author has chronicled the experiences of a patriot engaged in Cold War battles for our country. Rudyard Kipling wrote of 'The Great Game' that played out in Central Asia. James Waste has lived that game."
— Richard R. Pohli, Captain, USN (Retired)

DON'T SHOOT
THE ICE CREAM MAN

*A Cold War Spy in the
New World Disorder*

JAMES WASTE

RINGWALT PRESS

Ringwalt Press
Alta, California

This manuscript was reviewed by the CIA; that review does not constitute CIA authentication of information, nor does it imply CIA endorsement of the author's views.

Library of Congress Control Number: 2009909242
Waste, James.
Don't shoot the ice cream man: a cold war spy in the new world disorder / James Waste.

ISBN: 0-615-28343-8
ISBN-13: 9780615283432

Visit the author's website at www.jameswaste.com

To my sweet Marilyn, my Sno-flake...
you are the rays of my sunshine, the sparkle of my stars
you bring the flowers of my springtime and music to my soul
without your loving support I would have never found my way.

"Mr. Gorbachev, tear down this wall!"
– Ronald Reagan, June 12, 1987

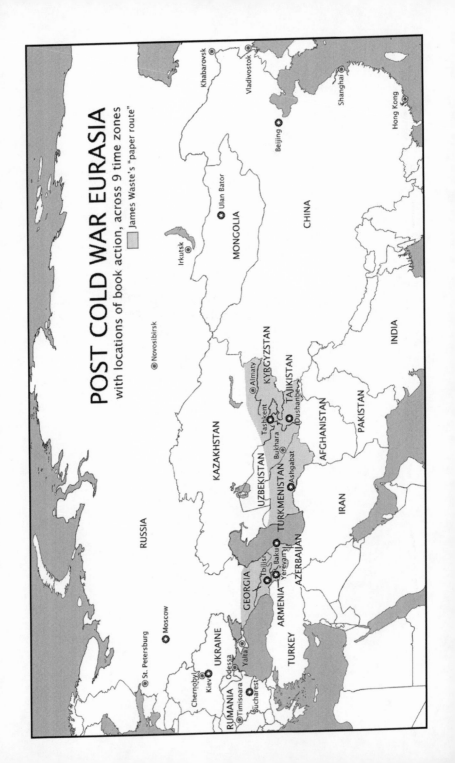

POST COLD WAR EURASIA
with locations of book action, across 9 time zones

☐ James Waste's "paper route"

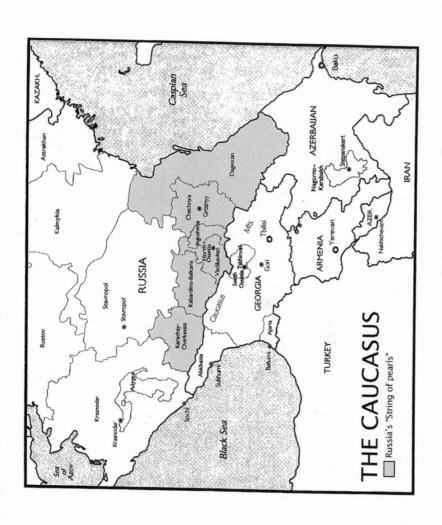

THE CAUCASUS

Russia's "String of pearls"

Contents

Introduction 1

Chapter 1: The Last Domino 3

Chapter 2: Or *Was* It Over? 6

Snapshot 1: The Greatest Generation 12

Chapter 3: Interperspective Corporation Is Born 16

Snapshot 2: Debriefing 29

Chapter 4: Evolution of a Spy 33

Snapshot 3: There Are No Coincidences 54

Chapter 5: The Job Begins to Define Itself 59

Chapter 6: Helena of Troy 67

Snapshot 4: The Rocky Silk Road 81

Chapter 7: Vigilante Justice 84

Chapter 8: Sink or Swim on the Afghan Border 93

Chapter 9: What Can I Tell My Children? 99

Snapshot 5: Nobody's Damned Business 107

Chapter 10: Light, Shadow, and Darkness 109

Chapter 11: Chernobyl 116

Chapter 12: California Dreamer 125

Snapshot 6: Passing the Baton 136

Chapter 13: Ancient Runners 140

Chapter 14: On Their Own 147

Chapter 15: Hot Caspian Night 151

Snapshot 7: The UPS Man   156
Chapter 16: Nagorno-Karabakh   160
Snapshot 8: Morning Run in Baku   168
Chapter 17: Spy in the New World Order   170
Chapter 18: Friends Are Where You Find Them   177
Chapter 19: Mirian   180
Snapshot 9: Illegal Procedure   187
Chapter 20: Bare Necessities   193
Chapter 21: What's in a Word?   200
Snapshot 10: Play It by Ear   206
Chapter 22: Seeking the Light   211
Chapter 23: "Skolka"   221
Snapshot 11: Lonely Are the Brave   226
Chapter 24: A Call to Arms   229
Snapshot 12: A Diamond in the Rough   240
Chapter 25: Paradise Lost   243
Chapter 26: Trick or Treat   254
Chapter 27: Don't Shoot the Ice Cream Man   263
Chapter 28: Uncivilized Behavior   272
Chapter 29: The Throwaway Republic   277
Snapshot 13: Muslim Creep   287
Chapter 30: Tribal Business   290
Chapter 31: Collateral Damage   296
Snapshot 14: String of Pearls   303
Chapter 32: On the Front of Over There   307
Snapshot 15: "Dr. Advil"   317
Chapter 33: Happy Days in Dutch Flat   320
Chapter 34: The Ultimate Betrayal   325
Chapter 35: Vladivostok and Ulan Bator   333
Chapter 36: Chechnya   345
Chapter 37: Business Administration 1B   351
Chapter 38: Alexander   365
Chapter 39: Networking   381
Snapshot 16: Scout's Honor   387

Chapter 40: The Third Man Theme   391

Chapter 41: Weaving Spiders   399

Snapshot 17: Many Wet Eyes   408

Chapter 42: Bohemian Knights   411

Chapter 43: End of an Era   416

Chapter 44: Rings on a Tree   427

Epilogue   432

Author's Note   436

Introduction

IN 1968, AFTER MORE than twenty years on the road, I left the world's biggest and best engineering and construction company. My wife and five children and I decided to settle in one place, Marin County, California, for the children's final school years.

My family had moved to Marin, across the Golden Gate Bridge and north of San Francisco, in 1941 when I was twelve. It was rural until the bridge replaced the ferryboats, and I loved the nine-mile school-bus ride to Mill Valley. There were no subdivisions in those days, but wetlands, marshes, and birds filled the view outside the school-bus window. We sang, joked, and played pranks as the bus stopped to pick up students at the dairy ranches, gas stations, and small villages along the route.

Marin was safe then, even though eleven million Americans were fighting World War II and ships for the war were being built nearby. The passion to enlist was tremendous. Six hundred former students at my school served and more than fifty died, leaving memories that shaped my thinking for the rest of my life. I was just a little too young to make those casualty lists, and later unable to serve in Korea, but this was my point of reference when my two oldest sons discussed dodging the Vietnam draft in the seventies. Sure, it was a bad war. Even so, I believed that we all must serve. When duty called, you had to go.

The debate continued over dinner for more than a year. I just couldn't grasp the fact that sons of mine did not understand their obligations. I was forty years old and the father of five, but finally, in total disgust, and, perhaps, with the help of a little alcohol, I laid it down—"If you guys won't go, I will!"

And, in a very real sense, I did. I entered the secret world of clandestine warfare that persists to this day. I couldn't tell my boys that, after a fashion, I had enlisted, but I felt that the family honor was preserved when I went into the intelligence business.

The Cold War is over now, but the world is being shredded by an epidemic of ancient nationalisms, religious extremism, and both old and new forms of terrorism. Scabs of feuds older than recorded time continue to plague us, and many of my countrymen still find it difficult to deal with other cultures from *their* perspective rather than our own. This attitude could end up destroying us all. The trick today is not so much to be able to look into the future, but to be able to look into the present and, with more than a little help from the past, realize that a war different from anything in our experience is all around us.

There is nothing cold about this war. It is a much more dangerous war than the Cold War. But, like the Cold War, it is a war in which, starting from my early childhood, I seemed destined to play a role.

I will reveal no secrets or hidden agendas as I tell my story, but it is my hope that this memoir will offer a glimpse into my long, silent journey though a lawless world darker than my own—a journey in search of my own redemption, through which I finally became one of the boys.

Chapter 1

The Last Domino
(Berlin)

IT WAS EARLY NOVEMBER 1989, and there was tremendous excitement in Eastern Europe and Central Asia. The diplomats had made 12,500 nuclear bombs obsolete—half theirs and half ours. The A-war was over. The "A" had stood for *"absurd."* I knew that history might well chronicle the twentieth century as the Century of Madmen. One bomb used by each side and there might not be a twenty-first. But the arms war (money war is better) had gone right down to the wire with the two Ks—Kennedy and Khrushchev—playing chicken over Cuba. Sanity ultimately prevailed, and the world was saved for that moment. It seemed that God still had things for the inhabitants of planet Earth to do.

On the night of November 9, 1989, Berlin was at the epicenter of communism's final convulsions in the West. The end was near. Reagan had commanded, "Tear down this wall!" and what he had described as the "Evil Empire" fell with the Berlin Wall.

The people in the street understood it. The reality that East Germany would once again be free was beginning to sink in and was being expressed all over the Free World. It was most dramatic at the tumbling Wall near the Brandenburg Gate. Visitors were being allowed to pass through Checkpoint Charlie.

Suddenly we could *see* the stark problems of the East and how obscenely they contrasted with vibrant West Berlin.

People poured into the east and the party was on with a vengeance. The joy was visceral, multileveled, and multicolored. Bottled up anger was released. Eyes trained to observe, from every corner of the world, showed up seeking the surfacing of secrets from an era submerged in darkness and intrigue. Others turned up just to share the end of the old order and the beginning of something new. Hope was in the air.

I joined a mixed group of Western observers—journalists, State Department people, and lots of military in civilian clothes—at the Kempinski Hotel. After a very "wet" dinner, we decided to go down to the Wall. The streets were wild. Booze was flowing and, in the turbulence, people cheered and fought at the same time.

I was unknown to most of the other observers and a lot older than all of them. Six of us rode to the Plaza opposite Brandenburg Gate where thousands of revelers were shouting, parading, and singing as only Germans can do. Newly acquainted and English speaking, we found a vantage point on a raised stone and concrete platform about 150 yards back from the Wall to watch those who were tearing it down.

We could see their frenzied activity clearly. They seemed almost desperate. It was as if they felt that if they didn't hurry it would be too late. It looked like dangerous work to me, but hundreds of them were demonstrating vaunted German engineering ingenuity in destruction as well as construction. Great slabs were pulled down with small ropes. As each slab hit the ground, another panel would open in the wall and you could almost feel the melding of darkness and light.

After an hour or so of watching the bonfires and sweeping floodlights, one of the men started quietly sobbing. I thought it was because he'd had too much booze, but then he said, as if he had made a great discovery, "Hey, it's over, isn't it?"

The man next to him asked, loudly, *"What's* over, P. J.?"

The fellow they called P. J. said, softly, "The Cold War." He paused before adding, "It really was a war, wasn't it?"

Then it hit me. This guy was P. J. O'Rourke, the well-known journalist. I think my mouth dropped open at his question. But, unlike those who truly knew the reality of the Cold War, maybe he was like the tens of millions of others in the West for whom the Cold War had merely been some sort of myth, an endless charade played by phony politicians over territory and profits.

Nevertheless, in my mind, O'Rourke's revelation came at a "biblical" moment when the world was redefining life on this planet. The Cold War had been *forever* for so many. It had been an accepted part of our lives. It had been a given, something that might never go away. And, now it had—suddenly and, seemingly, completely.

It was over.

Chapter 2

Or Was It Over?
(Bukhara, Uzbekistan)

I HEARD EXPLOSIONS AND GUNFIRE and looked out my Bukhara hotel balcony window at 4,000 screaming people demonstrating in the central square—their screams punctuated by pistol shots, the occasional burst of an AK-47, and a ranting voice on a scratchy loudspeaker spewing out words of hate. The crowd swirled and swayed like waves on a beach. Great guttural sounds of pain—like none I had ever heard—numbed my ears. Battle smells rose up to my open window. I was stunned. The fact that the Berlin Wall had fallen earlier that year made no difference to these people.

I had had a peaceful rest in Finland before starting on another trip on what I called my "paper route," which ran through the Soviet republics of Central Asia and the Caucasus. I was always excited about visiting such exotic places as Tashkent, Almaty, Samarkand, Ashgabat, and Dushanbe, for this was the old Silk Road. This particular run brought me to Bukhara, Uzbekistan's fabled desert city of sanctuary and menace, a place that still spoke powerfully of the caravan and the bazaar. It had been the capital of a Persian empire filled with schools and a library of 45,000 books in the ninth century. Much of Bukhara's ancient charm and mystery remained despite long Russian and Soviet occupation which, although "over" on the surface, was still very much present. Even without communism, the centuries-old ambitions of the Russian Bear had not changed.

Suddenly, as I watched from my hotel window, tanks appeared. A new kind of gunfire erupted, no longer random but more systematic. Ranks of white-clothed men were being cut down by fully automatic machine guns concealed in the robes of the front rows of opposing factions. Blood began to spread crimson on the white stone plaza floor, reflecting the late afternoon sun. Bodies piled up. In less than five minutes, the mob stampeded out of the square, leaving a hundred or more dead bodies strewn all around, with hundreds more wounded. Smoke and tear gas filled the air while tanks chugged, rattled, and clanked in all directions. People ran and fell, screaming.

More than six hundred Russian Army soldiers followed the tanks, with fire trucks and a water cannon washing away the blood. I thought, *The Cold War may be ending, but Russia's ancient drive for empire continues.*

Unclaimed bodies were gathered together in a corner of the square. Women poured into the square from side streets looking in disbelief at the wounded and dead. The shrieking and wailing echoed off the stone surroundings as loved ones were found.

A satellite might have caught this if it had been looking *at that precise moment*, but, as I later learned, no satellite was looking. Washington knew nothing about it, and, in an hour, it was all cleaned up and swept away. To the world, it never happened. Except my eyes had seen it.

I had just turned away from viewing the carnage through my hotel window when a loud knock sounded on my door. Three hard-looking men in suits—they always seemed to appear in threes—entered. The sullen third man, who didn't talk, is the one you never let get behind you. They looked menacing as they announced that it was time for me to leave Bukhara. One of them, in a heavily accented glottal baritone, asked, "What have you seen?"

Knowing this was dangerous ground, I replied in English, "Not much. Just some demonstrations. A lot of noise. It's really none of my business."

The man with the baritone voice nodded his head up and down approvingly, saying, "Good. You saw not much. Now it is time for you to leave."

Who, I wondered, did they think I was? I'd just arrived and hadn't even had a chance to get out into the country. Before I knew it, I was being hustled down some back steps and into a battered black Lada four-door sedan. Several other police types in soiled gray suits smelling of urine and strange tobacco smoke joined them, and they all seemed relieved to be getting me out of their jurisdiction.

During the twenty-minute ride in a closed vehicle filled with cigarette smoke, I began to hyperventilate. What did they mean by "leave"? I wondered. Was it a Muslim way of saying "leave this world for a better one"? I always made a point of sitting in the back seat to avoid the possibility of having a garrote put around my neck, and on this occasion I felt it imperative to do so. I had jumped in the back seat before it became an issue. They exchanged surprised glances. A small victory, I thought.

When we got to the rundown airport, it was ten o'clock in the evening and already dark. With one exception, the eight other passengers waiting to board the old Soviet Antonov AN-2 (Colt) single-engine cargo biplane were nondescript.

The man in charge of my escorts—bald, like Yul Brynner—told the other passengers in Uzbek that I was inspecting Intourist hotels for my tour business. Seven of them nodded and grumbled a bit. The eighth said in English, "Hi, I'm Anya and, oh God, am I glad to see you, whoever you are." Whatever her Uzbek blood mix—she obviously had some—I detected New England and good schools in her voice.

We all boarded, and in minutes we rattled into the air, heading for Almaty, Kazakhstan. The girl and I had a shouted conversation in the back row of bucket seats, and she told me that she had grown up in the States and gone to Bennington College, a private girls' school in New York State, known for its left-wing sympathies. She was visiting her grandfather in Bukhara and was a witness to what happened in the square earlier that day. Although her grandfather was safe—they had been hiding in a car outside my hotel—she was severely shaken. Limp and drained though she was, she was still a very lovely woman with short black hair, black eyes, and alabaster skin. She was quite slim in her jeans and sports jacket.

She told me what she had seen made her question her earlier belief in what she thought were the "great injustices of America," before adding, "With all its faults, America doesn't just shoot people and leave them spread out all over the streets as a statement of authority." Then she began to sob, and put her head on my shoulder.

We talked off and on for several hours, our conversation punctuated by the throb of the plane's engines as it labored over low mountain ranges. She told me she had been a real Bennington radical, vocal in her hatred for America, with no appreciation of American ideals, and that she had organized demonstrations against everything. It was, she said, in part a rebellion against her Uzbek-Russian-American physician father and her old-line Connecticut socialite mother. I told her of my love of America and its ideals and how, even with its problems, America was still the best country in the world. Then we fell asleep together on a pile of musty cargo padding in the space behind the last row of bucket seats. Early the next morning we parted ways at the Almaty airport.

Some years later, I was in the Russian city of Sochi, on the Black Sea just north of the border with the Republic of Georgia, trying to get to Moscow from Georgia the hard way. I had waited six hours when, finally, an empty plane that was dead-heading to Moscow became available. I climbed aboard the Ilyushin IL-62.

Just before take-off, a very attractive, sophisticated-looking young woman got on. She was wearing a long black leather coat and jeans and carrying the usual professional-type shoulder bags. In the otherwise empty plane, she sat across the aisle and one row forward from me. Without a word, she opened a small bottle of cognac and offered me a drink. I was intrigued, but thought, *Oh well! It's only three hours to Moscow, and she reminds me of Demi Moore.*

As I faked sipping cognac directly from the bottle, she said, softly, "You don't remember me, do you? We once slept together."

Startled, my first reaction was to think, *This has to be some kind of setup!* What was this woman up to? She spoke excellent English, was remarkably good looking, and here we were on an empty—or was it empty?—Russian aircraft. Suspiciously, I finally responded, "Honey, if I ever slept with you, I can assure you I'd remember it."

She laughed, saying, "I didn't say we did anything other than sleep." Then she recalled the flight out of Bukhara, how I helped her that night just by listening, and how grateful she was for what she called my "steady American presence at that terrifying time." She told me that her whole thought structure had been shattered at the bloody plaza and how she thought she would fall apart. She now understood that she had been corrupted by the radical left and had emotionalized their political philosophy. Indeed, she had gotten high on the power of the bullhorn and the frenzy of the mob.

But that day with her grandfather in the Bukhara Plaza, she'd seen the ultimate extension of her bullhorn and it had changed her forever. She told me it enabled her to see America through different eyes and, without knowing it, I had given her a different way to go. She returned to the United States and, after getting a law degree from Columbia, was recruited by one of our intelligence agencies.

When I asked her if this meeting was a coincidence, she smiled as she replied, "*You* certainly know that nothing in this part of the world is ever a coincidence."

The Greatest Generation

WHEN I WAS FIVE OR SIX years old, I used to play with an old World War I army cap. I remember it was coarse wool and had a brown visor. There were some other things in a carton, but all I can remember now is the cap, a thick leather belt, and canvas leggings. From an early age, I played outdoors in neighborhood vacant spaces and in Berkeley's nearby Tilden Park. We played cops and robbers, cowboys and Indians, and, best of all, War and Capture the Flag.

One Christmas when I was nine, my Uncle Frank gave me a dozen toy lead soldiers made in Japan. I had seen them in a Woolworth's five-and-ten-cent store. They were World War I soldiers with metal helmets. I collected them into the hundreds. I played alone with them, setting up battle scenes and using books from my father's den to make forts. I was the commander of both armies. I fantasized many little vignettes.

My dad served several years in Texas during World War I but never got overseas. My favorite relative, Uncle Corby, was in the Horse Cavalry and made it to France. A longtime family friend, S. D. Bechtel, rode a motorcycle delivering dispatches along the front lines in France. They all did their duty.

When World War II started at Pearl Harbor, I was living in Los Angeles, where my father was involved in military shipbuilding. I guess a lot of smart people knew war was coming. A year later, my family moved to Marin County, California, where my father was general manager of a shipyard that built Liberty ships and fleet tankers, employing 20,000 people.

During the war, gasoline was rationed and so was sugar and coffee. Kids had to buy War Stamps and Bonds before they could attend noon dances, pep rallies, and other school functions. We had blackouts to protect shipping from being silhouetted along the coast. We grew victory gardens. Almost every Friday at assemblies, boys who had just volunteered to "join up" stood on stage waving goodbye. Sometimes only a few months later the announcement of another Gold Star Student would send shock waves through the hallways.

Thirteen million U.S. men and women were in uniform at the end. Five hundred thousand died, including fifty-seven from Tamalpais High School. The courage and sacrifices of those who fought in World War II are well known and celebrated by a grateful nation. Newsman Tom Brokaw perhaps summed it up best when he labeled the participants "The Greatest Generation." There was nothing like them before World War II and, despite a world full of rancor and conflict, there would be nothing like them again.

The courage and sacrifices of the Greatest Generation are common knowledge. What is not as well known is the damage to the social fabric caused by their absence.

Of course, not belittling the women who gave their lives or Rosie the Riveter who was unavailable on the home front for months at a time, every time a guy got killed overseas, a wife, a daughter, a son was left with the aftermath. Whole families were destroyed. Whether a GI returned or not, the children suffered greatly by not having a strong male role model and sometimes the wives couldn't wait. Juvenile delinquency soared, as did alcoholism and depression. Gangs, as we know them today, got a big boost. And then there were the more subtle costs. Many wanted to do their duty overseas but were forced to remain stateside, or did not make it into the service at all. There was always the insinuation they never really wanted to serve and the discrimination that went with it.

The draft age was lowered to eighteen in 1945. I was excited. I would finally be able to serve with my peers even if my parents didn't approve. My older brother Bill served three years in World War II and would later be recalled for one and a half years in Korea. But a couple of A-bombs abruptly ended the war. I didn't make it.

Nevertheless, I enrolled in UC Berkeley and took lower-division ROTC in order to get a commission. Later, not seeing the need, I opted out of upper-division ROTC. When the Korean War broke out, I applied for a direct commission in the Air Force based on my college major of Science and Engineering. Expecting to be in the service in June of 1951, I got married the previous December. Then, rather unexpectedly, my wife announced she was pregnant. A week later the draft law was changed. "Expectant fathers" were not wanted. People wiser than I advised me to "stay out of the war if at all possible." I turned down the commission and spent the next fifty years regretting it.

I had already dealt with the consequences of not serving in World War II. During my four years of college, I'd competed with returning GIs who were three or four years older, smarter, more mature, and who had more money than I because of the GI Bill. The ratio of men to women in college was reversed from wartime with four men for every woman. This was a big problem for an eighteen-year-old who looked fifteen. I barely made the football team because of the backlog of returning vets. But socially, at least, most people accepted that I didn't go because I wasn't old enough.

Korea was a different story. For years after the war when men would ask me what I did in World War II, I would simply reply, "I was too young—just missed by six months." When asked about Korea, I found myself in the awkward position of explaining I missed that war because my wife was pregnant. Several of my friends who were members of a local Marine Reserve unit were called up on short notice and with very little training were dispatched to Korea. Three of them were killed.

Draft dodgers were treated roughly by the public. Movie careers were ruined. A conscientious objector was almost as bad as a traitor. Worst of all for me was that a few guys I knew spread it around that my dad got me out of the military because he had connections.

But I wasn't a draft dodger, nor was I a conscientious objector. I was just an expectant father who fell through the cracks, and the Department of Defense gave me its blessing. Lucky, I guess—circumstances had maneuvered me away from service and I would live with it. But even as I embraced my life as a husband and new father and began my career with Bechtel Corporation, the guilt I felt at not serving my country was flinging me toward the future.

Chapter 3

Interperspective Corporation Is Born
("Doing Business As")

Bᴜᴛ ᴡᴀɪᴛ ᴀ ᴍɪɴᴜᴛᴇ, maybe I'm getting a little ahead of myself in telling my story. What was going on?

In 1970, the United States and Soviet Union were mortal enemies locked into a political-military stalemate called the Cold War, each at risk of nuclear annihilation. The country was also in the midst of a political nightmare called Watergate, and turmoil in the Mideast between Israel and the Arab nations had, at one point, put our nation on full nuclear readiness. The resulting cutoff in Middle Eastern oil supplies crippled the American economy and had the entire nation questioning their own governmental institutions. It was not a good time for the United States.

I, too, had been struggling with my own personal crisis. I had been working for San Francisco's engineering and construction giant, Bechtel Corporation, for twenty years when, in 1968, I realized that for a number of reasons it was time to move on. I was finally facing the fact that something was missing from my life— from me personally and not from any of my personal relationships. This vague emptiness was only worsened for a time when fueled by alcohol. It wasn't from the high pressure of building huge grassroots industrial projects from scratch and the continual moving of my family. I suspected it was some sort of midlife crisis mixed with battle fatigue resulting from very little time off.

At any rate, when my low-grade unhappiness and feelings of lack of fulfillment became acute, with the help of my wife and several good friends I got help at Menninger Clinic, a well-known rehab center in Kansas. When I emerged a few months later, I had at least shed my brief but intense problem with alcohol forever and had gained a much better understanding of who and what I was, an understanding that would be the foundation in many ways for the rest of my life. Yet not long after I had adjusted to a new lifestyle, the inner voice, the voice without words, though fainter than before, was still a presence and stirred my remote, unfulfilled feelings in a slow simmer. I attended a few AA meetings in the early recovery period and learned the importance of "one day at a time." But the simmer was to last more than thirty years, although I soon would learn to manage the flame.

I spent most of that first year trying very hard at stock brokering and managing other people's money, which was a far cry from the robust outdoor work that required beating time constraints and the elements to produce a product useful to mankind. Construction was competitive but fun. Projects had a beginning, middle, and end, and no matter what your role, when the job was done and the project went into service, you could walk away and leave a monument to your efforts. It was hands-on and tangible. Virtually every worker had opportunities to be creative, and teamwork was paramount. As a stockbroker with the long, wet lunches at Paoli's trendy restaurant and hours just staring at the ticker tape, I was out of my element and my career was over almost before it began.

Somewhere along the line I had heard Joseph Campbell say "Follow your bliss to happiness and success." That sounded good to me while I was adrift. So one day in 1971, after a couple of Englishmen on my Olympic Club rugby team approached me, we decided to go into the antique business. And thus, James Waste Antiques was born. John Doughty and I, as cocaptains of the rugby team, got along real well. We connected with Murray

Tomson, a dealer and buyer in London, and started shipping containers of high-quality antiques to our shop in San Francisco's prestigious and historic Jackson Square, in the shadow of the Transamerica Pyramid building and within a couple of blocks of the Bank of America's world headquarters. We also opened an office in London. We sold high-end English furniture and dealt with a lot of interior decorators. I enjoyed dealing with the public, especially when it included people such as Richard Burton and Elizabeth Taylor, Shirley Temple Black, Robert Redford, Paul Newman and Joanne Woodward, Rex Harrison, and George Shultz, at that time president of Bechtel. The business seemed to satisfy my hunter-stalker-gatherer instincts for a while and it was a great central noontime rallying place for my rugby team, many of whom were grads from local universities and worked in downtown San Francisco.

One day in the early fall of 1971, I was seated at my mid-nineteenth century partners desk getting caught up on some shipping reports. I became aware that I was under a shadow. Without looking around, I half-consciously assumed that the sun had moved behind the tall pyramid building in its daily journey south for the winter. On nice days I left the front door open for my clients. For a moment, air pressure behind me adjusted to a presence, the 130-year-old wood floor creaked for a split second, and someone sniffed. I half turned in my swivel chair and immediately realized the shadow was of two athletic-looking guys with close-cropped hair wearing dark suits, belted overcoats, and sunglasses. Not showing my surprise, I said, "Hi, what's up? What can I do for you?"

The older guy said, "We don't know yet, but maybe a lot."

My first reaction was that they were a couple of Ivy Leaguers transferred to our fair city who wanted to play on our Olympic Club rugby team and get an athletic membership to the venerable sports social club. I asked, "What positions do you play?"

The older of the two (maybe thirty) broke in. "Can we talk, I mean privately?" I closed the front door and took them into my private back office filled with collectibles, sports trophies, and personal stuff and sat them on an imported, tufted brown leather sofa. As they sat down, the younger man picked up two spent twelve-gauge shotgun shells and held them in his right hand. They first confirmed my identity and then came right out and said they were with the CIA. The older man opened an attaché case and handed me a brief but rather complete summary of my life for the past forty-three years, including my recent rehab trip to Kansas and the fact that I had played trumpet in my high-school dance band.

In a way, these people were not new to me, but their approach was. They said they knew all about me and thought they could use my unusual combination of engineering construction, travel, sports activities, and language skills to gather some ground-floor observation and analysis of the general state of economic decline in the USSR. I asked, "You mean at home or abroad?"

They answered, "Abroad."

"Gee, I'm sorry, gents. I'm married with five kids and I don't drink. I wouldn't fit in."

They chuckled. The older guy said, "We're talking part-time as an independent contractor-observer at ground level. We've got the aerial view under control, but it comes up short. State Department and guys with diplomatic passports can't wander. But we've found that citizens can travel if they have a good cover story, and when it may be profitable to Ivan."

I asked, "How long would I be away?"

The older man replied, "It would be your call—you know, like where and how many fish do you catch on a trip. We haven't done much with contractors like this, but we'd like to inflate the program if a pilot operation like yours produces. You would be on your own but working within our general guidelines. According to our auditors' reports, the president is pretty sure the Soviets are going broke on their international financial affairs."

I inquired, "Is this really important?

The older guy responded, "I don't know what your values are, but aside from your family situation this will probably be the most important thing you'll ever have the opportunity to do. Do you hear me? We need you. Are you interested?"

To my surprise, my button had been pushed. I wasn't being sandbagged. I was their guy. They knew it and I knew it. I had been a member of numerous sports and business teams, but this was the ultimate team for me.

The older guy asked, "Do you want to think about it?"

I replied, "No."

He asked me, "Do you have to clear it at home?"

My response was, "No."

"When would you be available?"

"Now." I was being rushed into an elite fraternity. I said, "I do." I was a pledge.

The older one asked, "Can we get together this weekend and work out some details, such as how you'll be reimbursed, secrecy regulations, contract stuff? We also want to run you through some fitness tests and a medical check. If that goes well, we'll provide some intensive basic operational training and set you up for a six-week heavy-duty Russian language course. Here are a couple of phone numbers, but we'll call you." He handed me a card, then smirked. "I'm Tom and he's Jerry. I'm an attorney. I went to school in Massachusetts, and Jerry's a CPA from Chicago. I played lacrosse and Jerry played water polo. Do you think rugby is rougher than lacrosse?"

I answered, "Hell no, you guys use clubs."

Tom said, "Good answer!"

Jerry, clicking the two shotgun shells together, asked, "Oh, by the way, what's the story on these?

I asked them, "Got a minute?" They said nothing but listened intently as I began my story. I explained that the twelve dealers in the antique dealers association had recently terminated the night-security guy who had bought the franchise for our neighborhood, a protection racket approved by the SFPD. Not long after his termination, a number of big plate-glass windows were broken and, in my case, the flowers in my planter box were regularly uprooted and tossed on the sidewalk. At an association meeting, we decided that Pancho, the uniformed night-security guy on a motor scooter, was the culprit. The association president called Pancho to his office and suggested we were thinking of rehiring him but that he should first meet with Jim Waste in his store and see what he thought and, "Oh, by the way, Waste is a little wacky. He's sort of a macho man ex-Marine type. You know what I mean?"

A few days later Pancho showed up and parked his scooter in front. I shook his hand and asked him into my back office. As we discussed the problem, I became irritated, heated, then highly agitated, and said, "I'm gonna lay for that son-of-a-bitch every night until I get him. If I catch him pulling up my flowers, I'll shoot his balls off," and at that moment I grabbed my double-barreled shotgun in the corner against the bookcase, swung it menacingly under his nose and let one off in the air: BLAM! "Holy shit," I said, "that feels good. How about another?" BLAM! For a moment the pupils of Pancho's eyes had disappeared.

Pancho cried, "Hey, man, be careful with that thing!"

"Geez, Pancho, I'm sorry. I just get carried away when I think of that son-of-a-bitch pulling up my pretty flowers." I broke the gun open and the two shells popped out on the couch. "You want 'em?"

Jerry asked, "Did you rehire Pancho?"

I answered, "No."

"Did the dealers have any more trouble?" Jerry inquired.

"No," I answered.

"What happened to Pancho?" Jerry asked.

I replied, "Some drunk in a convertible knocked him off his scooter and broke both of his legs in front of the Pink Onion."

Jerry asked, "You weren't a Marine, were you?"

I responded, "I was that afternoon. Just ask Pancho."

For a moment I had met some unspoken agency standard. My recruiters beamed warmly and nudged each other as I spoke. We did a couple of high fives. These were my guys, and I really wanted to be one of them. And for some obscure impulsive reason I said, "Thanks for coming, I've been waiting for you." Their heads came together for a whispered moment. Jerry took off his coat and left separately. There were no more words. I only saw these recruiters twice more. They had done their job. That's how the agency works.

They already knew I had worked with the Royal Canadian Mounted Police (RCMP), the FBI, and MI5 (British Intelligence). Mafia and/or communist-dominated unions meant trouble for Bechtel's high tech projects, and sabotage was always an issue. I handled security as well as job health and safety matters in addition to my engineering duties for most of the projects I served on. As I walked the job several times daily, I was able to keep my eyes open for certain kinds of trouble and report same to the authorities. Through the years there were a lot of issues and I had developed a pretty good "nose" for trouble.

I was to learn that being an independent contractor was, in a way, like working for Accountemps, filling in where and when my specialty was needed. I was a jack-of-all-trades and opportunist, a consultant for anything that would allow me freedom of travel in the USSR. Unfortunately, without a diplomatic passport—a DIP—I didn't have any immunity if I got into trouble. When the subject of risk and potential danger came up during my training, they wanted to know why I didn't ask about it before signing up. My answer was simple. "It didn't matter to me," I explained. "I would and could deal with it." By that time, I had played in over four hundred rugby and football games, and not once had I even considered getting hurt and I wouldn't start now. I just wanted to play on their team.

As my intelligence work intensified, it became readily apparent that although James Waste Antiques was a fine cover for my operations in the States (I mused that movie characters like Peter Lorre, Sidney Greenstreet, and George Saunders frequently operated out of antique shops), I needed to have another, broader cover and company name so I could wear different identities as a consultant in Eastern Europe and Central Asia.

One day I was shooting the breeze with personal confidant Mike Kelly, a frequent overseas traveler, banker, and money man. I always spoke in cryptic terms about what I was doing. So did he. We hit on the name "Interperspective" (international perspective). It was a natural. Nobody else was using the name, and by becoming a "consulting company" I could use different covers, covers of convenience. My business cards were printed in English on one side, and Russian, Georgian, or Turkish on the reverse, and were handed out by the hundreds from Ulan Bator to Istanbul. My title was Consultant. In the years to come, I would consult on anything related to engineering and construction, but it turned out that my best cover was in humanitarian aid activities. I was also a rep for several international corporations like Kaiser Permanente and the Georgian Foundation.

Thus, Interperspective Corporation was born. Almost immediately I needed the right kind of help. The gods smiled. I never recruited, they just showed up on their own. I have since thought their personal needs were quite similar to mine.

Lou Jefferson, a Beltway Boy, a graduate of George Washington University in D.C., former security officer and confidant of Secretary of State John Foster Dulles under President Eisenhower, press secretary for Senator Hugh Scott, author and journalist, walked into my shop and eventually sold me a Civil War Sharps rifle with a brass patch box. At first we were just fellow recovering alcoholics. He was new in California and recently divorced. He liked my scene and I soon asked him to shop-sit for me during my short and long absences. I would brief him a little on my "business trips." Noting the frequency of my trips and the lack of details I provided, he finally confronted me one day and asked if I was connected with the government in some way I couldn't talk about. I blanked and blushed and knew this D.C. insider had my number. "I thought so," he said.

From then on, he told me a lot of his past and about the book he was writing. I had the agency check out his background, which included top-security clearance. They agreed to "limited exposure" when needed to operate Interperspective Corporation. He became the anchorman at home. He became the person my wife, Marilyn, would contact when I was overseas. As a long-time Washington, D.C. insider, he knew how to reach me most of the time. I would brief him before and after many of my trips. He also served an important function by managing the shop while I was gone. He was a year older than I and we had a lot in common including an interest in seventeenth, eighteenth, and nineteenth-century antiques. Earlier I had several people try to fill that role, including a well-known movie actor who was filming in the city and who quit when he realized I wasn't gay. Prior to Lou, whenever I went overseas I would have to close down.

One day in 1981, a young guy about twenty-five walked in off the street, unkempt, overweight, and wearing a cowboy hat and backpack. I asked him to check his cigarette at the door. Removing a pair of beaded Sioux Indian moccasins from his backpack, he told me he had seen my ad for antique guns in the yellow pages and thought he would give me a shot. Little did he know I was fascinated with Indian culture and history and that in my senior year at UC Berkeley in 1950 I had taken 250 West Coast boy scouts to the National Jamboree in Valley Forge, Pennsylvania. When our chartered train stopped at Glacier National Park, several other leaders and I were initiated into the Blackfoot tribe as honorary chiefs. My name was NA-TO-SE-NA, or Chief Sun, and I still have a doeskin document and photos for proof. A Japanese-American scoutmaster with a ukulele-playing group of kids from Hawaii—he happened to be the brother of Dan Inouye, currently the senior U.S. Senator from Hawaii—was especially thrilled with the ceremony and couldn't wait to hang his doeskin in his office in Honolulu. Only in America!

Back to Backpack Jack. I bought the moccasins and asked this flea market denizen if he could bring me more. After about the third visit, I asked him to give me a summary of who's who among the Indian and Western Americana trade people. Much to my surprise, he produced an elaborate chart rating the dealers according to the quality and price of their merchandise and, more importantly, the degree to which they could be trusted. As it turned out, Jack had a business degree from the University of Nebraska, was well traveled, and had a good working knowledge of history and geopolitics. His dealer analysis was no fluke. This guy was on the ball. I needed a smart go-to guy, and so it was that Jack Ringwalt became a provisional member of Interperspective Corporation. Jack lacked direction and was battling too many demons for me to tell him many details of my operation. However,

"Backpack Jack" first walked into my life with a pair of beaded Sioux moccasins.

I often entertained him on my return from overseas with anecdotes and impressions about my travels and general cover activities. And it was Jack who always took me to the airport when I was about to embark on a new mission. My wife—who always met me on my return—was uncomfortable saying goodbye.

These sessions and similar sessions with Lou gave me valuable feedback with which I could organize my thoughts and plan for the future. On most of my early travels, I took no notes or pictures, for obvious reasons. As it turned out, these conversations locked in my trip details for future book use.

It was Lou who eventually said to me, "You should write about all this! The area where you operate is little known or understood. You have a story to tell." Hearing that from a well-traveled pro—and a published author—was the beginning. When I made excuses, Lou got tired of my procrastinations and finally said, "Everybody has a book to write. The secret is to sit down and write it. Talk with your ballpoint pen. Don't worry about form, style, organization. Just start writing." And I did.

As things wound down for me, I hoped to have Jack join me on my "paper route." Unfortunately, by that time he was free of his demons but had gotten married and developed serious health problems and couldn't travel. However, his support and logistical roles continued to expand, and I came to rely on him as my personal assistant.

Sometimes my instincts from my undercover life spilled into my antique-store-owner persona. One day in the late eighties, an uninvited visitor about twenty-five years old exited my store with a $700 navigational sextant without paying for it. He had wrapped it in his ski jacket. As he lingered around with shifty eyes, I spotted him almost immediately. I waited until he opened the door to leave and confronted him. I asked the young man, "What do you have in your jacket?"

He responded, "Fuck you!"

As he turned to leave, I gripped his jacket but it tore loose and he took off running up Jackson Street with my sextant. Gary Near, a young criminal lawyer from upstairs in my building, saw the action. "What's up?" Gary asked.

I replied, "Shoplifter!"

Gary cried out, "Let's get him!" The main thing Gary and I had in common was we were both into competitive master's distance running and the following weekend was the annual 7.5 mile Bay-to-Breakers run across the city of San Francisco.

The miscreant had about a seventy-five yard lead on us but was headed uphill into Chinatown. We followed, slowly reeling him in as he tired. We dodged traffic on Columbus Avenue as he kept looking over his shoulder, and after about ten blocks he ducked into an alley, trying to hide behind a parked truck. Gary, who is not very big, waded right in and proudly retrieved the sextant in one hand and dragged the terrified man from behind the truck.

Barely breathing hard, Gary asked, "Shall we kill him? What do you think?"

The young man, seriously out of breath, gasped, "Who the hell are you guys?" (I was fifty and Gary was thirty-five.)

I answered Gary, "Naw, let him go. I got his jacket at the store."

Gary released the man and kicked him in the pants, saying, "It's your lucky day, Buster."

As Gary and I jogged back to the shop, I remarked, "Gee, Gary, are you black belt or something? You were fearless, you went right into him."

Gary replied, "Hell, no. I was with you. You're the rugby player. I've never done anything like this in my life!"

Moments later we both felt huge adrenaline rushes, not of euphoria but of survival. We had been foolish. The shoplifter could have been armed. I had used this adrenaline tool in sports and on my paper route a number of times. It can paralyze you or, if you manage it well, magnify your performance.

One night a few years later in a farmhouse in the former Soviet Republic of Tajikistan, I thought of Gary as I escaped into the night on the crest of another adrenaline surge, running for my life.

Debriefing

A T THE TIME Ronald Kessler wrote his highly informative book *Inside the CIA,* approximately 22,000 people worked full-time for the agency—about half at Langley Headquarters in McLean, Virginia, and in Washington, D.C., the other half in U.S. field offices and in embassies and field offices around the world. In addition, four hundred *operatives* (operations officers)—called "NOCs" because of their nonofficial cover—worked under commercial cover. A final category, hired for specific projects, consisted of subcontractors or annuitants who were typically hired for two years to perform duties such as paramilitary operations. The NOCs and contractors groups may together number 4,000 at any given time, bringing the overall total to 26,000 full-time plus part-time.

The Directorate of Operations is the spy side or clandestine services group within the CIA, employing roughly 5,000 people. The portion of the budget used to hire foreign *agents* or assets overseas is approximately 15 percent of the total budget. In other words, not enough.

Throughout my long association with the CIA, I worked both as a case officer and as an independent contractor. When perusing this narrative, the reader should keep in mind that my role-playing frequently changed according to the demands of the particular time and place, and the specific goals of my mission. The CIA was always my parent company; Interperspective Corporation was my cover company; humanitarian aid and economic research were my primary covers. For personal and security reasons, I've deliberately avoided mentioning my particular CIA classification during my various adventures. Besides, those details aren't important to my story.

Debriefing for *this* overseas observer, whatever hat I was wearing, was basically an interview held after accounting and documents were taken care of. I was "interviewed" in a number of places by various people or in small groups depending on my location at the time and whether it was expedient if the situation was too hot. Foreign embassies were sometimes secure and convenient, depending who was on station.

My home-office case officer changed every couple of years. I liked most of them, although you could never get close to them in this business. They ranged from lawyers, CPAs, and Ph.D.s to former military, including a former lady Marine major. By the time I retired, I must have worked with about ten of them, mostly from Langley, Virginia, who had received their basic training at Camp Peary (The Farm). A lot of them were Democrats and in their forties. Their equivalent military ranks would be captains, majors, and lieutenant colonels. To most of these case officers, I was an oddball, a freelancer, not a regular—maybe a guy they couldn't trust all the way. Yet my résumé of professional and personal achievements should have suggested otherwise. Actually, a degree of paranoia was considered a survival asset in the sometimes cumbersome operations of this great secret bureaucracy—an attribute I couldn't claim.

Meeting with the brothers (debriefers) was great sport. Through the years I met and briefed or debriefed intel officers in parking garages, on rooftops, in back alleys, public parks, and museum restaurants. It was an endless and necessary drill, particularly for them not to be seen with me. To many, I was a person of mysterious habits, an older-than-usual guy some supposed had special high-up connections. Sometimes I challenged smart-ass guys to race me in a 5K for a thousand bucks. There were no takers.

The briefing could be very specific, almost formal, with clipboards and prepared questions. Or sometimes, depending on the experience of the case officer, it could be a "kick around" bull session. I was most comfortable with these sessions because the officer in charge had a "been there, done that" background. I could tell experienced field officers by their first questions, just as I can almost always tell a real athlete from the "wannabes." There is an authentic tone, a perspective the "pros" had. When I heard it, I warmed up to the interview. The guys who got my goat were the intellectual, bookish, controlling types, showing off and pulling some self-anointed rank. They like to hear themselves talk and love to dig into you for their own ego, just to see how much more clever they are than you. I'm afraid I lost it on a few occasions when the "why did you" and "why didn't you"s started to pile up. The implied criticisms from guys who'd never had to march in the mud of a Third World assignment could become particularly offensive.

Usually I would outline my trip details just as they occurred. Then I would sort of fog over and play a few chronological reels from inside my head. I preferred most questions be held until I finished my summary. I spoke of what I saw, heard, and experienced. Conclusions were left for the Q and A period, where I could qualify my statements from the context of my summary. I could tell by the questions whether they knew how to listen. There were always two debriefers, and sometimes others would sit in depending on their technical interest. Most of the guys on station had very little or no covert experience in my area and, because of the Iron Curtain, had limited practical knowledge of the former Soviet Union. I guess I was some sort of colorful "007" type to the nonfield people, and they would vicariously enjoy my travelogues. I tried to be professional and not embellish events but, because of my lifelong tendency to theatrics, I got excited a couple of times during the Q and A. I made a point that I was among friends. It was several years later before my handlers found it necessary to dampen my enthusiasm by reminding me that I was a covert spy without a diplomatic passport.

On the other hand, this unconventional style served me well during my thirty-plus interviews with the Soviet KGB, Ministry of Interior, and local police. There, I played the "C-minus student" bit, which was usually appropriate because of the Soviets' limited world view. They would try to trip me up and aggravate me, and I would try to avoid sarcastic replies by giving them my best Miss America shit-eating smile. After a while, they would just shake their heads, concluding I was stupid and didn't know anything of interest to them. Oddly, these overseas interviews were sort of a game for me, although a serious matter at the time. I had a "pitch" for whatever my cover was, such as humanitarian aid, and to throw them off track, I made the rest of my story personal with questions like "Do any of you play rugby?" "Do any of you like the Beatles?" "I have five children and they're all smarter than me." "Are all Russian ballet dancers gay?"

At home, I had never liked taking depositions, executive reviews, or debriefing in general. I am a very open, straightforward guy and always felt violated when my reasoning, motives, or behavior were questioned. More than once I shot down a question with "You weren't there, butthead! You're out of my context. Let's move on." I would review transcripts later.

Many of the people I worked with stateside as well as overseas used assumed names in the event they might be assigned to undercover work and need a new identity. I was almost always me, Jim Waste, and it was easier to function as myself. I lost track of some good guys because of this practice, but it was standard operating procedure. Crazy business, huh?

Chapter 4

Evolution of a Spy
(The Early Days)

IN THE 1990s, the common perception inside and outside the government was that once the Soviet Union was vanquished, the world—or at least Eastern Europe—would be made safe for democracy. But as one of the more active observers in my ever expanding humanitarian and consulting roles, I could see that this was not necessarily so, especially in the Caucasus and Central Asia, those former Soviet republics that now made up my paper route. In fact, it was downright dangerous on my paper route, in many ways more dangerous than before the collapse of the Soviet Union.

But I didn't have time to reflect on this great policy debate or even on the lingering question of just why I always seemed to land in such hairy predicaments as the one in which I currently found myself. My thoughts were more immediate, more basic, as I was being pushed up the steps in front of a mob in the Central Asian city of Dushanbe, Tajikistan. I truly thought I was about to become the victim of an ancient custom and have my eyes gouged out. I had picked a bad time to go jogging. The locals were at each other's throats, and Russian tanks were waiting on the side streets for the opportunity to replace Soviet rule with the New World Disorder. All I could think about were the rugby players who talked about "Waste's thousand-yard stare."

They said it frightened opponents. Actually, it was my own apprehension and fear showing. Where would that stare be if I lost my eyes?

At that moment, I didn't feel like the hardened old rugby player and spy that I was, nor did I feel like one of those chosen few who have been at history's murky confluence of intelligence, diplomacy, military operations, and humanitarian assistance. Instead, I felt rather insignificant. Standing there, I remembered my boyhood and wondered what the boy I had been would think of me now. I had fantasized that I was Beau Geste and Lawrence of Arabia, little dreaming that I would become, like them, a working—if phantomlike—part of my country's intelligence community whose life might have been fiction, except that it wasn't.

I have always felt filled with a sort of raw and potentially dangerous force which has sometimes scared me, and I believe that, in many ways, I have become my own creation. It is as though I sculpted myself out of a large dose of smoke and shadows, or that I am the result of some conjurer's trick and that my "phantom" self is the conjurer. Of course, that's probably an illusion. I have a capacity for self-dramatization that makes for good company when I'm alone and leads me to think I'm spending time with the real thing. I often have to catch myself and remember that I am not an illusion, that I *am* the real thing, and that even though I'm a loner, I have several identities that travel with me wherever I go.

Most important is my Phantom self, which I'm never without. I am actually known by some friends as the Phantom. Over the years, I've acquired a reputation for not being there when I am there, and being there when I'm not there. I can't explain it, but it's true. I suppose it could have something to do with the fact that after I stopped drinking in 1969, I would frequently become bored with associates who were under the influence and just disappear. They would say, "He was here, he's not here, where is he? He's the Phantom." The name just stuck. But it also had something to do with the way I worked in the field.

Then, there are my companion identities that come and go depending on the circumstances. Because they are internalized and intimate, I would ask the reader to accept these several appellations for what they are—tools that have enabled me to survive. First, there's *Mr. Asshole*. He's with me most of the time and prevents me from making already bad situations worse. A typical internal dialogue with *Mr. Asshole* would start with something like, "Okay, Asshole, now what are you going to do?" Typical answers might be, "Stop! Think!" or "Jump! Run! Smile!" Then, there are Asshole's two close companions: *Mr. Stupid* and *You Moron*. They are self-explanatory. Of course, if my moves have been good and things are working for me, then I go with *Baby* as in: "Come on Baby, keep it rolling. Push it, Baby—it's going to happen." But my favorite companion is *Big Guy* as in, "Way to go Big Guy, it's happening. You're going to score. Do it! Whew!"

Some friends call me the Phantom.

The main thing I have truly learned is to listen to these companions. They are infinitely wise and much smarter than the lesser "I'm hungry, thirsty, or horny" voices that also seem to be constantly with me. Indeed, I've found that the secret to operating successfully as a loner is to listen to the right voices at the right time and accept their truths. They can make good company and ensure that, although I may be a loner, I'm never alone. Whether it was in San Francisco's Bohemian Club bar, the fine antique shops of London, a Moscow back alley, a running path in Santa Fe, or the office of Eduard Shevardnadze in Georgia's reborn capital of Tbilisi, my companions enabled me to do and say things that I didn't think I would be able to do or say otherwise. They proved useful over the years, undoubtedly saving my life on a number of occasions, although at times making me feel like a fumbling actor on a crudely lit stage. A friend of mine who was deep in Washington's security and intelligence labyrinth in the fifties and sixties told me that, in some ways, I remind him of Allen Dulles, godfather of America's intelligence community. He says that Dulles, who loved to talk of "dire and deadly deeds," always seemed to be somebody other than who he was, but, at the same time, was always really himself.

My interest in all things Russian began as a seven-year-old boy when, one warm spring afternoon, I first felt the melancholy effect that Russian music has had on my very being ever since. I was standing outside a window of my elementary school in Berkeley, California, listening to the glee club, when the mournful strains of the "Volga Boatman" came through the window. The crippled teacher came over to the window on her crutches and asked if I'd like to sing with them. When I said yes, she put out her hand, pulled me through the window, and sat me down with the others. Later, my mother took me to see a concert by the Don Cossack Chorus, and I was almost overwhelmed by waves of unexplained feelings. I believe my connection with Russian music is even more profound and visceral today than ever. There is a loneliness about it that brings forth images of the vast forests and empty spaces of Siberia and strikes a chord in my genes that goes back to my ancestors of the barren wastelands of the Scottish Highlands.

It was also as a boy on the playgrounds of Berkeley in the early forties that I began to realize that the fashionable idealism of the slogan, "It's not whether you win or lose but how you play the game," didn't quite do it for me. By the late forties, when I was wearing the rugby and football colors of the University of California at Berkeley, better known as "Cal," I had revised that popular slogan to, "It's not whether you win or lose but whether you're around to play another day." Those are still my watch words. I was a member of the Pappy Waldorf Cal football teams that lost three consecutive Rose Bowls. All three were lost in the last six minutes. But I never forgot that there is always another day and another game, and what really matters is that you finish well and are there to play again.

It was during those early years at Cal, when I was beginning to develop the philosophy of survival that has served me so well, that the Communist Party first attempted to recruit me. Moscow's instrument was a professor from England who taught one of my classes, "The Oral Interpretation of Literature." Although I had an uncle who was an avowed member of the Communist Party U.S.A. and secretary of Harry Bridges' Longshoremen's Union in San Francisco, I had no real idea what communism was back then—much less any knowledge about the black arts of spying and dishing out disinformation in the service of the Soviet Union. Indeed, California seemed barely connected to Washington, D.C., much less Soviet Russia.

However, in that class at Cal, I did begin to wonder if Shakespeare was not somehow a Soviet creation having nothing to do with the great voices of English literature. This professor liked to tell his students that in America's capitalist society, man is always going toward deterioration but, even as he deteriorates, he is growing. The guy would then proclaim, as if from on high, that Shakespeare understood this, and that he, speaking for Shakespeare and all the "other great Soviet heroes," was there to see that this deterioration led his students into a newer and more perfect world. A Soviet world. Today, fifty years later, the same tune is still being played at Sather Gate in Berkeley—the "Party Line."

Each semester, the professor's class was over-subscribed with a lot of mature-looking guys who were clearly not native Californians. They were all radical and outspoken, and, after a time, I noticed that they were all saying the same old thing. They talked class division—what I would later call "Hyde Park Corner crap." They allowed no discussion. But, as one who was raised in both Methodist and Episcopalian churches, in spite of my suspicions I was impressed at the time, as were many of my classmates, with what seemed to be great ideals and good intentions.

On a number of occasions, the professor invited me to his home "for coffee and talk" and, good recruiter that he was, stopped just short of asking me to sign up on the spot as an agent and disinformation tool of the Soviet Union. The professor knew that my father was executive vice president of the internationally known Bechtel engineering and construction company. Maybe he and his Moscow masters thought they'd just put me into Bechtel as a "sleeper" who they'd "wake up" twenty years later when, according to their way of thinking, I'd have my father's job and be able to place their agents in Bechtel's worldwide operations. Bechtel was already involved in developing Saudi Arabian oil, and the Soviets had targeted that part of the world early. I instinctively reacted negatively to the man's efforts, but he refused to give up on me. I think I frustrated him.

At the outbreak of the Korean War, when I applied to the Air Force for a direct commission as a psychological assistant, my old "professor" damned me with faint praise when he wrote that although I "sometimes had prejudiced points of view," they were "easily corrected" and I "rarely expressed underlying hostility or anxiety." The professor did give my "competence, intelligence, insight and good sense" passing grades. I never did figure out whether he thought I'd make a better agent for the Soviets in the U.S. Air Force or at Bechtel. Maybe they weren't clear on that either. Certainly they knew that my father had worked with John McCone, a cofounder of the Bechtel Corporation, who later achieved fame as Air Force secretary and as head of both the Atomic Energy Commission and the Central Intelligence Agency. In any case, although they didn't get me in college, they must have somehow figured that I'd be useful to them, and I believe they kept me in their sights after I graduated from Cal and began working for Bechtel.

After I graduated from UC Berkeley in December of 1950, I made what was undoubtedly the best move of my life. I married Marilyn Maas, the mother of my five now adult children. She's still with me after fifty-nine years which, considering the life I've led and led *her*, qualifies her for some form of sainthood, even if only in my heart. My wife's unexpected pregnancy kept me out of the air force, and, thus, I missed serving in the Korean War. I then began my career with Bechtel Corporation.

My specialty with Bechtel was cost analysis of all phases of design and construction of heavy engineering projects. I was often sent ahead to evaluate the local political and economic climate of where we were trying to build our latest project. It was during my early days in the field with Bechtel that I developed my "two-hundred-item mental checklist." It was kind of like a form set in my brain and I was constantly dropping observations into slots for later analysis. As a result, my memory was nearly photographic. This later proved to be most helpful in my intelligence-gathering activities because I didn't keep notes or, until the past few years, make recordings or take pictures. Only after the Soviet breakup did tourist Jim become comfortable taking pictures, and really, not even then.

My first big project with Bechtel was working on an oil refinery in Vancouver, British Columbia in 1952, the first oil refinery on the Canadian west coast, which was being built to connect with the big pipeline from the oil fields around Edmonton. We hired about eight hundred locals for the job, and some of the union people who talked the "Red Flag"—particularly the electricians and the carpenters unions—tried to recruit me. I listened because, having been born in 1929, I had grown up with and seen the soup lines and union-busting in San Francisco. At first, I just thought they wanted me in the union or, maybe, to organize the office workers and engineers. Finally, when I told them that didn't make sense because I was really on the management side, they got right up front about the Communist Party. Not long after that, the Royal Canadian Mounted Police approached me and asked me to keep an eye on the Red Flag people for *them*.

Suddenly, I was in what some would call "the game" and *not* on the Red side. I had begun to realize that there really was no middle ground, and I was beginning to believe there really was a left-wing conspiracy and that they were making progress. Although the Red Flag people didn't bring the Soviet Union directly into it at the time, I always felt there was a long, red fishing line somehow coming in to me from that professor at Cal.

Those union guys did use the word "infiltration" early on, and everybody knew the Soviets were interested in the pipelines and refineries being built in western Canada. Their true motive became painfully obvious when they shut down the project with strikes for no logical or legal reason other than to create chaos. Their goals were to split labor from management, and Canada from the United States. In other words, to divide and divide—the basic tools of their trade then and now. I had already figured this out when the RCMP contacted me.

The Mounties weren't just men on horses. Along with the horses, they were Canada's FBI and quite a few other things. They are very good. They somehow knew I was being approached and asked me to play along with the union guys, particularly the Red Flag types, and to report back to them. Which I did.

Although I didn't join the Communist Party in Canada and sign up to spy for the Soviet Union, I played a lot of rugby and spent a lot of time in bars with the guys trying to recruit me. I didn't know the term at the time, but I suppose I became something of a "covert operative," even though my cover was pretty much my reality.

My next Bechtel project in a foreign country, and the next chapter in my early experience with Communists and intelligence, came in 1963 when I went to work on the construction of a refinery for Texaco-Regent Oil in Pembrokeshire, Wales. I was an assistant area construction superintendent and, as in Canada, was also responsible for plant security, first aid, and labor relations, reporting directly to the project manager on these issues. This allowed me to see firsthand how much disorder employees without the proper motivation could cause, and it also put me in the position to see and hear matters of interest to intelligence people. The project was directly across Milford Haven Inlet from a British Petroleum refinery project that had taken six long years to build due to hundreds of strikes and slowdowns.

In Great Britain, communism was legal. Most of the labor unions were staffed and controlled by card-carrying communists and they made no secret of it. To many, communism seemed an attractive alternative to a war-poor economy, especially since there was no middle class at the time to combat it. There was no failed model of communism such as we have today. Bechtel built their refinery, a carbon copy of BP's, in two years for half the cost because, thanks in small part to some of my intelligence activities, we were able to minimize the strikes and slowdowns. There were sixty-one craft (union) work stoppages on my project, but the job was never actually shut down as a whole.

I was not officially a covert operative at that time, but I was learning the trade. While playing rugby and frequenting local pubs, I heard what I needed to hear about strikes, slowdowns, infiltrations, and subversive activities and passed this information on to where it had to go. I was active. I had some success.

Whatever my exploits in the secret world of covert operations, rugby is the great metaphor for my life—the life of a man who toiled in what would later become known as the "Pants Factory" within the intelligence community. I played rugby as a boy and, at the age of seventy, played my last full game with "seniors" (age thirty-five and over). When I was building refineries around the world for Bechtel, many of the muscular construction men who worked with me would hear that I was a rugby player and find it necessary to prove their manhood. They'd do what I call their "little hard man's swagger" for my benefit, forcing me to react. I always tried to show a "don't give me any shit" attitude, recognizing that strength has no value unless you demonstrate the will to fight. This attitude got me through a lot of tough situations.

In 1965, I returned to San Francisco from building an oil refinery in Wales and joined the Olympic Club rugby team. Because of my maturity and experience in international play, the club soon asked me to be the player-coach. In 1966, I took the team to the Boston Invitational Rugby Tournament, where we beat Racing Club of Paris, a team that included thirteen French international players. Because of that victory, we became the first American "club team" to go on tour in Europe since the 1928 Olympics. Sixty of us (players and supporters) toured Ireland, England, France, Scotland, and Wales. We won eight games, tied two, and lost two against major opponents.

The trip introduced modern American rugby to Europe, and the European papers wrote it up with surprised high praise. We were very good. I subsequently led the Olympic Club team for several seasons before forming the Bay Area Touring Side (BATS).

Not long after my initiation with Tom and Jerry, some new intelligence contacts asked me if it would be possible to "get that rugby team of yours" behind the Iron Curtain and, "using your construction cost-analysis skills, check out some industrial things while you're there." I told them good rugby was played behind the Iron Curtain and that I knew people in England who had played rugby in Rumania. When I asked them if they were serious, they replied they were very serious. I contacted my English friends, and they, in turn, contacted the Rumanians. Largely because of my Olympic Club team's earlier trip to Europe, the Rumanians agreed to four games, and the new BATS team was anxious to go.

It took about a year to arrange the 1972 Rumanian trip. Dealing with their officials was frustrating. A U.S. National rugby team made up largely of Northern Californians had beaten Rumania in the 1924 Olympics and repeated that victory in 1928. The two countries had not met on a rugby field since. I suggested to my handlers that we also play in Paris and London to submerge our trip from its specific intent. Al Moss of the San Francisco Chronicle validated us among the Rumanians by giving us a good press image.

When we finally got to Bucharest, the police followed us everywhere, creating a Keystone Kops sort of atmosphere. Bucharest, like all Soviet satellite cities, was a dreary place. Smokestacks billowed black soot into the air but produced little of value to the ordinary citizen. There was a general sense of unease—and worse—everywhere. Fear filled people's eyes. Our younger players noticed it the first day of practice, which was on the same field with the Rumanians.

Midway through the first practice, Rumanian officials asked us to stop until their players were through. I asked them why and they told me I was impolite and my players were rude. I didn't understand what that meant at first, but finally realized they thought our team was laughing at them. Actually, our guys were just getting loose. My teams have always had fun practicing. They would even do a few Globetrotter tricks, just horsing around. It was the politically correct coaches who disapproved, but a few days later we noticed the Rumanian players were doing a few Globetrotter-type tricks of their own.

We got—and were grateful for—the message. The athletes were acting out what they couldn't say. So we went about our business of playing rugby, even though the Rumanians, out of fear of their own government, were prepared to go to any lengths to keep us from winning. Indeed, they had been "ordered" by their government to win. The officials had also received the same instructions, and ultimately, thanks to the referee, the Rumanian team did win one game in Timisoara. Under the rules of international rugby, a game lasts eighty minutes with no time-outs and no overtime. However, the "neutral" referee of this game kept it going seventeen minutes past regulation time, which enabled his country's team to manufacture a score and a win. We did win the first three games of four.

After "losing" that game, we were invited to meet with the Rumanian players for dinner at a university cafeteria. We were still angry, but we cleaned up and were on time. They weren't. When they showed up an hour and a half later, their coach got me aside and apologized. His very good athletes hung their heads and avoided our eyes. He said his team was embarrassed. They knew they had actually lost to a better team, but the government had manipulated the referee. And they had been told that if they didn't beat the Americans, they could never play against a foreign team again. I told the Rumanian coach if he had told me how essential it was for them to win, perhaps we could have helped with the final score. He relayed this to his team. Having been embarrassed by their phony victory, their faces lit up with relief.

After that, athlete-to-athlete, we had a great time. One of our group started singing the "Battle Hymn of the Republic" and the Rumanians hummed along as best they could. Even the guys in overcoats who always followed them seemed to be having a good time. It was a warm evening and as we emerged from the building, students were leaning out windows all around the campus. *"Mine eyes have seen the glory..."* filled the air and I wept. I weep again as I write about it today.

I secretly viewed the Rumanian trip as a first step toward setting up a tour in Russia. We were scheduled to play in Paris when we left Rumania, and one of the Rumanian star players asked if he could come along as a "guest player" on our team. This was not an uncommon request among rugby players around the world. I said that, of course, he could come. However, when word of the man's request got back to the Rumanian managers, we never saw him again. They considered this twenty-year-old star player a national asset and were not about to let him tour with us, even as a guest. I was disappointed, but found the incident instructive.

Indeed, the whole trip was instructive and useful. I was able to report things you can't get from technical intelligence. Except for downtown Bucharest, most of Rumania was still unpaved and largely uncared for. I came to think of the ox cart as symbolic of the country's peasant economy. People were afraid to talk and couldn't have survived without the black market. Evil was in the air, and you could feel it. I so reported.

When I asked our Rumanian government-furnished guide, a thirty-three-year-old electrical engineer, if he wanted to accompany us to Paris, the young man told me it would be impossible because he had no hostage (wife or child) to leave behind, and that his own life would be in danger if he tried to leave.

His father, a lay leader in the Catholic Church, had been sent to Siberia for "reorientation" and died there of an unknown illness. The guide would walk with me and, when he felt it was safe to talk, usually on lawns between buildings, would ask if he could believe what he heard on Radio Free Europe and the Voice of America. He said he liked me and my team but that we didn't fit the image of Americans given to him by his government.

Incidents such as these taught me early on that sometimes when you thought you were doing someone a favor behind the Iron Curtain, you might actually be signing their death warrant. The young Rumanian's question about Radio Free Europe and the Voice of America was one I was to hear many times over the years.

As we were leaving Rumania, my camera was seized at the airport by two ragged, dull-eyed "soldiers" with machine pistols who couldn't understand why I would protest. They kept shouting in a deep guttural accent, "Airport, airport...no camera, no camera, *nyet, nyet...*"

When I protested loudly, "Tourist, tourist, civilian, guest, guest of your government!" they yanked back the bolts on their weapons and fired a few rounds into the ground in front of us. Peasant soldiers, with the opaque look of death in their eyes, can be very scary people to deal with. Nevertheless, they didn't shoot me. But I didn't get my camera back, either.

After my San Francisco based rugby team and I returned from Rumania and Paris, I passed my impressions on to my intelligence contacts. They were impressed and immediately urged me to take a team into the Soviet Union as soon as possible. I got in touch with a group in Boston involved in "cultural exchange" with the Soviet Union, and it was arranged for me to put together a group to play rugby in Leningrad, Moscow, Kiev, and Georgia's capital of Tbilisi.

It was not difficult to recruit a team from members of my own team, the BATS. Players from UC Berkeley and Stanford were also anxious to go. The Boston cultural exchange group was already involved in music and art exchanges with their Soviet counterparts and were anxious to get into athletic exchanges. The joining of the agenda of my friends in the intelligence community and that of the cultural exchange people was a natural. I personally wanted to take American rugby into the Soviet Union, and I was becoming more and more adept at lending my eyes and ears to the service of my country.

A great deal of talk, negotiation, and just plain bickering was involved, but, eventually, the approvals came through. In September of 1978, we flew to Helsinki and met with the Boston cultural exchange people. They were very helpful, but I wasn't always sure to whom they were reporting, nor did I really want to know, but at least they were on our side. They were good people and spoke Russian.

In Helsinki we encountered our first taste of what was to come with the Soviets. The Aeroflot people said they couldn't get our whole group on the Leningrad (now Saint Petersburg) flight, so they took off without any of us. We had to wait seven hours for them to return empty to Helsinki and pick us up. With a four-hour stop in London, we arrived in Leningrad for our first game after thirty-six grueling hours of travel. After we landed, our luggage was moved almost *too* swiftly through customs. We were told it was a courtesy, but I knew it had already gone through a highly professional and complete search during our long wait in Helsinki.

The next day, the Soviets took us a good ten miles out of town to some cow pastures (with real cows) where we were told we could practice. It seemed as if they were trying to hide us from public view, which, as it turned out, they were. The team from Leningrad wasn't going to be allowed to play us. So, after scrimmaging in a Russian cow pasture and drinking a lot of beer, we went on a several-day tour of the City of Leningrad. While this sort of manipulation went on, I kept my eyes open.

In 1978, Leningrad was still a city of ghosts, filled with destruction. Everyone was poor. Communism was the law of the land. We noticed there were very few young people, or men of *any* age. Just thousands of *Babushkas*—old, sad, and drab women with round, deeply weathered, apple-red faces and scarved heads, arm-in-arm on the streets, in support of each other and each other's tragic losses. There was an air of great tragedy all around us. One and a half million people had died here during World War II. We soon wanted to leave. But we had to practice, and they did continue to let us use the cow pasture.

Finally, without playing a single real game, we were sent on to Moscow, where they put us up in the world's largest and most "bugged" hotel, the Rossia, right next to Red Square. It was nice being on Red Square instead of in a cow pasture, and there were lots of available women around, but our team members had to watch themselves. The "honey trap" was an often utilized KGB method of compromising and sometimes turning foreign nationals.

We practiced a lot and saw the sights, but, again, we found a Soviet team that, for whatever reasons, did not seem anxious to play us. The Soviets paid most of our bills, but that was it. The team kept practicing and partying and wondering why they were there. Without competition, they began to lose their edge.

A Soviet sports official finally told me that although we might be allowed to play in Kiev, we would not be allowed to play in the then Soviet Republic of Georgia because we were considered "inappropriate competition." When I asked him what he meant by "inappropriate competition," after a long pause he told me, "They" (he didn't define "they") "have watched your team in the U.S. and Europe and have decided not to risk losing to you." The Tbilisi, Georgia team at that time was certainly one of the best teams in the USSR. They had played well against France, Spain, and Italy. *What's going on here?* I wondered. I began to feel that I'd let my players down.

Rugby provided my first Cold-War cover. Officials "manufactured" our only loss in Rumania. Later, in the USSR, they kept us from playing.

After a week in Moscow, we flew to Kiev. Finally, on our second to last day in Kiev, after the same cancellation treatment, what we called the "cow pasture bus" pulled up at our Kiev hotel and, in our practice suits, we filed aboard. Suddenly our cocaptains, Kip Oxman and Jerry Walter, shouted, "Everybody off the bus! Fuck these Commie assholes! Let's practice up the street in the park next to the grammar school!" Joyously defiant, forty-five young American rugby players spilled out of the bus and ran up the grassy center divide of the boulevard, to the consternation of our uniformed Soviet "watchers" and hundreds of other Soviets (Ukrainians).

God it was fun! There was nothing they could do but watch. We had a great practice, and many Soviets mingled and laughed with us. The bus pulled up with a dozen soldiers aboard. They got off the bus and before anybody realized what was happening, the soldiers were practicing with us. They seemed terrified at first, but then really got into it and loved it. When I blew the whistle, we all got back on the bus to keep the soldiers out of trouble. They will never forget us.

Although we didn't actually get to play in Leningrad, Moscow, or Kiev, we did finally meet some *real* Soviet rugby players at a sports banquet held in our honor the last night in Kiev. They told us that another American team, the Mystic River Rugby Club from Boston, a beer-drinking bunch of second-division players, had been there a few weeks earlier and had been billed by the Soviet government as the American national champions. They were destroyed by the Soviet clubs, and the Soviet press had made a big deal out of the fact that Soviet players had beaten America's "champions"—who were actually us.

The real Soviet team players took a look at our group at the banquet and wanted to challenge us on the spot, knowing it would be a real contest. But the government said no. The officials didn't want to risk a defeat after all the publicity their team had received for beating the so-called "American champions." I couldn't believe the manipulation of the facts. But it was early on in what was to become a bigger game for me.

Nevertheless, the Soviet players—mostly Ukrainian—seemed thrilled to meet us, and we ended up eating and drinking with them for hours. It went on all night, and various good-natured tests of manly skill, speed, and strength went on between the two sides in the hallways and parking lots, like *our heavy man against yours*, the *50-yard dash*, the *50-yard three-man car push*, or the *small guy piggyback race*. Most of the Soviet athletes I talked to would have preferred honest competition. Great athletes compete for themselves, not the politicians. So even though the "big match" between us wasn't played, I like to think that the sports relationship between the Soviet Union and the United States was forever altered for the better.

The next day, when we were finally ready to get on buses to leave for the airport, the increasingly disturbed Soviet officials accused us of stealing a towel, just *one* towel from the hotel, and delayed our departure for four hours. I got angry and asked a KGB man if they really wanted to check my team's bags for one towel. When they said they did, I called the team together in the lobby and told them that "on the count of three," they were to spread everything in their bags out on the floor. Forty-five American rugby players covered the Kiev hotel's extensive lobby floor with clothes, jock straps and toilet gear, and all activity in the hotel lobby came to an abrupt stop. The KGB men were bug-eyed and they begged us to pack up and leave.

When we got to the airport, we were told we had missed the scheduled plane and that there would be a five-hour additional wait. My eighteen-year-old son, Jamie, who was playing on our second team, took a walk, and when the Soviets suddenly moved up the team's flight time, he had vanished. I was told that the whole airport had been "sealed" off because of the arrival of a high Soviet official and that Jamie had been detained outside the "seal." I skipped the team plane when it finally left and waited for my son who, after the plane's departure, was allowed back into the departure area. The police had picked him up the moment he left the airport waiting room. Fortunately, he had his passport with him, but neither of us was ever sure whether his name helped or hindered him.

Had it been a warning to me? I wondered.

Taking advantage of the confusion, most of the team had gone on to Italy. Jamie rejoined the team in Italy, while I slipped onto a plane flying south and went to Tbilisi, Georgia, for three days just to have a look. Two Armenian-Americans on the team accompanied me, hoping to visit Armenia, which is right next door to Georgia. As it turned out, none of us got to Armenia, but we saw some local rugby in Tbilisi and I began what was to become a lengthy love affair with Georgia, the most European and Christian of all the republics in the Caucasus and Central Asia.

This trip was my first great learning experience in how to manipulate the system, play the angles, and get around the Soviet Union, with my athletic background helping to validate my various reasons for being there. I came to know the Soviet Union well. After the "no game" rugby Soviet stop, we did play games in Italy, France, and England, and I found ways to go back to the Soviet Union many times, although never again with my rugby team. More and more, I reported what I saw and heard to my intelligence contacts.

When Jimmy Carter courageously boycotted the Moscow Olympic Games in 1976, it delayed our scheduled rugby tour by at least two years. But the Olympic Games, nevertheless, created a permanent crack in the Iron Curtain. Several hundred thousand foreigners traveled into the Soviet Union for the games, and few appeared threatening to the Soviet people. The Soviets liked them, and the lies they had been raised on about the merits of communism were already becoming apparent to a new generation.

In addition, Western government officials and businessmen were exposed to the mighty potential of a vast land. It was not long before limited tourism was allowed by the Soviet government, and tourist bureaus already operating in Europe made arrangements with the Soviet Intourist Agency. This proved invaluable to intelligence and other agencies in the United States. Indeed, it proved invaluable to me.

There Are No Coincidences

I FIRST BEGAN TRAVELING to the Soviet Union as a tourist not long after Tom and Jerry recruited me. The early trips involved mostly reconnaissance to places where my associates thought that a "closer on-the-ground look" would fatten their file on certain areas of strategic interest. It was always important to feel the general pulse of the Soviet Union wherever I went and to get a sense of the national will and public interest in continuing to support an already declining military and economic regime.

Although each trip followed approximately the same M.O., that of traveling on a tourist visa to consult with the local governmental officials about various problems, I rarely hung around long enough for a follow-up meeting or a meeting with their superiors. When word got out that an American consultant was staying at the local Intourist hotel, business managers and low-level party functionaries would seek me out. The BATS trip to Rumania in 1972 had helped to make me less threatening to the KGB and higher officials, and the 1978 BATS rugby tour served to validate my presence.

Western Russia and much of the Ukraine were becoming accessible to standard intelligence reconnaissance, and I spent little time there. But during the 1978 tour, I met Nikolai, publisher of a controversial Kiev newspaper—controversial because of its interest in Ukrainian self-government and criticism of "Moscow Central." It is well documented that fifty years earlier, Joseph Stalin was so unhappy with the Ukrainian national movement that he conducted a program of genocide by starvation that resulted in the deaths of some eleven million people. When I met Nikolai, it was still—fifty years later—very risky to be involved with Ukrainian nationalism.

Nikolai, my new publisher friend, hung out with our rugby team trying to absorb, almost by osmosis, as much of our Americanness as he could. He laughed with us a lot and shook his head in disbelief that forty-five educated young Americans could get so much pleasure out of just being alive. Most of his ancestors had starved to death or died of medical neglect during the 1930s, although World War II conveniently obscured this holocaust from general view. After all, the Allies needed Russians to kill Germans, something they were good at, and, of course, the Germans killed a lot of Russians, something *they* were good at. Anyway, I enjoyed meeting and hanging out with Nikolai during that trip in '78 and told him I'd give him a call if I was ever in the area again. He promised me a personal tour of the Ukraine if I returned.

When I returned to the Ukraine in 1989 as a business consultant, Nikolai arranged a plane, train, and auto tour that ran south of Kiev to the Black Sea, including a short cruise on the Dnieper River. I particularly enjoyed Odessa. As we walked around the train station, I unexpectedly flashed back in time to somewhere around 1910 as I watched the locals going about their business. Sun-baked Ukrainian farmers and their leathery-faced wives lounged on luggage and giant bundles tied with thick rope. The men were mustachioed with massive hands, soiled clothes, and piercing blue eyes peeking out from under visored, woolen caps. The women were stout, muscular more from work than fat, and wearing bulky clothing. They reminded me of the photos of World War I that I had seen in the Encyclopedia Britannica when I was a boy.

There was no fast food anywhere. The mustachioed men and muscular women were all eating from packages wrapped in cloth. As they sat in groups and ate, I sensed an almost primitive partnership amongst them. Few words were passed, but there were a lot of glances, tosses of the head, shrugs, and nods that they all seemed to understand. I had witnessed the same sort of communication in Siberia.

During moments such as those in the Odessa train station, I somehow tapped into the world of my own pioneer ancestors who had settled in California 140 years earlier. Looking at those rough-hewn people evoked internal memories in me that did not have pictures, captions, or words of any kind but were nevertheless on my conscious mental screen. In these elusive moments of undefined awareness—awareness on a feeling level only—I was able to sense my own deepest origins.

My thoughts wandered more than I realized, and Nikolai nudged me as if to awaken me before saying, "I've been worried about you. We've been standing here for five minutes without speaking. Your breathing became heavy and your eyes were unseeing. I wasn't sure what was happening to you. Where were you?"

I snapped out of it, feeling a little insecure as I tried to explain. I asked him, "Do you know the words, 'Déjà vu'?"

Nikolai replied, "But of course. You were lost in the thought that you have experienced something before?"

I nodded affirmatively and we returned to our car.

The next day we drove south through the Crimean Peninsula to Yalta. I had asked to visit the historic site where Roosevelt, Churchill, and Stalin had met at the end of World War II to decide the future for us all. Fearing assassination, Stalin had refused to leave the Soviet Union, and the Black Sea resort at Yalta had been agreed upon.

The buildings were modest, and the main conference room where the historic meeting had taken place was paneled with different shades of Siberian wood. A few flags, framed documents, pictures of the principals, and a memorial plaque adorned the walls. Separate from the main display, halfway back in the room, was a framed copy of the front page of the June 26, 1945, San Francisco Examiner. It showed a full-page photo of the final meeting of the conference that founded the United Nations in San Francisco's War Memorial Opera House. As I looked at it, I could see myself standing with several other pages near the main stage. I could scarcely contain myself as I told Nikolai about how, as a boy, I had been chosen, along with several hundred other San Francisco Bay Area students, to serve as pages and gofers. My qualification was that I was student body president of my high school. I had spent seven days running errands for delegations from all over the world. It was a fascinating experience.

Nikolai joined me to look at the photograph, shaking his head in disbelief. He pointed to Molotov and the delegation from the Soviet Union and said, softly, "My father is one of those men, and I was seated in the last row of the highest balcony. My father brought my brother and me along because we were fourteen and sixteen and had been studying English since we were five. You and I were in the same room, in your country, when we both were teenagers."

We stood there together, disbelieving. "I loved your bridges and your friendly people," Nikolai went on. "I was never a Communist, and for my father the job was just necessary. He always thought he could best help the Ukraine by remaining inside the central Soviet government, and, for a time, it seemed to work. But a few years after this picture was taken, my father and several others who were with him were sent off to the Gulag and disappeared. So, you see, I have many reasons to be what you call an 'activist.'"

I stood there stunned...speechless. After a pause, Nikolai continued, "I don't know who you are or why you are here, but I think it is more than tourism or rugby."

And, that was that.

Chapter 5

The Job Begins to Define Itself
(The Devil's in the Details)

THROUGHOUT THE YEARS, I have often referred to America's intelligence community as the "Pants Factory." This term originated in cocktail parties held by Bechtel Corporation senior officials when I traveled the world for them building refineries, power stations, and pipelines. The wives facetiously referred to Bechtel as the "Pants Factory" because it was a company dominated by men. Perhaps more telling, however, is the fact that it is a "closed" company, which, by definition, is dominated by privacy, and many of its high-level officials have gone on to serve in sensitive government jobs. Among its more illustrious alumni are former Secretary of Commerce and State George Shultz, former Secretary of Defense Caspar Weinberger, and former Director of Central Intelligence John McCone. In any case, I started referring to America's intelligence community as the "Pants Factory" some years ago, and the phrase was picked up and used by some of my colleagues. It became, in a small way, my contribution to the mystery and mystique of that dark world.

During the thirty-some odd years I have been traveling the back roads of the Soviet Union and the "new" Russia and "independent" republics, I have spent most of my time and effort just surviving—eating, sleeping, traveling, communicating. During over forty trips to that part of the world, I spent what I estimate to be 43,200 hours in the many different parts that made up the Soviet Union. Only about 5 percent of that time was spent with "friends" and 10 percent with those known to be "friendly." The rest of the time was spent with total strangers, mostly poor, unhappy, and badly educated people who knew little about the West. They thought that if I wasn't a foreign intruder, I must be a part of the KGB or some other secret police. Ten percent of them would probably have killed me for my running shoes if they had the chance.

What it boils down to is that I've spent the equivalent of five years by myself, and this aloneness and isolation extended to the domestic scene as well. Today, because so much of what I have done is classified, it is difficult to see the look on my wife's face as she begins to understand the world in which I have lived. But it has been for that very reason that I have, over the years, had to keep her in the dark about the true purpose behind all my travel to Eastern Europe and the Soviet Union. Besides, it wouldn't have been fair to her for me to share my fears and the more deadly aspects of my experiences on a day-to-day basis.

For more than two decades, to my friends and neighbors I was "the guy next door without obvious employment" who traveled abroad three or four times a year to exotic places as a tourist. In reality, I made these trips in the service of my country—service I could not talk to anyone about. I often thought it must be kind of like space travel. Up to six weeks of being alone in the vast spaces of Russia and the former Soviet Union will do that to you, where you're never sure of anything and the only company you enjoy is your own. You have to like yourself or you're lost. I traveled alone. I worked alone. I *was* alone! Yet my country and culture were always with me. It may sound corny, but love of country sustained me in very tough moments. Sometimes, it was all I had.

The intelligence community has always been full of oddballs, and I guess, in my own way, I qualify. But this may have been my chief asset as well. As a specialist and independent contractor, I had limited conventional training other than Russian language, some weaponry, and a few parachute jumps. My only computer was my gut, and it was always "on." I always seemed to be older than the young men, and on occasion young women, who have been my colleagues. This helped the fact that in foreign eyes, I never quite fit their mold of an American sent there to spy on them. The human beings whom America's intelligence agencies had on the ground, whether official or unofficial, generally seemed to operate within mental as well as physical boundaries. They had to have an instruction, a plan, a specific objective, a place to go. In my case, I would just say, "What the hell!" and *go*, all the while acting like I knew just where I was going. This was an enormous advantage for me, not only as an intelligence operative observing the Soviet scene, but also after the Soviet collapse as my humanitarian and diplomatic roles began to emerge in the newly independent republics.

My being largely unscheduled made it difficult for the "watchers" to figure out what I was doing. But it also made it difficult for those at home to protect me, or even know where I was for three or four weeks at a time. I would just check in with contacts at home when I could. And unlike the Moscow Embassy people limited by diplomatic law, as an independent contractor I would go places the diplomats couldn't even think about. However, the risk was much greater because, as an independent contractor, I had no diplomatic immunity. I was often in danger, out on my own. The very real fear that I might have an accident or become seriously ill was always with me.

Even so, it was well worth it. As I moved around, I became adept at finding patterns in small, seemingly unrelated facts such as cutbacks in train schedules, fewer meat products and fresh vegetables, crop failures, unplowed ground, permanently parked cars, and broken factory windows. I got so I could tell a lot by how many potholes were in the streets, whether the paint on the buildings was peeling, how much rust there was on equipment, or whether it had been used recently. I purposely put no spin on what I saw, allowing those to whom I reported to draw their own conclusions. I just reported the facts and emphasized that they were facts only, no political spin by Jim— opinions only on request. These were facts seen by no satellite in places that rarely saw an American. I let my handlers connect the dots.

The Russian Intourist system generally worked well for me, although flying on Aeroflot was a cattle-train experience. The simple act of checking in and getting on a flight was like a street fight. Russians don't line up. They mob up. When you find a seat, you stay there because the aisles are piled with luggage and the "outhouses" overflowing with stowaway standees. Most men smoked during flight. On internal flights you carried your own food or you starved at high altitudes. I always carried my own fluids as well, usually canned orange Fanta. There always seemed to be plenty of cheese and salami around. Passengers would produce huge knives and hack off chunks. I generally refused kind offers because most hands were dirty beyond belief. Vodka was slugged straight from the community bottle, which I would politely decline, feigning stomach ulcers. Apple juice *(yablachniy sok)* was served on a tray, but the cups were never washed before being recirculated. The flight attendants were usually burly women who frequently engaged in shouting bouts with unruly passengers or just about anybody they didn't like. It seemed that *everywhere* the public was being served, the cry of shouting women could be heard. In restaurants, ships, planes, or wherever, there were a lot of angry people.

The flight crew, often filled with beer that was served them during the flight, always got off first. It was the custom. It was ridiculous to see overweight pilots fighting their way through standing passengers and luggage to get to the rear door. I have to say, however, that during hundreds of flights I never had a bad landing. I eventually realized the pilots knew they *had* to make soft landings because the planes were old and poorly maintained. Pilots and passengers alike generally thought I was Swedish or German because of my blondish hair and blue eyes, and they were surprised when I spoke Russian with a Moscow accent.

In the early Soviet days, I couldn't afford to be too choosy, as I knew my movements would be monitored and logged. I recognized that any means of travel was fine for me as long as it was productive for the people at the Pants Factory. My instructions to myself became, "Play it by ear, take what you can get, don't force it, but keep expanding coverage."

Although rugby had opened a lot of doors to the Soviet Union, the fact that for nearly thirty-five years I was also a competitive runner in Masters (age thirty-five plus) track and cross-country events throughout the world reinforced me as an athlete in the eyes of my Soviet watchers. They were undoubtedly aware that I had taken running teams to Europe and China, and even though I had never taken a team behind the Iron Curtain, my need for constant training was readily apparent. I ran around most of the Soviet industrial empire in my white Nikes, but my adversaries never seemed to realize that my legs and eyes could function simultaneously.

Most people did not run in public places in the Soviet Union, preferring parks and sporting clubs, and *nobody* wore white Nikes in those days. I was frequently approached about my shoes, as well as my trademark Porsche Carrera dark glasses. People lusted after both. But I also learned that people were less suspicious of me because I was so obvious. I did not *appear* to be programmed. I would just bob and weave my way around the Soviet Union, making mental notes about construction projects and the condition of roads, transportation, food supplies, maintenance, and pollution. I played it all by ear and just went wherever I could go, more afraid of being inconvenienced than killed.

My mission in the Soviet Union started out to be reconnaissance and analysis of enemies, both real and perceived, in the places they lived. But as the years rolled by and the Soviet Union collapsed, it evolved into conflict resolution, humanitarian assistance, and nation building. Already in the last half of the seventies, I began to see signs of the decay and failure that culminated in the ending of the Cold War. In the eighties, toward the end of the Soviet empire, I began to pick up on the fact that what roads they did have were falling into disrepair. Indeed, all across the Soviet Union you could see everything quite literally coming apart.

Few observers were giving the intelligence people in Washington this sort of thing. Satellite pictures can't monitor the mood of the people, and besides, there is no substitute for eye-level human observation. You just see more when you're on the ground. The diplomats were too busy looking at other diplomats, and the peek-a-boo boys from Congress saw little at all—only shallow impressions from managed and meaningless trips. They didn't see the scars that became part of my regular routine.

The embassy people were restricted in their movements. The satellite pictures could only show so much. But I was everywhere and saw everything! Of course, even though I moved around fairly unrestricted, I knew I was being constantly watched. I knew they were always on top of me. I was never alone. Even when I was alone, I was never alone. I could feel it like a loose net surrounding me, and, in time, I learned to ignore the constant surveillance. After all, I really had nothing to hide and so I never really tried to hide. It was the "trying" that got you in trouble. I saw what I saw, sensed what I sensed, and did a lot of economic and social pulse-taking. I noted changes, however small, tried to find patterns, reported to my handlers, and hoped it helped.

As the number of my visits to the far reaches of the Soviet empire increased, I think—at least I hope—my value to those to whom I reported grew because what I saw showed the decay and decline in ways few other Americans saw. I'm sure the KGB wondered what I was looking at when they saw me studying the rust on a tractor, a new hole in the road, or a building that never got finished. They were constantly baffled. What I was doing was just too broad for them and, I suspect, beyond their experience. They couldn't know what I was looking for because *I* often didn't know exactly what I was looking for either. Their limited background could not relate to mine. They could only speculate.

But, even though I managed to tune in to the Soviet way of life and traveled hundreds of thousands of miles in the Soviet Union as a part of it, I never lost track of the fact that I was participating in a war, a different kind of war perhaps, but a war nonetheless, and that I was constantly behind enemy lines.

I'll never forget feeling my stomach churn one day in Lenin's tomb when I stood silently, struck by how small Lenin was, how pale and bloodless. I wondered how this frail little man could have committed so many of history's greatest crimes against mankind—all in the name of a flawed system that was doomed to fail from the beginning because it was *contrary to human nature*. I just stood there thinking about the peach color of Lenin's long-embalmed skin and how this great criminal genius whose voice had shaken the world was actually so very small. "There he is, a little man," I said to myself. Stalin was also small. What did it mean? Why did they remove Stalin and leave Lenin?"

Suddenly, I could sense that unseen eyes were upon me. Two men with the KGB stamp all over them suddenly elbowed their way in, their eyes no longer unseen. I had a visceral, terrifying reaction. I was in the presence of primal evil. It was as if I had met Lenin and then been confronted with what he represented. A violent, orgasmic surge of terror convulsed through me that day in Lenin's tomb, a genetic meteor, a spark of savage memory, like a howling wolf. The KGB men stood frozen. They had seen me arch rigid and my eyes swell. I had been touched by a force they sensed best to avoid.

I walked briskly up the ramp and out into the winter darkness of Red Square. Lights twinkled in GUMS Department Store in front of me. Three goose-stepping young soldiers stomped up for the changing of the guard. The Kremlin bell tower tolled the hour. I walked, and walked, and walked some more. It was an hour before my adrenaline was back to normal.

During the Cold War, spies knew the rules of the game, and, to quote a CIA station chief in Athens and Paris in the fifties and sixties, "God, we had fun!" I never thought of the Cold War as "fun," and I doubt that very many other American intelligence operatives and spies did, either. But at least we knew what we were up against. This is no longer the case. Today, the multitude of national and ethnic conflicts that inflict our world cannot be settled by simply changing national boundaries to give each community a state of its own. Increasingly fragile bonds of order are the order, or disorder, of the day. The world is filled with troubled peoples for whom religious and cultural identity is more important than territory, whose conflicts know no boundaries, and for whom terrorism is a legitimate means to an end.

Whatever America's good intentions may be, there are those in power around the world who truly do not want peace or solutions to problems. Indeed, they thrive on instability and conflict. The only thing they understand is when someone else has more power *and the will to use it*. In a very real sense, most of the world has become a war zone, and my paper route is no exception. I would come to learn that although the Soviet Union may have collapsed, the Russian Bear merely went into hibernation.

Chapter 6

Helena of Troy
(The Orient Express)

MIKHAIL GORBACHEV CAME TO POWER in 1985. His task was to revitalize the moribund Soviet economy, and his policies were *perestroika* (restructuring), *glasnost* (openness), and *democratzia* (democracy). It was under these relaxed conditions that I was able to exploit the well-organized and efficient Soviet national tourist agency, Intourist, to my own advantage. Intourist previously served Soviet citizens only.

Under the communist regime, the Russians had to have the government's permission to travel. This was their way to keep track of people. There were different levels of service on trains, planes, and in hotels. I always booked into Intourist Number One, which was like a 1980s Holiday Inn, where the top apparatchiks and select foreigners stayed. They could watch me better, and I could see what kind of travelers were in town and why. Cultural exchange, humanitarian aid, and/or business development were my reasons for being there. I was bombarded with questions such as "Why are you here?" "Are you going to spend money in this area?" When asked what I was looking for, my general answer was, "Opportunities," and if asked what kind of opportunities, I would reply, "Any kind!" I sure met a lot of people this way, but because of my ad-lib approach I made very few friends. One meeting was unavoidable; a second meeting made me suspicious; and a third, if unsolicited, meant trouble of some kind. A lot of Russians wanted to make names for themselves by catching a foreigner doing something illegal. Hell, these guys used to get medals for reporting their neighbor or even a family member. They were despicable, and I used to think of them as human landmines—overzealous and paranoid. Sometimes while being interviewed by authorities, I could tell by their questions that someone had reported my presence.

To get *to* the Soviet Union, I frequently used a travel company called Travcoa (Travel Company of America). They had good connections in the USSR and a good staff of Americans who spoke Russian. As part of my job, I had been studying Russian for several years, but then, as now, I kept my proficiency in that language a "company" secret.

One of my early "tourist" trips, before the concept of my paper route was fully developed, was to take the train from Moscow across five time zones to Beijing and back again. The Russian version of the "Orient Express" ran 5,810 miles from Moscow to the then forbidden city of Vladivostok, Siberia. It was on this trip in 1985 that I met a woman I call "Helena of Troy."

I joined an American tour in Moscow and for fourteen days got off and on what was basically an ordinary passenger train for overnight or day trips, depending on where we were. I spent two nights in Novosibirsk, Russia's third largest city, situated on the banks of the Ob River just a short distance from the famed Akademgorodok, the Siberian branch of the Soviet Academy of Science. Novosibirsk is thousands of miles east of Moscow and still little known to Westerners. It has a population of several million, Russia's second-best ballet company, and, of course, its great science research center.

One of our party, a Livermore, California scientist, was dropped off at the science center to attend an international conference. He was looking for a needle in a haystack. One afternoon at an official reception while talking to an informal group of scientists, he heard the needle drop. We picked him up on the way back a week later. He could hardly suppress his pleasure. I had worried needlessly about dropping him off. When he met us at the train station, we stood nose to nose for a full minute, just beaming. Words were not necessary. He had been successful.

When we left Novosibirsk, Bill, the oddball New Zealander Travcoa guide with British manners, wrinkled seersucker coat, and boom box, and with whom I had been sharing a two-bed compartment, met me in the passage outside our compartment and very dramatically announced, "I have to tell you what I've done."

Startled, I responded, "Okay, what have you done?"

Bill looked distressed as he said, "I've been asked to trade compartments with Helena, the new Intourist representative. So she'll be with you."

I was disappointed. The guy was a colorful character, but I didn't argue. I thought perhaps he was more than just a Travcoa guide and might have his reasons. I usually will mentally float at times like these, which is what I did as I waited for him to continue. Finally he cautioned, "I guess I should tell you now that she can be difficult. What I mean to say is she's a moody bitch. But you may find her useful, or should I say helpful."

I told him it was okay. The train was already clicking along into the darkness. An Asian family was cooking some kind of food in their compartment. The female car attendant in a rumpled uniform was making tea, as she did all day long. When I opened the door to my compartment, Helena was already there. We had eyed each other at the station earlier, but I hadn't known who she was. The train was hot and stuffy, and the simple wall lights in the compartment were not bright. Helena rose to greet me Russian style—a soft handshake and a quick kiss on the cheek. She was in her early thirties with Slavic cheekbones and short but slightly wavy brown hair. About five feet five inches tall, she was wearing extremely tight-fitting Calvin Klein jeans and a light blue turtleneck sweater. There was something faintly erotic about her. When I told her blue was my favorite color and that the blue in her sweater brought out the "true blue" in her eyes, she seemed a little flustered but tried to be businesslike. Bill was watching us and commented, "I have blue eyes, too."

Helena arched an eyebrow at him and said, in perfect English with only a few New York language-teacher inflections, "I hadn't noticed."

I asked her, "Do you snore?"

This time she arched that eyebrow at me as she responded, "It depends on who I am with. I'm divorced now."

Her predecessor pointed to his left and said, "I'm in the next car."

I suddenly suspected that they had worked all this out beforehand, but I did like Helena's Calvin Kleins more than his baggy Russian pants. So I went along with it. It was about ten o'clock at night and I suggested that the dining car might still be open for a drink. She responded, "Let's go! I have a headache!" The dining car was old and shabby but had lots of character. The tables were uncleared, but the service was actually fast. We sat across from each other, and there were fresh flowers in a heavy cut-glass vase between us. For a moment I was in a time warp and thought it must be 1935. I like trains! I have since I was a child. There is a certain sense of adventure and romance about trains, and at that moment I was enjoying both.

Helena just sat there and smoked and drank vodka shots for about an hour and talked about herself. She was thirty-four and recently divorced from a chemical engineer. Her mother was a psychologist and her father an Air Force general. She said that she was a language professional and hoped to follow a career in the tourist and travel industry, and that she heard I was in the travel business, too. I told her that I was going to write a travel book one day, but that at the moment I just wanted to see as much of the USSR as possible. I said that millions of people would visit the USSR when conditions got better. She seemed to think that was odd because she said, "Many of our people want to leave here and you are saying that many will come from your country to visit."

As we drifted into more personal talk, I told her I had a large family and this seemed to make her uncomfortable. She dismissed some of my comments with, "That's your problem," or "That is not important." As the conversation got more intimate, she sort of erupted with, "I must go!"

"Where are you going?" I asked, seeing in her face that she had remembered we were sharing a compartment. "I'll be along in fifteen minutes or so," I added.

"Thank you," she responded and, pointing at the half-full vodka bottle, added, "bring that with you."

I let fifteen minutes go by and returned to our compartment. I knocked, heard a voice, and entered. Ignoring the upper bunks, Helena had pulled the other lower bed down from the wall opposite mine and was wrapped in a sheet on top of the blanket. When I put the vodka bottle down on the table, she asked me to pour her a nightcap. I filled a teacup two-thirds full of vodka. Her reading light was off, but I could see her bare arm reaching for the cup. She lit a cigarette. I noticed that her sweater and jeans were draped over the only chair. She sipped the vodka and started talking. "I do not have children. I don't think I want them. Tell me about your five children."

I answered quickly so she wouldn't register that I hadn't mentioned how many children I had. I'd just said that I had a large family. It didn't surprise me that she had this background on me, but it did make me wonder what those who employed her wanted. I gave her a rundown on my kids. She seemed particularly impressed that they had all gone to college and that my daughter Shawn was a jazz dancer.

After some thought, she said, "In another world, I would have liked to have been a ballet dancer, but, as you probably know, all little Russian girls want to be in the Bolshoi. Me, I was good at languages."

It was hot and stuffy in that small compartment as the train rocked and swayed under a red sky in an unending line toward Omsk, Irkutsk, and Lake Baikal. My black denim pants were now also on the chair. As I rinsed in the wash basin, she asked, "You were an athlete? Soccer and basketball?"

"American football and track," I responded.

She came back with, "And you are doing rugby, too, maybe?"

"That's my favorite," I said, thinking she wasn't very professional because she was ahead of the conversation, although she was obviously working off a briefing. Actually, all I really wanted to do at that moment was to pull off the sheet and see what her reaction would be, but she was still talking.

She said, "I am really too big for the ballet. I am five foot seven inches and weigh one hundred thirty pounds."

I responded, "You don't look too big to me."

Her voice smiled as she said, "Well, if you know what I mean, I am too big in certain, or should I say *special*, places."

I wanted to ask her where those places were, but we had six days to go and I decided to take it easy. I was learning that she could handle very complex English dialogue and that she might be extremely clever. I also knew that this very attractive Russian woman had already indicated to me that I could have sex with her if I so desired. This was not uncommon under the circumstances. Russian women can be very naturally uninhibited, and, of course, you always had to worry about the "honey trap."

But, I thought again, we still had six days to go. So I smoked a cigarette and eventually slipped into a deep sleep.

She didn't move all night. At one point I thought she was dead. When I woke up at six in the morning, the train had stopped. Helena had dressed and was outside trying to buy fresh pastries and hot food from some peasants. I wondered what she would bring back. I always ate carefully because I couldn't afford to get sick. I dressed quickly. As the train started moving, she returned to the compartment with two small loaves of bread and some pastries. She then brought some tea and added the few ounces of vodka left in the bottle.

I noticed from the beginning that she really wasn't a very good tour guide. She seemed to be reading manuals and writing reports continuously. This was obviously not her usual assignment. Before it became a problem for her, another Russian called Shaplis joined our fifteen-member party. Shaplis was obviously an Intourist professional, but I noticed he frequently acknowledged Helena was senior to him, sometimes with just a nod but the deference was there. They were both obviously not just what they said they were, but then, I thought, who was I to question this sort of thing? Nevertheless, I thought a lot about the dynamics between the two as the train clacked and rattled east through endless pine and birch forests, the *taiga*.

I felt as if I had been thrown into an endless odyssey and was reaching its outer limits. I couldn't have been further from home, and here I was wondering who was at my back and who was in front. Some of our American tourist group seemed pretty "normal," and I decided maybe I should hang out with some of them. The trouble was I had a problem with an overweight, widowed teacher from Texas. She was wearing a great mess of genuine gold bracelets, rings, and necklaces that had concerned the customs police. As we were both traveling alone, I couldn't avoid sitting with her on occasion, but she was a highly aggressive recovering widow—aggressive like a Russian in that she would pout if I ignored her. But I tried to be sympathetic and understanding. I don't think I succeeded, but I tried.

Helena, I suspected, was more than an Intourist guide.

The next night with Helena was uneventful. She drank four or five beers with dinner, saying it was good for her "meegraine" headaches, and kept writing in her notebook.

The train stopped often to pick up and drop off Russians and to buy produce, fresh meat, and eggs from the farmers who thronged the rural stations. Whenever we stopped, I would get off and mix in with the locals as much as I could. Helena would ask me to walk with her, and we would take short but delightful strolls into the rustic log villages with their split-rail fences, flowers, and cows. We'd walk the unpaved dirt streets with the sweet smell of vegetable gardens. The villages looked much like what America must have looked like in the nineteenth century. When we were alone like this, she would ask me a stream of questions, mostly about America and how its people were treated by the government. At first she would preface her questions with, "The trouble with America is…" but in time she began to open up with "Is it true that in America a person can…?" She volunteered that most of her knowledge of the West came from the Voice of America, and she would say things like, "I don't know why, but to me it sounds true that…"

I would respond, "If it wasn't true, they wouldn't say it," and she would come back with, "You really believe that it is true?"

She wanted to know about my daughters and why my wife didn't work, but she didn't ask some questions that she *should* have asked. In this business you have to build a bridge to the next place in the conversation. If you don't, the other person will wonder how you got there. Particularly if they didn't tell you. I knew that. Apparently, she didn't know it well enough.

During the fourth day out, the train stopped on a siding in a station switchyard to allow several military troop trains to pass. We got off and Helena jumped down from the passenger platform, crossed over five or six pairs of tracks and switches, and entered what must have been a train operations office. I guessed that she was checking schedules and, perhaps, making a telephone call to whomever she really worked for.

A half-hour later I saw her returning, stepping carefully over the rails. She was looking down, watching her steps, but not looking to her left or right. All of a sudden we both realized that a group of freight cars was being pushed down the tracks next to the platform I was on, tracks she had already started to cross. The freight cars were coming fast and, seeing that she was about to be crushed, I was by her in a second, shouting, *"Grab my hand!"* She did and I swung her up off the tracks and onto the platform just as the freight cars rumbled by, missing her swinging body by about a foot.

It couldn't have been closer. She was undone. She knew how close it had been, and that she had been careless. She hugged me and hung on for a long time. It felt good. Finally, she got herself together and said, with a touch of self-deprecation unusual for a Russian, "Now you know why I couldn't be a success with the ballet."

All I could think of to say was, "Big is beautiful where I come from, sweetheart."

She looked puzzled. "Who is sweet...heart? What is sweeet...heart?" she asked as our train whistled it was time to leave and we got back on board.

Two couples from Seattle had seen the close call and were chattering excitedly about it as we moved forward to the cocktail hour in the dining car. Helena turned negative and bitchy, probably embarrassed by her negligence. Very unprofessional for an officer of what *must* be her rank.

Although Helena had talked a great deal earlier, she said little now. After a heavy Russian dinner, she ordered a bottle of cognac and, without paying for it—she never seemed to pay for anything—started to work on it. In a moment of sadness, while nuzzling the bottle, she mumbled, "This is my only true friend. I can trust this. It makes my pain be quiet. I have two ways of finding peace, and this is one of them. You do understand, don't you?"

Ignoring her question, I asked if she took medication for her migraine headaches.

She responded, "Of course not!"

I came back with, "Do you see a psychologist?"

"Of course not!"

"Can't your mother help you?"

"No, no, no. Don't you get it? She doesn't know. Only you know."

"Why me?" I asked.

Her mumble turning into a melancholy snicker, "Because you don't matter."

Startled, I blurted out, "Thanks, sweetheart!"

Looking just a little contrite she said, "What I mean to say is that in my country if you admit you have a problem, then you don't have a good job assignment. They think you are unstable, maybe. If I am considered unstable after I get a job, I do not get promoted. I lose money. I have no future."

"So you just suffer?" I asked.

She nodded. "But of course. All Russians suffer in such a situation. That is why we do not have problems such as you do in America. We *ban* mental problems."

Feeling I was getting somewhere with her, but not sure where "somewhere" was, I commented, "You just deny they exist."

"Of course," she responded, a little music returning to her voice. "You can be sent to the Gulag even when you are not sick. So why risk being sick?" She took a slow deep breath. Her alcohol "medication" had made her more comfortable.

I speculated on promotions for Intourist guides who weren't Intourist guides but who, on the other hand, *were* Intourist guides. My brain cells were rattling with the wheels on the train.

About halfway through the bottle, she said, "This club you are a member of, this Bohemian Club in San Francisco in America...what is a Bohemian Club about?"

I couldn't recall telling her that I was a member of the Bohemian Club, but then I was getting used to the obvious fact that she had been well briefed on me. So I tried to describe to her a club that was private and existed for the pleasure of its members and was devoted to cultural and theatrical productions. As I told her that two of its first members were Jack London and Mark Twain, she interrupted with, "Oh, yes, I have read Jack London. He writes like a Russian. I don't know Mark Twain."

I went on to tell her that the club had members like band leaders, opera singers, and even Secretary of State George Shultz, who sang in a glee club. I told her that Shultz was a real extrovert.

Looking incredulous, she said, "He is?"

I replied, "Yes. And Henry Kissinger is in many of the club's plays."

Her face didn't hide the fact that she thought she was on to something, but she tried unsuccessfully not to let me know it, even as she leaned toward me so as to not miss a word I was saying. After a few more minutes of small talk about the Bohemian Club, she looked at me intently. Our blue eyes were momentarily lost in each other. Both of us were aware that the talk seemed to be going somewhere near an edge. Playing on the possibility that I might think she was a little drunk, she started tapping her index finger on the table, and in a light tone said, "You are pulling my leg."

"Not yet," I laughed as we got up and headed back toward our compartment.

She didn't laugh but continued the conversation inside the compartment. "This club of yours sounds very political to me. You have big summits there. It is like the Trilateral Commission I have heard of? No?"

"No, no. It's just what I said. Like a Boy Scout group or your Young Pioneers."

"Now you are *really* pulling my leg."

"Not yet."

"Do you expect me to believe all those men like Kissinger, Baker, Shultz, Reagan, and General Haig are meeting in the woods to sing and dance?"

"That's exactly what they do."

"Impossible. That could not happen. And who are *you?* You must be somebody special to be a member of a group with those kinds of people in it."

"Wrong again, sweetheart. In my country, people are free to join any club they want. People of different backgrounds and stations in life mix socially a lot."

"Mix! What is 'mix'? What you say is not true. I just don't believe it."

I thought to myself that she was protesting too much. And I hadn't mentioned Reagan or General Haig, besides which, where did she get Trilateral Commission? So, okay, she was KGB for sure. So what? This trip won't teach her anything special. Just don't let her know that *I* know, although she probably already knows that I know.

She interrupted my thoughts with, "Do you have a lot of money? Are you rich?"

"No. I'm just what we call upper middle class."

"What's 'upper middle class'?"

"It's just how I think of my place or level in life. Let's turn out the lights."

As was our custom, she washed up in the compartment first and then left the door ajar. When I went in, her reading lamp was off and her jeans and sweater were on the chair. She was motionless. Thinking she might be asleep, I slipped out of my clothes and got under the covers in my bunk. The compartment was overheated. There was a book under my pillow. I held it up to my eyes to see it better and heard her laugh. She threw another book at me and said, "Hey, sweetheart, you want to pull my leg now? Or maybe you want to pull both my legs now. You saved my life today. But I don't owe you nothing for that. I just want you to make love to me American style, and I'm sure you will like the little girl from Belarus."

I had not known many Russian women in the biblical sense. But this Helena spoke for all of them. Even now as I write this I can feel Helena imprinted on my total being—feverish, lusty, and laughing with no radio or props. Just the wheels on the rails. She would not speak in English while we made love. Russian was closer to her soul, so I didn't know half of what she was saying, but it didn't matter. I knew what she was feeling.

The following afternoon we arrived at Irkutsk and Helena was rotated out. We looked at each other and I knew the chances were small that I would ever see her again. That was it. It's the way it is in "the Business." She smoothed her sweater down provocatively and said, "Please don't write me. It would make things difficult for me and it wouldn't make my life any better than it is at this moment. I hope you will remember me, and thank you for being honest. She dug her thumbs into my belt and gave me a hug that didn't come from a dancer before kissing my left cheek, biting my right ear and saying, "*Paka,* sweetheart" ("So long").

Those I reported to learned little of Helena from me, but they learned much from the impressions of decay and unrest I had—with her unwitting help—gotten all along the way.

Snapshot 4

The Rocky Silk Road

D URING THE THIRTEENTH CENTURY, Genghis Khan with his Mongolian hordes galloped, slaughtered, and conquered his way west to Europe along territory that fifty years later would become known as the Silk Road when Marco Polo went the opposite direction, opening a natural trade route to China. Increasingly during the 1980s, I came to think of this same east-west corridor as part of my paper route.

The true Silk Road countries on my paper route include Kazakhstan, Kyrgyzstan, Tajikistan, Uzbekistan, Turkmenistan, and Azerbaijan, also known collectively as Central Asia. Moscow *manufactured* these six Silk Road countries after the 1917 Bolshevik Revolution with lofty intentions but little practical insight. From the beginning there was trouble, mostly because of this unrealistic plan by Moscow. As a result, the Soviets reengineered the Silk Road into a morass of unforgiving problems.

There are fifty million people living in these predominantly Muslim countries with such diverse cities as Tashkent, Bukhara, and Samarkand in Uzbekistan; Almaty in Kazakhstan; Bishkek in Kyrgyzstan; Dushanbe in Tajikistan; Ashgabat in Turkmenistan; and Baku in Azerbaijan. And if you heard any news coming out of these places, it was probably *bad* news about wars, riots, crop failures, and numerous devastating earthquakes.

The two other countries on my paper route, Georgia and Armenia, have ten million Orthodox Christians living in and around the Caucasus Mountains, where Christianity and Islam meet. Together, all eight members of my paper route form the southern perimeter of the former Soviet Union. The two Christian countries have suffered many of the same tragedies as their Muslim counterparts. Tbilisi, Georgia's capital, was trashed by the Mongol invader Tamerlane in the fourteenth century, over a million Armenians were massacred by the Turks in 1917, and, more recently, Yerevan, the capital of Armenia, was nearly leveled by an earthquake in 1988.

Are things any better now? With Iran, Afghanistan, and Iraq right next door, Russia finds it necessary to maintain a large military presence along its southern border and in the former Soviet republics because otherwise they would be "defenseless." Ahem! Defenseless against whom? The newly independent republics are caught between the proverbial rock and a hard place. With a collapsed infrastructure and unable to defend themselves from either the north or the south, they were easy prey for the Russians, who were able to manipulate the republics into joining the Commonwealth of Independent States after the end of the Cold War for their own protection. But how independent are they? Or do they just exist as a perennial buffer zone between the Russian Bear and Islam?

I have intentionally left out a lot of serious history because I am not a historian. I am an observer and an analyst. But the reader needs to have enough background to understand why I got into so much trouble in these places and why I was so often unsure what it is I was observing and analyzing.

The reader should also be reminded that for seventy years, the fourteen republics of the Soviet Union with its rocky Silk Road, the Caucasus, the Black Sea, the Berlin Wall, the Iron Curtain, the Arctic Sea, and its border with China were effectively isolated from the rest of the world, causing an obvious stunting of socioeconomic growth and self-esteem. This is crucial to understand because, when unrecognized, these deficiencies are crippling, and they have manifested themselves in a malaise of internal growth and foreign policy, thus skewing how the former Soviet Union has approached its international relations.

Chapter 7

Vigilante Justice
(The Pamir Mountain Court)

T O SOME EXTENT because of my trip with "Helena of Troy" in 1985, the Central Asian Soviet Republic of Tajikistan became part of my paper route. My cover was to try to set up possible itineraries for this heretofore unexplored region. Its capital, Dushanbe, was, on the surface, a safe place to go. The Tajikistan Hotel and the October Hotel (later home of the U.S. Embassy) were clean and well maintained. I preferred the Tajikistan Hotel mainly because most foreigners stayed there, and also because of the twin sisters, about seventeen years old, who could always be found weaving twin rugs in the lounge by the Intourist desk. They were the Central Asian version of actress Katherine Ross, times two. Nearby parks welcomed family outings and were filled with families of doting Russians picnicking on the grass. Statues of local heroes, and, of course, Lenin, were near the merry-go-round.

Dushanbe was not an old city. It lies one hundred miles north of the Afghan border and several hundred miles from Konduz and Mazar-e-Sharif in Afghanistan. It reminded me of a California Central Valley town. For the most part, the educated and the bureaucrats lived in the city, and there was no such thing as a middle class. The population consisted of "haves" and "have-nots," and the "have-nots" were 90 percent of the population. The "nots" barely benefited from communism. I used to tell people that if they wanted to know what "poor" meant, they should go to Tajikistan. The poor did what they were told to do, and when the Russians were there full-time, trouble was not tolerated.

When the end came for the Soviet Union in 1991, the Russians became "border guards" or "peacekeepers." A new dynamic appeared from the ruins of the past. Old tribal bonds were renewed. Jews rushed away on regular flights to Israel. The Russian civilian population declined rapidly. A phony aluminum plant that the communists had bragged about became a lost boondoggle. A civil war, little known to the outside world, raged for five years in the mid 1990s and tens of thousands were killed or fled to Afghanistan. Tajikistan was also one of the major staging areas for the Russian-Afghan war, home base for many of the casualty-laden "Black Tulip" flights—black, unmarked Soviet transport planes that brought the bodies home. I spent a lot of time there when the Soviet Union was still a going concern—my cover was to explore possible tourist itineraries for this heretofore unexplored region—and I knew its strategic importance. Its language is Farsi, the language of Iran, and it was and will always be an area ripe for extremist expansion.

On one of my early trips to this truly desolate region in the spring of 1986, I encountered a man I knew only as "the Colonel" (later assassinated on a Dushanbe street corner). He was a multilingual Intourist guide and interpreter at the old October Hotel. Balding, with a mustache, his clothes had a touch of the military. The first time I arrived at Dushanbe Airport, he and a driver were waiting. I knew he must be high up in the KGB because people deferred to him wherever we went. Around fifty years old, he seemed liked and respected more than feared. He looked like Robert Duvall, but with a bit more hair and prominent gold fillings. I told the Colonel that I was hoping to open what I called a Silk Road travel business. Actually, because this region was little known to those I was reporting to, I had been asked to scope it out politically and socially as well as economically.

The Colonel was cautious during my first couple of visits, but some kind of light seemed to go off in him in the spring of 1988 and he became friendly. Somehow he always knew in advance when I was coming. He would call me and we would dine together. He "pumped" me about the West because he had only been to Rumania and East Germany. He seemed curious, but cynical. At first, I thought he just wanted to practice his English, or maybe even get a job with my "travel company." But the real message was that the Colonel, like so many others I was dealing with, saw what was coming. He knew that Gorbachev's *perestroika* and *glasnost* were only first steps toward the inevitable end of the Soviet Union. Like so many, he was beginning to see options for himself for the first time in his life. I was almost embarrassed by what can only be described as his innocence about the future, because he was a very tough guy.

I liked the Colonel, in part because I think he had character. But I know that I was a puzzle to him. He kept trying to figure me out. Sometimes he would seem to catch himself when he thought he was on "scent." I wouldn't let him go too far.

As the nearby Afghan war ended and *glasnost* went into high gear, the Colonel really seemed to change. He was often out of town, his Land Rover covered with road dust and mud. The Russian garrison, although intentionally low profile, was large and hard to hide. There were thousands of Russian troops in the city and in their compound on the outskirts. By the late eighties he and I even began to talk politics, and he would volunteer updates or briefings on his view of what was happening. He was not always easy to understand, and he would leave gaps in his briefings, but the gaps were not difficult to plug.

With the end of the USSR, the situation along the fabled Silk Road of Central Asia became electric. Everything was in a state of flux, and, for a brief time, the window of opportunity was open. I told the Colonel that there would soon be a U.S. Embassy in Dushanbe—mainly for economic development—and that I had talked to our State Department about it. He asked me if I would be the American ambassador. I had to laugh. I told him I would be the ambassador only if he became president of Tajikistan. He smiled a beautiful smile of profound embarrassment, but I had gotten to him in some secret place. He had finally accepted me in an intimate way. Our cultures had overlapped—not merged, but connected. A certain trust was established.

Shortly thereafter, on a sunny May morning, the Colonel told me that he had to make a trip into the mountains and asked if I wanted to go. He said it would take all day and that we would be following a river on a new route I hadn't taken before. I said I thought we had done them all by now and tried to sound disinterested. He pushed.

I said, half jokingly, "Can I bring a book?"

He responded, "Do I bore you that much?" I laughed and he added, "You can bring a book only if you give it to me when you leave Tajikistan."

"That's a good deal!" I fired back.

He looked puzzled. "A deal? How is it good?"

I tried to explain. "I mean good for both of us."

He looked at me strangely. "But, you see, I think a deal is good when I win. Don't you want to win?"

I thought about the cultural divide between us, but said, "I just want us both to be happy."

His face lit up, and he nodded happily, saying, "Of course, but I still think that in a deal, I want to win."

After we started our trip into the mountains, the Colonel mentioned that we had to pick up a few passengers. That puzzled me because he and I were usually alone unless he advised me beforehand. I remembered a previous outing when we picked up some herdsmen (sheep and goats) and how bad they'd smelled and how much discomfort I'd felt in the heat with them. Then the Colonel's Rover had broken down and we'd hitched a ride on a dirty old bus full of more herdsmen. They'd all looked like they'd wanted to slit my throat.

But this time, thankfully, the Rover ran fine. About eight miles further up the road, across a river and through a grassy, rocky landscape, we came to a junction where the mountain road to Tashkent (three hundred miles away) and our road formed a "Y" intersection. There were thirty or forty houses and cinderblock buildings with corrugated roofs, a minor public facility, and a market, all tiered and terraced on a hillside.

We stopped momentarily, then turned up a rocky, rutted side road and pulled up in front of one of the houses. We got out of the Rover, and three of the Colonel's people (two lieutenants and a sergeant) came out of the house leading a prisoner with his hands tied behind his back. Everybody but the prisoner was smoking. The prisoner looked over at me, as if to ask for help. I let my eyes glaze over, sending a message—"No help here, this is *your* world." At times like this, when I was so far out on my tether, so alone, the thought often slipped past my "denial apparatus" that, *Holy shit! I may be on my last lap.* But I also get this same thought on British Airways when it gets bumpy over the North Pole.

The Colonel and I got into the front of the Rover and three officials climbed in back with the prisoner, who was shaking and hyperventilating. He was terrified, but the rest of us settled down and we drove another ten miles up the poorly paved road toward Tashkent. It was mid-afternoon and we were still heading away from Dushanbe. For most of the trip, the road paralleled a roaring mountain river cutting through gravel banks. The river was not more than eight or ten feet deep at this time of year and almost turquoise in color—probably due to silt from melting snow.

The Colonel made general conversation with his men in a language I didn't understand. They were silent, listening to him. Several times I leaned forward enough to see the prisoner in the Rover's mirror. Each time, our eyes locked, his pleading with unspoken force. Finally, I gave him an almost imperceptible headshake, which said, "No, I can't help you." He blinked, and didn't look up again.

We arrived at the end of the badly paved road and were confronted with an open gate made of pipes and a sign saying, *"Uzbekistan Border—Last Petrel."* At the end of the road were several earth-colored, corrugated-and-block buildings that had that "government look." There was also a large gasoline tanker truck that served as a gas station, a couple of small houses, and a café that offered half a dozen low tables where people could sit on the floor, lean back on pillows, and drink coffee or tea.

At a desolate café in Tajikistan, I was an unwitting participant in vigilante justice.

We all went into the café. The proprietors seemed to know the Colonel and his men. There was some discussion about me and then for the next three hours there was *lots* of conversation. They could really talk. They spoke with fierce Muslim passion. Muslims seem overly dramatic to me and I find them hard to believe at times. It was like watching a fiery, dramatic movie.

The prisoner sat alone. He could hear the conversation and was now and then asked a question. He stared at the floor most of the time, but occasional waves of fear ran through his body like a seizure. Even though all the talk was in Farsi (the difficult and not altogether attractive language of the Iranians), I was able to get the general drift of what they were saying. The prisoner didn't seem too bright, and the men with the Colonel would appear to sum something up before asking a new question. They repeated this routine a number of times.

Suddenly the Colonel and his men put their right hands palm down on the table. They all looked intently at me as if they were waiting. I finally put my right hand on the table, palm down. There was a moment of silence, and then we all stood up to stretch. The Colonel's men and the prisoner headed outside. It was almost dark.

I headed for the door, but the Colonel reached for my elbow and started to ask me something. As I stopped to listen to him, I heard what I thought was an old car's backfire, a *pop, pop, pop* sound. The men remaining in the room exchanged glances. I walked outside with the Colonel. I knew that the meeting to which I had been both a witness and a participant was over.

After a few minutes the lights of the Land Rover went on and, as we left the café's porch, I could see the leader of the Colonel's men in the glow of the lights, squatting and washing his hands in a shallow drainage ditch. Only five of us got into the Rover, which was parked next to a flatbed truck. I tried to shut the Rover's door, but it was so high off the ground that it struck the prisoner's feet which were dangling over the end of the flatbed. Not realizing his condition, I reached around the door, eased the man's legs aside, and was startled when I realized my sleeve was wet. At first I thought it was oil, but then I noticed the scarlet trickle running off the truck's tailgate. The others were directing the driver and I don't think they noticed my involvement with the prisoner, who was now a corpse being left for someone else to deal with.

My companions talked reflectively at first, probably justifying what they had done. The phrase, "Pop, pop, pop, and you're gone," kept running through my mind. We dropped off one of the men—I believe he was a sergeant—at the village where we had picked up the prisoner and then made the two-hour drive back to Dushanbe. It was late and I knew I would miss another meal. It didn't really matter. My own mind was churning.

As we drove down the slope of the plain, we could see the pale glow of the distant lights of Dushanbe. I was glad to see them. I was still alive, but I was a long, long way from home.

The Colonel said, "You Americans are always concerned with human rights. So are we. Today we have demonstrated for you our system. The prisoner was guilty of stealing military equipment, drinking alcohol, and raping a woman. There were witnesses. He was guilty! We had a hearing, and nothing had changed. The court voted unanimously, with our hands—including yours—palm down, that he must die immediately." I thought of my right hand—palm down. Jesus! I hadn't even known what I was doing. I thought maybe the right hand number had to do with who paid the café bill, or who was going to drive back, or what kind of dessert we were going to have. Now I realized I had been part of the "jury" that had condemned the prisoner to death, but I kept my thoughts to myself as the Colonel continued. "For now, this is the only way we have of dealing with problems of this kind. If the politicians get into it, the result will be anarchy. Our people know and understand *swift justice* because that is what we practice. When we are more civilized and democratized like you, maybe our 'justice' will be better. Yes?"

I wondered, but managed to choke out a weak, "Yes."

The Rover stopped by my hotel's front gate, which was chained shut and guarded by city police. As I got out, the Colonel spoke sharply to them and pointed at my upper body while making a scolding noise in Farsi. The hotel yard's floodlights were still on, illuminating the blood smears on the right sleeve of my navy-blue wool jacket and on my khaki pants. The Colonel murmured softly to me, "That may cause you problems. Take off your jacket when you enter the hotel." He escorted me to the door and through the lobby, screening my bloody side. He said, "It's been a long day for you and another long day for me. I'll call you. If anybody asks you about…"

Putting on as stupid a look as I could muster, I interrupted, "Asks about what?" He nodded. That was his only answer.

I had some bread and cheese and an orange drink before smoking a Marlboro in my room. Then I went to sleep in a chair facing my room's door. Nobody appeared. Nobody asked me *anything*. My pants didn't clean up, but the jacket was okay in the morning.

Chapter 8

Sink or Swim on the Afghan Border
(Before the Russians Left)

I WENT BACK TO TAJIKISTAN in October 1987 because it shared
a border with Afghanistan and there was obviously a lot of
interest in what was going on down there. I didn't really have
much of a cover other than adventurer, which I guess I was on
that trip. So out of curiosity and against my better judgment,
Mr. Stupid gained the upper hand and I hired a local driver to
take me into Afghanistan. Two other guys came along with the
van. I didn't question them, and just assumed they were some
sort of KGB types.

We went about twenty miles into Afghanistan and there was
military wreckage everywhere. Thankfully, *Mr. Asshole* asserted
control and I asked the driver to find a place to turn around. As
we did, the Russian-made van ran over an antipersonnel land
mine. It was not powerful enough to demolish the van, but it was
powerful enough to roll us over into a rocky ditch and almost do
me in. The door on my side of the van slid open and I was pitched
into a low arc for about a dozen feet. The last thing I heard was the
unmistakable sound of AK-47s firing down from the steep ridge
opposite the van as the vehicle went up in an orange ball of flame,
which instantly became a flash of sheet lightning in my head.

I thought I was hit as I fell backward, arms flailing and grasp-
ing. I felt weightless as it got darker and I could see millions of

tiny golden specs floating in my blackening universe. There was a humming in my head. Then I felt warm—no pain now and the ringing in my ears began to fade. I started sinking into a black velvet abyss—no bottom—deeper and darker, tumbling. I was smothered in silence. My mind started to race and I began having thoughts that all too often simmered just below the surface. My brain cells were crying to each other, *Poor Sno* (my wife Marilyn's nickname)—*I'll never see her again! What will she do? She needs me. Dig in and grab something, anything. Don't touch bottom or, if you do, push off. Where is bottom? Skip bottom—start swimming or flying or whatever it takes. You don't need bottom to push off!*

On some primitive, instinctual level, I realized this was a moment when I must choose to live or die, but, like tumbling in the surf, I wondered, *Where is up?* Then a semiround, coppery sun ball appeared through glassy foam and I felt an embryonic will to live. I had been swirling down in the vortex of the "in between," but now I was swimming upward, against a black cyclone. I had pushed off and suddenly flashed to the surface like a comet.

Battling to remain conscious, I told myself, *This is not it! Don't be stupid. You're not ready to go, not yet. You're not finished!* I was back. But, back where? God, I felt bad. Even so, pain feels good when you consider the alternative, and at least I could feel two of almost everything important. *Keep thinking,* I told myself. *You can't go home like this! Sno won't let you leave again.* But then I had a revelation. She won't know what happened because I'm here, not there! I had seen her sweet, warm, smiling face as I started to sink into that black abyss, and I knew I couldn't leave her alone to deal with what might happen to me. We had been together thirty-seven years and she deserved better than that.

Then, realizing I was back, I could hear men shouting and the crackling of the burning van. I thought I could smell rubber burning, or perhaps it was human flesh. All of a sudden,

I started mumbling incoherently as I became aware of a ruddy-faced Russian Army medic holding some sort of Slavic ampoule under my nose. "Good! You are back," the Russian medic shouted as he held a bloody bandage to the top of my head. "You have no bad holes, just a lot of blood. Your driver is dead, shot in the head and burned. Your companions are wounded but will survive. Judging from your eyes, I think you have been concussed. The next hour will tell us how bad. Keep talking, please." My monstrous headache supported his diagnosis.

I looked around, trying to find my bearings, when the young Russian medic added, "Our patrol is up on the ridge killing the bandits. You were a good decoy for us." He studied me and then added, "The Colonel wants to know what you are doing here?" The Colonel!—I thought he knew.

The medic continued, his Slavic accent more pronounced, "He has your passport. This is a very bad district." Pointing to the Russian convoy that he was apparently part of, he continued, *"We* don't want to be here, old man. Why do *you* bother to be here?" I didn't have a ready answer and he knew it, but I was vaguely offended at his calling me an old man. I thought to myself, *Fifty-nine is not so old.*

They put me in a Russian Land Rover, and by the time we bounced over the seventy miles back to Dushanbe, whatever the Russian medic had given me to ease my headache had worked. But I still hurt everywhere else when the Russians dropped me off at the Hotel Tajikistan. I decided not to notify anyone of my "accident" because the Soviet Union was still functioning and these were pre-U.S. Embassy days. So I struggled up to my third floor room above the Iranian Embassy. It was almost midnight.

I ate some pastries I had stashed in my room and wondered what Sno was doing at four o'clock in the afternoon on the other side of the world. I began to cry. I sobbed and shook uncontrollably for several very long minutes. Eventually, I caught up with my emotions and thanked God for their delayed release. An odd cocktail of fear and relief, I call such moments my "chokers." It is not uncommon for them to recur years later. Some things I just never get over and they have always left me a little scared. Landmines, in particular, are the devil's toys. They scare me the same way that screams of men being tortured do.

That night seemed much longer than it really was, and I had missed my internal Aeroflot flight to Moscow. It only flew twice a week, but a local official who seemed to have connections arranged for me to fly to Moscow on a P-79A military transport. In retrospect, I probably shouldn't have accepted the "favor," but at that moment I really just wanted to get the hell out of Tajikistan, and Tajikistan probably just wanted to get rid of me. I hadn't realized that I was being booked on the "Black Tulip" Soviet military funeral plane. It was a six-hour flight to Vnukovo Airport #2 near Moscow. About sixty cold, hungry, grubby, and battle-weary Russian soldiers were being unceremoniously rotated home, along with thirty-five rough wooden coffins lashed down in the back with plastic webbing. The Russians were so embarrassed over their involvement in Afghanistan that little recognition was given to their dead and wounded.

As the transport plane pushed its way through the sky, I feigned sleep and no one bothered me. The tank commander sitting next to me was so drunk he puked on himself and the smell was sickening. War really *is* hell! The best part of the trip was getting off the plane and walking out of the military area of the airport.

At four in the morning there were no taxis, but I talked a customs official into driving me to the city for twenty-five dollars. I got into Moscow safely and was relieved that nobody had caused me any problems. After all, this was 1986, when the Russians were unhappy—to put it mildly—with U.S. efforts to stop them in Afghanistan. As I slung my baggage into the lobby of Intourist Hotel #2, I glanced back into the dark street. Two black cars with small antennae were bracketing the car that had brought me in from the airport, and the driver was digging for his ID papers. I had known that the "free" plane ride was a setup but thought I picked my driver at random. But, of course, the KGB was always nearby.

I took Aeroflot to London as soon as I could and was scheduled to continue on BOAC to San Francisco. Instead, I decided to lay over in London for a couple of days until my face didn't look quite so bad and I was walking better. Marilyn knew that my consulting work often took me to Third World countries and that things didn't always go as planned. I think because of the primitive areas I was exploring, I was able to keep the true nature of my work a secret from her. Still, I wanted to look as good as I could before I went home.

Not long after I finally returned to California, I was picking up some things at the Ace Hardware store in Colfax (pop. 1,200, elev. 2,600') when I heard a voice ask me, "What happened to you? Haven't seen you for a while. Been out of town?" Looking at my face, he went on, "What *did* happen to you? But, hey, you left the lights on in your pickup truck. You gotta be careful."

After I turned the lights off, I asked myself, *What really did happen to me over there? Wasn't I careful? If that guy only knew.*

Then, as I drove out of Colfax and back onto Interstate 80 toward Lake Tahoe, a shiny red BMW nearly sideswiped me and the young woman driving it gave me the finger. As she pumped her arm up and down, our eyes made contact and a chilling wave swept through me. I had seen such flashing eyes, filled with anger and hate, throughout Central Asia. I wondered if the woman had any idea what had caused such a violent reaction in her toward me, and, more importantly, what might have been my reaction to her in such a moment of madness.

This was just a momentary flash of anger on an American highway, but eyes like those, filled with hate, had become a permanent fixture in my mind. Lee Harvey Oswald and Saddam

Hussein had eyes like that. I have learned to quickly walk the other way when I encounter such eyes, because I know there is no conscience behind them and that the only pain they will ever feel is their own.

Chapter 9

What Can I Tell My Children?
(The Law of the Jungle)

PARTICIPATING IN THE TAJIK JURY "procedure" was not my only experience with Tajik justice. On another occasion, when the Tajiks were, as always, fighting amongst themselves, I hitched a ride into the hills north of Dushanbe with two local officials. I didn't tell them I wanted to look at an air base I had heard about because I knew that would immediately result in some sort of detention. Instead, I told them that I represented International Rotary Clubs that were evaluating where to place humanitarian aid donations. Those fellows hadn't seen many Americans, and I didn't think they knew what a Rotary Club was. But, on the surface at least, they accepted my story, particularly when I also mentioned the Salvation Army, which seemed to ring a positive bell (no pun intended).

Whatever the case, I intrigued them. They welcomed me into one of those big all-terrain Russian vehicles that were very tough as long as you could keep them running. We started climbing up through rocky hills and passes, past decaying huts with rusting corrugated roofs, ragged children, and herds of goats. There was a feeling of desolation all around us. I remember a lone crow coming out of the sky like a black handkerchief floating in the wind. Sometimes I still see that crow just before I wake up in the morning.

We kept moving, up and up. I studied my two companions. They had decent enough uniforms, but I noticed there was something "wrong" about their socks. The socks just didn't go with the uniforms. I worried about that, but I felt comfortable enough until they suddenly announced they needed gas. We careened off the road to a farmhouse where ten truly tough and primitive looking armed men were gathered around two scrawny, dirty and very scared men, both with their hands tied behind their backs.

When we stopped, there was a lot of emotional discussion between the men I was with and the ten armed farmer-type tough guys. The two tied-up prisoners had stolen a military vehicle and wrecked it. As it turned out, the men I was with were not only intelligence officers, but a combined court and punishment unit as well. After more talk and hand waving, the prisoners were dumped into the back of our big Russian vehicle. We drove for ten minutes up a rocky side road before my "guides" pushed the prisoners out and started questioning and kicking them.

It was hot. Wild flowers were blooming. At five thousand feet, the air was thin and clear, warm but mild. It was a lovely day. I thought of my home in the mountains. I tried to hang on to that vision. My mind as well as my eyes glazed over. The kicking and beating went on for what seemed like forever. Finally, they "passed sentence" on the prisoners and "punished" them by repeatedly raising and dropping a fifty-pound rock on one of each man's legs, shattering and splintering the bones so the men would be totally crippled, and marked, for the rest of their lives. At least they didn't break both legs.

I was horrified. This was *their* world, not mine, but on that day I was a part of it. I kept silent until one of my companions turned to me and said, in Russian, "When this war we are in is over, what will I tell my children I did? Something for the cause? What if they ask what our cause was? I am not so sure."

Although I can still hear the screams and the sounds of legs being broken, there was something so human in that simple statement that, for a few moments at least, I felt better. But Tajikistan is a very rough place—rough in a sense that most Westerners can't really understand. As we drove back to the main road, the driver told the other waiting Tajiks, "At least we didn't kill them, and their neighbors can take them home." Tough as they were, they looked visibly grateful for that small bit of humanity.

I was always bothered by the slowness of any form of progress in Tajikistan. Their agriculture was and is marginal, and their engineers and other skilled people have all too often fled to more lucrative areas. It was as if the Tajiks were still in another century, and I was never quite sure just what century that was. Even the Russians were not able to bring them into the twentieth century. Of course, much of Russia itself has yet to see the twentieth century.

The thing about the Tajiks is that they don't just suffer from their own history, they suffer from and are affected by the histories of all those around them. Much of the damage from the Soviets' insane and ill-fated war in Afghanistan, for example, spilled right over the border into Tajikistan. Americans, always suspected of connections with some form of intelligence or another, were not welcomed by the Tajiks, not to mention the Russians, who were always hovering around behind them. This was not a safe place for me. The only other American who had gotten in there early was dead, and the Afghanistan war was right next door.

That day, for a moment—only a moment—I wondered why I was allowed, or forced, to watch Tajik justice for a second time. I asked myself, *Was it a warning, or should I feel complimented to be so trusted?* This, I knew, was a question that might not be answered and could only be understood by someone who had "been there." At times like this, I also asked myself, *What the hell am I doing here anyway?* I'm not a thrill-seeker, nor do I have a death wish. There was always the mission, but I really didn't *have* to be there. I just couldn't seem to help myself.

A lot of what I did, of course, was covert and off the books, but I was able to get a feel, a sense of both the present and the future and what it all meant. Human intelligence is often better than technical intelligence. Satellites could see a farmer peeing in a field, but couldn't reveal who was on whose side in Dushanbe, that legs were being broken, or that another coup was coming. Nor could they interpret the fact that, in all likelihood, only the Russians knew who would come out of it dead or alive. Generally when I went into these places, I was just trying to figure out which faction might take over, not necessarily why; and the only really *hard* information that Washington had at the time came from my observations. But I was able to take bits of information, scraps of conversation and pieces of perspectives and quilt them together for the "spy masters" in Washington and elsewhere. It was dangerous work, but whenever fear threatened to take over, I would ponder the meaning of the words of a British operative I once met on the shore of Lake Baikal in Siberia who said, "We spooks don't die unless they lose our files." I'm still not sure exactly what he meant, but thinking about it kept me alive a number of times while I went about my job looking, listening, and trying to make sense of what I saw and heard. And I *was* lucky, because I found people on the spot who could and would help me, including the Colonel.

I got to know the Colonel well and rode around with him often. The trip that included the palms-down jury was just one. Whenever we were together, he would describe me to those we met as his "friend" and "the man from the West." Although I never fully understood the basis of this "friendship," I never questioned it because it seemed to work for both of us. He spoke five languages and a half-dozen dialects including very good English. He was obviously disciplined and working under some kind of orders, and I believe he was probably the KGB's senior intelligence officer in the region, which means he probably suspected who I was.

My relationship with the Colonel, although cordial and frequently useful, did, however, continue to lead me into many hairy experiences. During a trip in the late 1980s when the Afghan war was winding down and I was attempting to determine which faction might take control of Tajikistan, I found myself near the Afghan border with the Colonel. He unexpectedly announced he had urgent business across that dangerous border and would, for my own protection, have to ditch me in a nearby farmhouse for several hours. At that moment, I really had no choice. I couldn't say, "Take me home, Kathleen!" So I traveled with the Colonel through the deserted and barren mountain countryside to an empty adobe farmhouse. The Colonel wasted little time in the farmhouse. He handed me an AK-47 and told me to shoot *anyone* who came through the front door. He added that if it was him or one of his men, they would tap on the back window first and enter through the back door where I would be able to see them.

I sat down on a chair that immediately buckled beneath me. So, moving to a corner of the front room facing the front door, I hunkered down on the litter-strewn floor and resigned myself to a long wait. I went into my airport meditation state where I visualize myself in Yosemite Valley. After four hours, I became worried and wondered what my alternatives were, if any. It was a desolate place. A dry wind blew sand under the door and a dead vine scraped against the window. I was at least a three-hour drive from Dushanbe and *too* close to the Afghan border. I was alone and without transportation.

Finally, as it began to get dark, I heard a vehicle coming up the road. When it stopped, I peeked through the window and saw several men get out and head through the yard toward the front of the farmhouse. The light was bad, but it was already obvious to me that it was *not* the Colonel or his men. I knew what I would have to do. I was committed. I was stuck! It was take them down, or I was out. I did have an ace—surprise. I knew I must not think—just act! I remembered a deer that had gotten away one winter in Idaho because I got "buck fever" and flinched. I would not flinch today.

There were three of them, heavily armed and cautious. They looked like Central Asian bandits from an old Hollywood movie about the British empire. They approached slowly, but carelessly headed straight for the front door. They were talking. It was all happening too fast. My hands shook as I backed up against the wall of the house and watched the front and side windows. The only questions in my mind were whether they would be bunched up or strung out, and if I nailed just one, what would the others do?

The Colonel had been *very* clear in his instructions: "Don't think. *Shoot* if they come through the door or windows!" I put the AK-47 on fully automatic. Its twenty-round banana clip was loaded. The game was on, and I felt as if I was in mid-air. Two of the strangers rushed through the door. I opened fire and rolled away from the wall. One of the intruders got off a pistol shot, but in a second both were crumpled and dead. I looked through the door and saw the third one crawling away. I fired another burst. He stopped moving. There was smoke and silence. My ears were ringing. The third man twitched and convulsed, then went flat in the yard. I stepped back through the front door and stumbled over one of the fallen. Recovering my balance, I quickly crossed the room to the rear in dark desolation, splashing blood "pat pat" like in the shower. *Oh, God, there go my white Nikes.* I actually thought that. It was wild.

My ears were still ringing as I went out the back door, AK-47 in hand. Running as fast as I could, I cut across a field and jumped a bramble hedgerow before heading up the unpaved road in what I hoped was the direction of Dushanbe. I ran and ran, trying to keep my pace, until my lungs hurt. Then, I slowed down to a more even keel. As I ran, I thought about the saying in the trade, "A field operative can't truly be trusted until he has killed another human being." I wondered if I was being tested. Maybe. Did the Colonel learn anything new about me? Of course he had. He learned that I could kill if necessary. On the other hand, maybe this had been nothing but a cleverly arranged assassination by the Colonel for me, the "Good Samaritan" from the West, to carry out. Had I done somebody else's dirty work? Was I being set up or sized up? I muttered to myself, "Go! Go! Go!"

After running north for maybe an hour, I stopped and looked for cover—a place to hide. I thought I had run at least seven or eight miles in the direction of Dushanbe. There was a faint glow in the sky, barely enough to define the faraway hill ahead of me. Running at night is an imperfect art. You don't try to see what you can't see. You stay in the middle of the road and react to lighter and darker objects. The road is light and the fields around you are dark. You get into a detached mode. You let your feet take over. If allowed, feet can see or sense where to land. You sort of let your right brain take over. The countryside was totally bleak. Silent. There seemed to be nothing growing or alive around me. I tried not to breathe too loudly. I couldn't dampen the sound of my shoes striking the sun-dried road and cursed my "sneakers." I also cursed the potholes and decided to ease up. I couldn't afford to sprain or break something. I was trembling from fatigue and, although I hated to admit it even to myself, unresolved fear. I had just killed three guys but at that moment didn't have the luxury to reflect on it. Instead, I had to concentrate on surviving the next turn in the road. The act of killing, in all its stark horror, might, as one of my mentors told me, "set the professionals apart from the amateurs," but that didn't make me like it. I looked up at the sky and shouted, "What the fuck am I *doing here?*" I might even be in Afghanistan

by now. They might trust me a little more now, but then...
"What the hell am I doing *here* in the first place?"

Just as I decided it didn't matter *who* trusted me now because this must be the place I was going to die, a vehicle's lights appeared bouncing along with men the Colonel had sent to look for me. They honked and called out, "Alu, Alu, OOO-SAY" *(Hello, Hello, U.S.A.)* until I realized that I was pointing my AK-47 at them. They smiled big smiles and shook their heads in a friendly fashion. Ironically, they had turned back once already because they had not realized how fast or how far I could run when scared.

After they picked me up, the truck stopped at the farmhouse on the way back to Dushanbe, where we found the three bodies neatly lined up in the yard for others to deal with. They wanted me to see this because they said they were proud of "Meester Jeem." The Colonel had already been there and, as he later told me, "cleaned things up a bit." He reassured me in approving and warm tones, *"Jeem, you deed what you need, what you had to do."* He took my AK-47 and examined it. Twelve rounds fired and eight rounds left. Like a good coach, he patted me on the back. I felt like I had been accepted into some jungle tribe. He was right: I did what I *had* to do, but I thought about the Colonel's remark for a long time, troubled by the fact that when you've seen or done the worst, and justified it, something happens to you and you never really recover. You are altered forever.

Nobody's Damned Business

A S MY TRIPS to the former Soviet Union became more frequent, more people, at home and abroad, became aware of
them. Not surprisingly, many wondered about the purpose of
my travels. It was not uncommon for some—idiots and friends
alike—to ask in front of just about anybody, "What are you—a
spy or something?" I remember one "old buddy" in particular
who got a kick out of referring to me as "Stealth," not realizing
just how close he was to my real "Phantom" nickname. I would
usually zig and zag a bit and, like a politician on a talk show,
skirt the issue.

Then there were the times when almost total strangers,
with little introduction or background, would ask smart-ass
questions that were *truly* out of bounds! My ears would ring
with: "How much money do you get paid?" "Do you carry a
gun?" "Have you ever *killed* anybody?" Indeed, they would ask
me everything except for the details of lovemaking with my
wife, and I have to say I was offended every single time. Combat
veterans, policemen, and others involved in life-and-death decisions as a rule don't like to talk about such intimate subjects.
I'm comfortable talking about such matters only with those of
my peers who may have actually had similar experiences, and
not very often with them. To all the rest, I would usually blurt

out something sappy like, "I can be violent if necessary." I have always had an ability to isolate myself, and this allowed me to do what was necessary, when it was necessary, without even thinking about it. There is never time for conscious deliberation—only reaction—when, according to the training manuals, God grants you "1.2 seconds" in which to choose life or death.

Most of the people in my business were formally trained in self-defense by the military. Perhaps it was easier for them. My "training" comes from being a cornerback or safety in football or rugby—positions where quick, aggressive, and reactive defense was the key. I have survived mentally by continually reminding myself that it was either *them* or *me*.

Over the years I *have* seen plenty of death. The thing about dead people that has always gotten to me is that one second they're with you and the next they're gone. When you see death, at that exact moment it seems so easy, so final, that I have found it difficult to relate to what's happening and rarely have adequate words for my wonderment. I just know it's over. They don't matter anymore. They are gone forever. The body is nothing. It was probably necessary. Only later does it occur to me that *I* could have been the one to die. But even though scared, seriously scared, scared *shitless,* I always knew that losing my own life was never a consideration. I rarely got badly hurt in hundreds of rugby and football games, or later behind the Iron Curtain. But, then, I didn't expect to get hurt. It's all a matter of *attitude*—survival, that is—and it is an attitude that has served me well.

Chapter 10

Light, Shadow, and Darkness
(Cat and Mouse)

THE SOVIET UNION was still very much the Soviet Union in 1987 the night an attractive Intourist guide came up to me in a Moscow hotel lobby and said, "I am so sorry to bother you, Mr. Waste, but if you could just come into the office for a moment or two and speak—only for a moment, if you please—with the gentlemen who are here, and, well, please come this way. Thank you."

I was *not* pleased. I was preparing to take another train ride across the vastness of the entire Soviet Union and, through eyes- and hands-on experience, report in detail on the condition of the country's economy and declining infrastructure. I was using my fine-arts-dealer cover on this particular trip, perhaps for the last time because I found it less useful outside the major cities where I was increasingly spending my time. I was anxious to get going and wary of bureaucratic traps and KGB tricks. But this was a particularly attractive Intourist woman whose original assignment had probably been to get me into bed with a camera rolling. And, besides the fact that her English was "NYU excellent," she had a certain hallucinatory clarity about her, as well as a set of provocative hips that I followed into the hotel office, a small room with a cheap disinfectant smell.

I was confronted by three men. One looked like a diplomat, another a cop, and the third a thug. To an experienced eye, all three were obviously KGB. The "diplomat," who appeared to be the leader, said in perfect English, "Thank you for speaking with us, Mr. Waste." He seemed to be showing off his English to the other two. The "cop" muttered something in broken English. The "thug" just looked quietly menacing as he let out a quiet fart. The diplomat continued, "We have just a few questions, if you please, Mr. Waste."

I gave the obvious leader of this KGB team my "rugby assassin's" smile, and the cop and the thug my "hard man's" stare. At least, that's what I tried to do. They obviously wanted to intimidate me but didn't succeed. I was used to guys like these. They see me and size me up and think they can take me, and it frustrates me because I know they probably can't—but I have to keep a low profile. I responded to the diplomat, "Glad to be of help."

The diplomat studied me before asking, "You are a dealer in antiques?"

"I am," I replied.

The diplomat quickly followed with, "It is true, is it not, that you were also an employee of the Bechtel Company for a long period?"

I nodded in the affirmative.

"Is it also true, Mr. Waste," the diplomat continued with a knowing smile, "that a Mr. John McCone, who was the leader of your Central Intelligence Agency, was associated with your company?"

I replied, "What do you mean *my* Central Intelligence Agency? The Bechtel Corporation is not *my* company, either. I *worked* for them, as did my father, who was a friend of John McCone. They built the Liberty ships that saved your ass during World War II."

The diplomat looked skeptical. "Yes, I see. But is it not true that they are an intelligence arm of your government?"

"What 'they' are you talking about?" I asked.

He ignored my question and continued. "And then there is the Mr. George Shultz who is very important in your government. He, too, worked for your Bechtel company and is a friend of yours as well. Is that not so?"

I replied, "My most recent contact with George Shultz was the day I sold him a grandfather clock. Did you know that he's a former Marine with a Princeton tiger tattooed on his ass?"

The diplomat wasn't sure how to handle that one, but said, "There is also a Mr. Casper Weinberger, who was very big with your Bechtel and also your government's defense…"

"Look," I said, "let's loosen up here. I'm just a rugby player and antiques dealer who used to be a construction stiff. I think Weinberger used to be a disc jockey." They shook their heads, probably wondering what "construction stiffs" and "disc jockeys" were, wound up the interview, and walked out with frustrated looks on their dour faces.

Not long after, on the same trip, at another typical Intourist "no star" hotel in Almaty, Kazakhstan, a similar threesome appeared and "invited" me into their establishment's office. The leader of this new trio asked, in English as perfect as that of his previous counterpart, "Mr. Waste, is it not so that you have an associate with the name of Louis W. Jefferson, sometimes known as 'Antofagasta'?"

Surprised by the boldness of this question, I replied, "In the antiques business in San Francisco, yes." My reply was true up to a point. Lou, of course, had traveled throughout the world with John Foster Dulles and was much more than just an associate. But, as I later told Lou, "I had no idea your middle initial was 'W' or any other letter, so when they came up with that 'W,' I suspected they were on to more than I knew about. That is to say, I wondered if *your* background might do *me* in, even though I was surviving my *own* checkered past. Happily, it didn't."

As it turned out, KGB interviews such a this were nothing more than an inconvenience, and so I pressed on with my trip. It was while traveling across the fertile plains and vast wastes of Siberia, with its days and days of endless forests, rough log cabins, and occasional gingerbread villages, that the sheer geographic power of the now former Soviet Union began to truly sink into my consciousness. Eleven time zones! Nearly halfway around the world! The experience was profound. I felt an almost primal relationship with the endless tracts of wilderness, the taiga, and the Russian music that was everywhere and often brought unexpected tears. But it also made me feel more alive and necessary. The vastness of Russia, along with the visible connection the Russian people had with the earth and the isolation of their past, was overwhelming to me at the time. It's a sad past that has not yet found a future, a hard place to live for most of its inhabitants.

I thought about the thirty million who had died fighting Hitler, and the thirty million more who died because they did not believe in Stalin's communism. My mind kept racing, in slow motion. I thought about those who survived, crippled by seventy years of failed development and dysfunctional ideology. What do they do without the gifts of history and social identity? *That*, I thought, is the great crisis of this social tragedy that was now entering a new phase. What would they build on when denied a valid past? I thought about death.

My preoccupation with death was probably a deep, and usually masked, emotion stirred loose by the vastness of the endless subarctic taiga forests that stretched out before me like a lawn of trees stunted by severe weather and short seasons. I knew that if you wandered into them, you could lose your way forever. Airplanes crash into them and disappear. It's like quicksand, in a way, with the train's rails going in ever deeper. It was pulling me inside out, reversing my very being. *Maybe I won't go home. Who cares?* I wondered if I would be sucked in and lost in Mother Russia's gut, and kept muttering to myself things like, "Survive or die," and "Stay on the mission." Of course, I knew this was about more than just my mission. My soul was being twisted by feelings without words as I was drawn into the darkness of my journey. Lost. *I'll just wander forever. Where is up? Where is down? Where is home?* I was feeling the rapture of a deep, obsessive involvement. Hang on, I tell myself, and check the tether from that faraway place I report to. Maybe it's time to go home! That little bird on my shoulder said to me, "*Baby*, you've been gone too long. Time's up!" The tether holds.

As I looked out at Mother Russia's vast emptiness, I began to have thoughts of my own mortality, such as, "If I disappear, who will know?" Normally my "Just go about your business" streak of fatalism would kick in at this point. But I became uncharacteristically preoccupied with death on this trip—not so much my own death, but those I had witnessed in Tajikistan and Afghanistan.

As the train rattled on, I began making cryptic notes for my next report, noting how odd it was that even in the most remote places, people seemed to place great importance on business cards. It got me wondering what might be the most appropriate card for me in that area of the world and, in a fit of inspiration, I wrote down that I was going to have my cards marked, quite simply, "The Unmarked Card"—perhaps in a number of languages. As I chuckled out loud at my own inspiration, a man who looked like he was in a saloon scene from *High Noon* pushed his way through the door into—for a Russian train—my sparsely crowded coach. For no apparent reason, the man in front of me started lurching around like a poisoned rat. As I continued to chuckle at the words "Unmarked Card," the "saloon man" and the "poisoned rat man" abruptly stopped their manic gyrations and stared at me. This sudden change shut me up. We all stared at each other and then burst into unexplained laughter. One of them opened a bottle of vodka, and during the conversation that followed I learned both men worked in a nuclear materials processing plant, one I had not known existed.

It was small, unplanned encounters such as this that both furnished important information and, at the same time, relieved the tensions of my double life. But, although it was fun and informative to be drinking (faking it) vodka with two nuclear engineers, I was always conscious of KGB eyes, seen and unseen. I knew my every move was monitored, and that even totally innocent actions might appear to my watchers to be something other than what they were and could land me in jail, or worse.

I generally knew when I was being set up. In this case I had to be careful not to show too much interest in the nuclear plant technicians. I talked to them about the U.S.A. and, conscious of nearby eyes and ears, stayed away from direct questions. I just let the vodka help them talk. On some trips I had not been able to spot my KGB watchers. This time I had, because two men who were obviously listening to the conversation looked much too bored for what they must be hearing. I had found that forced disinterest was always a dead giveaway.

After that particular trip, I told a colleague in America's London Embassy that one of the first things I always notice when I get off a plane in London after such a journey is that I sort of decompress. I don't have to be so careful and think about every move I make, like always arranging personal effects so that I can tell whether or not I've been searched. It's sort of like a cloud lifting when you're not fully conscious of it, since you *feel* it before your brain recognizes it's happening. For weeks, you've taken extra care in everything. The thump of a distant door sets your nerves on edge. Shadows under your door and the puff of window curtains when the air pressure in your room is changed, the sound of breathing in the darkness when you think you're alone, curious stares in the street—all are grist for your internal radar system.

Then, you're suddenly out of it. The built-in protective paranoia shield just lifts by itself—like thick storm clouds lifting from a mountain. All of the little pieces that go into the vigil that preserves your life are no longer necessary. Besides which, in London, cab drivers generally help you with your bags. In Russia, they never did. They just seemed to enjoy watching you struggle like foreign shadows in their darkened world, paralyzed by their own system, deadened to any prospect of what even a little initiative on their parts might produce.

Chapter 11

Chernobyl
(A Defining Experience)

THE EVENT THAT DEFINED for me my mission and evolving role as a spy in both the Cold War and the New World Disorder was the nuclear catastrophe at Chernobyl in April 1986. The Soviet government waited three days before announcing that an explosion had blown off the top of a nuclear reactor at Chernobyl. During these three days, a plume of toxic gases and dust, laced with plutonium, iodine 131, strontium 90, and cesium 137, some of the most deadly elements in the universe, was spreading across the western Soviet Union, Eastern Europe, and Scandinavia.

Writing in his 1991 memoir of his days as Soviet minister of foreign affairs and as one of the architects of the end of the Cold War, Eduard Shevardnadze said of the catastrophe: *"'Chernobyl Day,'* as I privately called April 26, 1986, marked a watershed in world history, a new criterion for foreign policy... How can you conceal something that can't be hidden? How could people complain about 'washing our dirty linen in public' when it was radioactive? How can you hide from millions of people the truth about a threat to their lives and health?" Shevardnadze continued, "Although I had been raised in a spirit of mystical veneration for the 'top secret' stamp, I nevertheless did everything I could to see that the truth about Chernobyl would be known to the country and the world in the first days after the accident. I was not able to do much..." But he did do something.

Eventually, going against all previous Soviet practice, there was *some* public disclosure. A few Western observers other than scientists were permitted to visit and view the site, although under a thin but very real veil of secrecy. However, there was still a lot of outrage at the Soviets for initially trying to "spin" the disaster. When the Soviet government finally realized that the only way to dampen worldwide condemnation was to exercise a public relations program of damage control, they decided full disclosure was the way to proceed, much to the surprise of many. They selected a number of experts and observers from various countries to go in and take a look. Shevardnadze wanted a more open policy, and I became one of the instruments of that policy when I joined one of these groups of twenty or so individuals. In an odd way, I think of this as the beginning of what is now a history with Eduard Shevardnadze, a man I have come to revere although I knew little about him at the time.

I was surprised but pleased to have been recommended for inclusion even though I was concerned it might jeopardize my various intelligence activities. But the word from the Pants Factory was that the opportunity to get into Chernobyl so early was worth any breaking of cover it might involve. As an ex-engineering and construction specialist with Bechtel, it was believed that I had the "right eye" to go in there and tell them what had happened, or at least observe and give them my own opinion. Besides, the Soviets certainly had at least a partial fix on me by that time, if only because of my years with Bechtel. Perhaps they viewed me as a channel to people back in Washington, and that, for whatever reasons, they could trust me to report only what I saw.

The Soviets ended up picking only ten from my group to actually go *inside* the mangled and radioactive Chernobyl control house and auxiliary buildings. I made the final cut. They said we would be safe if we followed proper procedures. But even so, I felt a rare form of paranoia. I couldn't help but wonder if I was being set up—by one side or the other—for something further down the line. I thought to myself, *Is this really what "somebody back there"wants? Have I become a marked man at home as well as abroad?* But ultimately, I just had to assume that people on both sides thought I would give a practical and balanced opinion and that my presence would add something. Although I was obviously concerned my health might suffer from exposure to radiation, it was an opportunity I couldn't pass up.

Some of us met in Geneva where we were briefed, and we then flew on to Kiev via Lufthansa. There seemed to be a general feeling that all of us wanted to give the world the most complete picture we could. We spent the night in special quarters in Kiev. An air of mystery surrounded us. Some of the people in our group seemed angry but kept their emotions in check. Nobody wanted to jeopardize what for all of us had become "the mission."

The next morning a very new and specially insulated bus with a number of Soviet scientists and "journalists" aboard picked us up in front of the hotel. We drove about sixty miles from Kiev, past abandoned farmhouses with everything obviously left behind because, as one expert put it, everything was "still cooking." Finally, we reached the totally deserted company town of Pripyat, where the plant operators and maintenance people had lived. We were deep in the "forbidden zone." It was eerie, strange, crazy, and, bottom line, a glimpse of what could be the end for all of us. An apocalyptic wind blew radioactive dust, like poison gas, around the bus in devilish swirls as it tried to get in.

I had seen dozens of these "worker cities" all over the Soviet Union. They were cold, tasteless, gray industrial complexes with three-story gray apartments, office buildings, and schools, all one mile or so from the plant. Often nearby were rustic villages with split-rail fences and vegetable gardens. Peasants and cattle mingled in the unpaved streets. The military decentralization of industry had kept cities small.

As we got closer to Chernobyl, I contemplated twenty-five thousand people being evacuated within forty-eight hours, leaving *everything* in place. I was told that the firemen and technicians who initially responded to the explosion were streaming into the local hospital, already gravely ill from intense radiation exposure, even as the children of Pripyat, ignorant of the danger, played in the streets. In my mind's eye, I could see women hanging laundry while young men kicked a soccer ball through air already filling with radiation. Hours had passed before they were told to leave, which they did immediately. All their plates and pots were still on the tables. Window curtains were blowing. Toys were tucked in beds. Toilets remained unflushed. Actually, I couldn't contemplate it. And then I saw for myself the abandoned cars and bikes stacked like skeletal bones in the center of town because the Soviets didn't allow anything other than people to leave. It was spooky. I thought of Pompeii, but Pompeii was quicker and more merciful. Chernobyl would continue killing for many years to come.

Security was extreme and heavy equipment was going in everywhere. We realized that we were close to ground zero. There were damp eyes in our group as heads twisted in disbelief. They drove us around the area for a while, but because the radiation levels were so high, at first they wouldn't let us out of the bus.

As we got closer to the plant, we noticed that they had been stripping at least six inches of topsoil off the ground in order to reduce radiation concentration. They were talking about doing this throughout the entire region because they believed that any wind, *anything* that would blow, could kill. An enormous undertaking faced them. Who knew who would survive?

The heroes were the construction workers who knew this was *their* war and that *they* might not survive. Like all good soldiers, they had received the call to die so that others might live. The question actually was not *whether* they would die but how long it would take, for the protective gear they wore was woefully inadequate. I can still see their terrified, pleading eyes glancing in our direction as they worked frantically, hoping that we might have brought some new reality that would reward them for their service.

The security fence was about half a mile from ground zero. Heavy equipment kept moving all around us. A concrete plant to make bulk concrete had been set up. The hope was that they could contain the radiation by encasing it in a massive concrete coffin. Activity, frenzy, confusion, and yellow barrier tape were everywhere. As we got closer, the faces we passed were increasingly terrified behind their clear plastic masks. Popular music blared from loud speakers and, for some reason, I was reminded of San Francisco's Playland at the Beach when I was a boy. For me, the sound somehow cheapened the heroics happening all around me.

The Soviets issued us white, airtight, hermetically sealed "moon suits" with respirator masks and heavy goggles before taking us to a conference room where some very serious-looking senior Russian officials appeared. They spoke to us through interpreters and gave us a rundown on what had happened, much of which we already knew. They said they wanted us and the world to know that they were not being evasive. However, there was pain and suffering in what we could see of their faces behind their masks, and it was obvious to us that they were not accustomed to telling the world much of *anything*, much less a major and top-secret disaster that forced them to admit that we all share this planet. Having never held a Western-style press conference, they seemed to go through a series of layered forms of communication trying to explain what they thought had happened without really wanting to understand it themselves.

Then, following men with Geiger counters, the serious-looking Russians led us under bent-outward girders into the heart of the plant and the control room. The damage was enormous and ugly. It was like an unimaginably huge bomb had gone off. I had personally seen the results of two large boiler explosions when I was with Bechtel, one in Anacordis, Washington, and the other in Pembrokeshire, South Wales. Both involved startup pilot error, which is not an uncommon problem when locals are hired and trained to run sophisticated equipment. But neither had even approached the scope of this. The world had never seen damage like this. The Hiroshima and Nagasaki explosions *evaporated* their targets, but Chernobyl left a gouged and ruptured industrial corpse. There was nothing to compare it to.

All told, we spent about three hours inside the perimeter of the plant, and when we got back on the bus there was very little talking or communicating of any kind. Mere words cannot describe what we saw, but I can tell you what the bus ride was like. The silence reminded me of the bus ride after the third consecutive time Cal lost the Rose Bowl in the last five minutes of play. But at least back then, we knew we'd survive.

I was told that Chernobyl would probably be "the greatest peacetime industrial disaster of all time" but regarded the statement as exaggeration until I was confronted with it and realized the implications of the radiation that was pouring out over the Ukraine and much of Europe—radiation whose effect would be felt for years to come. A very scary scene. I felt small. Hollow. Naked. Humble. Empty. Helpless. In awe of the implications, I didn't know *how* to feel. An unbelievably terrible accident.

I wondered how such an "accident" could have been allowed to occur. As I was familiar with the operation of such plants, it only made the question larger in my mind. As we headed back to Kiev, it came to me how easy it would have been for the right person to pull a pin on that place and have a controlled explosion if he knew what he was doing, an explosion that would hasten the end of the Soviet Union. The implications of what I was thinking shook me.

Later, I passed these thoughts along to my intelligence "masters" when they debriefed me. There were a lot of raised eyebrows, scowls, and the like. Not much else. Just fingers to the lips, and a long "Shhhh..." coupled with, "We will give your thoughts consideration and pass them along." It appeared my debriefers were catching an unexpected hot rock, something they hadn't foreseen or even thought of, or were they surprised that it was so obvious? For a moment, I almost wished I hadn't brought it up.

In my own mind, I linked this disaster to the nineteen-year-old German pilot, Mathias Rust, who, in May 1987, hedge-hopped his plane under Soviet radar and landed, smiling, right in the middle of Red Square. As a result, the top Soviet Air Force general was forced to resign. It could have been a bomb instead of a smile, and the Soviet people knew it. It further shook their faith in their government, which had already been shattered by Chernobyl. Taken together, I asked myself, were these signposts along the way to the end of Soviet power?

When we returned to Geneva from the site of this genuine disaster, there was a lot of curiosity. My questions about what I had seen, but not my suspicions, were noted. They really only wanted to know what we had seen. No projections, or analysis—just what we had seen. However, what we had seen proved valuable because they had already gotten lots of mixed scientific and engineering stuff, but very little first-hand practical reaction. The other members of our tour gave them that, and I guess they figured *they* were the ones to interpret it politically. Quite simply, their conclusion seemed to boil down to "just an accident—a bad one, but just an accident." Those we reported to didn't seem to see it as a sign on the road to the impending demise of the Soviet Union. And, they refused to look beyond what appeared to be obvious, namely, *why* it happened. "Just an accident!" they said. "It takes time to investigate these things even in the West, don't you know?" That was it!

However, my own nagging doubts persisted. Chernobyl, disaster and tragedy that it was, for whatever reason helped drive the final nail into the coffin of Ronald Reagan's "Evil Empire." There is no question in my mind that Chernobyl played a major role in the breakup of the Soviet Union and the end of the Cold War, and the real facts behind it may never be known. What we do know is that the night of the accident, the operators powered down the reactor in a way that made the core less stable. That, in and of itself, is not unusual, but what *is* inexplicable is the fact that they also disengaged critical safety systems so that when the reactor started to destabilize, a power surge in the core set off the explosion. Why no safety measures? Was it carelessness? Operator error like this happens even in the States. Operators are often hired locally and trained on the job, but still, it would be so easy to slip in a "ringer."

The Soviets under Gorbachev were already on a course that could only lead to radical change. Although I would never accuse Gorbachev of having anything to do with it, the disaster certainly pushed his policy of *perestroika* along. Young people in the Soviet Union responded to it, just as young Americans had responded to the much lesser but similar accident at Three Mile Island in 1979, and audiences had flocked to see Jane Fonda in *The China Syndrome*. And, for the Soviet Union, the mere fact that people were allowed to know about it was unusual, if not unique, and undoubtedly a major step toward the end of the Cold War.

Indeed, whether Chernobyl was an accident or something else, I sensed for the first time that the Soviets were on the ropes, and those at the top, although not saying it, knew it.

The national will was weakening. Everywhere I went in the Soviet Union after Chernobyl, I sensed a change in the attitude and mood of the people. Any remaining faith they had in Marx and Lenin was fading. They sought out Westerners to converse with in the open. Questions were everywhere. Of course, the climate being created by Gorbachev with his policies of *perestroika* and *glasnost* made them feel freer to raise questions. But Chernobyl, terrible as it was, was a big part of it. If someone had intentionally "pulled the trigger" to speed up the end of the Soviet Union, he or she accomplished his or her purpose. But what a frightful cost! When I ask myself if it was worth it, I have two answers: In the short run, no. In the long run, a resounding yes!

Chapter 12

California Dreamer
(Just One More Shot)

ONCE IN A WHILE I would get a call from my coordinator at the Pants Factory and would be told to pack my kit, given a destination, and instructed to check out something special, something that would benefit from experienced eyes on the ground. On this type of assignment, I worked directly with the American Embassy people and no special cover was necessary. It was just such a call in late September of 1993 that sent me suddenly to Moscow—not my regular beat by then. After I booked my flight, I got back to my coordinator and he told me I would be joined by a Mr. Jeremy Nodoff on the plane and that he would know me as "Cal Dreamer."

"He'll sketch it all out for you," my coordinator advised, "so keep in touch and, oh, yes, keep your head down." Keep my head down? Sure. But what stuck with me was his sense of urgency.

A day later, as I sat in the San Francisco Airport terminal near the British Airways desk showing Flight 265, I scanned the other passengers as they arrived. I was always two hours early and learned through long experience to look over those who would be on a flight with me. A half-hour before departure the flight crew, wearing white-and-blue blouses and sitting near the gate, rose and boarded. While I strolled around trying to be casual as I looked over the other waiting passengers, somebody swiped my San Francisco Chronicle, but I was through with it. Did that mean anything? No, but protective paranoia was taking over.

I boarded and put my two carry-on bags above my economy seat (contract personnel go economy) and then sat down next to the aisle. The Boeing 747 lumbered to the takeoff runway and, leaning back on its tail, lifted off and headed north over Canada and Greenland toward London. I did not relish the next twenty-four hours. No layover, five hours in the Heathrow lounge, and then five more hours to Moscow. The *Fasten Seatbelts* sign was still on and I wasn't sure the plane would stay in the sky where it belonged. I had been through the gas dumping and return bit twice. I felt like a drink although I don't drink, and didn't really notice the guy next to me, except that he was about my size. When we reached some altitude, he pulled out a newspaper and started to read. I glanced at it and recognized my missing sports section because I had torn a rugby article out of it. Then, I thought I heard a soft whistle come out from under the man's tongue. Sort of a *Mamas and Papas* sound. Whoops! "California Dreamer"? Ha! Actually, I was just having a little mental fun with myself because I *felt* I had another professional sitting next to me. I made some small talk about sports with him and then said that, as we wouldn't be served for over an hour, I was going to nod off for a nap. The man couldn't hold back. He said, "This is too much!"

I fired back with, "Jeremy, what is this—Hollywood Thrillerville?" as I gave him a soft elbow and we both laughed.

He said, "Well, it's working!"

He was about forty-five and had a small mustache. He was better dressed than I, and, as I found out later, had gone to MIT and was a West Point graduate. And, he was black.

He said, "I saw you looking for somebody you didn't know. You never even gave me a tumble and I was sitting right across the aisle from you. You must be a racist like all the rest." I am anything but a racist and was about to respond when he continued, "I'm glad you're offended. Anyhow, if you grew up in Northern California, at your age you probably never even saw, or at least knew, a black person until you were twenty years old." Actually he was right about that, but he refocused so fast, saying "Let's go back by the passenger doorway and talk sports!" that I let it drop.

I said, "I'll join you if you put away that needle of yours."

"But, of course," he said with a thick Russian accent.

As I peeked through the doorway's little round window at the snowcapped peak of Mount Shasta, rosy orange in the afterglow of the setting sun, Jeremy said, "Something *big* is going down in the 'Center,' and the president wants all available eyeballs to focus." By "Center" he meant Moscow. "We don't know what's coming. We just get strong vibes that Center is out of synch, that things don't make sense. Our perspective is that a putsch may be coming."

I fired right back, "They haven't gotten over the last one yet, and another one so soon could destabilize the whole Soviet Union. Jesus, this is terrible!"

He said, "Some of the players are obvious. Others are lying in the bushes."

"Do they know we know?"

"They *let* us know. Yeltsin wants us to be ready. He didn't want us to think he wasn't on top of things."

"What do I do?" I asked.

"Watch. Improvise. Get close to it on the ground. Break out into the open if necessary. Then, tell us what you see. There are others, but the more eyes the better—trained eyes."

"How long will I be needed?"

"Until the smoke clears and you're debriefed."

"What's the drop zone?"

"Downtown. The Kremlin. The White House, where Parliament meets."

"Last time somebody tried to destabilize, only six were killed. Pretty quiet coup," I commented.

"This looks different," Jeremy replied. "Sour old generals and ambitious young politicians. Dangerous mix."

"Where's the military in all this?"

"We don't know, but we expect casualties because the stakes are big. When you get there, drop your stuff at Intourist Hotel #2 near Red Square and contact me at the embassy. *Nordquist* is your contact. Wear Russian office worker clothes. Don't talk unless you have to, and if you do, only in Russian."

"Will I see you again?" I asked.

He replied, "At the embassy, for sure, and maybe outside. I'm fairly easy to spot in Moscow. You'll have some local assistance—drivers and such. But, you'll have to play much of it by ear." We returned to our seats separately and now only chatted about food.

London was gray and dripping, but I was intrigued and excited by the assignment and got a bit of that old pregame rush. I browsed six newspapers. Prince Charles was beginning to have marital problems. Moscow sounded foreboding. Extreme demands and a fiery new leader. But I felt Yeltsin could handle it. It's what he's good at. And I hoped that these were just growing pains for a very new, but very old, country. Anyway, he was the transition leader. He would be the one to take all the "arrows" for the new trial-and-error regime.

Ten hours after landing in London, I was standing outside Moscow's Sheremetyevo Airport waiting for a taxi. It was only seven o'clock in the evening, a time when things were usually bustling, but nobody was there. The place was empty, yet all the lights were on. I saw a few clerks, but the public had vanished. No people. No cabs. Nothing. It was like an eclipse, when normal becomes abnormal. Finally, I got a cab. Two

German businessmen rode in with me. They talked excitedly in German at first. One of them switched to English and said, "Have you heard? Another coup is underway, an attempt to overthrow Yeltsin's government. They're threatening the White House where the Parliament meets."

I asked, "When is all this supposed to happen?"

The German responded, "Now! It was on TV and radio at the airport."

I asked if they would mind if the taxi went a little out of the way to drop me off at the U.S. Embassy. The embassy was just a couple of blocks from "People's Park," where the activists were rallying. They said fine.

I went to the side visitor's entrance, identified myself, and asked for Colonel Nordquist. There was a lot of serious, efficient activity. You could feel it in the air. I wanted to get an update. Nordquist sent orders down to the Marine guard to hang on to me until he got there. In a few minutes an internal security door opened and a colonel in combat fatigues with a couple of plastic ID cards dangling around his neck came through. He returned the guard's salute and then saluted me. I felt like a general without a command.

Colonel Nordquist was also a black man of about forty-five, who had a striking resemblance to Jeremy Nodoff. In fact, it *was* Jeremy Nodoff. A hearty handshake was followed by a complex briefing in Russian which Nordquist/Nodoff told me to repeat back to him. I was able to play it back and he nodded, saying, "Follow me. I want you to meet a couple of guys who'll help you get around town." Both men were Russians in their mid-thirties and spoke good English. They were armed and I was not. We were all to wear flack jackets. My assignment was to get as close as possible to the "White House" and observe. The area would be unrestricted and there would be other "observers" and lots of journalists running around. We were given handheld radios that would enable us to communicate directly with the embassy. My

Russian companions took me to my hotel where I dropped my bags and changed into Russian-made clothes. I dressed warmly and took a day pack with an assortment of tools and supplies and left the hotel.

I didn't return for six days. The violence had started by the time we got to the White House. A political showdown had stalemated. I'd learned during my briefing that the revolt was being led by Vice President Rutskoy. They had taken over the White House, and fifteen guards and military personnel had already been killed. Hundreds of civilian workers had escaped but over two hundred more remained. Some were sympathetic to the coup. Others were not.

A very wide stone bridge crossed the river, perpendicular to the White House. Motorways paralleled both sides of the river and ran under the bridge. Concrete stairs connected the motorways passing under the bridge to a walkway on the bridge's top. A five-foot wall protected the landing at the top. I spent much of the next seven days behind that wall.

When we arrived, hundreds of soldiers and police were running around, ducking behind trees and behind parked cars. Occasional muffled explosions and shots could be heard from within the White House. Snipers started firing from upper windows. Ground fire began to respond. Military vehicles were parked in front of the building. Fifteen large T-34 tanks came rolling onto the bridge and deployed where they could see and be seen. A helicopter circled the top of the building. The two Russians with me scrounged together a makeshift "duck blind" for us to occupy on the landing. Nobody in command bothered us. It was chilly, but the cardboard barrier deflected the wind off the blind. It was a circus. Regular traffic moved along on both sides of the river. The weather was cool at night but quite comfortable. Thousands of Russians promenaded around the White House. Families with baby carriages strolled along the river. There were picnics! Most people thought the coup

Washington needed "eyes on the ground" during the 1993 constitutional crisis in Moscow.

would be bloodless and fail that first day.

However, by noon the next day, the White House had become a fort, and from my vantage point I could see military in the parking lot and civilians around the building being shot down and killed. People were hiding, and running between safe points. Tracers streamed into the sniper's windows. Small fires broke out. It was crazy. Street casualties reached a hundred, and the Russian command post across the bridge ordered the tanks to fire. They clanked to our end of the bridge and began selective fire at the snipers. Our "duck blind" was 750 yards in front of the tanks and they were firing right over us. It was loud. Concussion ammunition was being used, and the exploding shells did a lot of internal damage as the tankers raised their aim floor by floor. A racking echo reverberated between buildings and surrounding structures. Fires began to rage on the eighth and ninth floors.

Although we were in touch with the embassy, we got most of our information from Radio Moscow. Negotiations were not encouraging. I wondered what kind of misguided arrogance had allowed these rebels to think they could take over eleven time zones—the width and breadth of the Soviet Union—from their hunkered-down and trapped position in the burning White House. Ill-conceived "growing pains?" Maybe.

At the end of Day Five, we saw what we later learned were the neutral workers being allowed to walk out. We learned that the rebels were low on food and ammunition and that based on knowledge gained from the hostages, a plan had evolved. With several hundred workers out of the way and with casualties mounting on the outside, Yeltsin ordered a "show of authority" and more troops were called in.

At this time, the embassy instructed me to check out what had become a showdown at the TV and radio center in the Ostankino district, about five miles from the White House. It consisted of three- and five-story buildings grouped around a plaza in a mixed commercial and residential area. We were able to drive within two blocks of the plaza and nobody seemed to care who we were. There was intermittent rifle and automatic weapons fire. Hundreds of people lurked in the trees off the plaza.

My driver and I made a wide circle around the complex, then agreed to meet in half an hour. It was like the Old West. Everybody had a gun. My driver discovered that we were among the revolutionaries and we saw the government's backers holed up in the main TV building, which was smoking. A smaller building was in flames. Government reinforcements had yet to arrive to save the buildings.

Several helicopters circled out of range of the ground fire. My driver and I walked through the crowd for a closer look. We were definitely in bad company. Then it occurred to both of us that when the Russian troops arrived, we could easily get caught in the crossfire. For some reason, I remembered my mother always said, "You are judged by the company you keep." We knew the embassy was getting better reports from other observers and that the coup was flickering and sputtering beyond what would have been possible in communist days when civil disorder was slammed down immediately. We considered leaving, but the third member of our team had not returned, so we decided to sit tight. We could see the play from behind a long, low wall—people darting around, rocket grenades going off, small arms fire coming in from three sides.

We decided to move to the edge of the plaza where we found another vantage point. Light from fires lit up the battle scene. A dozen or so bodies were strewn in front of us. Some were moving and calling out. Others were still and quiet. Suddenly we saw a lunatic photographer running around shooting "action shots." Some of those guys seem to go *nuts* in combat situations. Their adrenaline takes over and the rapture of the big story becomes everything. I've seen it in sports photographers, too. "Gotta get a good shot!" becomes the battle cry. "Just one more!"

A truck careened toward the large glass doors of the TV Center. It ran over several of the bodies and crashed through. The photographer zigzagged behind it. Two men jumped from the truck and ran toward us and away from the building. As they passed the photographer, he took his last shot—a picture of two revolutionaries running toward the river at the moment they were hit by streams of AK-47 bullets. They dropped and died. The photographer tried to crawl away. He waved to attract attention, and then he died, too. All he wanted was just one more picture. His pictures made it, but he didn't. It turned out he was a well-known English photographer who had recently married another journalist and they had a child on the way. He had been wounded in the past. He knew the danger but thought he was immortal. I guess we all do at times. Sometimes it's helpful. Sometimes it's deadly.

We were worried about our missing teammate. Over an hour had gone by. We called the embassy and were told troops were on the way. The revolutionaries were dispersing and becoming a mob. We didn't need to see any more. Many of the drunken revolutionaries seemed relieved to run and faded into the city. One of them had earlier raised the question: "If we capture the station, then what do we do?" They obviously didn't have the answer.

We crouched and crawled our way from the square and back to our car, where we found our missing companion. His arm hung dripping by his side. He was obviously weak from loss of blood but glad to see us. He apologized repeatedly for "standing us up." He had been reconnoitering alongside the building when an internal explosion blew out a huge plate glass window. He had been knocked unconscious. When he realized he hadn't been killed, he cursed his "bad luck" and said he knew he shouldn't have gotten so close to that building. He was a tough character who, along with my other companion, spent two years in Afghanistan and then, when things changed in Moscow, had applied to the U.S. Embassy for a job. Fortunately, our four-door Lada car had not been stripped and we were able to get the poor guy to the embassy medical center where they gave him eighty stitches. He recovered fully, thanks to the embassy doctors. My driver went back to the duck blind at the bridge, and I joined him after grabbing some food and a clean coat. It was Day Six and during days like these, you don't stop to eat. You snack but you don't eat, and you slowly become altered. I try to keep running on my own adrenaline while practicing the old Boy Scout motto, "Be Prepared." (I always had some "uppers," which are fine on the upside but bad on the way down.)

News flashed around the embassy late that night that the TV station was finally safe in government hands. The next afternoon, a commando raid on the White House forced the rebels to surrender. Special Forces pouring out of helicopters entered from the roof, and others got onto the main floor through tunnels. Just before the final attack, rockets hit the offices of senior officials. There were struggles in the basement and on the main floor. A few more people were needlessly killed, but after seven days, it was finally over.

The world saw the surrender on television—Moscow's White House in flames as the crushed revolutionaries filed out, scared and unsure of their futures. I was watching the monitor in the embassy situation room, and you could see the question in their eyes: "What would be the price of treason?"

It had been a very moving experience. In its detail, it was pitiful and sad—truly tragic. But not only had the Wall come down, the New Russia had survived its first great challenge.

Passing the Baton

THE ENDING OF THE COLD WAR was a *process* that formally began with Reagan and Gorbachev's celebrated "Walk in the Woods" at Reykjavik, Iceland, in 1986. During this walk, the two leaders of the world's great superpowers agreed it was time to stop the insanity that had been the cornerstone of each country's foreign policy and, indeed, the world's foreign policy since the conclusion of World War II.

Reagan had superior intelligence, much of it gained from people on the ground, that the Soviet government was financially and spiritually bankrupt, and therefore when Reagan floated his "Star Wars" plan, there was no way for the Soviets to adequately respond. Incidents such as Chernobyl and the catastrophic war in Afghanistan only reinforced the inadequacy of the Soviet's position. More importantly, the *people* throughout the Soviet Empire had lost confidence not only in their military and technology, but also with the very system that had ruled their lives for seventy years.

When Western leaders demonstrated a willingness to work with the Soviets, Premier Gorbachev and Foreign Minister Shevardnadze knew the time was right. They had had their own earlier "Walk in the Woods" late in the 1970s in a barren park on a deserted shore near the Black Sea's Cape Pitsunda, when they decided, as Shevardnadze put it, to "no longer hold anything back." This meeting of the minds at Reykjavik, and earlier at Cape Pitsunda, created the atmosphere under which Reagan and Gorbachev, and Shevardnadze and Shultz, began working together in an attempt to ease tensions wherever they could.

Of course, there were many people toiling on different levels in the background who prepared themselves to continue the process when and if they got the chance, and when Vice President George Bush was elected president in 1988, he quickly named James A. Baker III as his secretary of state. I was always interested in, and eventually befriended, James Baker because we had so much in common. We had the same first name, were close in age, height, and weight, and he had been a very good rugby player at a very good rugby school, Dartmouth. I noticed during the summer camp sponsored by the Bohemian Club that he would hang out with the regular guys as much as he would with the hotshot guests. It didn't hurt my ego, either, that he remembered me on our occasional meetings. At first, I thought it was because of his association with Bechtel, but I would like to think it might have been because my Cal rugby team had trounced his Dartmouth rugby team during our college days. (I didn't remind him.) Later on, of course, he was to learn of my personal relationship with Eduard Shevardnadze.

Since his undergraduate days, Jim had racked up a number of achievements in government and industry which combined to give him the unique combination of skills that qualified him to serve with distinction under President Bush during the exquisitely sensitive transition period at the end of the Cold War. Much of his success can be directly attributed to the fact that he and Shevardnadze became close personal friends as well as partners during this time. When Baker would travel to Moscow, he would stay at Shevardnadze's home, and their two families became friends as well. As a result, Shevardnadze was able to convey in private, at some personal risk, foreign policy messages that would have been publicly unacceptable to the Soviet Politburo. This was only possible because of an enormous reservoir of trust that developed between the two, "the human factor," as Shevardnadze likes to call it.

There seemed to be two steps in their relationship and in the formal ending of the Cold War. The first groundbreaking step happened during September 1989. Baker invited Shevardnadze to meet him in Wyoming, even though at that time diplomats at the ministerial level were required to remain within a thirty-five mile radius of Washington D.C. and New York City. When the two arrived at Grand Teton National Park's Jackson Lake Lodge, they exchanged gifts, Baker giving Shevardnadze a pair of fancy cowboy boots and Shevardnadze surprising Baker with a beautiful enameled picture of Jesus, adding, "Even we Communists can change our world view." When the discussions were concluded they went fishing together and embraced as they parted ways. After that meeting, Shevardnadze commented that, "The Cold War confrontation was artificial," and he told Baker on a number of occasions, "We will not use force to keep the Soviet Union together."

The second solidifying step happened when Gorbachev and Bush met in Malta, after which Bush told Gorbachev, "We are no longer adversaries," and *they* embraced. This marked the real beginning of the end of the Cold War according to Baker, who further concluded that after Wyoming and Malta, "We decided we could trust the Soviets."

The policy of first confrontation, then cooperation, and finally partnership, paid off in Moscow when Baker and Shevardnadze met at the Vnukovo Airport. It was there that Russia agreed to the UN embargo against Iraq, which had just invaded Kuwait, because, as Shevardnadze proclaimed, "It was the right thing to do." As a gesture of goodwill on the American side, Baker had an American general brief Shevardnadze on what the United States' exact war plan was for Iraq. Baker felt this meeting probably saved the Desert Storm Coalition, and it was an incredible bit of statesmanship that Russia would actually support us in a war against their former ally, fighting together for international justice.

Baker had heard the call as had Reagan and Shultz. The baton of foreign policy was successfully passed to Bush and Baker, and the transition period was covered. The key to the success of this transition and the ending of the Cold War was the elevation of truth, trust, and goodwill. Good people on both sides intuitively recognized each other's integrity based on their mutual understanding of the natural laws of life. Ordinary people solved extraordinary problems, not with the latest technological devices, but with common sense. As Shevardnadze concluded, "It was time to end it."

Chapter 13

Ancient Runners
(A Change of Pace)

Sometimes the Pants Factory would send me off to exotic locales for no other apparent reason than to see what shook loose from the trees. As a result, I was able to get into China during the early 1980s before the Mainland began to open up to the West.

As I have already explained, rugby is the great metaphor for my life, but it was competitive running, not rugby, that got me into a still "closed" China. I was participating in the 1980 Masters (age thirty-five and over) World Championship Track and Field Games in Christchurch, New Zealand, when I was approached by a woman by the name of "Louise" who owned a travel agency. She told me there were representatives of the Chinese government at the event who wanted to talk to me about hosting a Masters running tour of what was then still commonly called "Red China." I met with them at the event, and about three weeks later Louise contacted me at home to offer me a scholarship to manage a running tour to China. Considering the nature and generosity of her offer, I chose not to ask any questions. Arrangements were made for Jim Puckett, me, and two elderly Chinese-Americans from Bakersfield to make an exploratory trip. This would turn out to be the first of three running tours to China.

On the second trip, in 1981, I took a group of men and women ranging in age from thirty to eighty, including the eighty-year-old Chinese-American couple from Bakersfield, California. The husband was a sprinter and broad jumper. On the third trip, in 1983, I hosted a thirty-eight member track team of the same general age group as the previous tour. They performed in six Chinese cities and Hong Kong. The first two trips were basically for distance runners racing 5Ks and 10Ks on roads, in parks, and around lakes, and the third consisted mostly of track-and-field events performed inside stadiums.

The Chinese were fine hosts. All events were thoughtfully planned out and the food was outstanding everywhere we went. The Chinese wanted to broaden such activities among their own older people. On a sports level the trips went wonderfully, and there were really no incidents of a political nature. The obvious economic changes each year were stunning. Much of it was visual and very dramatic and so broad-based that it couldn't possibly be faked. Something really big was happening.

I like to think these trips were my small contribution to the "opening up" of China. I was able to report seemingly unimportant things that, taken together, showed an evolution away from Marxist conformity. During my first trip, for instance, the Chinese, men and women alike, all seemed to be wearing Mao jackets. On the second trip, some of the women were wearing print dresses, but on the third, everyone seemed to be wearing colorful clothes and plaid shirts. Retail stores had appeared out of nowhere.

The Chinese, whatever they were wearing, were all fascinated with these middle-aged and older Americans running through their country. There's a respect and feeling for age in China that you really can't put on paper, but it's different from what we know in America or Europe. Literally translated, we were described as "ancient" athletes because there is no Chinese word for seniors in the sense that we mean it. And although generally guarded in their speech, I noted that after a few beers, the Chinese athletes were laughing along with us at the "right time" in a joke and telling their own jokes that fit right in.

During the first trip, we were invited to watch a soccer game in a stadium filled with 65,000 Chinese men dressed in blue Mao jackets. At one point, we were introduced to the crowd and taken down to the field to examine the track that ran around it, thinking we might run there the following year. Later, as we headed toward the exit tunnel, a great continuous roar went up from the crowd. It increased in intensity and one of my companions, Jim Plunkett, a blue-eyed, carrot-headed track coach from Mt. Hood College in Oregon, enjoyed the celebrity of being an ultra-racial-minority curiosity. People flocked around him. As Jim put it, "I'm one in a billion and never had it so good." But when the crowd noise continued unabated, we began to get scared, not knowing what it was they truly wanted. The crowd began jumping up and down on their seats, and about halfway up the stadium stairs we got ready to sprint to the exits! But our translator explained that the crowd was chanting, "Farewell, ancient ones" and merely trying to get a better look. As he began to lead us back to our seats, he told us the crowd wanted to know if we liked China. Then, shortly after we told him we did, he informed us that the stadium announcer had proclaimed, "The ancient, blue-eyed sportsmen from the East like China and approve of the track but do not like Chinese ice cream because it is too soft." There was a pause and then a wave of laughter, followed by a thunderous roar of *"Hue lai! Hue lai!"* (Come back!) Our interpreter explained that the crowd wanted us to come back out, and when we stood on our seats to give the thumbs-up and shake our clasped hands over our heads, the crowd went nuts. It was exhilarating, but I also sensed that it all could be turned off with a flick of a switch, if the government so wanted.

It was also on that first trip, in Shanghai, that I met the extraordinary Mr. Wu, secretary of the Anglican Church Association of China. Mr. Wu was about seventy years old and walked with a wobble, albeit a strong wobble. He greeted me warmly and told me that he had been in prison for nineteen years and had only been released the previous year. He had three years of religious schooling in Philadelphia where he had learned English.

I wasn't on any specific analytic intelligence mission during these trips to China, although I did report my impressions, and I suspect I served as something of a "front" for "Louise." While traveling with us, Louise went about her own business, which I'm pretty sure was Pants Factory business, as we ran our way through China. But she didn't draw me directly into it. Even so, I observed, and ultimately reported on, the crosscurrents of a curious population and a government filled with paranoia, a government I'm sure was quite aware of my connections other than track.

I was also fascinated with Mr. Wu on a number of levels. His story was a good one—almost too good. At first I wondered if the Chinese government had planted him on me. But as he talked at length about all his academic and other friends who had been killed or died in prison, I began to believe him and I finally asked, "Mr. Wu, do you really think things are getting better?"

To which he replied, "Well, they let me out of prison and they are allowing me to hold church services, and they asked me to give them a list of the books they destroyed when they sent me to prison years ago, and they have replaced them— almost all of nearly a hundred books."

"That," I told him, "is a good sign!"

Mr. Wu then went on to say that if we returned to China the next year, he wanted to entertain us and, perhaps, hold a service for us in his church there in Shanghai. When we did return

Our "ancient" athletes were welcomed throughout China.

the next year, in 1981, I had about fifty-five people with me with an average age of forty-five, and we raced in Beijing, Hankou, Wuxi, Hangzhou, Shanghai, and Hong Kong. Quite frankly, I had forgotten about Mr. Wu's offer, not thinking he would be able to pull it off. But when we reached Shanghai, Mr. Wu had not forgotten. He approached Louise and me, reminding us of his invitation. Louise was fascinated. She suggested that I ask the team if they wanted to attend an Anglican Church service in Shanghai.

I did, and all fifty-five of these aging runners, including Catholics and Jews, became enthusiastic about going. The church was a lovely big stone structure that Americans would have recognized in Kansas or Iowa, or in England or Scotland, for that matter. When we got off the bus, they took us to the rear door, and we realized that this was because the church was already full. There must have been eight hundred people in attendance and an organ was booming out those wonderful old Protestant hymns as they led us down the aisle. The crowd seemed to consist of either very old or very young people. You could see the excitement in their eyes, and feel their excitement as well, over this *first* international service in their newly restored Anglican Church.

When they sang, you couldn't understand the words, but you could understand the emotion. The emotion was overpowering, and the Chinese government, although involved in everything else, was not involved in *that*. We were all weeping. I felt we were all a part of history. Then Mr. Wu preached a sermon in both Chinese and English. The electricity in the air crackled all around us. It was as if we were being told that God had returned to China and had blessed us all for our faith. That day in the Anglican Church was one of the most moving moments of my life. Although I am not actively religious, I felt as if we were, indeed, present on the day that God returned to at least one small part of China. It was almost like a Biblical moment, at least for me, with my Sunday school background. I know that the Anglican Church is not the only pathway to God, but that's the way I felt as those hymns reverberated throughout the church. I treasure the memory, and the members of the team always bring it up as one of the great moments in their lives whenever we meet.

Later in that memorable trip, Louise, the aging Chinese-American couple from Bakersfield, a few others, and I were taken on a side tour into the mountains of northeastern China. At one point our driver was late picking us up at a small rural hotel. When he finally appeared, he apologized, saying that he had been required to attend an execution. He told us that one of his friends had been caught stealing for a third time and that it was normal practice to have friends of the individual to be executed in attendance. For a few moments, I was speechless. Then I asked him how the execution had been carried out. He said that his friend had kneeled down and an officer had simply walked up and shot him in the back of the head, after which the poor guy's other friends were told to go home. He seemed sad, but he also seemed to have a deep sense of fatalistic acceptance. For him, this was a normal and daily practice.

Later that same day, we heard from some other tourists that President Reagan had been shot. They weren't sure whether he was alive or dead. The news filled me with a great sense of insecurity because my leader at home might be dead and embarrassment that our nation is still, in some ways, so primitive. I momentarily felt as if *we* were the Third World nation, not the Chinese. I was chagrined and felt disconnected from my source of power. I'd felt this way once before, when Jack Kennedy was shot. At that time, I was living in Tenby, Wales, with my family, working on an oil-refinery project. I was amazed at my reaction, at my feeling of abandonment, but even more by the reaction of the people in rural Pembrokeshire, who were just as stunned as we were. How could this have happened to their big brother, their protector? They called for a minute of silence before the next rugby home game I was to play in and made me captain for the day. We were moved and grateful for their kind consideration and support at this difficult time.

Travel can isolate you in unexpected ways. It is essential to be secure within yourself, and, at times, it helps to be a little detached. Several days later, some Canadians sitting next to us at a concert in Hangzhou told us that Reagan had survived. Most of the Chinese hardly seemed to know who he was. But I knew. He had always been with me in my travels.

Chapter 14

On Their Own
(A Region in Transition)

A T THE END OF THE COLD WAR, there was a short period of
time when the former Soviet republics were truly free and
independent. Eight of the fourteen republics were on my paper
route. All eight, or perhaps seven (not including Tajikistan), had
qualities that other aggressor nations might find attractive, such
as oil and gas and geopolitical position. It was immediately obvious to me that the former Soviet republics along my route
should be integrated into the West as soon as possible to protect them from opportunistic intruders from such countries as
China, Iran, and Turkey. Few people making policy at the State
Department or other governmental agencies had ever been to
this region, and even fewer knew anything about the region's
problems or the nature of the various republics. For seventy
years the Curtain was down, obscuring these republics from
view. It was almost as if they had ceased to exist, and there was
very little written about them that was not Government Issue.

When the end came, it was the counsel of Western advisors
that the safest thing the newly independent republics could do
would be to join the United Nations, get tied to the West politically, and attract foreign embassies as soon as possible. As
the diplomatic infrastructure was being set up, the objective
became to "joint venture" with the West, thereby acquiring the

protection that investment by large political/economic entities such as "big oil" and "big banking" could provide. As a result, by the late nineties the republics averaged eight foreign embassies each, with Kazakhstan, Azerbaijan, and Georgia leading the way with sixteen, fifteen, and fourteen respectively.

This course of action worked well for independence and security. The giant Azerbaijan International Operating Consortium (AIOC) consisted of twelve international companies, with only two being Russian. Eduard Shevardnadze survived his second assassination attempt, in 1995, because he was riding in a special bulletproof car given to him by Germany. Most of our embassies were upgraded from a security standpoint. Our intention to more than merely recognize the new republics was fully demonstrated by our spending millions of dollars on the visible physical facilities in each country and seeing to it that only highly qualified personnel filled the top-level staff positions.

Membership in the UN opened many doors for the new republics but did not solve a lot of their problems. The Russians were quick to take advantage of the fact that these new nations no longer had a military to protect them against foreign intrusion or internal conflict, as that had always been the responsibility of the Russian military, the Interior Ministry, and the KGB. Therefore, it was not surprising that when the Russians left after the end of the Cold War, they left in a hurry, abandoning bases and military hardware worth billions of dollars. I got a lot of dirty looks and got backed up against a couple of walls, but was able to walk through five of these bases (some were vast) and see for myself this aspect of the collapse of the Soviet Empire. I was shocked at how out of control things quickly became. The corpse of this once mighty empire lay prostrate, and the formidable Russian military stores and supplies were there for the maggots to consume. Looters were both big-time and small-time, and they killed each other over the spoils. They would just drive in and loot and sack. Local *Mafiya* and foreign mercenaries fought over the stores and supplies. At one depot, in Dagestan, two headless bodies were hanging from a light pole as a warning to the uninvited. I couldn't help but remember the abandoned fortress in India where a religious sect took their dead to be scavenged in the sunlight by the massive black cloud of vultures circling overhead. And, of course, there was the ultimate nightmare of "loose nukes." It was a surreal, ugly, and dangerous phenomenon to see firsthand.

During the unstable period following the breakup of the USSR, Central Asia and especially the Caucasus were the scenes of ethnic cleansing and the killing of many tens of thousands of citizens. I was witness to a half-dozen of these local wars. I investigated and reported what I saw. I was appalled by the brutality on both sides. The mentality of these wars was not of our times. Old cultures, uncivilized, evoked the savagery of the twelfth century, even more unforgivable in the twentieth. Ineptitude and lack of leadership and organization magnified the senseless slaughters. Because of their ignorance and apathetic viewpoint, the Western press minimized the importance of these newly independent countries, and the uninitiated new president from Arkansas faked his way around the problem by objecting to the bloodshed and then shucking off the matter as "their problem" and letting things slide until the next election. After all, the Chechen problem and others had been around for a couple of hundred years and it was now time to enjoy the "peace dividend." When in my efforts to attract attention to the situation I even went so far as to say, "This part of the world is on fire, and a third world war could start here." And the usual response was, "Uh-huh. Yeah, maybe."

Late in 1991, with civil wars raging in Georgia, Armenia, Tajikistan, and Azerbaijan, the Russians created a special organization called the Commonwealth of Independent States (CIS). As sudden and complete as the Russian overall departure was, the return of the Russian military along the former borders via the clever and *apparently* necessary CIS was equally impressive. The new republics were totally vulnerable to outside forces, and Russia had lost its greater USSR buffer states. The question quickly became who would police internal struggles such as Nagorno-Karabakh and Abkhazia? Many of the republics fantasized that the UN would protect them from the Russians. They were wrong! Who was the greatest threat in the region, deliberately creating civil wars and assassinating people? None other than the Russians!

This was a hard lesson that only revealed itself over time. In the heady days of 1991, the region was full of hope and, although I knew I would always be involved in intelligence gathering, I looked forward to being able to use my legitimate consultant and humanitarian roles to help these struggling countries find their way.

Chapter 15

Hot Caspian Night
(Pre-Embassy Days)

I HAVE OFTEN THOUGHT of one hot summer night in 1991 when I was staying at the old Azerbaijani Hotel on the Baku Harbor. There was chaos, wars, and domestic strife throughout the region, and I was specifically asked by the agency to take a look at a serious conflict developing between Armenia and Azerbaijan.

I kept the agency apprised of the war and, as I did so, I noticed the presence of a large number of oil men from U.S. and Western countries as well as Russia. They were easy to spot, as I had spent so much time with them while working on refineries and pipelines for Bechtel. Even the *Mafiya* was there. The region was wide open, and the grab was on. Although other parts of our government may have known what was happening, the CIA didn't seem to have a good handle on it and so they sent me to Baku to check it out. It was pure field intelligence.

That night in Baku, I went for an after-dinner stroll along the waterfront park. I eventually found myself outside a dingy café at the end of a long, broad pier used for loading ships' cargo and passengers. The smell of oil from the Caspian Sea was everywhere and extended for miles inland. I passed young men happily playing ping pong and smoking cigarettes under the lights in the recreation area. As I leaned against the railing trying to get a better look at several luxury yachts anchored nearby—until recently a rarity in this area—I noticed several cars halt abruptly at the base of the pier two hundred yards away. A moment later the phone rang in the café and a muffled Turkic voice spoke briefly. Then the light in the café went out and the door was latched shut. I could see bobbing figures with flashlights coming toward me silhouetted against the city's evening glow. Before I had a chance to say, "I haven't done anything, officer," my internal companion, *Mr. Asshole,* told me something was wrong and I didn't need to find out what.

I ducked behind the café and went down a flight of steps to a passenger loading barge. The bobbing lights were halfway there, scanning the wharf and railings. I took my shoes off, tied them together, hung them around my neck, and slipped over the side into the smelly Caspian. For some reason, as I did so it passed through my mind that this was the same Caspian Sea that produced all the caviar I had recently enjoyed in Baku. I dogpaddled under the pier toward the shore, trying to stay in the middle of a fifty-foot wide pier that rose fifteen feet above me. Hoping I couldn't be seen or heard, I slid from one piling bent to the next piling bent about thirty feet away and stopped to listen.

The search party reached the café and went down the stairs with flashing lights. Another light was poking over the railing looking for a swimmer. There was a lot of shouting back and forth, then broken glass and half a dozen shots, more shouting, then a single shot, and a moment later a splash. I waited for the lights to stop dancing and peering. I was close enough to the beach to hear car motors start up and the spinning of tires at the head of the quay.

I waited for maybe an hour, clinging to a piece of rebar protruding from one of the pilings. Obviously they had not come for me, but I clearly had no business being out there at that time of night and didn't want to appear complicit. I knew if they were Azerbaijanis they would not return, but if they were

In chaotic Baku, I evaded gunmen in the oily water beneath the pier.

Russians they would hang around and double back. I decided not to go ashore at the quay head but managed to swim about a hundred yards down the water's edge to a construction project. I climbed out on a cofferdam made of sheet steel piling.

It was still warm, and an oily breeze had come up. Fortunately, I was dressed lightly in dark colors. I found a barrel of petrol and cleaned off some of the tarry patches on my hands. I wrung out my clothes and swung them around my head to dry like a crazy, naked windmill. I waited. It was late. The lights in the recreation area were off now. There was no traffic on the boulevard between me and the hotel, and the hotel lights were reduced to the entrance area and a few rooms in the fourteen-story structure. Semidry, I jogged along the front of the hotel for half an hour, hoping my body heat would improve matters.

It was now one o'clock in the morning, very late for Baku.
I finally crossed the boulevard, dodged through the hotel garden and up the ramp into the delivery area behind the kitchen.
I knew there was a service elevator because I always check for
back doors. If I was in luck, it would be operating. It wasn't,
but the adjacent narrow stairwell door was open, so I climbed
up eleven stories to my room. I had my key out as always.
I quickly went quickly inside, peeled off my clothes, turned on
the warm water, and glanced in the mirror! *My God,* I thought
to myself, *who is THAT? Al Jolson, or maybe an East Indian?* It
took the rest of the night to clean up. Fortunately, I had just
arrived in town and had a lot of soap and shampoo. I ordered
three quarts of 150 proof Russian vodka, which helped cut the
grease. My skin was red and sore for a week, and I was afraid to
light up my nightly Marlboro for fear of immolating myself by
accident.

At the time, I was too tired to be afraid. But off and on for
the rest of the week in Baku, I had unexpected waves and shud-
ders followed by little aftershocks. None of this attached to any
conscious thought or moment, but, as always, the little man
who sits on my shoulder noticed and would remind me that
I wasn't on the beach at Malibu, California, you know.

So what was this all about? Maybe it wasn't even about me.
The U.S. had yet to set up an embassy. I was on my own, and
Azerbaijan was on its own and fighting Armenia in Nagorno-
Karabakh. The Russians *never* left Azerbaijan at the end. There
was too much at stake oil-wise. Baku was well on its way to
becoming a boom town. It reminded me of Calgary, Alberta,
Canada in the fifties. Big foreign oil companies were setting
up. Perhaps the third language in Baku would soon be Oklaho-
ma-American. And with the boom came the bars, dance halls,
hookers, petty crooks, and big-time gangsters. The gangsters
were tougher than anything you find in the States. There was
no law and order to speak of, and most of these guys didn't

have much hope to live past thirty. Life wasn't that important, particularly if it was somebody else's life.

These guys were a type I had not yet seen in Georgia. But I knew they would come. They were already next door in Armenia. Many of them had been enforcers for the Russians, really scary guys. Now they were freelancing on their own, rent-a-mob style. They viewed the former Soviet Union as fertile ground. The great oil strike (re-strike) in Azerbaijan justified for them *any* kind of behavior.

So what actually happened that hot, smelly Caspian night remains a mystery. I was pondering the question a few nights later in a small Baku lounge. Perhaps it was my turn and I got lucky, or was it that the pier café owner didn't pay his protection money—"no cash, go splash"? The El Paso roughneck sitting across the table from me said, "We pulled another 'floater' out of the cofferdam this week." He drawled, "That makes four since I've been here. They all had holes in the same places."

I nodded, "Yeah, this is their town, friend. You gotta play by their rules—if you can figure out what they are!"

The UPS Man

MORE AND MORE I was seeing the harsher side of life in parts of the world little known to most Americans. The clandestine aspects of my work inevitably began to change my outlook on not only the world, but on myself and my family.

The few guys I met along the way who actually knew what I was doing in Central Asia—Special Operations types, intelligence officers, and senior embassy officials—treated me in a variety of ways. My advancing years, forty to seventy, always brought a mixture of disbelief, respect, and disrespect. Some American ambassadors didn't want "maverick" intelligence people roaming around their temporary kingdoms, and they certainly didn't want "rogue diplomats." Others were supportive of the idea of a "loner" observer and solicited my observations and cooperation.

When I arrived in one of those "temporary kingdoms," I would always check into the embassy consular office to advise the ambassador or chargé d'affaires that I was about to hit the road to do some business for my consulting firm, Interperspective Corporation—most of it in the realm of humanitarian aid and economic development.

I have to say that I really enjoyed most of the Special Ops and military guys I met along the way. They generally liked me, too, because I could talk sports. Although today each military service has its own specially trained units, in the early nineties they were mostly CIA operatives who could be inserted into special situations anywhere in the world within thirty-six hours. I particularly remember Dick Martin and Manny Gonzalez in the former Soviet Republic of Georgia. Dick was always showing up in one of those big black C-5A cargo planes bringing in USAID materials, and I ran into him in a number of countries. He had a Masters degree from Louisiana State and wanted to get into construction after he retired. Manny was the military attaché at the embassy; he was a Mexican-American graduate of West Point who spoke pretty good Georgian and played the guitar. Trim and handsome, he wowed the Georgian women with his ballads sung in Georgian.

The last time I saw the two of them together, they politely asked me what my *real* mission was. When I told them I was an independent contractor, they wanted to know who I reported to when I was on the road and what happened if I dropped off the radar screen. Feeling nearly indestructible, I was always in denial about dropping off the radar screen. A CIA operative had recently been murdered near Tbilisi, Georgia. There was an impressive memorial service, and his body was shipped home in a regulation coffin, complete with U.S. flag. It was apparent to all three of us, however, that would not be the case with me. Dick again asked, "So, what happens to *you* if you go down?" Manny, showing off his knowledge of such things, said he heard that people like me—independent contractors—got "smoked" (cremated) and sent home by UPS in a special cardboard box. He added that the intelligence services would deny their existence but later engrave their names on a bronze plaque inside a building somewhere in Virginia. We all laughed, but I noticed that they watched me closely to see if I could handle just such a prospect. It seemed to relieve them when, in a light tone, I told them I'd prefer FedEx Overnight because I owned several shares in the company.

I never told my wife, Marilyn, about this conversation. Our home is in the Sierra Mountains near Lake Tahoe and we get a lot of UPS and FedEx deliveries. Marilyn later told me about one such delivery and I was reminded never to underestimate her intuition. I had been gone on one of my longest trips— almost six weeks—with no access to telephones for three of those weeks. There had been trouble at the time in Tajikistan, and although Marilyn didn't know the covert aspects of my work, she understood I went to very dangerous parts of the world.

Marilyn was home watching our grandchildren frol-icking in our pool when she saw the UPS truck crunch its way into our circular graveled driveway. The local driver, Charlie Bates, studied his clipboard and punched some data into a computer before getting out of the truck. He seemed troubled and Marilyn winced as she watched him because she wasn't expecting any deliveries. Her entire being began to clench into a knot as she signed what she thought was a special international form and accepted a fifteen-inch square box from Charlie, who had been delivering to our house for years.

The box was from Baku, Azerbaijan, and her imagination took off. Could it be her Jimmy? Charlie sensed a problem and offered to help. Marilyn felt incapable of walking to the house. Her throat almost closed as she handed the box back to Charlie, saying, "See what it is." Charlie used a box cutter, and a moment later the box revealed a shiny metal container. Marilyn shud-dered and held her breath. But then, although the writing on the rim was in Turkic script, it became clear that the container was filled with six pounds of Caspian caviar. A poorly written note in broken English said:

> *Mister Jim regrets missing another birthday but*
> *hopes this thought can count. Further, there is*
> *nothing here to buy but rugs.*
> > *Loving You!*
> > *Mister Jimmy*

Marilyn began to breathe again, and then, or so I was told, she smiled.

Chapter 16

Nagorno-Karabakh
(An Open Wound)

T HE CAUCASUS MOUNTAINS have cast a spell over travelers
for countless centuries. Greek, Roman, Byzantine, Arab,
and Mongol armies all passed through before the region was
carved up by the Ottoman and Persian Empires in the sixteenth
century. Russia also made its first tentative moves at that time,
but it wasn't until 1864 that Russia could say with confidence
that it had become master of the Caucasus. With jagged peaks
higher than the Alps and glaciers tinged crimson by iron oxides,
the Caucasus added new dimensions to both life and death for
all who challenged them. Stretching eastward for seven hundred miles from the Black Sea to the Caspian Sea, the area em-
braces the farthest reaches of Europe and serves as the frontier
between the Muslim and Christian worlds.

In addition to the lush vineyards of Georgia, the region
includes treeless and earthquake-prone Armenia as well as the
oil fields of Azerbaijan. On the border between Armenia and
Azerbaijan, rocky streams and dried-up offshoots furrow the
withered brown hills and ridges. Peasant villages cling to the
sides of narrow roads like beads on a string. The border, sometimes almost impossible to find, snakes over the ridges and
around the streams and roads. Bandits, territorial rivalries, and
ethnic violence characterized the first years of independence

for these three nations that make up the "border lands" and are known collectively as the Trans-Caucasus.

The trouble is, all the old issues stay alive. One of them has resulted in tens of thousands of people being killed in recent years. Azerbaijan includes within its boundaries the long-disputed enclave of Nagorno-Karabakh, an area largely populated by Armenians and a place of constant conflict between Armenian peasants and Azerbaijani herders. The roots of the conflict go back to the early 1920s, the years between the departure of the Turks and the arrival of the Russians, when the Khanate of Karabakh straddled the eastern edge of the historically Armenian plateau. The population of Karabakh was largely Muslim except in the highland area known as Nagorno-Karabakh ("Nagorno" means "mountainous"), where the people were mostly Armenian. The local rulers were Armenian princes, and they considered Nagorno-Karabakh to be part of Armenia. But it lay within the borders of Azerbaijan, like an island fifty miles from the border. With the formation of the Soviet Union, the Russians might have solved the problem by readjusting provincial boundaries. However, the creation of new tensions—or the maintenance of old ones—was part of their method of control. It still is.

In 1991, mobs carrying clubs and Turkish flags with crescent moons spilled out into the streets of Sumgait, Azerbaijan, fifty miles east of Baku, looking for Armenians to kill, and what Armenians describe as a "*pogrom*" ensued. Hundreds of people were stabbed, stomped on, and burned, and the threat of landmines became a part of the fabric of everyday life. This is a controversy that stirs the emotions of those of Armenian descent all over the world, including the United States.

I remember having lunch in August of 1993 at the University of California's faculty club with Professor Armen Der Kiureghian of the UC Berkeley Engineering School. He was a handsome, energetic guy in his late forties and had the

*Lives were shattered on both sides in the conflict
between Armenia and Azerbaijan.*

best of intentions, but he had never been to Armenia until
recently. Nevertheless, in his childhood he had sat by summer
campfires in the mountains near his Fresno home in California's Central (San Joaquin) Valley and listened to his elders sing
stories of another home, half a world away, and of hunger, invasion, and massacre—the very reasons his family had come to
the United States in the first place.

Professor Der Kiureghian had been invited by the American Academy of Sciences to travel under their auspices to Armenia along with Mihran Agbabian of the University of Southern California, another American of Armenian descent, because of their special interest in earthquakes. Their mission was to determine what role American science could play in correcting the planning and engineering flaws revealed by the great 1988 earthquake in Leninakan. The American University of Armenia, with an emphasis on civil engineering, had already been established, with Agbabian as president and Der Kiureghian as dean of engineering. Since Armenia's next door neighbor, Georgia, had similar seismic problems and a large number of bright young people to deal with them, I suggested that perhaps Armenia and Georgia could get together in some way to combine their resources. It was a very civilized and cordial conversation until I facetiously asked, "When are the Armenians going to stop beating up on the Azerbaijanis?" Much to my surprise, or maybe I should have known better, Professor Der Kiureghian slammed his fist down onto the table and logic, discipline, and friendliness disappeared from our conversation. This Armenian-American engineer pounded the table and for a minute or two expounded that the Azerbaijanis were *Turks*, and that the Turks had massacred over a million Armenian people between 1915 and 1917. (The Turkish Government officially admits to three hundred thousand, but it was *genocide* nonetheless.)

When I pointed out that the Azerbaijanis were Turkic, but not Turks, Der Kiureghian insisted, "*All the same!*" When I added that it was the *Russians* who had maintained the boundaries of Nagorno-Karabakh as a means of keeping the Armenians and Azerbaijanis at each others' throats and thereby controlling them both, he wouldn't have *any* of it and just kept voicing his deep hatred of the Turks. Ancient emotions run deep, violent, and unyielding.

Two years earlier, during the summer of 1991, I was afforded the opportunity to see and hear firsthand what this hatred could do when the already simmering tensions in Nagorno-Karabakh exploded into open warfare between the two countries. I was having dinner with the new ambassador at the American Embassy in Baku, which had been set up in an old Intourist hotel. A newly hired Azerbaijani staffer joined us at the table and almost immediately pointed across the plaza toward the steps leading up into the park overlooking the Caspian Sea. He said, "The last time I sat here, they were killing and burning people out there." An Armenian woman named Lola Avakyan had been stripped naked and forced to dance, her breasts slashed and her body burned with cigarettes before she was mercifully killed. Her body was then draped over a statue in a fountain near the entrance to the park that would ultimately become the national burial ground for thousands of Azerbaijanis who couldn't match up to the better trained and better equipped Armenians in the battle for Nagorno-Karabakh. After hearing all this, the American ambassador concluded that, "The Azerbaijanis have no national will to fight!"

I witnessed that war from both sides and sometimes feared for my life. But when I was with the Azerbaijanis, I *always* felt their insecurity, not only because of poor military capability or the criminal activity brought in by "big oil," but because Mr. Heydar Aliyev, president of Azerbaijan, had formally been a member of the Soviet Politburo in Moscow.

On this particular trip, after observing several days of fighting around Stepanakert, the capital of Nagorno-Karabakh, I had actually been trying to reach Lake Sevan, an Armenian lake whose beauty compares with that of Lake Tahoe near my home. I was looking for what I had heard was a very old monastery in the vicinity, which had continuously operated during the Soviet era and was still operating today. Instead, I inadvertently wound up at a picnic where the participants took a live goat out of the trunk of a car, slit its throat, skinned it, and barbecued it. I couldn't help but notice how casual they were about the throat slitting. No need for refrigeration here!

During the summer of 1991, Russian peacekeepers were stirring up as much trouble as they could in Armenia and elsewhere. It was so bad that the president of Armenia finally had to *ask* the Russian Army to help "police" the conflict with Azerbaijan. When a Russian soldier accidentally fired a shoulder-launched rocket into a school bus carrying fourteen Armenian soldiers, burning them to a crisp, all hell broke loose in Yerevan, the Armenian capital. "What the hell were the Russians up to?" I wondered. The Armenians blamed the "Turks" (Azerbaijanis) and began shouting an Armenian version of "Remember the Alamo."

I represented myself as a journalist and quickly produced a phony press card. I was allowed to go into the mountains with three European journalists to inspect the burned-out bus. The charred bodies inside were grotesque and unrecognizable. Russian troops were in the area policing the road to Stepanakert when all of a sudden, two young Armenian boys on motorcycles smuggling illegal weapons tried to run a checkpoint. They shot a Russian soldier and took off. They were later pinned down in a field by a Russian helicopter. After being warned by loudspeaker to surrender, they fired at the helicopter, which was hovering near the roadblock where our Land Rover had been stopped. A squad of Russian soldiers went into the brush and killed them. Their bodies were draped over the hood of one of the Russian scout vehicles and delivered to the main road where we were parked. It reminded me of deer hunters I had seen in Idaho, slinging deer they had shot over their saddles. The Russians didn't look happy. They didn't want more trouble, not this kind at least. A scowling Russian major walked over to me and the other journalists and, shaking his head, wanted to know what we had seen. A cautious Frenchman assured the major that it all looked like some kind of accident during "normal maneuvers." None of us wanted to spend the night there on the mountain. After a few more questions, the major let us go. Amazingly, the Russians didn't even check our papers. How times had changed!

It was late in the day and there were no food stops on the road out of the hills back to Yerevan, so we smoked a lot of cigarettes and marveled at the fact that we had been released so quickly, in fact, released at all, without so much as a witness interrogation. As we sped away, a Swedish journalist produced a bottle of cognac from the back of the Rover, which quickly disappeared. We all agreed to meet at the press conference the next day, which was being held in Yerevan at the presidential palace.

Yerevan is a bland city that, nevertheless, gives you the feeling of a very old culture. To the south, snow-capped Mount Ararat—reputedly the resting place of Noah's arc—rises spectacularly from the Turkish plain like Japan's Mount Fujiyama, and as you look into the southern Islamic sky, you think about Christianity's fourth-century roots in Armenia and Georgia. Yerevan was a relatively obscure provincial town until after the Bolshevik Revolution. It was affected by a horrendous earthquake in 1988 which devastated Armenia's second largest town of Gyumri (Leninakan) some fifty miles away, no thanks to the inexplicable design failures of the newer Soviet-constructed buildings. More than 25,000 people were crushed during the night and an estimated one million left homeless. Gorbachev's promise to rebuild Leninakan petered out due to the economic problems associated with the impending collapse of the Soviet Union. Armenians still feel jilted to this day!

The next day, I was escorted into an elegant salon in the presidential palace with my group of journalists and about eight or nine more journalists (a couple of whom were Russian), where President Levon Ter-Petrosyan, a philologist by training (semantics and linguistics) and a three-pack-a-day chain smoker, spoke to us. In his forties, he had been born in Syria but was educated at Yerevan State University. His father had been a member of the Syrian Communist Party before becoming a member of the Soviet Politburo in Moscow. I had met the Armenian president before under more confusing circumstances. I was impressed that he recognized me, although I don't think he could quite place who I was. I said to him, "Mr. President, I am James Waste of *Interperspective Corporation*, an international economic and industrial consulting company headquartered in California, which has many citizens of Armenian descent. I have played rugby with some of them."

Some wine was served and the French journalist described what we had seen to the president, who leaned back and thought for a moment before looking directly at me and saying, "When you go home, tell George Bush that Russia is a massive, dysfunctional country and it will take centuries for them to overcome what they have done to themselves and all of us."

Dysfunctional? I thought to myself. *He's got that right!*

One of the president's colleagues interjected, "Those boys were stupid! They didn't know what they were doing."

Armenia's president just smiled and responded softly, "Ahh, maybe, but the day they stood up to the Russian Army will never be forgotten. My people will sing songs about them for hundreds of years. The ballads of hate for the Turks still live and now will include a chorus about the Russians."

As we left, an aide grabbed me by the arm and said, "The president wonders if you will have lunch with him."

I replied, "But, of course." And off we went.

Snapshot 8

Morning Run in Baku

ONE MORNING IN 1993, I got up early—early for Azerbaijan and Central Asia, that is—to go for a one-hour run along the waterfront, up the stairs, and around the Parliament building. The sun had been up for about fifteen minutes. As I crossed the boulevard to get to the sea wall, I could already feel the heavy late May humidity and smell the oil of Baku as I ran by the bay.

Suddenly I saw a partially uniformed young man with the ever present AK-47 slung incorrectly over his shoulder. He looked sad and too young to be lighting the cigarette he held. He had a brightly colored schoolboy knapsack at his feet, which his mother had probably given him to carry his personal things and maybe a snack. I wondered if he would lose it when he got into the fighting or if it would just make him a better target.

As I ran further along the sea wall, I saw perhaps a dozen such lonely figures and wondered about them. Finally I saw an old, dirty, and dented military bus starting to pick these boys up on street corners along the waterfront. I asked a passerby, "Where are they going?"

The answer came back, "They are going to die. They don't know why, but they are going to die. The bus will take them to the hills around Nagorno-Karabakh, where the Armenians will kill them like the rest."

What could I say? An ancient feud over ancient land.

*I counted nearly 4,000 graves in Baku at the height of
the Nagorno-Karabakh War.*

I mumbled, "Thank you, good morning," and continued
running until I reached the broad stairway that leads to the Vista
Point and Park, one thousand wide stone steps up and overlooking the Caspian Sea. It was a tough climb. The great white
Parliament buildings stretched in front of me.

As I got close to the top of the stairs, I heard wailing and crying. Early morning burials were already taking place. The hillside, which had once been a park, was now a national cemetery.
I remembered back in 1991 seeing the first hundred graves,
with family pictures, trinkets, and flowers, and the wailing that
never stopped. I knew there would be significance in how many
graves were there now. The number was 3,800, with thousands
more buried in small village cemeteries around the country.
Almost four thousand graves just in this one location. All with
pictures and trinkets. That told a great deal about the little-
known war between Azerbaijan and Armenia over Nagorno-
Karabakh. A satellite might have been able to count the graves,
but it would not have captured the wailing and the air of hope-
lessness and doom among the people. But I did—I was there.

Chapter 17

Spy in the New World Order
(A Paler Shade of Light)

Long before the Soviet Union broke up and the Cold War ended or changed form, my job for years had been to analyze industries, study firsthand the failure of infrastructures, and determine who the players were in the various regions on my paper route. I had come to know Georgia, Armenia, Azerbaijan, Turkmenistan, Kazakhstan, Uzbekistan, Kyrgyzstan, and other republics of the former Soviet Union well. But for me, the years following the breakup of the Soviet Union—the New World Order—had become dominated by my relationship with Georgia and its leader, Eduard Shevardnadze.

After a nationwide referendum in March 1991, a majority of Georgia's population had voted for independence, and the Supreme Council of the Republic of Georgia had passed the Restoration of Independence Act, the first republic to do so. This Act acquired real significance when the Soviet Union was formally dissolved in December 1991 with the denunciation of the Union Treaty of 1922 by twelve Union republics, including Georgia.

Almost immediately, Georgia became involved in civil war, resulting from a split among the leaders of the new ruling bloc. The capital, Tbilisi, became a war zone, and the new president, Zviad Gamsakhurdia (son of famous Georgian novelist

Constantine Gamsakhurdia) was in the middle of it. A genuine struggle for power ensued, punctuated by bloodshed and suffering.

Gamsakhurdia took control of the media and arrested his political opponents, most notably Jaba Ioseliani, commander of the Mkhedrioni (the "Horsemen"). The Mkhedrioni was a near legendary group of about six thousand fighting men whose symbol was a black horse. Although Gamsakhurdia was popular among the masses, his campaign was marred by slanderous campaigning, harassment of opponents, and physical violence. Many believed, myself included, that he was an agent of Russia whose mission was to keep the pot boiling.

Open warfare engulfed much of Georgia. Battle lines formed through the fall of 1991, and many of Gamsakhurdia's former supporters joined the opposition, which he portrayed as "a coalition of disgruntled intellectuals, the communist *Mafiya*, and the 'criminals' of the Mkhedrioni." Paranoia and intolerance dominated his every move, causing one observer to describe him as "Georgia's version of Macbeth."

Shortly after he took power, Gamsakhurdia's opponents launched attacks on the Parliament building in central Tbilisi, demanding that he step down. I was in Tbilisi as part of my CIA directive to monitor the region following the formal dissolution of the Soviet Union. People and groups had demonstrated and marched for nearly three weeks when the situation began to really deteriorate. Random gunfire punctuated everything. It was very tense. Speakers shouted from the Parliament building's steps, one after the other, without stopping. Loudspeakers blared static-filled rhetoric. Words, static, and shots intermingled. It was very tense, even volatile, but I tried to move among the demonstrators as if out for a Sunday stroll. Signs and placards were everywhere. Gamsakhurdia refused to quit. He was holed up in the Parliament building for nine days as bullets bounced off its walls and the center of the city burned. When I would jog the side streets of Tbilisi, it was like running an obstacle course between hotspots of militant activity. Very few of the fighters on either side were soldiers. Their weapons included hunting rifles, shotguns, and World War II Russian surplus. Some of the "generals" of the opposition were actually movie directors and college professors. Alcohol flowed freely.

On one of my jogs, I returned to the bar in my hotel near the Parliament building to call Lou Jefferson in California to tell him what was happening. His wife, Margaret, answered the phone and the *pop, pop, pop, brrrrrrtt* of gunfire bombarded her ears. When she asked me if she was hearing what she thought she was hearing, I told her, "Now, you can always say you participated in a change of government in Georgia." When I went back outside, bullets still whistled by my ear. People shouted that I should get down, that snipers were firing from roofs, but the real question wasn't whether *I* would survive, but whether *Georgia* would survive.

Later that night, an extraordinary thing happened. The head of the Georgian Orthodox Church, which had somehow survived seventy years of communism, called for a last-hope, desperation-filled prayer service on the carpeted steps of the Parliament building where all the fiery speeches were being made. It was a warm fall evening, and the summer crickets were already silent. The Orthodox leader, in his black robes and with his long, black, glistening beard, spoke in ancient Georgian. Flickering candles appeared, as if from nowhere, in the hands of the majority of the crowd, which now numbered over ten thousand. When he recited the age-old words of Orthodox ritual, the crowd, as if from some tribal memory, replied with the correct ancient phrases. Even the people themselves seemed amazed that they remembered. Religion was alive in Georgia. Actually, it had never gone away.

I knew that Georgia would survive a revolution that had been both brutal and comical, and I knew that I was participating in history. History had seemed to reach at least an interim culmination during that memorable service when men in all manner of uniforms slung their guns over their shoulders and held candles in their hands, singing Georgian hymns. For those few moments, the factions in the civil war seemed to have come together as they joined in the ancient liturgy of the Orthodox Church, their candles creating a warm blanket of light above them, and at that moment I knew that somehow Georgia would come through its time of troubles. I became very emotional and had a vision of Georgia emerging to play a leading role in bringing the former Soviet republics into the community of nations.

Gamsakhurdia fled, but even after the "coming together with the candles," chaos and catastrophe still appeared to be Georgia's destiny for the foreseeable future. The prayer service had provided a lull, but the conflict continued in a number of ways. Georgia was still vulnerable to the whims of the Russian Bear. It had been the garden republic of their empire, the birthplace of much of their rich culture. It also provided a buffer zone to protect the Russian flank from Islamic extremism. And, it was an outlet to the Black Sea right next door to oil-rich Azerbaijan. So, the chaos continued.

An acting Military Council set up by Gamsakhurdia's opponents realized that until order was restored, the new Republic of Georgia was unlikely to achieve the international recognition it needed if it was to *remain* independent and avoid the embrace of a Bear that had changed its colors but was still the same old Bear when it came to claiming Georgia. Decisive action was required. In early 1992, Eduard Shevardnadze, the former Soviet foreign minister but Georgian to the core, was invited back to his homeland to lead a newly formed State Council, and with the new position came the official title "Head of State." (My associates and I facetiously referred to him as "Mr. Head.")

This was the first of several steps that would eventually lead to Shevardnadze's being popularly elected president of Georgia in 1995. With an illustrious new leader, the problem of finding a way out of international isolation was quickly resolved. What became known as the "Shevardnadze factor" secured international recognition of Georgia's independence. Georgia joined the United Nations and encouraged rapid establishment of foreign embassies, with fourteen major countries doing so almost immediately. Shevardnadze knew better than most other Georgians that Georgia must quickly become part of the "outer" world or slip back into the arms of the Bear.

Although the voters gave Shevardnadze a huge mandate to govern when he was elected chairman of Parliament in October 1992 and he quickly achieved international recognition, that didn't immediately end the troubles. Gamsakhurdia's forces kept up their armed resistance to the Tbilisi government through 1992 and into 1993. *Then*, the Abkhaz leader, Vladislav Ardzinba, declared the province of Abkhazia—which had been part of Georgia for hundreds of years and was ethnically 75 percent Georgian—an independent republic.

Shevardnadze reacted with tough measures. He broke up the Mkhedrioni who had backed him against Gamsakhurdia and found it necessary to jail the Mkhedrioni leader, Jaba Ioseliani, who was suspected of being in touch with Moscow and was blamed by many for the bombing that had nearly claimed Shevardnadze's life. The Russians continued to test Shevardnadze as he looked over his shoulder at his other neighbors, Turkey, Azerbaijan, Armenia, and Iran.

The civil war in Abkhazia continued and intensified, but the rest of Georgia began to calm down. In the early 1990s, the country's best hotel, the Metechi, had a sign at the door warning guests to check all weapons. It was difficult enough trying to sleep with the sound of automatic gunfire in the background, but at least they tried to control the dining atmosphere.

However, by 1995, the sounds of gunfire and explosives in the city, which had so often punctuated dinner in the fine dining room, had been replaced by violins and flutes. A simple metal detector at the door became sufficient for security purposes. Things were getting better, and they were getting better because of the courage and tenacity of Eduard Shevardnadze. I have heard numerous people describe him as a truly brave man. "He walked toward the fire, not away from the flame!"

By 1995, bullet-pocked buildings were under repair. People again walked the streets at night. Roadblocks in and out of the city were less frequent. Thousands of illegal weapons had been confiscated, and searches and identity checks were no longer a way of life. When I rode into Tbilisi from the airport, I smelled apples and pomegranates instead of gunpowder and blown-up toilet facilities, and *Diet Coke* was everywhere. In some ways it was more like a ride into town from San Francisco International Airport, except when I passed the spot where a couple years earlier I had seen a burning van or another place that made me remember the screams of rebels being incinerated in their tank.

At a Ray Charles concert I attended in Tbilisi in 1995, I heard Ray Charles sing the song he had made famous. I even heard a man singing "Georgia on my Mind"—in Georgian!—in a very primitive, smelly men's room. When Ray Charles arrived in Tbilisi, you *knew* things were better. He packed the concert hall, standing room only. The crowd sang with him in English and then in Georgian. A joyous time for everybody. Wow—what a night!

Georgia had come a long way and so had I. My maturity, experience, and independence made me uniquely qualified to not only see the changes over time, but to appreciate them as part of a larger picture as well. Unlike my line and staff colleagues, my *lack* of specialization was becoming one of my primary strengths. As I became more involved with Interperspective Corporation in Central Asia and the Caucasus, my freedom of movement allowed me to *participate* in the history I was witnessing. In my efforts, particularly on behalf of Georgia and Shevardnadze, I began to see a certain culmination of purpose in my own life, a better reason for walking for a time on this planet. I suppose I had been preparing for it for thirty-five years, and sometimes I wondered if it was all part of some *greater* plan. What I didn't know then, and do now, was that, more and more, my cover was becoming my mission.

Chapter 18

Friends Are Where You Find Them
(More Than Just a Shadow)

THROUGHOUT MY TIME behind the Iron Curtain and later after the Soviet Union had dissolved, I noticed people tailing me who I presumed were KGB or intelligence agents from the new republics. Most of these people were probably on local or at least specific assignment, but there were a few for whom keeping tabs on me appeared to be an ongoing responsibility. In the early days, when the Cold War was hot, I had to assume their role was adversarial, if for no other reason than to catch me doing something I wasn't supposed to be doing, which would provide them with a propaganda victory. But even then, I realized they were often there to protect me as much as to track my movements, and at times I was grateful to have them by my side.

There was, of course, the Colonel, who guided me around Tajikistan and set me up for the skirmish in the Tajik farmhouse. But there were two others in particular, both Georgian, who also filled this role. I never knew the name of one of them, or what he ate or when he slept. The other would eventually become one of my best friends.

I first became aware of my nameless "guardian" at odd moments during the late 1980s. It struck me how much he resembled actor Anthony Quinn, so, not ever having been introduced, this is how I chose to remember him. I didn't notice him again until 1993, when, totally unsolicited, he picked me up at the Tbilisi Airport after a late-night arrival and gave me a ride into town. This was during the civil war and, although Shevardnadze had quieted things down, Tbilisi could still be a dangerous place. The road in from the airport was dotted with burned-out vehicles. At one point, the tall, lean driver, the man who turned out to be my angel but looked like Anthony Quinn, tossed an AK-47 to me in the back seat and told me to use it if I had to.

As we approached the city on the darkened parkway, we saw a van lying on its side in flames ahead of us. Cars were scattered around it. Somebody was shooting. "Quinn" skidded to a stop, leaped out, and let off a few bursts from his AK-47. We pulled two men out of the burning van—one bloody and dead, the other bleeding badly and on fire. We rolled the burning man around on the grass and were barely able to get away as the van exploded. Police cars arrived and Quinn had an animated conversation with them. Apparently satisfying the police, Quinn pushed me back into his Lada and rushed me to the sixties-style Iveria Hotel in Tbilisi, fifteen miles away. It was three o'clock in the morning. I hauled my luggage up three floors to what I called the "bug room," because I knew it was crudely wired with listening devices.

At seven-thirty the next morning, Quinn appeared again, this time with two Georgian policemen and what appeared to be a KGB type. After inquiring about my state of health, they told me they wanted my bloodstained clothes and an agreement that I would not send a story of the previous night's happenings to Western newspapers. It was 1993 and the world would not understand an incident like this out of context. They said it was an "internal matter" and resulted from some "extremists" who had refused to stop at a roadblock for a weapons search. The extremists had used their weapons and the Georgian police had been forced to return fire. They told me the explosion and resulting fire was caused by illegal ammunition and grenades. I complimented them, saying something to the effect that they were tough hombres, that I hadn't seen anything worth reporting, and I was glad nobody had gotten hurt—which, of course, was a diplomatic lie. That seemed to do the trick! Quinn and I exchanged glances as they left—the kind of look rugby players exchange when they come off the field after winning a close game. It felt good. Nevertheless, when they left the room I was shaken. They had been deadly serious about not reporting the incident. I knew the only way I could gain these people's trust was to cooperate with them as much as possible. Also, if I showed any limitations on what I could do, that would be a dead giveaway that I was not working on my own. So I did report the incident to my handlers but kept my mouth shut to the media.

I saw Quinn at least ten times over the next couple of years, once when he came to my assistance after a shooting incident in my hotel room, but generally in a crowd and from a distance. Sometimes I noticed how his eyes would soften in a moment of recognition, and sometimes there would be a brief hint of a nod, but I never really conversed with him again. My shadow. My dark shadow. He was good—very good. I would like to have known more about him, but, of course, never asked. Even so, I always had the feeling that somehow he was on my side, and I wish I could have thanked him in some way but never got the chance.

Chapter 19

Mirian
(By My Side)

I WOULD NEVER have been able to get to know "Georgia like a Georgian" or find my way around much of Central Asia without another Georgian, Mirian Meskhi. Without Mirian, I probably wouldn't even be alive to write my story.

Mirian, like the Colonel and Quinn, was sometimes both my shadow and my shepherd in the murky world of the Trans-Caucasus. A former KGB operative and native of Tbilisi, this man who became the "Shadow of the Phantom" spoke five languages and was the son of a legendary Georgian soccer coach. He had served in the Soviet Army as a senior noncommissioned officer with responsibilities for intelligence and security matters. He often said the Russians didn't usually allow Georgians to become full-fledged officers but liked to pick their brains, and so they made them noncommissioned officers. Not surprisingly, he thought that most of the Russians he had encountered were "stupid."

Even though the Russians had controlled Georgia under both the czar and the Soviets, Mirian believed they always had a social and cultural inferiority complex with regard to Georgians, whose history went back to before the New Testament. He had been in Afghanistan with the Soviet Army and would sometimes wryly remark that, "The Soviets were always trying

Without Mirian, I wouldn't be alive to write my story.

to *one up* on the United States. In everything. Even when things were bad, the Soviet 'bad' was worse than 'bad' anywhere else. So when they went into Afghanistan, they made their involvement there much more horrible and senseless than the U.S. involvement in Vietnam."

Mirian returned to Georgia from the army before the breakup of the Soviet Union and became a tour guide for the government's Intourist travel agency. This, of course, meant that he reported indirectly to the KGB, and when asked about it today, he answers with a laugh, "Everybody who worked for Intourist reported to the KGB because Intourist *was* KGB. Every person needed permission to travel in the Soviet Union—even the Soviet people. Intourist watched all of them for the KGB, and sometimes it seemed as if everybody was reporting to everybody for the KGB. It was a joke, even though it was serious. The KGB was an internal police force as well as an international intelligence organization."

I recall first meeting Mirian in 1988, just after my plane landed at Tbilisi Airport. He looked like a muscular Omar

Sharif. Like Quinn, the Colonel, and all the others, he just sort of showed up to meet and assist me. All I really knew about him in the beginning was that he spoke good English, had a car, was reliable, and was very, very smart. At that time, the Soviet Union was still alive, if not too well, and Mirian was still wearing the dual hats of Intourist guide and KGB agent. He jokes today about the long forms he had to fill out each evening and how difficult it was to put me on paper.

Immediately after we first met, Mirian spent many days with me in transit as we drove down to Armenia and Azerbaijan. I learned very quickly that when serious trouble was imminent, Mirian could get me in and out of places that might otherwise be closed to a blue-eyed American. Even though I assumed he would report on me to the KGB, I sensed something in the Georgian that I liked and, up to a point, could trust. I think I overworked him that first year. We went everywhere possible in Georgia, Armenia, and Azerbaijan. I don't think he had me figured to be anything other than an adventurous tourist, although, of course, he must have had his suspicions.

Even though it became obvious to me that Mirian's masters might be in Moscow, it was just as obvious that his heart belonged to his native Georgia. Indeed, Mirian hated the Russians because, having worked for them, he knew how their minds worked and what they really thought of Georgia. Plus, he professed to love America. Despite this, in the early days, there was always a sort of invisible wall between us. Then, when the *not* so invisible Berlin Wall fell and the Soviet Union broke up, I sensed a new freedom in Mirian as well as in his country. He had listened to the Voice of America for years and wanted Georgia to be like us, which is one of the reasons I get so upset when some of our so-called "leaders" are dishonest or corrupt. You spend so much time and effort trying to influence these people, and then for as simple a reason as raging hormones, in an instant you lose credibility. I remember seeing Eduard Shevardnadze at his first U.S. press conference as president of Georgia, standing at separate microphones with Bill Clinton. What should have been noted as an historic occasion was hijacked by the press reporters' obsession with Monica Lewinsky. Clinton did nothing to stop them, while Shevardnadze just looked on. This was one of the four men who engineered the end of the Cold War, a historic statesman! I was embarrassed for America and told Shevardnadze so during my next visit to Georgia. And, of course, he was gracious about it.

But at the time, it was still too early to know how deep Mirian's love and respect for America truly was. All I could really be sure of was that often when I thought we were in deep trouble, Mirian would step forward and say, "I'll take care of this." Mirian always seemed to know just what to do.

When Shevardnadze returned to civil-war-torn Georgia after the breakup of the Soviet Union, he had no regular army with which to fight the rebels. Under the Soviet Union, the Russians had been the army. Shevardnadze was forced to turn to the Mkhedrioni (the "Horsemen"), an "elite" group of unemployed young men from good families mixed with ex-cons and criminals, to help defend the territorial integrity of the newly free republic. The Mkhedrioni, although a black force now outlawed, had proved crucial at that time. One night in 1993, Mirian and I were out in the countryside of Western Georgia tracking some "out of control" members of the Mkhedrioni who were fed up with the civil war. They were wearing their emotions on their sleeves as they hunted down rebels who had deteriorated into ragtag gangs. Many members of the Mkhedrioni had themselves deteriorated into gangs that were *not* ragtag, but more like animal packs. Many were just animals. They proved it that night. The Mkhedrioni had cornered four rebels in a crossroads farmhouse, and Mirian and I were following right behind them as observers. After a brief conversation during which the rebels denied any wrongdoing, the Mkhedrioni began shooting them in the legs. They were leaving their "calling cards." There was blood all over the place. One rebel was screaming and another was in deep shock, obviously bleeding to death. But when Mirian and I started to head for the door, thinking it was over and just wanting to get out of there, the Mkhedrioni lowered their AK-47s at us, saying that we would not be allowed to leave until we had drawn a little blood as well. My stomach churned a sickly dance. It was one of my life's most horrible moments—barbaric, ghastly—and I was trapped. The thought of shooting unarmed farmers to make a political point and join their "fraternity" repulsed me, but the other options weren't very good either. A refusal might bring on more shooting. Caught in the middle, I hesitated, but Mirian grabbed one of the AK-47s and began shooting at the ceiling, the windows, and anything with glass. Then he handed the automatic rifle to me, pointing it at the floor as he did. I let off a few bursts at the floor and the back door, put on what I like to describe as my "shit-eating Rambo smile," and did a kick-boxer spin. The Mkhedrioni began laughing. A tense moment had passed. They were punching each other's arms and doing thumbs up. Mirian and I did a slow high five. The Horsemen walked away.

Mirian nodded toward the wounded, and followed the Horsemen out into the farmyard. I inspected the shattered legs. Three were hopeless, but the fourth had only flesh wounds. I spoke to him in Russian and told him we would send help. I pulled some dirty, old lace curtains off the windows and made a quick tourniquet for his bloody leg. Mirian called from outside, "Let's go! I told these guys you had a bad meal and had to take a shit!" I hurried outside. A bottle was being passed. They were all smoking. One of them smirked at me, or was it a sneer? We quickly got out of there.

This was only one of many times that I felt Mirian's quick feeling for a dangerous situation and instinctive understanding of the Central Asian mind saved my life, or at least my reputation. Yet in the world of the post-Soviet Trans-Caucasus, incidents like this were not unusual. They would generally happen suddenly, with no warning, and when I would describe them to embassy personnel, they would usually shake their heads, wondering what it all meant. After all, it wasn't why they were there and really was not their problem. Incidents like these generally meant very little *except as part of a larger picture*. Most regular employees of American diplomatic and intelligence agencies follow a much more structured path than I, acting on information from "authoritative" or government sources, and they are usually smart enough not to get into shootouts at country houses in Georgia. Nor do they find themselves caught in Chechnya between Russian units and Chechen rebels. But I did. Often. That's why I was there. It allowed me to report that I didn't see many dead Chechens, mostly dead Russians. But I also knew that the Chechens recovered their dead quickly, not only for religious reasons but so they wouldn't be counted by the Russians. Being there and getting to know the locals allowed me to put what I saw and experienced into a larger picture. I learned what to look for and what to make of it when I saw it.

A big concern of Mirian's was the growth in power of the Russian crime syndicate, better known as the *Mafiya*, because he could feel its tentacles spreading into Georgia and the other former Soviet republics. I shared his concern. By the mid-nineties, between three and four thousand gangs had undermined reform in Russia and spawned extraordinary levels of violence. A hazy boundary between criminal and legal business existed in a country with no tradition of *legal* free enterprise. *Mafiya* groups penetrated most areas of the Russian economy, giving them a disproportionate influence in everything that happened in so-called "free" Russia. Sadly, many Russians increasingly identified free-market democracy with organized crime and corruption, and its power and influence continue to spread throughout the old Soviet Empire.

As the Russian *Mafiya* grabbed a foothold in Georgia, Mirian worried that it would destroy the beginnings of free-market democracy in his native land. He shared Shevardnadze's concern that Russian policymakers made what he believes to have been a fundamental error by trying to develop a free-market economy before constructing a civil society and infrastructure. Shevardnadze did not make that mistake in Georgia, and Mirian, like Shevardnadze, was hopeful for Georgia's future. I, too, am hopeful for Georgia, and have been so active in trying to help Georgia that an associate once jokingly suggested, "Shevardnadze ought to put up a statue of you in the main square."

I jokingly replied, "Yes, maybe a statue that nobody could see—just its shadow—because, as you know, my friends like to call me 'the Phantom.'"

Snapshot 9

Illegal Procedure

THE NEWLY INDEPENDENT country of Georgia elected two presidents before they even had a constitution. The first president, Zviad Gamsakhurdia, had been fired during a dramatic and bloody revolution near the end of his first year in office. The people in Georgia were devastated. The hero of Georgia's fight for independence, their first elected president, became a fugitive. His inadequacy as a governor with its accompanying corruptness could not be offset by his cinematic good looks or his talent as a writer and poet. His power-hungry wife ("the Dragon Lady") and a very suspicious connection to the Russian intelligence services ultimately landed him in a grave somewhere in Chechnya. Whether his wife had him killed or not, he certainly had been in over his head politically and beyond his character limits, and the intelligentsia recognized this almost immediately. But the general population, particularly the women, were swept away by Zviad's charms.

So with their first president gone, the obvious choice to lead Georgia was Eduard Shevardnadze, who had resigned as foreign minister of the Soviet Union and retreated to his native Georgia. When I first met him in 1992, he was in real limbo. The Russians hated him because he had helped end their reign as a superpower, and the Georgians considered him a traitor when he went north to work for "Central" a few years earlier. At this awkward time, he was misunderstood and without many public friends. However, it soon became obvious that Georgia was blessed with the presence of this man who not only possessed extensive international connections and experience, but was also a devoted citizen of his beloved Georgia.

So, to legitimize Shevardnadze's rule, in 1992 the second election was held. The election was overseen by the OSCE (Organization of Security and Cooperation in Europe) monitors. This is what brought me to Georgia at this particular time. In my role as a U.S. private citizen, I would eventually assist in monitoring three Georgian elections. Although this election was technically a plebiscite, it was a wonderful experience for me to see the country coming alive and to witness the rare birth of a democracy. The outcome of this election was 99 percent in favor of Shevardnadze and 1 percent opposed. Shevardnadze commented at the Metechi Hotel press conference the next day that he "was embarrassed by the numbers and that it would have looked better had there been more 'no's." This was greeted by a low rumble of friendly, understanding laughter. I was sitting next to "my man" Mirian, taking notes. I offhandedly leaned toward him and facetiously asked, "How did you vote?"

Much to my astonishment, he answered, "I voted 'No.'"

"You're making a joke?" I asked.

"No, I am serious," he replied.

Mirian and I had gotten pretty close during the three years I had known him. Sort of a father-son or mutual admiration kind of thing. I thought I knew him well. We had spent hundreds of hours together scouting Armenia, Georgia, and Azerbaijan. I could hardly wait for the press conference to end, even though some of the former Soviet Pravda-types were trying to embarrass the new chairman. They were unsuccessful, failing to recognize that this smiling Georgian is one of the great political figures of modern times. His name is right up there with the likes of FDR, Churchill, and Ronald Reagan.

Arm in arm, I marched Mirian out onto the café deck in front of the hotel. It was nearly noon and warm. I motioned for the little Russian waitress to bring "two of the usual." The world press crowd was surging out of the conference hall. I couldn't wait to ask my friend why he didn't vote for Eduard Shevardnadze. "He certainly is qualified to run your little country, isn't he?" I said.

Mirian replied, "He is okay. He is qualified and so on. But..."

"But what?" I asked.

Turning serious, Mirian continued, "I am very troubled by the process in which this took place. Do you remember just a year ago when Zviad Gamsakhurdia was the overwhelming popular choice? We were all proud of Georgia. We were no longer a republic under Russian rule. We wanted the world to know about our success, and then the elite, deciding our first president was a bad choice, staged a revolution and deposed him. Just like in South America or Africa. So, I think, here we go again. Is it just a coincidence that Eduard Shevardnadze was here and waiting, available? It is not that I dislike Eduard She-vardnadze, or all the politicians for that matter, but I, for my own self-respect, could not vote for Eduard Shevardnadze or anyone else who would be elected after such a revolution."

His tone was angry and loud for him. Reporters and guests were staring from tables near us. I felt embarrassed for not even noticing this aspect of the man's character. His guiding light as a young Soviet soldier and KGB guide had been Radio Free Europe and Liberty Broadcasting. Truth meant *everything* to him. He only understood *truth*. The big man's eyes watered and he dropped his chin to his chest. Cocking his head sideways and looking up at me, he asked, "Who did you *think* I would vote for, 'yes' or 'no'?"

"*No*," I said quickly, "of course."

He smiled a huge smile and clasped his hand over mine on the table top—a Georgian "high five." He looked at me sternly and said, "Sometimes I don't think you get it *or* me!"

I chuckled and said, "Mirian, you are very perceptive. You are a very special guy, and your sense of integrity has great meaning for me."

Mirian asked, "So, Jim, do I make my point?"

"Profoundly," I replied.

"So next election," Mirian responded, "if Eduard Shevard-nadze does a good job, I will vote for him, but this election I can't."

Looking him square in the eyes, I exclaimed, "Gotcha, cowboy!"

And with a look of great personal satisfaction, Mirian replied, "Cool, man."

This former Soviet soldier was a remarkable young man. His values were so clear! This was the first of two conversations which made me fully appreciate just how profound Mirian's understanding was of the rights and obligations of freedom and democracy. A couple of years later, I was somewhat humbled when Mirian caught me off guard while driving back to Georgia from a few days in Azerbaijan. After listening to me prattle about politics for a while, he interrupted with, "You just don't get it, do you? Communism is *not* a political or economic theory. It is *not* a religion or ideology, although it seems like it at times. Communism is an *attitude*, a mentality, a characteristic of the mind, as you call it. That's why its appeal is still international. It consistently transcends logic. Its appeal is emotional. It is the ultimate manifestation of 'the haves versus the have-nots' issue. If you don't get this, you will never successfully deal with the communist mind."

When I finally did get it, I turned to him and said, "Okay, Mr. Smart Young Man, what is freedom?"

Without missing a beat, Mirian replied, "Freedom is *also* an attitude, a positive attitude. It is the ability to choose between peace and conflict, right from wrong. It promotes individual responsibility and social accountability, and with freedom, you will always be able to deal with communism." Mirian beamed with joy. He really knew what freedom was. As did Shevardnadze, he understood freedom better than most of my friends at home. He and Shevardnadze had been without freedom. Shevardnadze's 1991 memoir, *The Future Belongs to Freedom*, made that unmistakably clear. After reading this book, I no longer had any doubt that Shevardnadze truly did abandon communism. Often, it is recognizing what's missing that matters most.

That evening, over dinner at Betsy's Guest House, my table buddies and I had a rousing discussion of recent events, during which I spoke out on the subject of political correctness. In the years since college, I'd been increasingly jumped on or corrected for verbally expressing my opinion, perspective, or point of view in public. This often happened with people I hardly knew, and I wondered what they'd heard, or thought they'd heard, or whether it was my tone of voice that had pushed their buttons.

Although I speak knowledgeably about things, I avoid being authoritarian. I'm basically an upbeat, tolerant, and constructive guy. In a word, I consider myself politically polite, not politically correct. I've been told that my sin is that I'm judgmental. But isn't everybody? My correctors certainly are!

Over time, I became gun-shy and drifted into the great silent majority, preferring peace over conflict. The price I paid is that my correctors saw my retreat as weakness and continued to attack. Conversely, I saw them as the negative and belligerent victims of their own terminally unexpressed hatred and anger.

Somewhere along the line the now popular term "politically correct," or PC, rose out of the swamp and became the not-so-subtle power tool of the radical left to influence public thinking on such subjects as religion, class envy, and politics. Mirian once pointed out that the term originated in Moscow a hundred years ago when the Communist Party leaders appointed "political correctness" officers to control and eliminate illegal thinking—thought control. There were no alternate ideas to the party line, so free speech was not necessary.

This is the attitude of the bully who says, "It's my way, or no way" and gains power by using fear and threats of retaliation to intimidate contrary views. The ultimate impact of these PC people has been to stifle natural human social interaction and ideas, limiting the freedoms needed to ensure justice and political balance.

One of the first things Shevardnadze did when he came into power was to promote freedom of speech, press, and media in general. I was there when this happened. The dramatic result was like when a long silent crowd at a football game suddenly and spontaneously bursts into an ecstatic roar when a last-minute score brings a needed victory. It is a miracle moment, uninhibited and free. When sixty-thousand-plus are united without reservation in one glorious voice, a flash moment occurs, a glimpse of what ultimate unity and freedom can be.

At Betsy's, I spoke of my awe at the incredible range available in man's communication processes. I compared the drip, drip, drip of political correctness to the flash flood of the sudden touchdown or a Pearl Harbor.

At this point the Irish bank guy leaned forward and with a half smile said, "And that's just your opinion."

And with a half smile I replied, "Yep. That's all it is." And we all laughed.

Chapter 20

Bare Necessities
(Planting Seeds)

W HEN THE RUSSIANS pulled the plugs connecting the fourteen republics to the Center, the most dramatically affected aspects of infrastructure were water, power, petroleum products, and public health, and these are all still critical problems today. Oh, and of course, the rule of law. When the Soviets were in charge, at least their police and military provided *some* law and order. However, this was one of the first things to go during the power vacuum that developed immediately following their departure, and, at times, *local* martial law was the only law that was effective, and I began to feel more danger than ever.

Overnight, like mushrooms following a rainstorm, kiosks not much larger than phone booths sprung up everywhere selling almost anything, but mostly foreign goods. The most popular items were ice cream, cigarettes, candy bars, Coca-Cola, and Fanta. The frontier scouts of marketing could be found everywhere, often and early. They could *smell* an idle ruble or lari (the currency of Georgia) ten thousand miles from the factory. Only six months after the breakup of the Soviet Union, I was able to buy a Mars Bar and a pack of Marlboro cigarettes at the trailhead high in the beautiful Pamir Mountains in Kyrgyzstan where the mountain climbers parked their cars.

Ladies' cosmetics and underwear were in great demand. Communism had never addressed the brassiere problem of its defeminized women. Standardization of cup size had provided support only for the more abundantly endowed "babushka" types. Some of these items were previously available on the black market, but now it was all out in the open.

I noticed two things that sped up commerce in the Caucasus more than any other—the cell phone and the inexpensive Yellow Cabs brought in by a Turkish company. The pace of the cities quickened overnight. A visitor could now get a lot more done in a day with much less frustration. It had previously been difficult to plan social or business engagements more than a day or two in advance because unforeseen matters might arise and commitments would have to be broken.

Gambling was everywhere after the first year, usually in hotel lobbies. Casinos would be opened, with the usual accompanying criminal types in the not too distant background and the flashily dressed hookers hanging out nearby.

The nouveau riche had fancy cars like BMWs and Mercedes that almost always *looked* good but were, in fact, rebuilt or stolen cars from Europe, especially Germany. Due to a lack of driver's education and an oversupply of macho mentality, auto accidents were frequent and usually horrendous (my biggest fear next to land mines and being swarmed by gypsy-kid pickpockets).

TV sets and household appliances began appearing surprisingly at the same prices as in downtown Los Angeles. And then there were the *clothes*—clothes for women—and what a difference that made on the street! I had seen the same phenomenon in London during the early 1950s when Britain finally began to recover from the war. People just wanted to look better. It's fascinating how the world comes together simply by wearing similar clothes. Visually perceived cultural differences are diminished and self-esteem is bolstered. Just watch how the well-dressed walk on Tbilisi's Rustaveli Boulevard as compared to their unliberated and poorly dressed counterparts.

I also witnessed the birth of a new Georgian appellation—the sudden appearance of the *goimi*, which refers to certain individuals in the emerging middle class. Caught in the class gap and using U.S. and European magazines for fashion hints, clothing ensembles, makeup, and accessories were often inappropriate and poorly coordinated. One day while walking on the Boulevard, I asked my close friend and personal physician, Maya Sharashidze, how she knows a *goimi* when she sees one. Maya chuckled and said, "See that handsome young man waiting in front of the chancellery? He's wearing a beautiful navy blue gabardine suit and expensive Italian shoes. His shirt and tie are okay, but look at the high-riding trousers and white sweat socks! That's a *goimi*," and then she laughed at herself for wearing a pair of jeans from the Gap along with white Nike shoes and white women's tennis socks. Pointing to herself, she added with a blush, "But this is different?"

Although promising indicators of the future, all this activity could hardly be called infrastructure development, something Americans take for granted because it has always been there. It took almost four years to create pedestrian crosswalks in Tbilisi and another four years to teach the public to use them. One-way streets and sober traffic cops eventually made things safer, but at least it was a start. However, what most Americans don't know or fully appreciate is that a country has to "grow" an infrastructure to meet the varied needs of its people. Georgia, after a chaotic start, is still in the "planting stage" and has begun to focus on such basic infrastructure needs as water, power, roads, and medical and communications facilities. The hope is that as Georgia develops, the growing infrastructure will also include such diverse sectors as financial services, telecommunications, and, of course, tourism. But it requires vision and exposure, something Georgia was sorely lacking when I conducted my first meeting with Eduard Shevardnadze.

The meeting took place in the spring of 1992, just after Shevardnadze had been brought in from Russia by a Military Council to try to establish some order out of the chaos that occurred in Georgia after the Russians withdrew and Gamsakhurdia was overthrown. It was merely an introductory meeting with Shevardnadze, and I gave him one of my Interperspective Corporation cards. He took it and showed it to Gela Charkviani, his Chief Foreign Policy Advisor, who had studied at the University of Michigan and spoke perfect English. After a short conversation with Charkviani, Shevardnadze asked what my specialty was. I explained that I had extensive experience in construction, engineering, and infrastructure development and that I would like to schedule a follow-up meeting to talk with him about matters I felt would help his new country. I was struck by his openness, accessibility, and, perhaps most, by his humanity. We seemed

I first met Eduard Shevardnadze in 1992; we spoke about his plans for Georgia's future.

to have an instant bonding, and I could see why both George Shultz and James Baker called him a friend. When you were with Shevardnadze, you knew you were connected to him. The man really listened and, more importantly, really *heard* what you had to say, taking notes on a yellow legal pad as you talked. Not only did he answer your questions thoughtfully, he responded to them in depth. I chuckled as the thought crossed my mind that we all wear masks and Shevardnadze was, in a way, like a spy probing behind other people's masks. I was surprised and flattered that he opened up to me the way he did and shared much detail about his personal background and his view of the world.

A second meeting was quickly arranged, during which I hoped to offer some ideas and guidelines from my background with Bechtel to help steer Shevardnadze away from the failed communist system toward a true market economy. He was, after all, a career politician and statesman, not an administrator. Typically he knew what he thought should be done or what he wanted to be done, but had little knowledge as to how his goals could be accomplished, and unfortunately he was surrounded by people of similar qualifications and often dubious integrity. He was submerged in a stunted culture. I was someone who had nothing to gain, so he listened.

After exchanging pleasantries, I stopped beating around the bush and asked Shevardnadze just what *were* his plans for Georgia's future? My question was met with vagueness, which I attributed in part to his fatigue and preoccupation with the raging civil war that had almost derailed his return to Georgia. I decided to play my consultant hand, and made the pitch I had often made during engineering feasibility presentations and reviews. I offered, "Mr. Chairman, I don't mean to be presumptuous, but I'd like to share with you my preliminary checklist or shopping-list system that I used when I was involved in project development with Bechtel Corporation, and, I might add, it will be at no cost to you."

Shevardnadze glanced at Charkviani, arched his eyebrows, and, with his characteristic smile like the sun bursting from behind a cloud, shoved his notepad across the conference table toward me and handed me his pen, blunt end first. I knew the list well, but for readability I printed it carefully instead of writing. I was excited! On my shopping list, I included the three main components of infrastructure development: UTILITIES, FACILITIES, and SERVICES. I broke each main category down into its constituent parts, e.g., water and energy for utilities, roads and airports for facilities, and education and medical for services. In turn, I broke each of *these* constituent parts down into further detail. I tried not to comment on each item as I wrote but noticed that Gela was expanding on them for me as he translated into Georgian. I did state that all these things are necessary sooner or later, but that there was a natural sequence to building an infrastructure (or a *nation*, for that matter). I numbered the items, starting with power generation and ending with tourism. I slid the list back to Shevardnadze. He stared politely for a moment as if he could read English, then tore off each page, waving it gently like a flag and handing it to Gela. They chatted for several minutes in Georgian and then Gela said, "The Chairman thanks you for consultation and also that it was free—like in free enterprise!"

Now feeling Shevardnadze's acceptance, I asked if we could talk a little longer. He replied, *"Ki, ki, kargia"* (yes, yes, it is good). And then, as an afterthought, he asked, *"Ramdeni puli?"* (how much money?)

I replied, *"Upasod"* (no charge), and we both laughed. It was at this time I realized that Shevardnadze possessed a real sense of humor. On a more serious note, I asked, "Are you going to build a pipeline to export Azerbaijani oil?"

"Probably," he responded, "but it is very risky. You know, easy to sabotage and subject to outside political forces, and it would be very costly. Georgia has no money."

I replied, "The twelve 'big oil' companies will finance the line and protect their interests. I have been involved in pipeline construction in both the U.S. and Canada. A suggested pipeline through Georgia to the Black Sea might be six hundred miles long and, at a hundred million dollars per hundred miles, it would cost six hundred million dollars. The right-of-way is not difficult," I added. I was on a roll! "A second, alternate line would perhaps be longer but would provide insurance against hostile intervention." Shevardnadze shook his head in contemplative disbelief. Then I asked, "Do you have any idea how many barrels of product can be pumped through the line from production to market outlet? How much a barrel is worth? How much Georgia can charge in royalties per throughput barrel?" His eyes revealed that he didn't know, but I skidded to a halt. He did *not* have the slightest idea, nor did most of the people around him—past or present. They were politicians, not managers, and besides, things had always been free! Records had not been kept on such matters, or, if they had, they were all in the Center and not only unavailable, but useless at best. I realized that when the Soviets withdrew their support for the infrastructure, such as it was, the former republics, including Georgia, had essentially been castrated, and the horror of their dependency on Mother Russia was everywhere. Shevardnadze did not have the basic information he needed to make fundamental political and economic decisions. How was this super-diplomat going to rebuild his beloved Georgia? No help from the Bear, that was for sure!

Our U.S. infrastructure is always there for us, even if relatively unnoticed. It is decentralized, yet integrated and efficient. *Their* system was centralized, but *not* integrated *or* efficient, and through the years I watched it collapse. This is what happens when everything is free! But, in order for Georgia to make the sea change necessary to resuscitate and grow its infrastructure, the rest of the country must embrace the vision at the top.

Chapter 21

What's in a Word?
(Georgia's Professor)

SHEVARDNADZE SEEMED TO APPRECIATE my consultation, but I'm not sure he understood the need for a vision to rally his country around. He was preoccupied with setting up a government and dealing with the civil war that had broken out when Gamsakhurdia was forced to leave. The western government was interested in seeing Georgia succeed, as were many private people and institutions. I realized that I needed to enlist influential and untainted individuals to help define a vision. The name that surfaced again and again was Professor Alex Rondeli, Chairman of International Studies at Tbilisi State University and later Special Advisor to President Shevardnadze.

I met Alex Rondeli in 1992 at the private home of Betsy Haskell, who was already developing a reputation as "the Perle Mesta of Tbilisi" with a little "Georgette Mosbacher" thrown in. Betsy was hosting one of her elegant dinner parties, and I knew that Rondeli would be there. At this first meeting in 1992, not long after my revealing conversation with Shevardnadze, it was only natural for me to corner Rondeli after dinner and ask him, "What's happening with Eduard Shevardnadze? What's next? What's his plan? Does he have a vision? What does he tell his people?" I wondered if anything had even registered during my previous discussion with Shevardnadze.

Alex Rondeli remains one of the best-known think-tankers in Georgia.

Alex replied, "Stop, please for now. But please, let's meet together when you visit in the fall."

On my next visit, I flew to Moscow and took a Georgian National Airlines (ORBI) flight south to Tbilisi. The situation there was in transition and very unstable. There were roadblocks in and out of the city and gunfire could be heard at unscheduled intervals, especially at night. Drive-by shooters were marauding around the city, shooting mostly at buildings just to be macho. The only person I knew who would walk around at night under these circumstances was none other than Alex Rondeli. He didn't own a car, so it was his only way of getting around.

When I arrived in town, I called Rondeli (it took two hours to get through) and we agreed to meet for coffee at a sidewalk café on Rustaveli Boulevard. Alex had recently been to the States and lectured at Williams College in Massachusetts. His English was excellent. By the second cup of coffee, we had decided that Georgia must seek a new identity and set aside the old macho chest-pounding "I am a Georgian!" form of nationalism.

I again asked Alex what Eduard Shevardnadze's vision was. He muttered something about peace, freedom, and prosperity, but that wasn't going to do it. Then I got excited. "No, I mean he needs a gimmick, a slogan, a one-liner that he can lay on the people that gives them a sense of *now*, of direction—a goal, something to unify them in a common cause!"

Now Alex perked up and said, "We need a new identity. The Russians nearly destroyed our self-esteem. But, of course, Russia has an even worse identity loss. Russia suffers from a monstrous loss of self-esteem. I'm wondering what do you think that gimmick could be?"

I replied, "As a political scientist and a student of the United States, you must know some of our political slogans."

He did and proceeded to rattle off, "'Remember Pearl Harbor,' 'Remember the Alamo,' 'Remember the Maine,' 'Fifty-four forty or fight!' and, oh, how about 'The New Deal' and 'Reaganomics'?" I was amazed. We were greatly amused with ourselves as we brainstormed our way into a *third* cup of Georgian coffee. What became clear to us during this brainstorming session was that no progress was possible without a vision or goal to hang one's hat on. Rondeli saw Georgia as a possible "Switzerland of the Near Abroad." I saw it as the "Headwaters of the Transport Corridor." He saw it as the "Flagship Republic" of the region and, at that same moment, we both remembered Marco Polo and the Silk Road. Now both of us were truly excited! The Silk Road gave us a whole fresh perspective. It was a new way for the people of Georgia and the region to look at themselves—a way for them to see themselves as part of an old vision made new. Acceptance of this sort of vision was essential for internal and external socioeconomic growth. Without such a vision and realistic goal, Georgia would surely fail.

So was this talk of the "Silk Road" and a "transport corridor" anything more than just talk? It was, and seeing the region in ways not previously possible, these concepts helped stimulate

Eduard Shevardnadze's move to establish a regional council of nations with common history and common problems. The East-West Regional Council was dedicated at Tbilisi State University on October 10, 1995, and among the many dignitaries present were George Shultz and his wife, O'Bie.

The "Eurasian transport corridor" concept got traction and is flourishing, and, indeed, there are now multiple oil pipelines running throughout the region. People don't realize that you can board a boat in San Francisco and get off at any of three Black Sea ports in Georgia—Sukhumi, Batumi, and Poti. And from these Georgian ports, goods and people can travel by rail or road all the way to Beijing. People have been doing this for countless generations! Interdependence is the reality; regional coprosperity is the goal. Even without oil from Baku, the concept of a Eurasian transport corridor is needed. If the nations of the region do not develop a sense of codependency and cooperation, *really* big trouble could result. Carried to the ultimate extreme, the region could be the starting point for World War III! An economic battle over oil profits and/or a religious reign of terror brought on by Muslim extremists could ignite it, with, of course, a little help from the Russians.

But in an ironic twist, the way the Russians had historically dealt with their subservient republics may have inadvertently made it easier for a regional mentality to emerge. As a frequent traveler to the eight republics of Central Asia, I could communicate to some degree with all the people in Russian. Eighty percent of the population of fifty-five million are Sunni Muslim and speak a Turkic language (the sole exception being Tajikistan where Farsi, the language of Iran is spoken), but *all* of them have absorbed a lot of Russian culture. The Russian presence may have been distasteful and oppressive, but everyday life was relatively smooth in spite of monumental inefficiency and corruption. Certainly what infrastructure remains in these countries is left over from the "Russian occupation," and although it nearly collapsed when the "colonialists" withdrew, just enough of it survived so that each republic, in its own way, is rebounding. The need for a regional concept makes great sense!

Alex and I believed that some form of regional organization similar to the European Union (EU) must be convened to deal with regional problems and opportunities. Why be second-class to Europe? History was born in this area. There is a collective memory of ancient origins in addition to a substantive religious connection. Even the Russian period left *some* starting points for regional growth. Alex and I never doubted that the region could prosper. But, as is the case in many parts of the world, it will take more time than it should because of ignorance, greed, and corruption.

In 1998, while visiting his daughter, an honors student at the International School in Monterey, California, Alex came to visit me at my mountain home high in the Sierras near Lake Tahoe. I will never forget driving him to the lake in mid-winter and standing on a pier as we decided that if only "they" would let "us" run things for five years, Central Asia could leap ahead thirty years and save a trillion dollars and millions of lives. As we spoke, the winter wind blew an opening in the snowy sky and a sharp shaft of sunlight spotlighted us. Alex squinted up at the light in the sky and said, "I think we are being called on to try. I am not a very religious man," he continued, "but I *am* a believer and a student of religious history. I believe this breakthrough of sunlight is a sign—a sign that we are on the right road." We knew we were right! And then, as before, we chuckled at our sense of self-importance before becoming a little embarrassed at our "revelation."

Then, as we were returning home, we saw another sign that day—a sign that said: "Gasoline, toilets, cigarettes, and post cards—preferably in that order." It was a Chevron station looming out of the blizzard engulfing Interstate 80. We laughed this time at the *symbolism*. Chevron was already big in Kazakhstan.

I was impressed by this very big man of very big dreams speaking of signs, and I will always love him because he never sold out to the Communist Party (even though he was, of necessity, a member) or the corruption of the bureaucrats. Alex suffered financially and healthwise at the hands of small bureaucratic minds, but he survived on *truth!* He became one of President Shevardnadze's chief advisors on foreign affairs, a position for which he was eminently qualified. He later set up the Georgian Foundation for Strategic and International Studies, and remains *the* guy the foreign wire services call to find out what's up.

So, what's in a word? Almost everything not readily apparent to the naked eye. I know that knowledge is power, and that words implement that power. It fascinates me that a phrase can unite or destroy civilizations. Ronald Reagan's careful choice of words was more effective than six thousand bombs. When Reagan recognized the Soviet Union as an "Evil Empire" and said "Mr. Gorbachev, tear down this wall," his words were among the most powerful ever spoken. For now, Alex Rondeli and I will settle for Georgia as the "Switzerland of the Near Abroad."

Alex's legacy will be his students. Georgia needs him to help bridge the generations lost during the transition. His joy will always be walking around the city being greeted by his former students shouting (usually in English), "Hi, Alex!" You can see it in their eyes. In Alex, they see hope! He doesn't *need* a car.

Play It by Ear

MY FATHER WAS A SELF-TAUGHT banjo and piano player. When he returned to UC Berkeley in 1919 after serving in the army during World War I, he played in Horace Heidt's college band to pay for his college expenses, until one night Heidt noticed that Dad's music was upside down. Heidt said Dad was faking it. But I know he wasn't. The music was already inside his head. He could hear it and was just letting it out. Heidt went on to become a famous bandleader and showman. My father eventually became executive vice president of one of the world's most diverse engineering and construction companies. Not bad for a history major who couldn't read music.

Former secretary of state and Bechtel Corporation president George Shultz referred to Dad as the company's "living legend." I grew up with Dad and know he merely had some tricks, or perhaps I should call them "knacks." Dad would listen carefully to a set of complex problems, analyze them, and reduce them to simple truths in manageable form. For example, after remaining relatively silent during several hours of discussion at a board meeting, Dad would say, "Well, it all boils down to…" or "So, until more facts emerge, we'll have to play it by ear."

The press reported that Ronald Reagan fell asleep at cabinet meetings, but I know better. He was just monitoring and editing.

Remember, he was older—been there, done that. So he would let the cabinet vent for a while and then, to nobody's surprise, would pick up the ball and throw a strike, such as, "Well, it all boils down to..." or "Let's play it by ear." Then he would toss down some jelly beans (he liked the green ones), pass the bowl around, and crack an appropriate joke: "That reminds me of the story about..." Dad and Ronald Reagan could get their point across, as can George Shultz.

I remember in particular the 1995 dedication of the East-West Regional Council in Tbilisi. Shultz and his old friend Eduard Shevardnadze were due to be the featured speakers at the newly formed council of regional leaders. An elite group of over a hundred government officials, academicians, and prominent public officials from the Caucasus region were in attendance. Among them, in the front row, were Nanuli Shevardnadze and O'Bie Shultz, along with my friend Gela Charkviani, whose formal title was Chief State Advisor, Head of the International Department, the State Chancellery. He was all of that and often served as Shevardnadze's interpreter, but not on this particular day.

Earlier in the day, Shultz had toured several sites of historical interest and attended a luncheon at the *Sameba Joint Venture Winery* in the town of Sagaredjo, about twenty miles from Tbilisi. The luncheon was hosted by Bob Medearis, a consulting professor of engineering and management at Stanford and UC Davis, and an entrepreneur extraordinaire on the side. Bob had been a friend of Georgia from the beginning, from organizing seminars on business development to sponsoring student internships. The winery was originally Bob's baby, and George Shultz along with a golfing buddy had anonymously invested $50,000 of their own money into it years earlier without telling Shevardnadze. Shortly before Shultz's visit, I had the privilege (and the fun) of telling Shevardnadze of Shultz's involvement in Georgia's new experiment with free enterprise. When I mentioned the $50,000 investment, Shevardnadze asked Gela to repeat the amount, and when he did, there was a long reflective pause followed by several deep breaths. His eyes welling up, Shevardnadze tilted his head and with a slight quaver in his voice said, "Isn't that typical of George? He doesn't seem to need credit for good deeds."

The luncheon at the winery was what the Georgians call a *tamada*, and, as is their custom, there were a lot of toasts. The toastmaster proposed individual toasts to all ancestors, friends, heroes alive and dead, sports figures, deities, deceased pets, phases of the moon, etc., etc. These toasts were fun but *deadly* after a while. As a nondrinker (there *are no* nondrinking Georgians), I had a hard time explaining why I didn't participate. "What do you mean you don't drink? This glass is not filled with gasoline, it's only vodka!" After an hour and a half of this, a sumptuous lunch was served.

The party left the winery late in the afternoon and went directly to the dedication at Tbilisi State University. Shevardnadze gave a thirty-five-minute, thoughtfully eloquent, and humorous account of several historic moments he and Shultz had shared, especially at Reykjavik where they, along with Reagan and Gorbachev, had begun to gain each other's trust and respect. The well-dressed and dignified audience was thrilled to hear their man, their hometown boy, sharing the intimacy of these moments while being validated by the presence of his counterpart.

*Eduard Shevardnadze and George Shultz share a long
history of cooperation and friendship.*

Then it was *my* guy's turn! Shevardnadze is a good public speaker, warm and almost poetic when he speaks. Shultz's style, on the other hand, is long on content, solid, logical, and to the point, although often with a twinkle in his eye. The match was on! After lengthy applause and a change of interpreters (both pretty young Georgian women), Shultz led with a good opener and then followed with his own recollections of the historic events, speaking highly of his Georgian friend who had been one of the principal engineers in saving the world from possible nuclear annihilation. Fourteen minutes into it, George asked the audience if it was okay for him to take off his navy-blue suit coat. The conference room was not large and many attendees—including Mirian and me—stood along the walls, making it quite warm inside.

For the next forty minutes, George (in shirtsleeves) did yeoman service for the U.S.A. and gave those assembled some choice inside political comments and predictions. But he went on a bit too long for the comfort of his wife, O'Bie. I was near the front of the room and noticed as O'Bie nudged Nanuli with her elbow, which drew a smile and a nod. O'Bie then tried, on several occasions, to signal George with a wifely sort of salute, drawing her hand across her throat as if to say, "Cut!" She finally caught his attention and his pace quickened. The two women exchanged an international, knowing glance of wifely victory.

George, like the cool professional he is, dramatically glanced at his watch and said, "Now, in conclusion, I would like to say that as some of you might know, I served in the U.S. Marines during World War II." (O'Bie was a Navy nurse.) "I remember in boot camp that when the day was done, the top leatherneck sergeant would have us stand in formation before dismissing us by saying, 'It's time for you jarheads to stack rifles, get chow, and hit the sack!' *Thank you!*"

As he turned to find his coat, he missed seeing O'Bie covering her face with both hands in mock horror. The young interpreter was overwhelmed and struggling with what Shultz had just said. Mirian pulled on my arm with a quizzical scowl. Gela Charkviani sprung to his feet and, being very savvy in English and Americanese, gave a clear explanation of George's "closer," though the audience still wondered what language had been spoken. Everyone rose and Shultz, now wearing his suit coat, warmly greeted the audience as they exited the room.

Gela leaned toward me and asked, "Did I get that right?"

I replied, "Bull's-eye!" and was rewarded with a huge smile of relief.

As we walked to the limos, George caught my eye and said, "Maybe I should have sung 'Georgia On My Mind,' but I only know it in English and Russian, and this is a Georgian crowd!"

All I could think to say was, "Semper fi!" as Mirian continued to shake his head. And to this day, whenever I see George Shultz, he says, "It's time to stack rifles!" and we both laugh.

Chapter 22

Seeking the Light
(The Good Samaritans)

"GEORGIA IS SITUATED between the borders of both Europe and Asia, at the ancient crossroads of the most important migrations of peoples and civilizations. It is a point on the globe where cultures, faiths, and the strategic interests of the powerful have intersected and clashed, ensuring Georgia an enviable, glorious but, in many ways, torturous fate." These words were written by Eduard Shevardnadze in his 1991 memoir. Thanks to the leadership of this architect of the ending of the Cold War, his native Georgia, in many ways, became the leading republic of the post-Soviet Caucasus Mountain chain, and its capital, Tbilisi, an important financial and political center in an area whose geopolitical importance is still not well understood by most Westerners.

Shevardnadze often sought the advice of Rusudan Gorgiladze, one of his most trusted assistants and representatives, a woman who rapidly achieved an international reputation of her own. Rusudan is a startlingly beautiful woman with coal black hair and flashing eyes that grab you and seem to draw you into her country's culture and three-thousand-year history. Just looking at her gives you an insight into why historians and archeologists view Georgia as one of the cradles of civilization. There are some who view her as a darkly attractive and mysterious woman, but, to most, her voice is a barrage of passion when she speaks of what she believes lies ahead for Georgia specifically, and the whole Trans-Caucasus region in general.

Rusudan believes in the old axiom that you can't reach into the future without having a firm grasp of the past. And yet, there has been such little common history with the United States, it's hard for most Americans to understand what's happening in the Caucasus, especially Georgia, or the potential that exists in the region, both good and bad. For Armenians, including the many Armenian-Americans who support their ancestral homeland, the scars from early twentieth-century massacres still run deep, and they compare them to their present-day feelings about Nagorno-Karabakh. America's Armenian immigrants and their descendants have made their fellow Americans at least aware of the existence of their ancestral homeland, and as for Azerbaijan, it has triggered the word "oil" in the minds of Americans for decades. But, largely due to the fact that there never really was a Georgian diaspora, the American experience with ancient and now once again free Georgia has been minimal. As a result, the Soviet's bloody annexation of Georgia after Lenin consolidated his power received little if any attention in the West, even though production of every kind fell to less than one-third of its pre-revolution capacity.

American industrialist Armand Hammer received enormous publicity for his "capitalist ventures" in the then new Soviet economy of the 1920s, even though, in actual fact, they had very little value. He *did* set up a pencil factory, but that was about it. On the other hand, Averell Harriman, another American industrialist with an otherwise much publicized life, tried to organize a pipeline and refinery project for transporting crude from Azerbaijan's Baku oil fields through Georgia to the Black Sea (an idea that oil companies are acting upon today), which received little publicity at all. Harriman *did* manage to get and operate a manganese concession on the rugged

Georgian plateaus of the Caucasus Mountains near Chiatura, one hundred miles from the Georgian port of Poti. However, the Soviets killed the project by flooding the market with Ukrainian manganese and charging an annual fixed royalty that made it impossible for Harriman to cover the costs of his supplies and equipment.

Harriman's ultimate failure in Georgia during the winter of 1926-27 was not, of course, due to the Georgians themselves, but to their Soviet masters in Moscow. The Soviets took and held absolute control of Georgia right up to the end of the Cold War and, when the Soviet Empire collapsed in 1991, Georgia and the thirteen other republics were left to fend for themselves. So, in each of the former republics, one by one, the infrastructure, which had always been administered by Moscow during the Soviet Empire, suddenly no longer existed.

This particularly affected Georgia's hospital and medical-care systems. Most of Georgia's medical supplies had not come from either Georgia *or* Russia. On the contrary, Czechoslovakia and other Eastern bloc countries were the main—although not the only—suppliers. But *all* supplies first went through Moscow, or Center as it was known throughout the Soviet Empire. Nothing was imported directly into Georgia. *Everything* was arranged for and shipped through Moscow. At the time of the collapse of the Soviet Union, Georgia had 120 hospitals and clinics and 30,000 doctors and medical technicians. But when Moscow cut them loose, none of the healthcare professionals knew how to bring so much as X-ray film and surgical tape into the country. Then when the healthcare professionals looked toward Center for assistance, Moscow thumbed its figurative nose at them as if to say, "You wanted to be on your own, now *you* deal with it!"

Moscow, of course, wanted to see the new republics fail and have to come to Mother Russia for help, thereby creating a new dependency, and soon opportunistic doctors took advantage of the system by taking over some of the hospitals and operating a sort of medical *Mafiya*. They dispensed minimal health care, while most of the rest of the system shut down. The ordinary medical establishment did not see the medical world as a business. It had always been *free!* Even Georgians of Shevardnadze's caliber had difficulty dealing with what to most Americans would seem like a relatively simple situation, because, after all, they had grown up in—and known nothing but—the old Soviet system.

Shevardnadze had a unique ability to cut to the chase of a problem or an idea—"pearls" as I prefer to call them. One such pearl came from a conversation in 1993 in which we were discussing the medical crisis, especially the criminal aspects of it and the corresponding lack of national awareness of the importance of civil law. Shevardnadze quite rightly pointed out, "You must understand that, at this time, much of what *you* might consider illegal is not illegal in Georgia. As a result, the current match-up of systems is not conducive to doing business here. So don't send your lawyers here! They could be lost in our culture. It would be much better to send *our* young lawyers to learn *your* system because it is more clearly defined, and let *them* represent you here." Although Shevardnadze may have understood the essence of this pearl, there still hasn't been adequate remediation of the problem.

In June 1997, I attended the "Georgia-Turkey Joint Investment and Cooperation Opportunities Seminar," organized by Bob Medearis and Nick Frank of the Chalice Wine Company and cochaired by a brilliant twenty-seven-year-old Georgian, Constantine Rizhinashvili. A breakdown of projected GNP was presented by the minister of finance, and the healthcare sector was not even considered to be a constituent part. Amazed at the oversight, I rose to point out that in the United States, health care comprised 17 percent of GNP! The looks on the faces of the Georgian participants were incredulous. A reply was out of reach. But the omission had *not* been a mistake, and all that the foreign participants could reply with was an astonished murmur. Not having had to deal with the financial aspects of health care, the Georgians didn't even know how to account for it. Who would pay? It got so bad that Georgians were taking food to family members in the few hospitals that were still open because nobody seemed clear on how hospitals could feed their patients.

I had first become aware of the impending medical crisis back in 1994 through conversations with various Georgians at parties or "salons" throughout the city and at the Tbilisi home of a colorful and attractive American woman from Baltimore named Betsy Haskell. She frequently entertained a diverse group of foreigners—businessmen and women, journalists, and intelligence operatives—for whom her home had become a hangout. Betsy first appeared in Tbilisi in 1991, just after the collapse of the Soviet Union but prior to the fall of Gamsakhurdia, representing the Soros Philanthropic Foundation by giving workshops on public administration. However, Georgians who had spent their entire lives under the Soviet system did not seem too interested in American concepts of public administration, and Betsy soon found the experience about as rewarding as lecturing to teenagers. Georgians are highly intelligent and well educated, but for the last seventy years public administration had not been relevant in their world and the people weren't yet equipped to grasp—much less utilize—the valuable information given to them. Unfazed by it all, the former debutante, union organizer, and Lauren Bacall look-alike, having recently lost her third husband, decided to stay on in Tbilisi and go into the real estate business.

Shortly thereafter, because of *Mafiya* violence, the U.S. Embassy declared the Grand Metechi Palace Hotel off limits to American citizens. I had previously stayed at the Metechi only one night, but it was a memorable one. I remember standing out on the ninth-floor balcony of my room, admiring the lights along the river and the floodlit castle on the hill and thinking how it reminded me of a movie set, when all of a sudden I heard a distinctive *pop...pop...pop!* Instinctively, looking below at the hotel's parking lot, I saw two men loading a limp body into the trunk of a Mercedes. As a result of this sort of thing, Betsy was asked by the American ambassador, Kent Brown, and others if she could use her real estate connections to find a decent place for foreign visitors to stay, especially those from the States.

I first met Betsy toward the end of 1991 when Ambassador Brown mentioned that she was suffering from the flu and would appreciate any aspirin or Tylenol I had to spare. At the time, Betsy lived in a wonderful eighteenth-century Georgian house filled with antiques located up the hill from Rustaveli Boulevard. I dropped by and thus began my ten-year friendship with this lady from Baltimore, who was a really classy broad, tough as nails—the ultimate capitalist. For the next three years, when I was in town Betsy rented one of her bedrooms to me, and I was graciously included in a number of her elegant dinner parties, which provided great networking opportunities for me.

One day in the summer of 1994, Betsy spotted a glorious but understated chandelier with crystal and emerald drops in a house she was marketing. Having heard that I was in the antique business, she asked my opinion. I told her the price was too high, but she loved it and bought it anyway. After she paid for it and put it on a blanket in the back of her much-used Jeep Cherokee, she lit a cigarette and said, "Now that I've bought the fucking thing, I'm going to have to find a place to hang it." So Betsy rented and remodeled an old four-story building at 21 Gogebashvili, a cobbled street five blocks up the hill from the main boulevard, Rustaveli Prospect. After remodeling the place into fourteen tastefully appointed bedrooms, she hung the chandelier there, and that's how *Betsy's Guest House* just sort of happened.

Betsy Haskell is a true entrepreneur, and her guest house became the Grand Central Station of Tbilisi.

The guest house quickly became the "Grand Central Station," the "Raffles," the "City Plaza"—in other words, the communications center of Tbilisi, filled with people whose common bond was their concern for the future of Georgia. Betsy led the way for real-estate revitalization throughout the entire neighborhood. Her dinner parties, which had their genesis at her private residence years before, were punctuated by the animated discussions of people trying to get things done, and laughing at their adversity and inconveniences in order to survive. Her guest house became so popular that within two years she bought a six-room annex across the street, which was where I preferred to stay.

It was on the rooftop at Betsy's where she served dinner and adult beverages during the summer months that I first got involved with the Georgian Foundation. It was there I met Merle McQueen, who headed up—indeed was the brains behind—the foundation, which had first been led by her former husband, David Sigua, a Georgian doctor. Merle, who worked in the legal department of the Kaiser Permanente Health Group in the San Francisco Bay Area, established offices for the Georgian Foundation in Martinez, California. Utilizing her Kaiser connections, she began to ship surplus medical supplies (four million dollars' worth) into Georgia to help them meet the crisis created by the cutoff of supplies coming through Moscow. With Dr. Ward Flad, Dr. Chuck Clemons, and others, we developed the idea of Kaiser Permanente setting up a whole new healthcare system in Georgia. During this time, also on Betsy's roof, I met Stan Music, a senior U.S. Public Health Service Officer who was also in Georgia trying to figure out what could be done about the healthcare crisis in Georgia. He compared the level of 1995 Georgian public health care to "that in El Paso, Texas, in 1915." When I asked him what he thought about the "Kaiser idea," he said, "It would be like a blessing from on high!" His enthusiasm gave us all a great lift.

One of the brightest phases of the Georgian Foundation's activity was supporting the establishment of the Jo Ann Medical Center specializing in pediatric cardiac surgery headed up by Dr. Irakli Metreveli. When I first met Irakli, he was hammering, sawing, and painting a twenty-room wing of an abandoned hospital into a state-of-the-art children's medical center. By the time he was in his late thirties, he had performed over twelve hundred corrective surgeries, typifying the brilliance of many young Georgians. Shevardnadze spoke at the opening of the pediatric center and often referred to it publicly as an example of what could be done with "imagination and a will to work."

Several other bright stars from our exchange program include Dr. Akaki Zoidze who, like Irakli, interned at Kaiser Permanente in Oakland, California, before returning to Tbilisi, where he served as deputy minister of health and later, in his early thirties, became his country's deputy prime minister.

Perhaps my favorite Georgian is Dr. Maya Sharashidze, a cardiologist and the daughter of one of the former Soviet Union's most noted oncologists. At thirty-eight, she became one of President Shevardnadze's personal physicians and also supervised the Georgian Foundation's tuberculosis program. She, too, interned in California. Widowed in her thirties, she raised a son, Mamuka, who went on to study medicine at Oxford University. It was quite natural that she became my personal physician while in Tbilisi and treated my major problem with recurring gout, which, of course, required the attention of a top-flight cardiologist. A delightful and beautiful lady, she described her genealogy as "half *Sputnik* and half Georgian." The Georgian half included some Greek and Armenian bits and pieces. We became good friends and associates at the Georgian Foundation and laughed a lot. She usually worked long and late hours at the hospital but would always make time for me when I was in town. I was always delighted when after work she would drive her little old white Lada sedan up the cobbled streets to Betsy's Guest House and throw stones at the metal shutters outside my second-floor window and "shout up," as is the custom, "Come on down, Blue Eyes. Let's go have some ice cream!" I can still hear her giggly laugh.

Like most little Georgian girls, Maya always wanted to be a ballerina. Although that didn't happen, she will never lose the lyrical grace of movement she developed in her early training. I would watch her glide through a crowd at the opera or in a soccer stadium. I swear her feet barely touched the ground. Everywhere people seemed to know her. To follow her was to walk on a path of smiles. And yet, if a Georgian footballer made a bad move, Maya would let him know about it! The predominantly male fans seated around us were always clearly impressed with her knowledge of the game. Heads craned to see where that female voice was coming from. Mamuka had a great mom and, at times, I felt like I was back in high school when I was with her. So you can probably tell that my attraction to this dark-eyed Georgian lady was strictly personal. The fact that she commented from time to time on Shevardnadze's health was purely coincidental. "Honestly, Maya!"

All in all, the Georgian Foundation was an obvious activity for me to be involved in. What an opportunity to make a difference! It has been said that history is rarely found on the main road but, instead, in the remote valleys or in small side streets and back alleys. Or, in this case, on an American woman's Georgian roof. I've been in many remote valleys and small side streets, as well as *too* many back alleys, where between the bursts from AK-47s you could still almost hear the clank of medieval armor and the echoing of primitive chants. Sometimes the shape of a window could be like a poem connecting you with a thousand years of history. Even the bandits, who were everywhere, gave you a feeling of times long past, although they were very much a part of the present. I often felt as if I was on a long and still largely uncharted path. And I always remember the wise words of another traveler who said, "Never look over your shoulder because only God knows how much stuff gets left on the trail."

Chapter 23

"Skolka"
(How Much?)

INEVER HAD MUCH BUSINESS for the Pants Factory in Uzbekistan. The country's capital and largest city, Tashkent, is known to many foreigners as the place a terrible earthquake in 1966 killed thousands of people—estimates range from 50,000 to 500,000. The Russians lied about such statistics. There had also been an earlier, but just as devastating, earthquake in Ashgabat, Turkmenistan, in the 1950s. It flattened all the ancient buildings, and now there is hardly anything old to look at in the entire city. The losses there were never announced, but hundreds of thousands of people died. It happened in the middle of the night when most people were sleeping. Nearly all the unreinforced roofs dropped and, as a result, more were killed than injured. Thousands of Russian rescue and relief workers were sent to what was a strategic border republic of the then Soviet Union and formed the nucleus of the 500,000 Russians living in and around oil-and-gas-rich Ashgabat today. The Bear is forever opportunistic.

In the 1980s, Tashkent was the transportation hub for me. I could reach Tashkent from several directions—two regular flights from Moscow daily and three times a week from Baku and Irkutsk. From there I had daily flights of one or one and a half hours to Bishkek, Dushanbe, Samarkand, Bukhara,

Ashgabat, and Almaty. This was Central Asia—seven republics, all quite different economically and politically, but each sharing an ancient Silk Road history.

Uzbekistan has a predominantly Sunni Muslim culture with a unique Asian appearance. For lack of a better description, Uzbeks look slightly Chinese. They are Asian, but not what I was used to in San Francisco or Hong Kong. They are successful cotton growers. Tashkent is noted for corruption on a grand scale. Fortunately for me, after the collapse of the Soviet Union, Uzbekistan was on someone else's paper route and I generally spent only layover time there. Still, I went there from time to time on specific assignment or just to check it out. With a population of two million, Tashkent was a dusty place with a slightly tired Moscow-appearing central area and park, mostly rebuilt after the devastating earthquake. Oddly enough, the city had a very good art gallery, and I always stayed at the Uzbekistan Hotel—a 1960s, twenty-story modern building that was better than most state-owned hotels.

Uzbek women can be very beautiful. Tariana, the Aeroflot manager in Tashkent, was just such a creature—fair skin, greenish-blue almond-shaped eyes, and jet black hair cut medium short. She was also an artist and a musician. Her father was a general in the Russian Army. Tariana, who swore she was 100 percent Uzbek, even showed me a picture of her parents. She did not like being called Eurasian and was proud of being from an "old family." About thirty-five years old, she could not control her smile. She worked twelve-hour days at the big hotel with one day off a week and never complained or protested conditions. She felt lucky to have a regular job in a clean, safe place with meals provided. She claimed she could never get away for a drive in the country because she never knew when I would show up. When I would arrive at the hotel, she would stride up to the Aeroflot counter and give me the "kiss, kiss," and say, "Can we go now before you change your mind? I know you have come to take me to America, haven't you? I have been waiting. I am ready!" And then she would squeeze my hand and reach out and touch my lips with her index finger and say, "I know, I know—not yet." We had talked about her life there, and she would wistfully suggest that if I took her away she would be my slave. She was a classy lady. Her personality had the elegance of Audrey Hepburn. However, the real story I want to tell is about an economic study I made one night at the Uzbekistan Hotel of a not so classy lady. In fact, she was no lady at all.

My room, as usual, was on the mezzanine floor—you had to go up two flights of carpeted stairs and through a lounge to get to it. The key lady, Inga, sat at a desk near the elevator. She was an attractive but hard-looking East German who had somehow found her way to Tashkent. The lounge was dimly lit and decorated with potted shrubs and small palms, all of which needed more frequent watering than they were getting. When I crossed through the lounge to my room, I would see well-dressed men lurking in the shadows. They were not locals. Most were Japanese, Indians, and Pakistanis, with a few Russians. They were in Tashkent to do business related to manufacturing and agriculture, especially cotton production. Usually there were several pairs of young women, well dressed for Tashkent, sitting on couches and smoking. They were, of course, hookers, and Inga was their Madam. The men in the shadows obviously didn't want to see or be seen by each other, so they would station themselves behind the palms and potted shrubs or the marble columns that supported the ceiling, waiting to be served. I had paid attention to the increased hooker activity. Sex for money meant there was money on the move and people were doing business in Tashkent.

For a couple of years, Inga never hustled me for girls, although one time she did come to visit me in my room a few doors down the hall from the lounge. She thought I was Swedish at first and wanted to talk and smoke on her break. We spoke in Russian. She was an erotic creature and seemed a little lost in Central Asia. But on a later trip in 1993, it got a little more complicated. I had just finished a sumptuous dinner in their big Russian Art Deco dining room with its Asian dance band and gay Russian waiters, who must have been deported to Tashkent from the old Soviet Russia. They seemed happy, no doubt because in Russia gays simply don't "exist." The place had a smoke-filled nightclub atmosphere. A hundred or more single women danced with each other, most of them wearing home-made "dream" dresses. They were given a special price for the tables and, if they left with a man, the hotel expected a kick-back. It was actually kind of sad. Most of the girls looked young and unworldly. They looked like Iowa girls at the Elks Club. But this was not Iowa and they weren't in an Elks Club, and such scenes were being repeated all over the former Soviet Union.

Anyway, after dinner, as I was crossing the mezzanine lounge, Inga waved, saying, "You are leaving tomorrow?"

"*Da,*" I replied.

She smiled seductively, saying, "I have something for you." A few minutes later, Inga came to my room with a small prayer rug, asking, "You want to buy? I sell you cheap."

I asked, "What is cheap? *Skolka?*" (How much?)

She replied, "Thirty-five dollars."

"Too much. Rugs like this are fifteen dollars in the lobby."

"I come back!" she said. Fifteen minutes later, Inga returned with a silver bracelet with coral stones and asked, "You like this?"

"*Nyet. Skolka?*"

"Twenty dollars," she replied, rubbing the bracelet on her ample bosom as if to shine it, adding, "It is good for you. Ees Lucky!"

I came back with, "*Nyet!* It was ten dollars downstairs."

"Okay," she responded. "I come back." A few minutes later she returned with a determined smile and several gaudy silver rings with big semiprecious stones.

"Skolka?" I asked.

"Fifteen dollars," she replied.

"No thanks! They are only three dollars downstairs."

Standing to her full height of five feet ten, she said, "Okay, I will make you a bargain you must accept. I will give you a special arrangement because you have been kind and talked to me as a friend."

"Okay, okay," I responded, wanting to find out what she had in mind.

"Good," she said, almost demurely (for her) and asked, "How about girls? I get you girls." I was startled. *"Two* girls!" she added. I was speechless. "Two girls all night."

I managed to get out, "Two girls all night?"

"Yes," she replied, "and I will be one of the girls. You like me...yes?"

This was fun, I thought, but wondered if she was putting me on. She knew I was leaving. Nevertheless, I had to be polite and at least consider her offer. So, for the last time, I asked, *"Skolka?"*

"Eight dollars," she responded. "All night. Two girls." It was the free market at work. It was an offer only I could refuse. I was perspiring. Inga looked dejected, but then smiled and said, "When are you coming back? Maybe I try again." I gave her eight dollars just for the conversation. In any case, one age-old form of the free market was alive and well in the former Soviet republics.

Snapshot 11

Lonely Are the Brave

URING THE DAYS of the old Soviet Union, I tried to stay away from making friends and acquaintances. The whole point was to get information, then move on when I couldn't deliver or somebody found me suspicious. I was still almost entirely covert and didn't want a careless word to screw up an assignment. The Intourist people were often helpful, but I certainly couldn't carry on a romance. Too risky and I had to remember who they worked for. I didn't want to get caught in a compromising situation, or call special attention to myself. But after the Soviet breakup, as my humanitarian and consulting roles expanded, I was able to make a few friends and acquaintances, which at least temporarily eased the loneliness I think we all felt in the field. Unfortunately, I still had to be careful.

From time to time, I would run into other foreigners, mainly Brits, other Americans, Australians, and Germans, who seemed to be floaters like me. Over a few meals, cryptic acknowledgements might be made, usually with a broad paintbrush. Because of my northern European appearance, I found a different experience among fifty million Muslims in the Central Asian republics. They looked different and spoke a Turkic language. I felt more comfortable in Armenia and Georgia even though I spoke only a few phrases of Armenian or Georgian. Both Christian countries and their obvious ethnicity and culture were more acceptable to my subconscious natural-selection tendencies. I couldn't help profiling wherever I went. I think we all do it every day at some level; it's a natural and necessary part of survival. Selectivity is a primal function, a constant conscious and subconscious process, like an automatic pilot. It screens and evaluates and makes choices. It's an intuitive intellect that must always be considered, particularly in the spy trade.

Most of the time I hung out with the expats (expatriates), many of whom were involved in humanitarian aid and infrastructure development. Groups such as Doctors Without Borders, USAID, UNICEF, and Salvation Army represent the United States well. The U.S. public is largely unaware of the good work these people do. These good Samaritans sometimes paired up for the current tour of duty. There were continuous conferences, business meetings, cocktail parties, and mixers of all kind. It was not uncommon for men to find a local lady to play with. It wasn't so easy for the visiting NGO (nongovernmental organization) women because the local men, though educated and attractive, didn't have any money to spend on the rich foreigners.

In my case, being older than most, for the most part I was able to control my hunter-stalker needs reasonably well. Because I was a "short termer" with a suspicious business card, the regulars were often quite leery of me. I was not the mainstream type of NGO. I must add, there were some natural safeguards that made casual romantic liaisons less attractive. For example, the irregular supply of hot water made bathing difficult on a regular basis. Getting clothes cleaned was almost impossible on my paper route. Women's hygiene and public health facilities were limited. Dental issues and bad breath were a really big problem. Ugh!

One of my favorite ladies, just a friend in Tbilisi, a former Intourist guide, worked at the front desk of the four-star

Metechi Hotel. About thirty-five years old, slender, with jet black hair, she reminded me of TV's Courtney Cox. She rarely smiled because she was missing one upper front tooth. She had been that way as long as I had known her. One night at dinner, five of my NGO friends and I got together enough money to buy her a new tooth. Wow! What a difference. She cried and cried at our generosity. After the repair was completed, she had an uncontrolled, beautiful smile. A few months later, she met and married a wealthy German contractor and moved to Stuttgart. We felt her joy but missed her smile.

What we all had in common was that we generally cared about people, and as humanitarian aid workers we tried to help as much as possible. This is in stark contrast to the Russian men, and I get a big kick out of watching Moscow's women today. Moscow is a great city. It is Russia's central metropolis. Like Rome, Paris, London, and New York, its money attracts its country's beauties. Not only are Moscow's women more attractive than most, but they are often ethnically interesting and downright provocative in those mini-shorts so many of them wear—shorts so tight that they left nothing to the imagination. It bothers me that so many of Moscow's men are still so grossly political, or hung over, that they don't even notice.

However, in a strange way, this attitude of Russian men is understandable. No matter how blatantly Russian women show off their physical charms, there is an almost unique mystery about them that few Russian men seem able to grasp. But then again, Russia is not the Fatherland—it is the Motherland! Mother Russia. I think Russian women are the true survival force. They give tough love to their daughters, but they spoil their little boys. I don't know why. Nor do they.

Chapter 24

A Call to Arms
(Georgia in Crisis)

POUND FOR POUND, for its size Georgia has produced more than its share of "Red Stars," including Stalin, Beria, and Shevardnadze. Georgia's contributions to America include the choreographer George Balanchine (name shortened from Georgi Balanchivadze), as well as John Shalikashvili, former Chairman of the Joint Chiefs of Staff, who arrived in America at the age of sixteen and entered the Army as a draftee. Also, many of the former Soviet Union's great soccer players, rugby players, wrestlers, and chess competitors were actually Georgian, not Russian. And then there's the fact—not known to most Westerners—that Tbilisi was once a top filmmaking center. Maybe it's the weather, or maybe it's the European nature of most Georgians.

I have wonderful memories of Tbilisi. A walk in the old city at any time of day was a treat to the eyes and ears. Lace curtains blowing in first-floor windows, sounds of students practicing the piano, violin, flute, and even occasionally a jazz guitar, a look into darkened rooms with secrets only hinted at—a nineteenth-century world complete with paintings, sculptures, and heavy Russian baroque furniture. Whole families lived under the same roof. The grandparents and the groom moved in with the bride's family. No childcare centers or old folks' homes here. The matriarch presided, and we were often treated to the sight of young boys and teenagers walking around hand in hand with a grandfather. Women and girls held hands a lot with each other as well, but they didn't hold hands with men and boys. Everybody kissed everyone else on both cheeks. Lots of hugging. Many crossed themselves as they pass the Orthodox churches. You very quickly perceived that this was a genuinely peaceful, friendly, civilized, and intelligent group of "nearly" European people who never wanted anything to do with communism. The Greek ambassador once told me that, "Georgia is Mediterranean like Northern Greece." I think it's like the Sacramento Valley in Northern California. It's at the same latitude but 12,000 miles away. The Caucasus Mountains that separate Georgia from Russia are taller than the Sierra Nevada and feature the three tallest mountains in Europe, with peaks such as Kazbek, which you can see from Tbilisi, rising 16,500 feet, and, further west, Mount Elbrus, rising 18,500 feet. Europeans come to ski at Mount Gudauri, two hours from Tbilisi, which has an excellent facility on the Georgian Military Highway at an elevation of 8,000 feet.

The great Georgian poets and writers documented this civilization one thousand years ago. Magnificent Georgian Orthodox churches and monasteries were being built from the fourth century on. The Bible refers to fine wine from Georgia when it was an outer province of Rome, and, of course, there is the Greek legend of Jason and the Argonauts' quest for the Golden Fleece.

Since Georgia was a military doormat for most of its history, it must be desirable and geopolitically important. Although no battles were fought on its territory during World War II, 400,000 Georgian lives were lost (the cream, not only the peasants), which amounted to about 6 percent of the population. And because of the resentment toward their Russian occupiers, many Georgians chose to fight alongside the Germans.

Shevardnadze could not raise an army of consequence even as late as 1998, when I attended the Great Independence Day Parade in Tbilisi. Though wonderful, it took only seven minutes for the procession to pass the president's stand and seven more minutes for it to pass by again while going in the opposite direction, giving the impression that it was twice the actual size. It was practiced and timed so that the flow of perhaps six thousand soldiers, sailors, Special Forces, and police, along with twelve tanks and scout cars, looked fine and the bands sounded great, but this could hardly be called "military might." The chanting of soldiers and clumping of marching boots were medieval. The sense of history was everywhere and very moving, but it was still largely a charade. The military didn't pay well or offer a future, and many Georgians had served in the Soviet Army and vowed to never serve in *any* army again. But at least in 1998, the situation was stable and there were even American Special Forces helping train the Georgian Army.

But, with visions of Cossack sword dancers, galloping horsemen, mountain warriors, brawling wrestlers, and rugby players in my head, it still came as a surprise to me that when Shevardnadze first came into power, he didn't have *any* army to repel the Zviadists and later the Abkhaz rebels. And yet it is not so surprising when considering that for the last seventy years, Georgia hadn't had a standing army of its own. The Soviets had fulfilled that role with regular army troops bolstered by a contingent of elite Ministry of Interior forces. However, back in 1992 during the civil war, what few regulars Shevardnadze *did* have were getting bloodied everywhere, and he was forced to call on the Mkhedrioni for help. They were tough and corrupt, but that was the best he could do at the time.

I decided to check out the situation firsthand, so Mirian and I returned to Tbilisi late one night after several days in Armenia on the Nagorno-Karabakh run. There were an unusual number of roadblocks, and we were stopped after we crossed the Kura

River Bridge and were at the bottom of Rustaveli Boulevard. Dark figures were leaning on parked cars. Their cigarettes were red embers in the night. It was three o'clock in the morning. Mirian said to me, "You stay here. I'll see why we can't pass." He returned a moment later and motioned for me to follow him. We left the car behind and crossed a broad plaza that was a flower market during the day. We went down a flight of stairs and then onto the porch of an Old Town produce market across a smaller plaza from the police station. Milling around the dimly lit square were forty or fifty police. Two senior police officials were arguing in the middle of a cluster near the front door of the old building. The one wearing a suit and thick-soled shoes clearly outranked the drunken police captain. It was obvious that the "suit" was in charge. Moving freely among the police, Mirian got a few nods of recognition, which I never questioned. He glanced at me and rubbed the back of his neck, which was our sign for "let's go." I followed him toward the stairs, and then he said, "We must wait and watch. It won't take long."

I just sort of stood there, not knowing what to expect. Some of the police remained in the shadows behind the police cars parked near the station. Mirian, who smoked a lot, lit up a cigarette. Suddenly, two blindfolded men with their hands tied behind their backs were brought out of the police station. Mirian said that the argument was not about whether or not these men should die, but who should execute them. The police didn't want to do it because these men were fellow officers who had been caught smuggling drugs and explosives. The prisoners were seated on a stone water trough a few feet from the side of the police station. The assembled group became silent as a hooded figure came out of the police station and walked briskly to the prisoners, who were facing a wall. Some in the crowd looked around to see if they could figure out who the executioner was by who was missing! Just like that, he placed an automatic pistol at the base of each man's skull and fired. He checked to see that each man was dead and then left the scene.

Mirian told me, "That's what they deserved." He then added, "Everybody knows about the executions, but nobody likes to talk about them."

The executioner and the police captain kissed cheeks and left. They were swallowed up in the darkness. I noticed dozens of pockmarks of quick justice on the wall behind the trough. Finally we went back to Mirian's car and by then the street blockade had been removed. It was five o'clock in the morning and we went on to the hotel.

Mirian and I planned to be at the Parliament building that morning to see who answered Shevardnadze's call to join the army. Shevardnadze had only recently returned from Moscow to replace Gamsakhurdia to try and restore order. Just as he seemed to be gaining the upper hand on *that* situation, the western Black Sea province of Abkhazia, though an integral part of Georgia, decided to declare itself "independent." A *new* civil war was on, and the call had gone out on radio and TV for young men to volunteer for the fight to save their new republic and preserve its territorial integrity. Shevardnadze's army, such as it was, was getting its ass kicked in Abkhazia, and so Mirian and I hoped that the president's stirring speech would muster five or six hundred patriots to deal with the bandits from the west. However, by ten in the morning, only fourteen men of various shapes and ages had volunteered, although a crowd of several hundred had come to cheer the historic occasion of this first assemblage of a Georgian army by *Georgians*.

It didn't help matters that only a few weeks earlier, a company of 150 young Georgian volunteer soldiers had been routed by the more experienced, mercenary-led Abkhazian rebels. They had broken and run from the battlefield. Even as a non-combatant I could understand why the young Georgians cut and ran. They could see their efforts would be futile and that the outcome would be fatal. I probably would have run with them. As I would soon learn, watching the Georgian irregular army fighting the Abkhaz semiregulars was a surrealistic nightmare of chaotic indecision, misdirection, panic, and scrambling. There was much individual bravery but failure as a group, not unlike the American Indians fighting the U.S. Cavalry in the nineteenth-century American West. Ignorance and confusion prevailed over the battlefield. The University of California Marching Band with one blow of a whistle was better disciplined.

Through the years, tens of thousands would die during these futile war games. But for the moment, the mercenaries (and the Russians) had carried the day with their ostensible cause being the Abkhaz desire for independence and the result being the cleansing of ethnic Georgians from their rightful homes. The prize for the victors was the property and other loot left behind. A sweeping sense of national shame only added to the already depressed mood of the nation. They were being mauled by the Bear, even though it had supposedly left of its own accord. Where was the will to fight and defend their new country?

In Tbilisi, the pool from which Shevardnadze could draw consisted largely of young men between the ages of seventeen and twenty-seven, mostly high-school dropouts, wearing black denim pants and white socks, who could usually be found hanging around in groups on street corners smoking cigarettes. When I would pass by these guys, ten or twelve otherwise disinterested eyes would note my presence, but except for the few that would check out my white Nikes and wraparound sunglasses, that would be about it. Disinterested eyes reflected disinterested minds and, through no fault of their own, time had moved on without them. School was out for these fellows and there were no jobs on the horizon. Setting goals had not been a part of their upbringing, because for the last seventy years their lives and futures had been arranged by others. They were in a vacuum. There was no beginning or end to where they were, and the street corner had become their world. Given the freedom of choice for the first time, many did not know how to handle it or understand the responsibilities that went with Georgia's new independence. They couldn't see what was in it for them: that they now had a future to consider but must first *earn* the benefits of this new freedom. Freedom is not free! They were already a lost generation. Except for the few that went for the pure adventure of it, they ignored Shevardnadze's call!

In 1992, Georgia was poor and in bad shape, but certainly not a lot poorer than the America of my childhood during the Great Depression or the England and Europe I witnessed a few years later after World War II. It was during these dark times that people's characters were forged or refined and they had to be at their best merely to survive. During the 1930s, my dad and his coworkers at Bechtel were involved in building both the Bay and Golden Gate Bridges as well as Hoover Dam, massive projects the likes of which their young company had never done before and which, quite likely, could never be done again. These great engineering and construction marvels were built at the height of national distress because they were building on a legacy of freedom and three hundred years of experience with free enterprise. They could see the future! I was raised at a time and in an atmosphere that generated the *attitude* that anything is possible, and the people I later worked with at Bechtel didn't know there were things you couldn't do. Failure was not an option. It was just a matter of how. They set no limits and didn't contend with suffocating bureaucracy. It was this pioneering spirit, this "intentionality," that carried the day.

In stark contrast, these young Georgians, as well as most of the Third World, could *not* see the possibilities for the future that hard times often provide, and the call went largely unheeded. But there were exceptions, including seventy-two-year-old Alexander Khaindrava, a language teacher and veteran of a Japanese prison camp in Shanghai, with whom I became friends. He was so disgusted with the cowards around him who wouldn't join up, that *he* volunteered. Not taken seriously at first, he got himself out of a street blockade unit and went to the fighting near the Abkhazian provincial capital of Sukhumi. Alexander boasted of killing two Russians and two Chechens during ambushes. He was an inspiration to many Georgians, and I personally think he settled some old scores in his heart with the Russians. The Russian KGB had treated him badly when he returned to Georgia after being liberated from the Japanese at the end of World War II, and Abkhazia provided the perfect opportunity for revenge.

More typical, however, of those who *did* show up for duty was a young Georgian movie actor named Levan Abashidze. He missed the initial call to duty because he was working on a film. When he returned from location to Tbilisi a few weeks later, he heard that three of his best friends from Tbilisi State University had volunteered to go to the Abkhazian front. He also learned that planes left for Abkhazia several times a week with reinforcements. Levan decided to join his school friends and was able to get a flight to the Black Sea battleground. His combat training consisted of having had a part in a gangster movie! But he was an athlete and, like the others on the plane, was bright and clean cut. They thought they would fight for a few weeks and be home for Christmas.

For most of these recruits, it was a week or two training and "bring your own uniform." Officers were mostly former NCOs in the Soviet Army or police, and some of the recruits got on the plane without even knowing how to fire an AK-47. For many it was a lark—a great experience "for a couple of weeks." But there *were* some who went out of a sense of duty and because it was the right thing to do. However, a walk down Rustaveli Boulevard any time of day would soon show you what the results were: missing arms, legs and faces. Land mines were used in Georgia, too.

Levan found his friends in a farmhouse in the Gaja Valley, about fifteen miles east of Sukhumi. They rejoiced at being together again. It was like old times. Levan brought along bottles of wine with his as yet unused AK-47. The others had been involved in skirmishes, but made light of it. They drank and smoked and sang songs about Russian whores and Turkish whores and Georgian virgins.

The next morning, they were assigned the job of sweeping the woods along the road and up the valley to the next town about two miles away. It was believed that there were about fifty Abkhaz soldiers with artillery hiding in the woods, and their mission was to capture the artillery if possible. Levan fumbled with his AK-47. They all laughed and then, with thirty others, spread out on both sides of the road. The four school friends could see each other as they entered the deep forest. Firing was heard, but they kept walking. Brush and uneven ground made visibility poor. Shots continued coming from the right of their position. Suddenly, in a blinding flash, the four Georgian friends were down, two killed immediately by a hand grenade, and the other two, including Levan, wounded by fragments. Levan was still alive, but dying. He would die if help could not be obtained. His friend, Giorgi Jagjaladze, crawled to the road and was able to stop a passing truck driven by an elderly Georgian farmer. They got Levan onto the flatbed, where he died in Giorgi's arms. The farmer drove them to the airport and promised to collect the bodies of Levan's two other friends. They probably hadn't been missed. Nobody knew where they were.

Giorgi managed to stay conscious as he was loaded onto a Georgian Airlines transport and told his story to a Georgian volunteer doctor. He and sixteen others on the plane survived. Twenty others were rolled up in coats and blankets, some missing shoes. Giorgi lay next to Levan. I was there on the transport plane as a hitchhiker and sat on a medical chest. The volunteer doctor, looking shocked, said to me, "That's Levan Abashidze, the movie star. He's dead!" The dim light illuminated Levan's handsome, boyish face, a face in a world *not* at peace. His two missing friends made it home for Christmas and were buried in the snow.

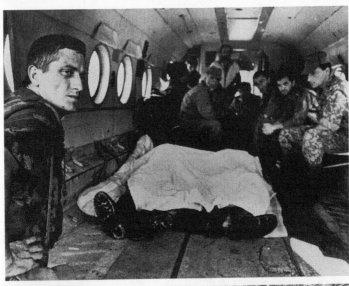

Transport planes carried thousands of fallen Georgian soldiers home from Abkhazia. It was a brutal, low-tech war.

I interviewed Giorgi later in his home and couldn't help but think of my own three sons. I promised Giorgi that someday I would tell the story of his heroic loss of innocence. He was grateful and I will always remember him saying, "I would go again, if necessary. I would not fight on foreign soil, or fight for others. But I would fight for my country and on my own land. I would do that again."

Levan is buried near the chapel high up on Mtatsminda, the Mountain of Saint David, overlooking the Georgian capital of Tbilisi. He had answered Shevardnadze's call.

A Diamond in the Rough

WHEN I FIRST MET Constantine Rizhinashvili in 1992, I was shocked to think he was fifty years younger than the old army veteran, Alexander Khaindrava. I met him through Nancy Ann Coyne, a freelance photographer and historian who got caught up in the Georgian Civil War. She told me, "There is this Georgian guy you really should get to know. He speaks English with a New York accent and has even appeared on Larry King Live." This was just what I was looking for, a young "go-to" guy to back up my friend and driver, Mirian Meskhi.

Through various networks and because he understood the social and economic realities in Georgia, Constantine quickly became tied in with several U.S. companies, including the *Sameba Joint Venture Winery*. Bob Medearis discovered Constantine and soon had him on the Stanford University campus studying law (not a bad place to study, with Condoleeza Rice on duty as chancellor and George Shultz's office in the Hoover Institution nearby). We kept in touch during the time he was in California, and two years later, law degree in hand, Constantine returned to Georgia.

One day in 1995, when I was passing through Tbilisi, we met in the reception area of Betsy's Guest House. It was good to see him again and I was proud of his perseverance. As we waited for our coffee, we could hardly *not* notice Betsy and the reception-ist dispensing information and giving directions to the guests, almost like traffic cops. I remarked to Constantine that Betsy's was a natural power station, the real hub of Tbilisi. "She's got the answers," I said. "She's the 'go-to' person for out-of-towners."

We sat there for a while quietly taking in the scene, and then I said, "When I did feasibility studies for Bechtel construc-tion projects, the first thing I did was visit the town where the projected site was located. I checked around and found the guy or guys with the most answers about everything local. As the go-to guy, that person became my facilitator during my in-spection tour. This person was usually eager to get in on the ground floor of a future project and realized, of course, that there could be some fallout in their direction." We savored the moment and thought about the ramifications of what I just said. Then I added, "Betsy clearly serves this function." And then, after a pause, I said, "You know, somebody could come in here and probably make a good living by charging money for what Betsy does for free."

It was at this very moment that Constantine asked, "Jim, how do you spell 'facilitator'?"

The next time I passed through Tbilisi, a year later, I met Constantine in his new office in the bank building on Rustaveli Boulevard. He and his engineering buddy, George Bazgadze, had formed a new company called GCG—Georgia Consulting Group. The company brochure listed twenty-four companies as customers (almost all foreign), with about a dozen of them being "Cadillac" accounts. Looking out the window of his of-fice, I pointed to a group of young men standing on a corner near the Opera House half a block down the tree-lined street. I asked, "How come you're not out there with your classmates, Constantine?"

Constantine thought for a second and then replied, "I tried it for a couple of weeks and nothing happened, so I decided to try another location. Most of those guys were waiting for something to happen. They were stuck with the old mentality. I saw Betsy create a real-estate industry and start a hotel against impossible odds. She just made it happen. She saw unlimited opportunities when most others were blind, so I said, 'Why not me?' I had nothing, so I had nothing to lose."

I haven't seen Constantine recently, but the last I heard he had politely turned down an offer to become Georgia's minister of finance. Unlike his counterparts, Constantine did get off his old street corner and change locations. He set up law offices on a new corner a block away from Moscow's Red Square and across the street from McDonald's. He was able to recognize and take advantage of the opportunities provided by the new freedom in Georgia. He and people like him were able to implement the new versus the old style of thinking, and, as such, Constantine and others of his ilk represent Georgia's best hope for the future.

Chapter 25

Paradise Lost
(A Perilous Journey)

B Y AUTUMN OF 1993, Shevardnadze's first recruited army had all but won its first war, fighting its way north through the rich farmlands of West Georgia, over the Kura River, and across Abkhazia another 130 miles to the port city of Sukhumi, one of the true garden spots of Eastern Europe. After much bitter combat, the city fell and trucks rolled to within a few miles of Gagra, which was north on the coastal highway leading to the Russian Black Sea resort city of Sochi, where the Russians have their luxurious dachas and sanitariums.

With Abkhazia almost totally under Georgian domination, military matters suddenly turned sour. Somehow, the Abkhaz minority of 20 percent was able to miraculously reverse the military situation. They had pushed the numerically superior but poorly commanded Georgian Army back on its heels, and Sukhumi, a city of 125,000, once more became a battle-ground. With fighting house-to-house and building-to-building, Sukhumi was under siege and being bombarded with random artillery fire from the foothills rising seven hundred feet in a crescent, ringing it on three sides.

Shevardnadze made four or five tours during the heaviest fighting. On one occasion, due to concentrated shelling, he had to seek safety in the basement of a state office building. It was during the bombing of the office building, while Shevardnadze negotiated with the Russian regional commanding officer, that I was able to hand-deliver a personal letter from George Shultz pledging his support. Shevardnadze seemed grateful. On an earlier trip, his helicopter was almost forced out of the sky by the downdraft—no doubt intentional—from a separatist Abkhaz helicopter flying above him with a Russian crew. His comment at the time was, "A cat has nine lives and I have used half of them."

I went to Sukhumi four times during the fighting in 1992 and 1993—three times by land with the help of people who are still there. But the first trip had been by trawler at night because all the roads were blocked. The trawler had been buzzed by MIGs and a helicopter gunship, so after Russian destroyers

As the building was shelled in Sukhumi, I handed Shevardnadze a letter from George Shultz.

ᲡᲐᲥᲐᲠᲗᲕᲔᲚᲝᲡ ᲞᲐᲠᲚᲐᲛᲔᲜᲢᲘᲡ
ᲗᲐᲕᲛᲯᲓᲝᲛᲐᲠᲔ — ᲡᲐᲮᲔᲚᲛᲬᲘᲤᲝᲡ
ᲛᲔᲗᲐᲣᲠᲘ

თბ-ლისი, 380002 რუსთაველის გამზ. №29 ტელ: 99 92 92

CHAIRMAN OF THE PARLIAMENT
HEAD OF STATE
OF THE REPUBLIC OF GEORGIA

29 RUSTAVELI AVE. TBILISI
Fax (481)/6029690 ext — 18) phone 999292

22. Oct 1993

Dear George,

At the time of extreme hardship that fell upon me in recent months the moral support of my friends was and remains to be my sole sustenance. Being an exceptionally warm-hearted man, you are one of those who showed loyalty to our cordial relationship established at hard, albeit relatively happier times. Today when hardships have become almost unbearable the life-giving power of our friendship has been fully manifested.

I was in besieged Sukhumi when your last letter arrived in Tbilisi. My assistants read it to me during one of those wireless communication sessions and I told myself that if I was destined to survive, I would find due means to express my utmost gratitude to you.

I am now seeking appropriate words but fail to find them. I feel more indebted to you now that Jim Waste let me know about the project that you intend to head. This would be an invaluable service to my country and to me personally.

God bless you for your efforts and contributions towards the well-being of my mutilated country. Hearty thanks to all who are with you.

Nanuli and I send our best regards to O'Bie and wish happiness to your wonderful family.

Yours

Eduard.

To Mr. George D. Shultz.

began patrolling the Black Sea coast as well, I decided the sea approach was too risky.

My mission in Sukhumi was to verify who the actual combatants were and to check their equipment whenever possible. Except for some Asian AK-47s, virtually all of the weaponry I saw came out of abandoned Russian military depots. More importantly, I was able to inspect four Russian T-34B tanks as well as the wreckage of an MI-24 Hind gunship and a MIG-21 Fishbed low-level tactical fighter—the "Mongol," as the Russians like to call them.

My Georgian "techie" was stunned to discover that although the Russian-manufactured equipment was standard, it *was* the latest design and—as the Abkhazian military could barely read a street sign—could only be operated by skilled *Russian* drivers, pilots, and technicians. But we were unable to find any Russian bodies because their dead had been evacuated so quickly.

With the assistance of my local connections, I was able to unobtrusively question prisoners during my four trips. Wearing local clothes and taking a "second-row seat," I became just another bounty hunter, paying guys fifteen dollars a head to interview prisoners who were *other than* Georgian or Abkhaz. Mirian helped with the interviews and we both wanted to know who the foreigners were. The box score went like this: 2 Russians, 6 Armenians, 5 Afghans, 9 Chechens, and 2 Ossetians. They were all mature and experienced mercenaries. *That's* why Shevardnadze's army was being routed! They were facing hired guns, but hired by *whom?* It was becoming self-evident to Mirian and me that it was the Russians. But why? That one's simple. They wanted to control Abkhazia. So, after hundreds of years, the great resort area of the Georgian Republic decided to become an "independent country." From a practical standpoint, this could not work! The professional people (doctors, lawyers, and engineers) were mostly Georgians. The brains fled, and what remained of an infrastructure disappeared.

As the minority Abkhazians regained lost ground, they committed "ethnic cleansing." Lovely towns, fine homes, pretty lawns, and luscious gardens were burned out and looted, and eventually 250,000 Georgian refugees from Abkhazia were forced to flee to Georgia, mostly the big cities—a crippling burden on the struggling new country. The ethnic cleansing is a horror that both sides have written little about and which seemed so senseless. But it was not senseless from the Russian standpoint. The Russians simply wanted to annex this lush land and used their standard tactics to do so. In this new era, it never occurred to them that they could simply coexist peacefully with Georgia, and as a result of their old mentality, fifteen thousand ethnic Georgians were killed fighting for their homeland. Trapped by the Russian border, the Black Sea, and heavy fighting in Gali and Zugdidi, thousands of refugees began to retreat from Sukhumi and other cities over a steep and poor mountain road, which only took light traffic at first and then really deteriorated. The seven- or eight-day walk to safety was about eighty-five miles long, cresting over an 8,900-foot pass via the small mountain village of Chuberi.

When the refugee exodus first started, hundreds made the trip over the mountain pass okay but thousands more, who were not used to walking, lined the road. Then the temperature dropped severely and snow began to fall. Freezing weather made it impossible for them to move forward or backward, and hundreds perished along the road. The living couldn't even bury the dead. When I flew aerial reconnaissance over the road, I counted 130 bodies just along a several-mile stretch. The old, the sick, and the children were the most vulnerable.

The Abkhaz didn't interfere with the exodus, in fact they encouraged it. CNN and the world news agencies soon learned of the thousands trapped in the winter snow. Relief came from many quarters—from the Ukraine (which provided mountain choppers), Armenia, Turkey, and, of course, Georgia, among others. A Georgian chopper crashed on the Georgian side of the mountain pass, killing its two pilots along with two refugees.

Just hours after I returned from my own aerial inspection, I got a call from Jack Morgan, the captain in charge of the Tbilisi Salvation Army unit (along with his wife). A former major in the U.S. Sixth Cavalry Division, he said, "I'm flying up in the hills tomorrow and I need some help."

I responded, "Sure, what's up?"

He explained, "Some of our Georgian pilots want to re-trieve the bodies from the crashed chopper and then go up in

the mountains to a village near Mestia to drop off some supplies and other goods for the local police and government to
distribute."

I had only one question, "What time?"

"I'll pick you up at Betsy's at eight." Which he did.

When we got to the airport, we went out onto the tarmac
through the civilian baggage entrance. The security personnel just waved us through and we drove about a quarter of a
mile onto the landing field, past a few parked Aeroflot Tupolev
Tu-134s and some old MIG-17 "Fresco" (NATO code name)
fighter jets.

I thought to myself, *Oh, shit*. I had taken off and landed at
this military/civilian field many times and had noticed twenty
or twenty-five old planes, but I also noticed that they never
seemed to move. Now I understood why. No spare parts! After
all, the Russians were gone.

There were two husky fortyish Georgians standing next to
a butterscotch-colored MI-8 Hip utility helicopter. They smiled
and saluted us with greasy hands. Due to the shortage of helicopters, the government would not risk one of their active military craft to rescue people already dead. But these Georgian
pilots had known the dead men and were willing to risk flying a
retired aircraft. They had worked on the chopper all night. One
of them got in and eventually it kicked over. It ran. But for how
long? I wasn't sure I wanted it to run.

The Salvation Army officer had brought several drums of
gasoline with him and, as the pilots made final adjustments, he
pumped the gas into the chopper's tank. As usual, I was most
impressed with this "Soldier of God." The pilots tossed out some
junk and we loaded supplies. I noticed that three of the four
landing gear tires were flat, and the fourth was half buried in the
dirt. Weeds were two feet high, and a hot wind blew across the
tarmac. I tossed my daypack through the big middle door and it
skidded across the floor to rest against four empty body bags.

After forty-five minutes of revving the engine, the pilots pointed at the snow-capped mountains and then pointed at me. I jumped in after my pack. The copilot then jumped out and used a big screwdriver to chop the hard-packed clay loose from the fourth wheel, which was locked into the ground. Suddenly, the earth let go of our struggling craft and we bobbed up a few feet and hung stable until its rescuer could clamber aboard. Our ascent was gradual.

After about forty minutes, we arrived at a small mining town at the foot of the mountain pass and landed at an abandoned MIG-fighter base where refugees were being collected and treated. With fifty dollars of my own money, the pilots were able to buy more gas from a Ukrainian pilot whose chopper had broken down. An hour later we bounced back into the air and started up a steep canyon where we spotted the crashed Georgian chopper against the canyon's side. Local mountain people had reached the crumpled chopper a few hours earlier and removed its four dead occupants, marking a spot for us to land near the bodies. When we got down, the pilot kept the motor running while Captain Morgan, the copilot, and I loaded the dead Georgians into our helicopter. Captain Morgan knelt and said a few prayers in Russian. Everybody crossed themselves. The bodies were mangled and a bit "ripe" from being in the sun for forty hours. They were silent forever, but heroes for what they had done. We got them in the body bags and strapped them along the floor against the rear wall. We closed the door and the chopper lurched off our perch and continued up the canyon. The pilot seemed very busy and I later learned he was doing double-manual, seat-of-the-pants flying. But I didn't know it at the time.

After about fifteen minutes, we reached the top of the ridge where we saw a picturesque alpine village with a small church. Next to the church was a schoolyard, teaming with refuges waiting to be taken off the mountain. A government loudspeaker truck advised us to kick the supplies out at about twenty feet over the schoolyard, which we did, but not to come down any lower because the crowd was hysterical. We decided to try the church instead, but even at the church there was near panic. Soldiers had to push the people back, so we didn't actually land. We just hovered a few feet above the ground so the pilot could gain altitude in a hurry.

Seventeen people were loaded aboard or just scrambled through the sliding door into the cabin. The pilot refused to leave his dead comrades behind, which meant we had two pilots, four body bags, Captain Morgan, and myelf, for a total of twenty-five people on a retired, out-of-service helipcopter with a maximum load capacity of twenty. The pilot later commented that he hadn't counted the body bags. As I stood by the door, which was stuck open, I avoided the eyes of those we were about to leave behind. I told myself to look like I knew what I was doing—to be professional. I froze myself into a kind of half-assed smile and didn't let anybody know I was scared shitless, as the pilot said "Fuck it!" and gave it the gas. The chopper shuddered and shook, and it crossed my mind that maybe I should jump out and *walk* down the mountain. The pilot eased the chopper up, but the air was warm and thin and the chopper wouldn't fly much above the ground. Immediately below us was pure madness. Captain Morgan crouched beside me and squeezed my arm just below the elbow and forgot to let go. He was scared shitless, too, but was making funny gestures with his other hand to try to amuse a pregnant evacuee who was about to give birth at any moment.

Suddenly, the whirling blades seemed to grab enough thin air to do the job, and we went straight up about fifty feet, where we just kind of sat. Then, in what seemed like a moment of desperation, the pilot moved the chopper sideways off the top of the ridge, before leaning it over at a forty-five degree angle and sliding it sideways down the deep gorge. The passengers, having no idea what was happening, screamed as if they were on a roller coaster ride. I wondered to myself whether it was all over. I was having one of those *This is it!* experiences. But it wasn't. Maybe a ten-second lifetime later, the blades began to beat faster and the sound became more uniform. By sliding off into the canyon, the pilot had bought some heavier air and increased the lift.

I started giving everybody a big dumb smile and even let them look into my eyes. Captain Morgan let go of my arm, which had purple finger marks for a week. The pilot caught my eye and then held his nose, wiping his brow in jest. I gave him a thumbs up. Hugging the ground all the way, we slid back down to the town at the foot of the canyon just after sunset, where some foreign humanitarian aid people took over our passengers. We again found the Ukrainian pilot and I bought the rest of his gas.

I thought about returning to Tbilisi by Red Cross Land Rover, but not seriously. This had been no ordinary trip. There was nothing routine about it. We had done it together and I needed to finish this mission with the team. If you haven't done something like this, you may not be able to relate to the power men can have in a crisis. My God, these men were brave! I can still feel their eyes of joy and knowing hugs as we finally parted ways that evening on the tarmac back in Tbilisi. We will always be connected by those hours on the ridge.

Captain Morgan drove us back to the city, a city grieving over the tragedy occurring on the mountains. I arrived at Betsy's Guest House and checked in with the night manager. She told me everybody was still having dinner because it was the last time for dinner on the roof this season. I was hungry and bolted up four flights to Betsy's roof. Twenty people were still there, drinking wine and finishing dinner. My table gang, all regular customers, were already half-loaded. One wag yelled, "Hey, you're late! We finished off the ice cream! We thought you were out of town!"

I was about to get into my harrowing day with them when I noticed, there in the moonlight, a table for four with only three seated. One was Gary Mansavage from USAID (Agency for International Development). Handsome and friendly, Gary was sitting with two of the most beautiful women I had seen in Georgia, or anywhere else for that matter. He called me over and said, "I'd like you to meet Nina Ramishvili, Prima Ballerina of the Georgian Dance Company, and Rusudan Gorgiladze, Special Advisor to President Shevardnadze." Of course, I already knew about Rusudan ("Rusico" to her friends), but this was the first time I had actually seen her. I instantly knew I had to have Gary's black-haired, black-eyed companion, even if only as a friend! It was like—*shazam!* Speaking from long experience, I have learned that when your eyes lock onto a woman's and *shazam* happens, you should probably turn and walk the other way.

Rusico loosely held a pack of cigarettes. I took one out of the pack, lit it, and gave it back to her. Nobody had ever done that for her. Gary asked, "How 'bout some wine?" I surprised myself by reminding him that I had not had a drink in twenty-seven years.

Rusico responded, "You don't drink and you don't smoke. What *do* you like?" She paused and I could see she knew where she was going.

I replied, "Ice cream and girls. Not necessarily in that order. Or, maybe at the same time?"

We looked at each other, and, with a heavy Russian accent, Rusico concluded, "But, of course." I would see Rusico many times later as our friendship blossomed over the years.

Captain Morgan was transferred to Kazakhstan. He wrote me a brief note before he left, thanking me for helping make the chopper trip possible and enclosing a receipt for "$100 worth of aviation petrol for rescue performed November 7, 1992." I marvel at how resourceful these Salvation Army people are.

At a later meeting with Shevardnadze, Gela Charkviani remarked in an aside, "The president wants you to know that he has a lot of respect for the Salvation Army. He says they know how to get things done and have good leadership and principles." And, with an intimate smile, Gela told me that Shevardnadze wished his government were half as efficient. I agreed and told him this was true wherever the Salvation Army serves in the world.

Both Georgian pilots got jobs with the newly formed Georgian Airlines, and as long as I was traveling to Tbilisi, the butterscotch chopper remained just off the tarmac about a quarter mile from the new air terminal. I could always see it as I took off to return home. Only later did I learn that I had been on its last flight.

Chapter 26

Trick or Treat
(Don't Forget to Knock)

A s THE SECOND ROUND of the Abkhaz breakaway intensified, tens of thousands of ethnic Georgians fled the lush Black Sea coastal province to escape the "slash and burn" ethnic cleansing being carried out by the so-called Abkhaz natives defending their "homeland" from the Georgian Republic. Even though in the minority, with the help of their Russian manipulators, they were able to separate over 250,000 Georgians from their ancestral homes, where most Georgian families had lived for at least 250 years.

As the Abkhaz conflict escalated, floods of displaced Georgians from Abkhazia who had relatives in Georgia's two major cities of Tbilisi and Kutaisi poured into those cities, cities already stretched to the limit. The people faced food and water shortages as well as power rationing, but somehow they managed. It was unfortunate, however, that the refugees were more connected to people in the city than to people in the countryside, where life was easier. The two "modern" Intourist hotels in Tbilisi, the Adjaria and the Iveria, each consisting of fourteen stories and three hundred rooms, were built in the early sixties and were pretty good by Soviet standards. Both were immediately turned into quarters for the refugees, with as many as six or eight people to a room. Balconies became shelters, and hand-washed clothing was hung out on the railings.

Perestroika and *glasnost* had seen the advent of a flourishing new tourist business. Tours from the U.S. had been stopping regularly, and one of the last groups of foreigners to stay at the Iveria was a motor coach full of people from UC Berkeley. I remember chatting with some of them. They must have figured I was some sort of KGB type, especially when the bus pulled out and gunfire broke out a few blocks away. The wide-eyed Californians stopped the bus and wanted to know what the hell was going on. I asked them where they were going, and when they replied they were going to Yerevan, Armenia, I said, "Good! And don't slow down!"

As they drove away, they were all pointing at me, and I could hear one of them asking, "Who *is* that guy?"

The Iveria Hotel's "bug room," my favorite, overlooked the Great Cultural Plaza with its giant modern architectural art objects and spectacular fountain. It was my favorite room because I *knew* it was bugged, and it was only three flights up a wide marble stairway. In case of trouble, it was good for easy in-and-out access. Also, I could use the stairs when the power went down, which was often, or when the four small elevators were jammed with all kinds of people and supplies. I never felt safe in crowded elevators after seeing two young men kill a third, stabbing him from both the front and the back in an Azerbaijani hotel elevator in 1990. When the elevator door opened at the next floor, my fellow passengers scrambled out and down the hallway, leaving me staring into the dead eyes of the unfortunate victim.

In Tbilisi, through all of 1993, only a few of the rooms were reserved for tourists, mostly celebrities, and the rest of the hotel, with its refugees, quickly degenerated. The huge banquet hall with its black-and-white marble floor overlooking the river was used for serving breakfast and early dinner. Refugees did the

A human lost and found sprung up in Tbilisi.

serving. Hundreds would congregate in the lobby before meals. Most people would try to look presentable, wearing Western-style clothes, but it was a loud and unhappy crowd. Many were sick. The young men who had been wounded in the fighting were usually drunk.

A human "lost and found" operation was set up in the park behind the nearby Church of the Virgin. Trees and walls were covered with a patchwork of scraps of white paper giving the names of missing friends and relatives. Occasionally, there would be shouts of joy when people found each other, but just as often, you would hear shouts of anguish.

Each day as more news of setbacks in the war was posted on the hotel's bulletin board, there would be frequent shrieking and wailing as news arrived of a friend or relative who had been killed. Usually three or four coffins rested in a corner of the hotel's lobby, containing remains waiting for identification or a proper burial service. Most people thought they would be in the hotel for a few months and then get billeted somewhere else. Ten years later, many are still there.

Although I was one of the few paying guests of the hotel, I did not eat with the refugees. They spoke mostly Georgian and were generally suspicious of people who looked like me. I *would* on occasion walk through the great banquet room to size up the mood of Moscow's latest victims. Sometimes an associate would join me, but my good friend and colleague, Mirian, thought it best that we not be seen together under those circumstances, and I learned early on not to question his judgment on such matters.

One evening in November 1993, after a long delay due to a power and water stoppage, dinner was served around 9:30 instead of the usual six o'clock. By that time, some of the young "veterans" were getting very drunk, and there was what can only be described as a feeling of bad karma in the dining room. Just after I entered the room with a companion, some moron jumped on the bandstand with an AK-47

and did a Cossack dance step, before turning to write his name with bullets on the large eight-by-ten-foot glass window overlooking the river. A full clip going off in the marble hall was hard on the ears, not to mention the splintering, crashing glass and the shouting of the crowd. Half the people in the room hit the floor. My companion drew a pistol. The police, usually useless anyway, were nowhere to be seen. Immediately, several men from the crowd tackled the shooter, and an old man with faded World War II ribbons on his coat kicked the shooter's head from side to side until the blood flowed and he lay senseless. There was a little talk about what had happened, but within fifteen minutes everybody settled into dinner. My companion, who had stayed out of it, got up and began to sing to relieve the tension. The crowd joined in. It sounded good. Everything got better. The crisis had passed quickly. After all, these people were from the west—the wild, wild west of Abkhazia.

I should note that the Iveria Hotel was one of about thirty modern, high-rise Intourist hotels built throughout the Soviet

Union during the 1960s. You could rate them at the early Holiday Inn level. They were mostly for the new travel needs of Russians in the post-World War II USSR. It was a good way to control all travel, and, of course, Soviet citizens needed special visas to go anywhere. These visas limited travel time, determined the specific means of transportation, and identified the purpose of the trip and the people who would host or do business with the traveler. I was always amazed at how well it all worked, considering the lack of internal communication. Little pieces of waxy paper seemed to get you in and out of eleven time zones fairly easily. Most of the hotels must have been designed by the same guy, and his calculations were never checked. Typically the rooms had a hall door, a bathroom to the left or right as you enter, and then an inner door to the sleeping quarters. They generally had two single beds in an L-shape, alongside separate walls. Common to at least fifteen of the hotels I stayed in was the fact that you could not close the second or inner door because one of the beds would stick out several inches into the doorway. For quiet sleeping and better safety, I would always push my bed away from the wall, close the second door, and then push the bed against the door. Although I frequently laughed to myself about this, it proved to be a worthwhile security device on several occasions.

After the tumultuous dinner, I took the elevator to the third floor, carrying some baggage. As I slipped out of the elevator, the key lady had a message for me regarding a meeting I had arranged for the next day with Shevardnadze. There were always half a dozen or so people hanging around the elevator "socializing" and talking on the telephone. This was *their* street corner! For two days I had noticed several of the same drunk and obnoxious young Georgian evacuees loitering there. When the key lady mentioned Shevardnadze's name, two of the drunks started getting on my case. One had a crutch, the other a head bandage. I tried to brush them off politely in Russian, but drunks are the same anywhere in the world, and these two drunks were real assholes. They were trash, full of self-pity and looking for trouble. All my life I have avoided these particular kinds of drunks. I walked down the dark hallway. People stood in open doorways while kids darted in and out of rooms. I was a new neighbor to a lot of these people, but we all shared common problems. As I dug out my room key, I could hear the key lady down the hall giving some stern advice to the two drunks. Not thinking much more about it, I went inside my room.

In those days, I had a certain routine at night when retiring. After washing my T-shirts and shorts, I would check my money and passport and pack for a quick departure. Next, I'd check my shortwave radio for Radio Moscow and the BBC, while smoking a single Marlboro. Sometimes I'd write a postcard and then turn to the local "belly dancing music," as I called it, or, if I was lucky, to some country and Western. Finally, with one eye open, I'd go to sleep.

On this particular night, I had just started writing a postcard when I heard a hard thumping on the hall door, then shouting voices. I thought to myself, *What next?* The second door was already blocked by the bed, to which I gave another shove. Then there was a really loud, smashing thump and two loud, incomprehensible voices. *Somebody* obviously wanted to see me and, without even politely knocking, had kicked open the outer door. Maybe they hadn't counted on the inner door. I tried to turn off my light and pulled the cord. The bulb broke as the lamp hit the floor, which was probably a good thing as now I had the advantage. My two visitors heaved against the second door, shouting obscenities as they did. The bed began to give way in the darkness. Suddenly, an AK-47 and an arm slipped through a crack and I shoved the door as hard as I could. The door didn't close, but the first asshole was forced to let go of his AK-47, which bounced off the bed and onto the floor. Now it was mine! I thumbed onto semiautomatic as the guy silhouetted against the dim hallway light stumbled over my bed into the darkness and hit the floor. The guy behind him was making noises but staying put. Now it was close quarters and there wasn't any time to work out a strategy. Enraged, the number-one asshole wheeled to his knees looking around for me. The next thing I knew, the AK-47 I now had in my possession went off a couple of times and sent a bullet at a perfect angle through the guy's left butt cheek. The other guy vanished, and the first one, moaning and whimpering, retreated over the bed and out the door, hobbling toward the elevator, wounded for the second time that week, and, unbeknownst to him, this time by a *benefactor*. What a world!

AK-47 in hand, I pursued in my Jockey shorts and Nikes. Heads peered through open doors. Men came out and women held children back. Knowing trouble was brewing, the key lady had called the lobby for help. We all arrived at the elevator just as four men rushed up the wide stairway. One of them was my silent associate who looked like Anthony Quinn. Another was a leader of the refugee group. The other two were police. I detached the clip, ejected a live round, and handed the AK-47 to Quinn. He half smiled, shook his head and, in Russian, asked, "*Shto novava?*" (What's new?)

The drunken asshole number two was scared. He knew he was in big trouble. Asshole number one's blood was trickling down his leg into a puddle on the floor. The area was ringed with people wondering what the hell was going on. Somebody was saying that the two guys were troublemakers even *before* they were refugees. Quinn spoke roughly to the first one, who stupidly sassed him back. As a result the chair he was sitting on was knocked out from under him and he quickly felt the weight of Quinn's foot on his neck and the cold steel of an AK-47 barrel against his temple. The man finally got the message. One of the elder refugees led him onto the landing and down to the lobby. Quinn talked briefly with the key lady and then pointed at my Jockey shorts and said, "Stupid American" and everybody laughed. He then cocked his head to the side and gave me an exaggerated wink. He offered me the AK-47. I put up my hand and said, *"Nyet!* Not today!" I had had enough for one night. Quinn gave me a medium love punch on the shoulder and said he would take care of it and left. As I headed for my room, a woman passed me with a mop and a bucket. Quinn had come through for me again.

The last time I saw Quinn was in 1995 on a casualty-laden aircraft flying out of Abkhazia. I happened to glance down at a face sticking out of a body bag and was startled to be looking into Quinn's eyes, which, even in death, seemed to catch and hold mine. It was a sudden body blow, a shock to my core, a profound sense of loss. To me, Quinn was immortal. I knew very little about him, yet saw him as my guardian.

The day after the skirmish in the Iveria Hotel, before seeing Shevardnadze, I was visiting with Gela Charkviani, who joked in a friendly way about what had taken place the night before. He asked, "What's the matter? Didn't you like the food?"

I replied, "The food was okay, it was the company I didn't like. Some drunks came to my room and wanted to play 'trick or treat,' so what I did seemed right at the time."

"Yes," Gela responded, "I'm sure. But what is 'trick or treat'?"

I tried to explain it to him. He sort of *half* got it and was polite. I sometimes wish I wouldn't come up with those smart-ass one-liners over there. Gela spent about fifteen minutes with Shevardnadze while I waited. I could hear the two of them laughing. That was good. When I entered his office, Shevardnadze couldn't hold back a big smile. Through Gela, he told me of a big holiday they had in the fall, something to do with the harvest, and how he himself had grown up in the small town of Mamati in the Province of Guria, where they would play pranks on people. But, he added, they weren't destructive pranks. Then he asked, "What was it you did to the hooligans? Was it 'trick' or 'treat'?" We all laughed. That was the best part of the meeting.

The real high point for the whole day, however, occurred when I returned to my room expecting to have to do my nightly routine by flashlight. Much to my surprise, I was delighted to find that my broken 25-watt bulb had been replaced and that a new bulb had also been put in the bathroom. The next morning, I thanked the key lady and asked her to thank whoever gave up their light bulbs for me. She was a Russian, about forty-five and not bad looking. I think she must have lived there because she always seemed to be at her desk, twenty-four hours a day, acting as sort of a "house mother." She was a refugee—this must been the only world remaining to her, and she clung to it with a rough grace. Later on, as I left town, I gave her five packs of Marlboros in the red box, like in the advertisements (new in Georgia). She became undone by what she saw as my generosity and announced that the next time I came back to her floor, "I am yours!" Although she probably meant it, a Russian could say that and laugh and get away with it, but not a Georgian lady. Georgian women are sort of *1930,* Muncie, Indiana.

Chapter 27

Don't Shoot the Ice Cream Man
(Maverick Diplomacy)

O NE SPRING DAY in 1994, I was standing quietly in the Tbilisi office of Eduard Shevardnadze waiting to meet with him. He knew that in addition to my consulting and humanitarian functions, I had also been monitoring the various conflicts. I don't think he minded. I think he liked to hear information from totally different perspectives.

Shevardnadze was in somewhat of a precarious situation. He was now misunderstood and even hated by most Russians because they believed he sold them out. And even though he was Georgia's best hope, many Georgians were suspicious of his years in Soviet government as well. I still had easy access to him, but I knew this wouldn't last long as many government officials and bureaucrats had begun to assert themselves. Still, as late as 1994, I could just poke my nose into his office and he would often wave me in, as he did today.

Shevardnadze quietly studied a briefing paper while I studied him. I was struck by the Georgian leader's road map of a face, a map lined with signs not only of laughter and pain, but with strong evidence of a creative and compassionate mind. I was reminded of the Episcopalian bishop at my childhood communion. Both he and Shevardnadze exuded strength, warmth, wisdom, and humor, as well as a strong sense of realism. I could almost see the aura I felt in his presence. Like the bishop, he had moral authority. History's music as well as its tragedy seemed to surround the Georgian leader. I thought of Teddy Roosevelt's declaration that he liked to "grab hold of history and make it do the right thing." Shevardnadze was like that, even though he had some very tough history to deal with.

As our meeting began, I told Shevardnadze the story of recently being pinned down in a field in Abkhazia. I relayed to him the story about the ice-cream man on a bicycle who rode right into the middle of the shooting in Abkhazia as some of Shevardnadze's own "hard guys" approached the action from another direction. It was surreal. Somebody flung a grenade into a farmhouse as my two bodyguards and I got out of our car. We quickly took cover in a drainage ditch. We heard moans and groans from men who'd been hit earlier. It was just before noon. I peeked over the edge of the ditch, trying to figure out who was fighting whom—just who the Abkhazians rebelling against Georgian rule actually were. It was difficult to tell. They all somehow looked alike.

Shevardnadze listened closely and chuckled when I said they all looked alike. It had flashed through my mind that they all probably even knew each other. It was obvious to my bodyguards they were Russians, Chechens, and northern Caucasus Muslims fighting with the locals. The scene was chaotic as virtually all civil war scenes were, but, strangely—almost comically—like a bizarre game of cowboys and Indians. The shooting went on for some time. The adversaries also seemed to be dressed alike, and few seemed able to shoot straight, although there *were* two dead bodies on the edge of the road a dozen yards from us—victims of an earlier action. Flies had already found the dead men, and a mongrel dog sniffed at one of the bodies until sent on its way by gunfire. We stayed there for several hours, hoping the firing would die down.

Shevardnadze nodded appreciatively as I told him that eventually, when there seemed to be less gunfire, one of *my* "hard guys" suggested we make a run for the car. As we hunched up to go, in the distance we saw a man in a dirty white jacket on a bicycle struggling toward us on the loosely compacted dirt country road coming from the city of Sukhumi some six or seven miles west of our ditch. He had somehow tied a cardboard box onto two wheels in front of the bike. As he got closer, we could hear him crying "ICE CREAM!" in Georgian. After some frenzied shouting from both sides, the ice-cream man stopped and was allowed to meet with representatives from both sides of the "battlefield," one side at a time, to sell his ice cream. He even made change. When he started to leave the field, one of the Abkhazian mercenaries raised his rifle and one of my bodyguards started shouting, "Don't shoot the ice-cream man! Don't shoot the ice-cream man! There is an American observer here and he really wants some ice cream." The ice-cream man approached the ditch, and I stood up slowly from concealment in full view of everybody to validate the negotiation. I could feel dozens of eyes peering cautiously at me, wanting to know what I looked like. I pulled out a five-dollar bill. That made the very frightened ice-cream man smile, and he gave me the ice cream.

These were my bodyguards the day an ice-cream man pedaled through an Abkhaz battlefield.

"What happened then?" Shevardnadze asked.

I replied, "The ice-cream man pedaled madly down the dusty road and, in a few minutes, they started shooting at each other again, but their bursts were shorter and their hearts didn't seem to be into it as much. Maybe they were embarrassed. After all, this was a local issue not worth the inspection of an American observer." Shevardnadze was amused at the sheer absurdity of everyone stopping their efforts to kill each other so an American could have some ice cream.

In retrospect, this scene has become my metaphor for most of what was happening on my paper route. I called it "culture lag"—senseless addiction to a vague, distant past with no plan for the future. Crazy. No hope.

I also told Shevardnadze about the dead bodies I had recently seen stacked up like cord wood, lined up row after row in a Chechen warehouse. A year earlier during the first Chechen War, I had been asked to try and get into strife-torn Chechnya, a Russian province on Georgia's border, to give the Pants Factory a firsthand report on what was happening—who was doing what to whom, who was winning and why, and what was *really* at stake. And, of course, I wanted to know, just for myself, *what the hell was going on there.* Oil was somewhere in the mix, but to what extent? America's press was showing the Russians stomping down the iron heel of oppression, but not much else.

I had stayed several miles outside the main city of Grozny, but eventually went into the city itself with two of my Georgian companions. The Russians were taking quite a beating, and evacuating their dead had become impossible. A trainload of Russian women had just arrived after a rally in Moscow. They were *supposedly* mothers of the young, minimally experienced, and barely trained Russian soldiers. They were scouring the ruined city of 180,000, yelling the names of their boys, many of them already dead and laid out in the warehouse. Several of the women were drunk, crazy, and in tears as they screamed out names like "IVAN" and "SERGEI" into empty, burned-out buildings. Some of the women even looked familiar to me. Could they be Moscow "rent-a-moms"? I didn't really think so, but maybe a few were. They certainly didn't hide from the press.

I told Shevardnadze I had discovered that rather than mature "Russian professional murderers" being killed by "heroic Chechen rebels," as portrayed in the Western press (reports believed by many Washington spy masters), most of the dead were pink-cheeked Russian boys with toe tags—if they had legs at all—who had hardly known how to operate their equipment. They had literally been drafted onto trains to Chechnya where they were met and killed by highly experienced Chechen soldiers and murderous Muslim mercenaries from Afghanistan. It was no contest. A total mismatch. The Russians had shown no mercy from the air, so the Chechens had felt no guilt in running up the score on the ground.

As I relayed what I had seen to Shevardnadze, it struck me how ultimately *ironic* it was that I was giving intelligence to a former Cold War adversary. At the same time, it was becoming clear to me just how much my role had evolved since the tearing down of the Berlin Wall.

Shevardnadze, who knew the Russians so well, shook his head sadly as I relayed what I had seen. I told him of the awful smell of burned flesh in one village just over Georgia's border, the bloated bodies in the streets, and the Chechen women wearing black mourning scarves sobbing in the burned-out shells of their homes. I told Shevardnadze of looking into one of those shells and seeing nothing but burnt bedsprings holding a few charred bones. I *didn't* tell him how some in Washington found it difficult to believe my reports. I knew that Shevardnadze had no problem believing them at all. But I had seen more than I bargained for.

The Chechen capital of Grozny was only a hundred and twenty miles from Tbilisi, and at times the roads in between must have looked like the roads just ahead of the German Army in World War II—filled with chaos and fleeing civilians. Dead animals and burnt-out cars were everywhere. So-called "armies" operated as little more than autonomous armed gangs, detaining, robbing, and often murdering travelers at random. Strangers and the Western media were not immune. It was a *war*, not a civil revolution! I wrote in my report that, "In most war zones there's a certain method to the madness, and after a while you learn the ground rules. In Chechnya, there are no ground rules." It truly *had* been awful. The whole center of Grozny had been flattened—bombed repeatedly and scorched.

That day in Shevardnadze's office, I continued to unload pent-up thoughts and feelings. I shared some of what I had observed of Russian involvement in Georgia's own recent civil war in Abkhazia. It didn't seem to bother him that the Russians were being badly beaten in Chechnya. He had warned them about messing around in Abkhazia, saying it would come back to haunt them, and, indeed, it *did* in Chechnya. I also told Shevardnadze about the chopper overloaded with casualties that had flown me out of an artillery barrage in Abkhazia during the fighting with secessionists from the Abkhaz ethnic group. I told him I could still see the faces of those we didn't have room for. He said he was glad that, as someone from the West, I was seeing what was happening—seeing that the great Russian Bear was still everywhere.

Listening closely, Shevardnadze said, "I resent the Russian presence there, but then Yeltsin is in great difficulty. The entire territory that used to constitute the Soviet Union is in deep trouble today. These countries have not had independence for a long, long time. Georgia was part of Russia for two and a half centuries. Conflicts like Chechnya, or ours in Abkhazia, rage everywhere. In my opinion, these are not the last conflicts.

Other conflicts are to be expected. I wouldn't be surprised if eastern Russia or Siberia were to break away. They don't need Moscow and, in fact, resent Moscow. But I think the law of necessity ultimately *has* to work."

He rapped on his desk with the palm of his hand as if to emphasize the point before continuing, "Abkhazians and Georgians, for example, *have* to live together. Even though the civil war in Abkhazia has been a tragic event with heavy casualties, it is my hope that it will increase the responsibility of both sides."

Shevardnadze continued, "You know, people in America wonder why I still seem friendly to the Russians, not to mention Iran, Turkey, and Iraq." He laughed. "Tell them that those countries are my neighbors. *Of course* I must do business with them! Besides, they are much bigger and stronger than Georgia. We always have to be clever, or we will lose our way once again."

Then, turning serious, he asked me what *I* would do when it was over about all those on the opposing side in Abkhazia who had fought so hard against him and the stable government he was trying to establish. How should he punish them?

I thought for a while before answering. Then, out of nowhere, I recalled that during our own Civil War, Abraham Lincoln had been asked how he intended to punish the South and he had very simply replied, "The best way to deal with a defeated enemy is to make him a friend."

Shevardnadze quietly repeated Lincoln's words in Georgian. Then, through his interpreter, he told me, "That is profound. It will be the basis of my policy."

We sat quietly for a few moments as Shevardnadze contemplated Lincoln's words, apparently trying to adapt them to his time and place. Then I recalled the candlelight services that, at times, seemed to be the only thing holding ancient Georgia together and remarked that it was my hope Georgia would never again have to face the horror of civil war. The former communist leader looked up at the ceiling and murmured, "*God willing.*" He hesitated, reflecting on what he had just said, and then, seeming inwardly happy with himself, added, "I have not said that often. Until three years ago, not at all."

We sat silently for a time. I was moved. I knew that Shevardnadze had been baptized into the Georgian Orthodox Christian Church earlier that year. Some cynics thought it was a political ploy. I knew better. Seeing something in my face, Shevardnadze said slowly, in English, "It *was* a miracle, you know."

He got up from the table and stared out the window at a hillside crowned with a small, ancient chapel glistening golden in the afternoon winter sun. Then, turning back to me and speaking again through Gela, he said, "Perhaps the *real* miracle was the way we came together—Gorbachev, Reagan, Shultz, and I. We had each climbed our own separate ladders. The time was right, and we were each prepared in our own way to do what was necessary. It was very clear that the key was we were all men of principle, men of integrity. We could recognize this in each other. We were ready to act together, and together we were ready to end the lunacy." Shevardnadze laughed as he added, "Reagan told us one night that none of us was smart enough to do it alone." I thought to myself that books are full of theories, but it finally came down to four men of integrity, each finding a way out of his own darkness. Looking back at the ancient chapel on Mtatsminda, the mountain of St. David, Shevardnadze concluded, "There is life up there once again. But without what the four of us were able to do together, that would not be so. It *was* a miracle."

I felt privileged as I listened to the former Soviet foreign minister describe his crucial role in the ending of the Cold War. And I was moved when I considered how he had become leader of his own troubled homeland, where fifteen hundred years of religion—its spirit as well as its substance—had survived seventy years of communism. Hearing the aging statesman (actually, he is *my* age) utter the name of God affected me. This was the man who now *thanked God,* and had forced me to realize that my own exposure to danger and difficult situations over the years had brought even me into some form of communication with a higher power, a God I was not always sure about but one I would always believe in.

Suddenly, as we sat quietly lost in our own thoughts, my attention was diverted by snapshots thumb tacked to Shevardnadze's back wall. And *there*, in one of the small pictures, I saw *myself* talking to former Secretary of State James Baker. It was a moment I will always treasure.

I had come to love Georgia and its culture, a culture that had survived a thousand years of invasions. And I felt fortunate to be involved in the fate of a Georgia that, with the Russians *mostly* gone, was finding its way into a new future.

Chapter 28

Uncivilized Behavior
(To the Rescue)

WOMEN WERE EVERYWHERE in my travels. Not many, but *some* of them were gorgeous young KGB agents who came on to me blatantly, if somewhat clumsily. That was not all that unusual. I knew it was not my "hard guy" rugby looks that attracted these women. They had a job to do. But certainly not all the women I met on my paper route through Russia and Central Asia were out to seduce, compromise, or marry me for a ticket to the West. There was, for instance, Sibi, that English and Iranian girl—dual passports—an Oxford student, who, or so it seemed, half the Turks, Armenians, and Azerbaijani had propositioned. Slender and attractive, she wore Western clothes, and many of the men in those male-dominated societies assumed she was a lady of the night.

Sibi was frightened the first time I met her. She spoke fluent Farsi, the language of the Tajiks as well as the Iranians, and had come to Tajikistan to teach children in a small rural community. But that afternoon she was shaken and distressed. She had traveled previously in Turkey with her mother but had never traveled alone in a country such as Tajikistan, a country that my friend Professor Alex Rondeli calls the "throwaway republic." For me, the place always ranged from unpleasant to terrifying, so I understood the fear in Sibi's eyes.

Our paths first crossed in mid-1993 when I was in Dushanbe on personal assignment, checking out the clearly deteriorating situation in Tajikistan. I was returning to my hotel after jogging when a white Land Rover with International Red Cross markings pulled up in front of the hotel and Sibi got out followed by the driver, a big, burly looking man who appeared to be German or Swedish but turned out to be South African. Sibi looked like she was trying to escape. When she saw me, she asked me for my room number and dashed into the lobby. After watching her disappear and wondering why she seemed so frightened, I went back up to my room. My phone rang almost immediately. It was Sibi and she wanted to come to my room. When she arrived, she seemed petrified. She grabbed my sleeve and didn't let go for an hour, not seeming to realize what she was doing. She said the South African had offered her a ride to her teaching assignment in the hills northeast of Dushanbe, and then, mauling and slobbering, had tried to force himself on her. It was obvious that she was in way over her head. She poured her heart out to me. I just held and comforted her. It seemed like the gentlemanly thing to do. I had dinner with her that evening. Her real problem was that the school was about sixty miles away and she couldn't get there by herself, and wasn't even sure she wanted to commit to the assignment. I talked to her for several hours, calming her down.

The next morning I cornered the South African, who seemed more like an overgrown, lovesick schoolboy than a mad rapist. I gave the big fellow my "hard-man rugby-player look," while telling him that Sibi needed safe transportation. He apologized to me about Sibi, saying he had been out there for so long he had become "uncivilized."

I added that I had some work to do for my publisher, and would accompany them. The work was merely part of a cover that I frequently used in conjunction with my very real consulting, sports, and humanitarian activities. I often found myself moving within covers that enclosed covers, to the point that sometimes I was not altogether sure whether who I am, or who they thought I was or who I was supposed to be, was actually who I was.

Before leaving Dushanbe with Sibi in the South African's Land Rover and heading northeast, I checked in with the Colonel. He told me to be careful and to remember to "walk like a ghost," and, in fact, to "become a ghost" because there were "a lot of crazies out there." When I replied, in an attempt at humor, that my friends often called me the Phantom, the Colonel responded with a very thin smile and said that "the word would be passed" that we were coming, and that we "would probably be all right." Although the Colonel had been helpful at times, I assumed it was because this made it easier for him to keep tabs on me rather than out of the goodness of his heart. There was always a healthy screen of suspicion between us. But he *was* helpful.

So, with the Colonel's blessing and advice to watch out for crazies, Sibi, the South African, and I left Dushanbe in the Red Cross Land Rover. It took about three relatively uneventful hours on graveled roads to get to Komsomolabad, a small town of about 6,800 people in the Pamir Mountains where Sibi hoped to teach. The local Tajiks had been anxiously awaiting her arrival and implored her to stay. Sibi got caught up in their excitement, saying, "Yes, yes, I want to stay. I *will* stay! I am here to teach."

Because Sibi's luggage was still in her hotel room in Dushanbe, the South African and I suggested that she go back with us and we would see to it that she returned to her teaching assignment the next day. On the way back to Dushanbe, we had some engine trouble. We had barely managed to get the Land Rover across an old stone bridge when we came to a crude roadblock and were confronted by three heavily armed and very stoned young Tajiks. When the wild-eyed young Muslim men saw Sibi in her Western clothes, they went crazy. One of them had a face like a rat and kept spitting out a constant stream of unintelligible words through teeth that appeared to have holes in them. Another was wiping his nose with one of the fingers of his right hand while he waved an AK-47 around with his left. Speaking fluent Farsi, Sibi tried to talk to them and then told me with disbelief in her eyes, "They want to take me home to meet their mother!"

I put my arm around her and told her to tell them, "She belongs to me. *I* am her mother." When the rat-faced Tajik heard this, he quickly shoved the barrel of his AK-47 into my chest and started yelling at me that they wanted to talk to her in private. The wild young Tajik with the runny nose grabbed at Sibi. At this point, the South African erupted and grabbed two of the half-crazed Tajiks, cracking their heads together like melons in each hand. I took their guns away, we pushed Sibi into the Rover, and fortunately it started. As we drove away, the South African shouted at the stunned Tajiks that he would drop their guns off down the road where they could pick them up, but if they gave him any more trouble he'd kill them. I knew that the South African was being very smart by allowing them to retrieve their weapons, and thereby keep at least some of their dignity, because Sibi would have to come back through here to return to her teaching assignment.

The South African had really come through in a jam. I decided he *must* be okay when he happened to mention that he had tried out for the "Springboks," the South African national rugby team. I learned that we had both played rear row positions in the back of the scrum. Fortunately, Sibi had attended Oxford and gone to rugby games and parties, so she endured the male bonding thing as we bounced along the rough road back to Dushanbe. The South African didn't put any more moves on Sibi and, in fact, helped her return to her school. Sometimes you desperately need people like him in that part of the world. They know how to deal with it. They understand the local game and can be invaluable when you're feeling way out of your element.

Sibi was typical of my many contacts and sources of information, both small and large. I was later pleased to learn that she was safely teaching school in the small Tajik town that had been so happy to see her. She and I kept in touch during the months and years following her teaching assignment. The last time I heard from Sibi was an email from Peshawar, Pakistan, in 2002. She married a Scottish engineer who had played rugby at Edinburgh University. Peshawar in the year 2002 was on the State Department's "No Go" advisory list, and I couldn't help but wonder why the hell she was there and just what the hell she was doing. Whatever, we genuinely liked each other. I'm not sure exactly why. She was, of course, grateful and trusted me. Maybe she thought I was too old to be dangerous, like Billy Graham in the tour posters on the walls of the Dushanbe Hotel. Perhaps of more importance was that she understood, in a way few people did, that I genuinely liked women. One reason is that the good ones are generally dangerous, but it's a different kind of danger from, say, a firefight in Tajikistan, although both heighten my sense of gratitude for being alive. Women renew the life-giving forces within me. AK-47s on the Afghan border take life away.

If you will forgive me for a moment of philosophy and personal reflection, I think women are remarkable. They not only give life, they teach the next generation how to survive. They're survivors themselves—Susan Butcher, who won the 1,150-mile Iditarod sled-dog race four times, is just one example. They live longer than men, often end up with more money, can have multiple orgasms, etc. etc. In the final analysis, women give men whatever power they have other than muscular. Most women understand this fact and administrate it judiciously. Most men, on the other hand, think they're the dominant sex and don't have a clue as to how things really work.

Chapter 29

The Throwaway Republic
(A Voice in the Crowd)

THE TRANSITION during the early 1990s was a particularly tough and strange time to be in Tajikistan. Going anywhere in Tajikistan was dangerous. Tajikistan is sort of like Afghanistan at low tide. It's a very, very scary place, and its politics are murky. And its "boss" city, Dushanbe—scary and murky. Russia was like a gigantic piece of fine clay that had been pummeled and molded and shaped over the centuries, but remained, nevertheless, a gigantic piece of clay to be pummeled, molded and shaped again. Yet, as had been the case for centuries, it was still hanging there over all the other Asian republics. For me, it was both exciting and frustrating, with many off-the-wall things happening in places I hadn't planned to visit.

I remember in particular the time my journey of exploration along the ancient Silk Road was interrupted by a mob that forced me onto the steps of the Parliament building in Dushanbe. I had just flown down from Tashkent, Uzbekistan, and wanted to evaluate the current political unrest among the city's 300,000 population, as well as what I knew was a continuing Russian presence. The 35,000 Jews who had been settled in Tajikistan by the Soviets were already abandoning the new republic in a systematic evacuation, many to Israel.

The first thing I noticed was a blanket of unusual military activity at the airport. An embassy official and the new American ambassador's working wife were hustled into an embassy van. On the plane ride in, they had known me simply as a tourist, so I grabbed a ride in a very ancient taxi. I had to walk softly with our embassy people, who sometimes resented my independent method of operation. The American Embassy in Dushanbe was very new and had only recently become operational. It was staffed by six middle-aged Americans, who were using rooms in the city's October Hotel as both offices and living quarters. It was centrally located and decent enough.

Dushanbe, with its tree-lined streets, is both very Asian and very Russian—in many ways reminiscent of one of the Central California Valley towns of my youth. It lies about an hour and a half south of Tashkent by Aeroflot on a sloping plateau one hundred miles from the Afghan border.

Tajikistan, as a whole, is very Third World, with a thin Moscow-generated veneer. It was frequently on the State Department's "No Go" travel advisory list, which not only did not stop me, but in an odd way, I suppose, was a big reason I was there again. My mission was always to go where the trouble was, to get on the ground where Americans didn't go and to see things our technology—advanced as it was—couldn't see.

Riding into Dushanbe that evening, I heard a growing crescendo of street noise, trucks, buses, and carloads of chanting protesters, loud speakers, and a tent city in the square filling up with a gigantic "rent-a-mob." It was not a good sound, and all I wanted to do was check into the Tajikistan Hotel.

The next day, I could see some of the activities from my hotel-room window. It was October and the ground was parched hard. The park gardens were withered, and dried flowers, no longer colored, rattled in the breeze. The neglected children's amusement park had rusted to a halt. Concert halls were unattended and crumbling. Tiles in mosaic murals were missing.

Cars were skidding around without brakes. At home, I would have thought it was a nice mild fall afternoon, but in Dushanbe it was not. Dark figures darting between the rival camps at opposite ends of the main boulevard about half a mile apart were working themselves into a frenzy. What was already bad was getting worse. An almost unbroken line of big blue trucks in convoys unloaded thousands of poor, dirty-looking, chanting farmhands into the courthouse plaza. I decided to take a walk to check out the scene up close.

I made the mistake of having a camera in my hand as I walked amidst the snarling, writhing mass of angry people. My rather ordinary tourist camera, like a beacon, made *everybody* automatically aware of me. The man who first grabbed me wore very bad clothes and had so many scars he seemed to have been stitched together. I kept hoping that the stitches would burst. It was an illusion. The whole happening seemed to be an illusion. But it was not an illusion when two other armed men grabbed me and proudly led me into the plaza through squatting masses shouting for the blood of the foreigner with the camera. As they led me to the steps, I thought they were about to gouge my eyes out in front of 5,000 Muslims who were doing a dance that made me imagine some sort of ancient fertility rites in primitive parts of Asia. Swaying, bowing, twisting, delirious with evil and hate. Frantic now, they seemed to be clawing wildly at their oppressive heaven. They would chant, then go silent, dance, and then go silent again. It was eerie. It seemed ghastly, pagan—godless. I was reminded of how the old Red Devil fireworks used to go off when you least expected them to. You lit them and ran, expecting them to explode. When they didn't, you started back and all of a sudden the little red tubes would start popping off in a chain reaction. The mob out there in front of me was popping off like that.

Was I on the outskirts of hell? I didn't know. As I looked into the crowd, a woman lifted her veil and stuck her tongue out at me. It slipped out of her mouth like a wide red carpet under the black curtain of her veil. A mob has a face. This mob had a mouth, too. Out of that mouth came a great primitive rumble. A subterranean sound—the sound of dirt, rock, and fire mashing and screeching.

As I looked out over the crowd, for some reason I will never know I thought of a bad dream I had in Baku one night in which a single pistol with ivory grips had suddenly pierced through a mass of faceless bodies and found its mark between my eyes. Was I hallucinating? In retrospect, I think I must have been.

My two rag-headed escorts led me up a dozen steps to a loudspeaker and with proud smiles and a more-than-gentle shove presented me to a guy in his forties wearing a white shirt, tan military-style pants, and black shoes. He was slim and balding, with a Slovak mustache. He held a black leather clipboard. I knew without knowing that this man was a Russian intelligence officer—the only non-Muslim in sight. "Who are you?" he asked in German, with an East German accent.

I responded in deliberately sloppy Russian, "I just got into town. What kind of party are you throwing? I'm an American tourist. Haven't you seen any of us before? The toilets here are worse than in Tashkent. What's the big celebration? Hey, what are these guys smoking... Can I be on *your* side?"

He laughed a small laugh and gave me a nudge, but his eyes glistened cold. He had the face of a man enjoying some internal power force. There was a chill in his laugh. His "nudge" was meant to hurt a little, just a little. It didn't. But I did feel fear. He was definitely in charge.

In order to handle my fear, I kept telling myself this was no big deal and that I would get through it by pretending I was giving a speech in front of my high school graduating class. I tried to laugh, but couldn't. Deep breathing helped a little. I just smiled and smiled, and finally asked the man at the microphone (I later learned he was a Russian from Belarus), "Can I speak to them?"

Finally, through a tight smile, he mumbled, "Why not?" Actually, he was probably being pretty smart, thinking, "Why not give the Yank a chance to say a few words nobody will understand and then shake his hand and get rid of him?"

I shouted in English, putting as much feeling as I could into it, *"I am Jim Waste from California, U.S.A.! You have a beautiful country! I love Dushanbe!"*

The Russian intelligence officer gave me a Lee Harvey Oswald sort of smirk. He did not translate my words, but looked as if he wanted to abort my performance and get me the hell out of there. He didn't know what to do with me.

I was scared silly. I remembered my dad telling me in the late 1940s about a similar mob in Lebanon dismembering several Bechtel executives who had been my family's friends. They were taken from their hotel rooms, ostensibly to the police department, but never made it.

The crowd had quieted down and seemed to be studying me, waiting for the next act. I dug deep into my inner survival kit and began shouting, still in English, *"Mars Bars . . . Marlboro smokes . . . Coca Cola . . . Hey!! . . . Horseman pass by! . . . YOU ARE A HERD OF TURKEYS!"*

Some of the crowd laughed and pointed at the crazy American, but they didn't kill me. They didn't gouge my eyes out either, although they *did* make little circles with their index fingers around their eyes. They just shook their heads—a great mass of mumbling heads shaking at the crazy American. But, when somebody in the crowd shouted in Russian that I was not with British Intelligence, they suddenly just let me go.

Bowing politely, I shook the hand of the German-speaking Russian. By that time, I knew I had seen him before and that I would probably see him again. He *also* betrayed faint recognition. When I think of his face today, I think of the face of evil, an intellectual façade backed by unmistakable, deeply embedded hate—a face I saw often through the years.

I carefully picked my way to the back of the squatting crowd where some Australian humanitarian relief workers had been watching the whole thing. They had been joking and speculating on what I might have done to be in so much trouble and what kind of punishment I might receive. They thought it was clever of me to give my name and home address over the loud speaker in case I was given to Allah without my permission. It helped to joke around a bit. I always liked Aussies. Although it was difficult at first, I found myself able to laugh with them.

I then turned to walk back to the hotel. As soon as I cleared the plaza and was out of sight of the steps, I had an almost overwhelming adrenaline rush! My inner survival kit, which had pulled me through so many rugby matches and races, was obviously still in good working order, but it had definitely been in overdrive. At that point, I felt like running at top speed to get comfortable, not out of fear, but out of relief, release, and joy. My "reserve tank" was still full. I was alive and grateful that when *somehow* they realized from a voice in the crowd that I was *not* with British Intelligence, they had simply let me go and even the Russian with the face of evil had seemed relieved.

In spite of nearly meeting my maker, I was amused by the fact that the Tajiks were still preoccupied with British Intelligence. It was at this moment I realized that the voice in the crowd must have been one of the Aussies! Wow! Three cheers for the Aussies! We *do* take care of our own! Many Tajiks believe that all spies (and all foreigners to them were spies) work for British Intelligence. British Intelligence had been in that part of the world for centuries. But I felt elated to be alive, and pleased that my wife wouldn't have to be misinformed by some dispatch of my "accidental" demise.

I rushed back to my hotel and called the American Embassy to see if they knew how bad it was in the streets. One of the staffers asked me to please get over there and tell them what I had seen and what I thought about it. The embassy was on the

*Trucks carried a "rent-a-mob" from the countryside to
a demonstration in Dushanbe.*

third floor of the October Hotel and had a clear view of the boulevard intersection, which was blocked by two old blue buses.
When I got there, I could see three embassy personnel peeking
fearfully out the window. As I passed through the garden, now
abandoned, the summer's last heat swirled scraps of paper and
dust against the stone borders edging the empty flower beds.

I hurried up the stairs into the lobby and ran up to the third
floor where we could see the boulevard and the groups at each
end. One group was made up of intellectuals and the more
stable and conservative elements. The other was a pure, primitive mob—most of them brought in from the country by the
Russians to cause trouble. They were dirty, sullen, and ignorant.
When the mob started start moving down the boulevard, the
intellectuals started moving, too. Shouting erupted and shots
were fired as the two groups came together at a roadblock.
AK-47s sprayed and splattered. It was like watching weed-eaters
at work as rows of men pitched forward. There were dead and
wounded all over the street. Screams and smoke filled the air, as
slowly spreading crimson pools of blood reflected the sunset.

Then, seemingly out of nowhere, hundreds of real, uniformed Russian soldiers appeared and separated the rioters. The Soviet Union might have broken up, but the Russian Bear was still there! Within an hour, the smoke and smell in the streets had faded. The screaming had stopped. The Russians had removed the dead and wounded and hosed down the streets with a water cannon. Dump trucks filled with bodies vanished. Many of the dead had slit throats and *coup de grace* shots in their foreheads. The Russians moved quickly and brutally, and in less than two hours they, too, had vanished into the countryside as if nothing had happened.

One of the embassy officials, obviously new to the newly opened post, asked me, "Why are the Russians here?"

I pointed down at the few remaining bodies deliberately left on the boulevard and responded, "That's one reason, but only one. They like the unrest. They create it. It helps them to keep some form of control. But they don't want it to get out of hand, either."

"Are you serious?" he asked.

"Of course. If there's no trouble, there's no need for the Russians to be here. So they create the trouble."

The embassy official looked at me as if I was crazy, and continued, "You mean it was staged?"

I replied, "Of course it was staged, because the Russians want the rest of the world to believe that their former republics—the CIS—need protection. So they light fires, and then put the fires out." I explained to him that for seventy years the Russians were the fire department and the republics had gotten used to their coming in when there was trouble. Then, of course, Iran was just down the road, and militant Islam was everywhere.

Most of the other embassy guys listened in on our conversation intently. But I will not soon forget the highly educated—but lazy and a bit stupid—embassy officer who, when he heard about my experience on the steps, giggled and then said, "You're a real defender of the faith, aren't you?" A painful silence ensued. That's how I chose to answer. I supposed he was okay in some ways, but mostly he was an asshole, and I let him know I knew it. I wouldn't have died for *him*, and now he realized it.

My rugby team had two basic rules. "No assholes allowed," and "No practice, no play." I finally fired back, without thinking but with a heavy load of sarcasm, "When I talk to fellow Americans like you, I often wonder just where you guys fit into that faith, if at all."

From the standpoint of my later report on the incident, I was able to determine that the political differences were both real and violent. And with the U.S. Embassy watching but saying little publicly, even though they would evacuate their quarters five times during the next couple of years, the Russians were maintaining their presence in force.

It was a valuable stop, although I did pay a price. For seven days after that confrontation on the steps, I could feel my nerve edges dancing just under my skin. But I didn't have to be put on steps in front of a Dushanbe mob to make me feel uncomfortable in Tajikistan. I *always* felt uncomfortable in Tajikistan. So much of life there is both primitive and cheap and often of no value at all. There were many times when I was not sure if I would ever see my home or family again, and it bothered me that I might die, or worse yet, just *disappear,* in a place so aptly named the "throwaway republic." It was *almost* enough for me to change my personal travel agenda so that I would never go back there again. I could just hear two of my friends at home saying, "He was killed overseas in Tajikistan!"

One would ask, "Tajikistan! Where the hell is *that?*"

Followed up by the other with, "Tajikistan! What the hell was he doing *there?*"

Of course, they would never find out the answer to the second question, nor would my wife and family, and knowing *that* was hard to deal with.

Muslim Creep

HISTORICALLY, MY PAPER ROUTE through the former Soviet Central Asian republics was devoted to trying to figure out for the U.S. who was doing what to whom. Long before the breakup, I was well aware that six of the eight former republics on my route (not counting Georgia and Armenia) were inhabited by fifty-five million people, fifty million of whom were Muslim. For obvious reasons, when atheistic Moscow set up *this* particular region, they made an exception to the banishment of religion, mainly because it would have been impossible to enforce. Instead they cleverly *used* religion to their advantage, going so far as to set up governments with Muslim leaders who were acceptable to them as figureheads. Once these governments were operational, the less cooperative Muslim leaders were eased out of power or simply disappeared from sight. It was a very effective means of control. By controlling the Eurasian corridor in this way, Moscow created a dike or buffer zone to fend off the inevitable spread of Islam from their Muslim neighbors to the south such as Afghanistan and Iran. This, of course, required a constant military presence in the republics along the Soviet border.

When the final collapse of the Soviet Union happened and the inevitable security vacuum brought on by the Russian disengagement followed, I realized, *virtually for the first time,* that much of the chaos I had been reporting on was the result of Russia's own seventy-year struggle with the Islamic presence. This had been a *gigantic* problem for the Russians to service through the years, and in the final days of the Soviet Union, Gorbachev and Shevardnadze had very serious concerns over the future behavior of the newly independent, Muslim-dominated states. They were afraid, with good reason, of a massive intrusion of Islamic extremism into the former border republics. Therefore, out of necessity the CIS was born in 1991, and with it came the quick return of Russian troops to their old Soviet borders.

But until that time, "Muslim Creep," as I call it, had been kept under control and managed. The ever crafty Russians understood from the beginning that if they withdrew the economic infrastructure, including the "border patrol," the shit would hit the fan. At first I had not recognized the full implications of this issue—that the Russians had their own problems with Muslim extremism—and I had not reported about it.

This "ethnic problem," in general, had received little exposure in the West and had been obscured and denied by Moscow, which continually stirred things up to provide opportunities for future intervention. Although the continual mischief was nothing new and their types of tactics had been employed by colonial powers throughout the world, the growing seriousness of the larger, more dangerous problem of Muslim extremism was not fully recognized in the West until recently. The Bear had never solved their ethnic problem, and Muslim Creep was waiting to get up and walk!

During an early meeting with Shevardnadze in which he had urged me to tell George Shultz that Georgia *had* to join the CIS, I thought it was a backslide or reversion to the old Russian order. But, after coming to appreciate the *ordeal* the Russians had experienced with their own ethnic problems, I became a little more sympathetic. Indeed, it had been a revelation for me. The Russians had a legitimate need to control their borders and, in a way, the CIS now seemed to be a less devious ploy than before.

Unfortunately, the Bear would again get caught in his own honey trap, in the Russian autonomous region of Chechnya and elsewhere, just as Shevardnadze had said they would. If the Russians had played it straight from the outset in these troubled areas, maybe they wouldn't be in the current mess. But, of course, flawed thinking provides flawed results.

Chapter 30

Tribal Business
(Thank Heaven for Little Girls)

O NE DAY IN 1998, having finished my humanitarian work in Tbilisi, I was killing time walking around the city and decided to drop by the newly refurbished Metechi Hotel. It was there that I was reminded of Mirian's concerns about the *Mafiya*. Unlike the earlier days, the Metechi had been cleaned up and was now free of the stains of previous abuse and mismanagement. The hotel was built by a Czechoslovakian company to the finest European four-star standards—stairs of marble, glass and

By 1998 the Metechi Hotel had become civilized—at least on the surface.

brass, water fountains, and three glass elevators running up and down on golden tracks in the fifteen-story lobby. A grand mobile shimmered in the morning light. Drinks, sandwiches, and pastries were served in the spacious atrium throughout the day. The chocolate torte, along with the flute player who alternated with a violinist and cellist, created a classy and cultured atmosphere. For me it was like the town square and I went there often to monitor the ebb and flow of international activity.

I had just slipped off my Nikes and sat down in the atrium when there was a sudden hush in the room. A side door normally used as an exit banged open and a group of five or six men marched in. Bypassing a security officer, they headed for a reserved table in the back, near what was called the "golden elevator." At about the same time, a similar group entered through the revolving front entrance and seated themselves at a table near the reception counter, not far from me. I tried to ignore them and went on eating my cake and reading my English-language Georgian newspaper, but heads were nodding at me and a fellow with a crew cut in his mid-twenties, built like a tight end, came over to my table and looked me over. I gestured for him to sit down and, in Russian, told him I would order more cake. He didn't seem to understand, so I rattled a little English at him and produced my passport, saying, "OO-ES-AY—tourist." He kind of tossed his head back and returned to his table.

As he walked away, I could see the outline of his flak jacket and the bulge of a skeleton stock machine pistol. He was obviously the "chaperone" at that table. A moment later, a linebacker-looking chaperone from the *other* table made a sweep of the room. As he walked past my table, he made a sort of hesitant gesture, like he was jamming his thumb through a door. I wasn't sure what it meant, so I waited for another sign. None came.

In the meantime, the two groups seated at their separate tables were served tea and pastries. The elevator had stopped running, and only one person remained behind the big reception desk. Recorded rather than the usual live music played in the background. Six or seven of the younger men at one of the tables looked like cousins, or at least as if they came from the same part of Georgia. They sat in positions that allowed them to see in all directions. Two of the older men at the table became engrossed in conversation, and I couldn't help but wonder what they were talking about. The scene at the other table was almost a carbon copy of the first except the men looked just a little rougher, were not as neat, and had rounder eyes and longer hair. I decided they were probably from Guria on the Black Sea in West Georgia.

The linebacker and the tight end kept moving around the room in an invisible perimeter. Papers were passed back and forth and studied and discussed. This went on for over half an hour. Everybody was smoking cigarettes and most of the men were leaning forward, elbows on knees, keeping low, eyes scanning the room as they listened to each other and lit each other's cigarettes. One of the guys, who looked to be in his forties, took some sort of paper to the table where the rougher-looking men were sitting, while a Godfather-type at each table talked on a cell phone, maybe to a higher power in the parking lot or maybe to each other.

Finally, after an hour of negotiation, the groups' postures changed. The men sat up straighter and became more animated. Half-smiles replaced sullen looks, and both groups rose and, without flourishes, left the way they had come in. Whatever they had been negotiating or discussing had obviously been settled. I felt like waving goodbye, but suppressed what was only an urge to relieve the tension I had felt. Then, I noticed that the linebacker and the tight end had returned to the center of the room. I got ready to dive under the table, but to my surprise, the two guards from rival tables kissed each other on both cheeks and—I couldn't believe it—gave each other "high fives." I guess it was a job well done for both. As the tight end went out the side door, he looked over at me and flipped me a thumbs up. This time I waved, and smiled as well.

After a few minutes, the elevator started to move again. The pianist and the cello player also returned. The other desk personnel reappeared and got busy. Business was over. Although it had been done in almost a ritualistic tribal style, this meeting characterized a new way of doing business in Georgia. A small step from a thousand years ago, but perhaps that's the way it will have to happen—incrementally, one day at a time. I couldn't help but think that at least it was Georgians, and not the Russian *Mafiya,* who were taking over the economy in Georgia.

I motioned to the waitress for my check and she laid my bill, which had a big circle in the center, down in front of me.

"What's this?" I asked.

She replied, "The convention split their bill and included you as their guest. Soliko from Guria, one of the head men, said to thank you for being there because you added an international flavor to their meeting."

"Wow!" I responded. "I thought they might shoot me or something."

She smiled. "That's happened right here in this room, but not recently. The mob, or Georgian *Mafiya*—they *can* work together if there is mutual gain." I couldn't help but wonder what the issue was *that* day.

After witnessing the Metechi meeting, I made my way back across town and decided to stop in for a Big Mac. One of the most dramatic signs of the invasion of free enterprise was the two-story McDonald's by the Metro Station on Tbilisi's Republic Plaza. Once an elegant Russian bank with marble columns and neoclassical ornamentation, it was still one of the finest buildings in the Georgian renaissance capital. It was clean, efficient, and staffed with bright, hustling young Georgians who served food identical to the U.S. version. The restrooms were the finest in the Caucasus.

In the States, I prefer Burger King, but for Americans like me, Tbilisi's McDonald's represented a touch of home, even though the background music was Central Asian rock and roll and the place was jumping from eight in the morning until midnight. There was frequently a birthday party atmosphere with pink balloons, attractive and smiling mothers in their thirties, and cute kids munching and slurping away. The crowd was, by Georgian standards, generally well-to-do. Everything tasted exactly the same as it did in the States, and even the prices were the same. If you didn't speak Georgian (the Georgian language is *only* spoken in Georgia), all you had to do was point to "#3" and say, "To go."

I had just started eating my Big Mac and was looking out over the plaza with its robust fountains and statues of Georgian heroes when I noticed a handsome young father in black slacks and the traditional well-pressed white shirt sitting with his seven- or eight-year-old daughter. She was a Shirley Temple look-alike with a pleated plaid skirt, vest, and puffy-shouldered blouse, knee-high checkered stockings, and brass-buckled patent-leather shoes. A large white butterfly bow adorned her shoulder-length auburn braid. I was immediately infatuated with the child. Looking at her somehow linked me up with my own daughters when they were at that same delightful age, as well as with my third-grade class in Berkeley, California, where I had experienced my first feelings of "true love." The little girl was involved in assembling her Happy Meal toys when her father rose. As he headed for the order counter, I noticed a medium-sized Beretta pistol holstered in the small of his back. I was only mildly surprised by the pistol, as lots of people in that part of the world were armed, but as my eyes momentarily locked with his, I felt a surge of suppressed recognition. I had learned *not* to acknowledge such moments until my brain had sorted out what I was seeing. I sipped my chocolate shake and glanced toward the pigtailed girl, then allowed my eyes to return to those of her father. He gave me a seemingly embarrassed smile, held up a Happy Meal animal, and sort of shrugged his shoulders. He seemed to be seeking my understanding.

At that moment I realized he was one of the bodyguard-messengers I had encountered earlier that day at the Metechi tribal enclave. Now, without the flak jacket, Uzi, and scowl, he was a family man, just like me. I raised my milkshake to him, as if making a toast. Then, putting up the five fingers of my hand, hoping he would get the message that I had five children, I nodded toward his lovely daughter and clutched both hands over my heart as if to say, "Oh, how precious she is." Something passed between us. It was a good moment. Georgians are great family people. It's the basis for their traditional culture. Even so, I'm glad I had arrived at the McDonald's first, so he didn't think I was following him.

As I walked up the cobbled street to my quarters at Betsy's Guest House, I reran the McDonald's scene in my mind. I thought about how seeing the little girl had put me in touch with feelings from my past. I marveled at the power of such feelings, stored so long in some private place. For a moment, I was deep into my own long-gone past, a gift from the tribal bodyguard and his gorgeous little girl, and I thought about the *power* of memory. Memories of violence and horror can linger in a person for a lifetime and in a culture for centuries. Such memories, stored as pain, can express themselves in a subterranean tendency to exact revenge and seek more violence. This was the curse of Central Asia, an eye for an eye, a policy often ruthlessly practiced by the Russians. As I reached the last block before Betsy's, I again thought of the bodyguard's beautiful daughter and the violence of revenge being expressed in all the countries around me. I couldn't help but mutter to myself, "God, show us a better way."

Chapter 31

Collateral Damage
(Things Aren't Always What They Seem)

T HE SUMMER DAY IN 1999 when I almost stayed in bed developed in stages. I was feeling a little down after a long week of travel in Armenia and Azerbaijan. But rather than hide out in my room, I decided to walk across the city to the Sheraton Metechi Hotel and drop off some papers at the embassy on the way. It was Sunday and sunny, and I was beginning to allow thoughts of home in the High Sierras to filter into my consciousness. I needed a wake-up walk, and the prize would be a piece of chocolate torte and Georgian coffee.

As I crossed the parking area in front of the hotel, I passed through a garden of pink and red roses. Although it was late in the summer, the fragrance was sweet and I thought that alone was worth the price of admission.

As I approached the massive revolving door, I saw a tall, slender woman in a miniskirt approaching the door from within. It was Maisa, the leggy (5'9") "Michelle Pfeiffer" of Tbilisi, a flute case tucked under her arm. She often stood by the grand piano in the lobby to entertain passing guests. We entered the slowly spinning door at the same moment, and she stopped and caught me as I stumbled out after a full turn. Laughing, she said, "I tried to call you, but you must have been hiding. I can't see you on Tuesday because it is my twenty-third birthday and my mother is having a *tamada*. You know, the Georgians look for any excuse to celebrate and make many wine toasts."

"No problem," I replied.

Then she said, "That Fred I met, the Boeing engineer, he is a nice man. He has tried to help me. He is also too young for me—maybe he is early thirties and is a bit provincial. I am a city bird, but Fred is just a well-educated cowboy from Seattle—well-meaning and boring, and I don't love him." She repeated for emphasis, "I don't love him."

I was amazed at her sensitivity. She had seen me writing in my binder on and off for several years. I had told her I was writing a book and screenplay about the "new" Georgia, so it was not inappropriate for me to ask her for a list of the songs she and the cellist played with the pianist. I let her know that I had recorded some of them. I told her I'd be needing authentic background music for my film and, being first flute in the world-class Georgian National Symphony, maybe she could provide it. "We could have the shadowy silhouette of a willowy Maisa, playing her silver flute as the credits roll by," I said.

She caught on and even sang a few bars of "The Shadow of Your Smile." She continued, "But, of course," and suggested that some popular Russian and Georgian songs must also be included. She did a little Central Asian wiggle and bump and said once again, for her own satisfaction, "I don't love Fred. You know that now. He is kind and decent."

I interrupted, "I am not always kind and decent."

She replied, "Oh, good. You will not bore me. Now, I can love you even more."

More than what? I wondered. *Whoa!* At this point, I couldn't get those legs out of my mind, so I jokingly said, "Forgive me, Maisa, but I think you have the most beautiful legs in all of Georgia."

"Maybe the Caucasus," she replied. Then after a pause, "The legs were good for climbing trees when I was a little girl. It felt good. It was maybe my first sex, I guess. You think?" She reached out and poked my arm with a pointed finger and said, "You think there is something wrong with the rest of my body? Why just my legs?"

Flustered, I replied, "Your mind also."

She laughed, "But, of course." She had to move on, as the blue-suited house security guard was watching. I sensed in some way that she belonged to the hotel. She added, "Next time we are together, I want to consummate our relationship."

I said, "Consummate? Really? How?"

She replied, "I remember one day you said you had never kissed a flute player before and that you had played the jazz trumpet in high school. Then suddenly you left before I could tell you that I had never kissed a trumpet player. We must explore this together." She then got a little academic, asking, "Do you know aperture, staccato, glissando?"

I blurted out, "Yes! I know all that stuff. Doesn't everybody?"

She replied, "I must be the only one not to have experienced it yet."

I asked, "Where shall we conduct this experiment? My place or yours?"

"Yours," she replied, adding, "my mother might become suspicious."

I began to hear the faint sound of "California Dreamer" in the back of my brain. It wasn't the little man who usually sits on my shoulder and whispers in my ear. This was the Mamas and the Papas, and they were getting louder and louder. Catching myself, I mused, *These people are so clever! When she performs, this baby can scan the whole roomful of action. She can pick and choose. Who pays for her clothes? She speaks excellent English. She's twenty-three, maybe going on thirty-three.* And then I admonished myself, *Hey, Mister! You're thirty-nine years older than she is! Doesn't that tell you something? "California Dreamer." Yeah, right!*

As Maisa passed on through the Rose Garden, she paused, turned her head to sniff the flowers and then, shifting her flute case, disappeared to a lower level. It was then that I realized I had once again survived one of the more seemingly benign hazards of my line of work. I mean, I did genuinely care for her and wished that she could have been whisked off her feet and taken back to Washington by the Boeing engineer. But maybe she didn't really want to be, and maybe she didn't care for me quite as much or in the way that I thought. I had to remind myself that she was still a possible adversary, and I noticed there was always the same guy in the vicinity whenever Maisa and I talked. Relationships had become more ambiguous since the fall of the Berlin Wall, as former enemies became something different.

I was a long way from home! As an independent contractor and a loner, I was not immune to the problems and pressures that affected the "regulars" in my profession. If you trace the evolution of the modern American intelligence community, you'll quickly notice the peaks and valleys of its success. Unfortunately, all too often, the goals and personalities of the various intelligence agencies were affected by the domestic policies currently in fashion. As a result, intelligence policy often lacked continuity or was short-term and ill-conceived in the first place. Intelligence gathering and its contributions to the effective operations of the State Department should be an ongoing and continuous operation. The intelligence baton *should* be passed from one administration to the next. Intelligence gathering is at its best only when it is objective and its collectors are trained to be objective. Therefore, passing the baton should *never* be linked to partisan politics.

During the past fifty years, I saw up close much of what went on in the intelligence community. The game changed frequently and so did the stresses exacted on those who played the game. Government-funded, directed by the executive branch, secretive, and badly treated by the press, operatives understand that high skill and personal danger are frequently accompanied by low pay. Sometimes, when I was functioning as an independent contractor, I put up my own money just to get the job done. For those few thousand assigned to foreign posts, the living conditions are not conducive to family life with the accompanying stability that family brings. In fact, many agency people marry within the agency, a practice that is encouraged for obvious reasons. Hiring policies tend to favor men because of the nature of the dangers faced by female operatives, including pregnancy and vulnerability to barbaric interrogation. But women also possess unique skills that can be especially effective in certain situations as part of covert operations.

Military engagements last a day, a week, even a couple of years, and when they are over, the participants go home and try to achieve some sense of normalcy and closure. A key element to this process is the recognition they receive—if not by the public at large, then by their government. Intelligence field personnel, on the other hand, especially those involved in lengthy covert activity in hostile places, are a very special breed. Uniquely qualified for special operations, many survive and retire while others quit. Unfortunately, hundreds more have been unceremoniously killed while on duty. In addition, there are the "walking wounded," those members who are psychologically scarred and damaged by the abnormalities of covert work.

Through the years, I met a number of these men in a support group where we could discuss our common problems in private with people who could understand and were willing to share their experiences. Women were not deliberately excluded, but at the time there were very few female covert agents and none ever showed up. We met in various locations throughout the San Francisco Bay Area. This group had a divorce rate of about 75 percent, alcoholism 60 percent, and drug use

30 percent, mostly prescription. Abusive behavior was also a common problem. During these group sessions, there would be a lot of sadness, a lot of laughs, a lot of *ignorance* about where the pain came from, and a giant need for approval. This was the wreckage of the silent war, and sometimes all we could do was cling to each other's commitment to God and country.

The members of my "walking wounded" group changed continually although, as in Alcoholics Anonymous, a few attended *every* meeting lest they slip over the edge. During the past twenty years, I probably met forty such troubled people. They were always checked out for "background," but out of the forty, there was only one I would consider truly psychopathic. There were, of course, always a few assholes (misfits by nature) who would attend, but basically they were a fine group of men, colorful by their diversity. The most interesting characteristic they had in common was the almost total lack of self-pity and cynicism that is so pervasive among bureaucrats and politicians today. They had chosen to serve their country and had accepted responsibility for their actions. Yes, there was a lot of griping about policy and the like, but for the most part, this was a tough-minded bunch of guys—hard-nosed professionals who had volunteered to play on an elite team.

New members often thought I was some sort of guest speaker as I was always older than the rest of the participants. We were all at different levels of maturity. I was often amazed at how mature some of the young men were. I viewed myself as sort of a late-bloomer emotionally. You know, forty-five going on twenty-five. More recently, I was labeled "Painless Parker" by one of the wittier chaps because of my lack of guilt or regret when referring to some of the more difficult moments I had experienced "on the road." I didn't need to rationalize things. "Yeah, shit happens. Maybe I compartmentalize. Maybe I'm insensitive. Maybe I'm in denial. Or, maybe I've just got my 'zone' and know how to use it when I need to!"

I always remember reading the inscription in my dad's bible given to him by his mother when he graduated from grammar school in 1909. It said:

> *Yesterday is gone, forget it.*
> *Today is yours, use it well.*
> *Tomorrow belongs to God, leave it alone.*

I had already had a breakdown of sorts in my early forties. I wandered off the straight and narrow for a year or two and took refuge in booze and women, which I discovered was a natural consequence of not dealing appropriately with my emotions. But, with the support of several good friends and my beloved wife, I pulled up my socks and kept on marching. I never lost hope, and with hope you maintain your will to win.

I love it when my heroes—George Shultz, James Baker, Ronald Reagan—unabashedly call themselves "eternal optimists." The great Antarctic explorer Ernest Shackleton asserted that "optimism is true moral courage." This is the only way to go. Hope is God's gift. Without it you are lost. Sadly, some of my friends lost hope and didn't make it.

Snapshot 14

String of Pearls

ALONG THE NORTHERN SLOPE of the Caucasus Mountains are the six Russian republics of Karachay-Cherkessia, Kabardino-Balkaria, North Ossetia, Ingushetia, Chechnya, and Dagestan, strung west to east along a line from the Black Sea to the Caspian Sea—a sub-Islamic necklace waiting to be pulled taut, thus decapitating the newly independent republics of Georgia, Armenia, and Azerbaijan. These inaccessible and inhospitable ethnic enclaves, each with its own language and separate dialects, have populations ranging from 400,000 to 700,000. Literacy is low. The Chechen and Ingushetian languages are considered among the oldest in the world, traced back as far as seven thousand years.

Over the course of twenty years, I traveled occasionally into these backward mountainous areas and often noticed a sort of local religion or cult common to most of them. My various Georgian drivers, most of whom were Christian, generally didn't know much about these places and cared even less, referring to the people who inhabited them as "hillbillies." They and other visitors passed off their religious activities as some sort of carryover of pagan rituals from the not-too-distant past, perhaps more out of denial than ignorance, thus blinding them to the simmering Islamic threat.

A more recent traveler to the region, Erla Zwingle of the National Geographic Society, said, "There are no trees, no telephones, and no Jesus" in these mountains. And it's true. As civilization falls away below the clouds and as the great jagged peaks give way to an even greater sky, you can easily give in to some sort of *natural piety* in awe of such grandeur. This is where the world ended according to the ancient Greeks, but *now* there is a peculiar combination of Christian and pagan elements. Lay priests perform animal sacrifices at pre-Christian shrines called "khati," and the vendetta, the obligation for revenge, is practiced. It is not advisable to call these people pagan because they think they're Christian.

What I have also noticed during my travels to the region is the extensive presence of a primarily Muslim ethnic group called the Kist scattered throughout the Caucasus. Their presence is somewhat obscured by their use of local language and customs, but their religious practices and Islamic style of architecture have not gone unnoticed by the people of Kakheti and there has been a lot of bloodshed between these two vaguely organized groups. Preserving land rights by the Kakhetians and extending territorial influences by the Kist are ongoing sources of conflict.

All this and heaven, too, above the clouds, where crystal torrents streak down dark-shadowed canyons, sheep graze on rocky hillsides below time-eroded peaks, and where, as Zwingle says, "the gods were first feared by Man." As you see heaven and earth merge together, is it any wonder that there is a confusion of spirits here—pagan, Christian, and Islamic—a good mix for the communist deity to stir and swirl?

The Russians have always had their eye on the Islamic expansionism on their southern border and were grateful to have the very high Caucasus Mountains to protect their southern flank. Until recently, only one highway crossed the mountains, the Georgian Military Highway, a second-class road in very poor condition that always shut down during the winter.

I thought I was the only outside person who had noticed the Islamic influence until one day when Eduard Shevardnadze commented that, "The Russians will regret messing around in South Ossetia, Abkhazia, and Chechnya, using them to manipulate regional power. It will come back to bite them." As had been their practice throughout the former Soviet Union as a method of control, the Russians would stir up the latent hostility in these autonomous border provinces, which would then require intervention. They eventually found out what Eduard Shevardnadze already knew—that Islamic extremists have been plucking on the necklace string for a long time. As a result, the Russians got more than they bargained for.

Traditionally, the Russians would blame the Chechens and the Georgians for endless political misdeeds and terrorism. "Georgian" and "Chechen" were dirty words in Moscow. During World War II, 600,000 Georgians served in the Soviet Army and 40 percent of them did not return home. And because Stalin didn't trust the loyalties of the Chechens, 400,000 of them were shipped eastward to Siberia for ten years until Khrushchev finally allowed them to return home. Little wonder the Chechens despise the Russians, and guess who was living in their homes while they were away? This hatred manifested itself more recently, of course, in the two disastrous Russian-Chechen wars of the 1990s and in subsequent terrorist bombings in Moscow. When speaking of Chechnya, Mirian would gloat over the "stupidity" of the Russian policy in the region, "An eighteenth-century mentality for a tenth-century situation."

Realistically, it is probably too late for the Russians *or* the Islamic extremists to take over the Caucasus because major oil and gas development in Azerbaijan, Turkmenistan, and Kazakhstan has brought huge investments from major foreign investors to the area. Also, there is no doubt that the Kremlin-controlled energy giant, Gazprom, would consider the Caucasus to be of vital interest to their overall natural energy strategy and would fight to oppose any future encroachments on their activities.

What are the Russians really afraid of? Loss of oil rights? Loss of subservient autonomous provinces for their political game-playing, allowing Chechnya to harbor terrorists, or Muslim Creep? What I have found is that many of the separatists have outside Islamic connections as well as Islamic-supplied weapons, and even Islamic names in their top leadership. No real progress has been made in resolving these problems, and at least 75,000 people have died for nothing. So, for now, the pearl necklace remains intact, but the Islamic luster continues to grow, even if in a somewhat dull fashion.

I wouldn't go into these areas today for any reason. If you don't get kidnapped by terrorists and held for ransom, you might get caught in the crossfire between skirmishing local militants and the Russian Army. And, of course, there is always the clear and present danger of diabolically placed land mines; nobody knows for sure where they were hidden or why. So what else is new? This is a very expensive string of pearls!

Chapter 32

On the Front of Over There
(Too Close for Comfort)

O N A WARM, SUNNY MORNING in May 1995, twenty "approved humanitarian aid workers" were at the Tbilisi Airport, standing by the loading stairs of a twin-engine Tupolev TU134, a plane much like our old workhorse DC-3. There was a party mood in the air. Working under the auspices of the United Nations High Commission for Refugees (UNHCR), most of the people knew each other from previous joint efforts, both in Georgia and in other trouble spots, some most recently from Rwanda. All of them had been trying to inspect the civil war scene in Abkhazia but had been unable to get access because of government restrictions on southern Georgia as well as Abkhazia. Finally, during the preceding week, a peace agreement had been secured which would, for the first time, allow some outside assistance from accredited nongovernmental organizations (NGOs).

An elite group of UN military police supervisors, mostly majors and captains as well as a colonel, had been stationed at a posh former Soviet officers' compound near the center of Sukhumi. They had been monitoring the action for several months. The job paid well and was noncombatant, and they were official observers at best. At the same time, Russian "peacekeepers" were being positioned south of Gali on the

Inguri River, ostensibly to maintain a cease-fire. However, one look at a map would show you that by doing so, it really moved the Russian border two hundred miles inside Georgia, effectively isolating Abkhazia.

The party started when the plane left the ground. Cognac was splashed into the morning coffee. Burt Arbuckle, a bearded South African with an enormous stomach framed by suspenders, had a small suitcase made from a crocodile killed in the river near his home in Mombassa, Kenya. A Hemingway-like character, Burt was sixty, but looked seventy-five. He turned his small suitcase into a makeshift table and placed it in the middle of the aisle, serving Georgian champagne to his inner group seated around him. Obviously he had done this before. Burt was a pretty good crooner and an excellent whistler. For the next two days he would take requests. He knew the words to about forty songs. The group would sing along—a favorite was *"Ochi Chyornye"* ("Dark Eyes"). Three Frenchmen kept to themselves on the plane and seemed disgusted by it all.

As a whole, the group was a tough, combat-hardened collection of intellectuals, and there wasn't a phony do-gooder among them. They all were immediately interested and skeptical of this Mr. Waste from the Hoover Institution and Kaiser Permanente International. The major topics of conversation during the flight were getting laid and writing position papers to justify their next grants. They lived from grant to grant.

We landed at Adler Airport, just inside the Russian border, about ten miles from the Black Sea and the Russian resort city of Sochi. We tossed our night bags aboard a waiting bus. Our leader, originally from Bangladesh, was the Deputy UNHCR Director in Georgia. He wore a suit and tie and took care of all the amenities. Crossing the border into Abkhazia required *somebody's* political approval, which we had, and two armed Abkhaz guards got aboard to accompany us.

A white UN Land Rover led the bus south for seventy miles along the semitropical coast road with its rocky beaches. Every third house or so was damaged. No doors or windows, some blackened by fire, others stripped of their roofs. Signs of looting were everywhere. I started counting the number of "cleansed" homes. By the time we entered the outskirts of Sukhumi, I had counted more than one thousand such houses along the seventy-mile stretch. Sukhumi had been shelled for months from a crescent of hills overlooking the city. The shelling was not systematic, but many government buildings and apartments had been badly damaged. A number of ten-story buildings were windowless and blackened, and the City's famous Victorian-style Botanical Gardens were a tangled mess of broken glass, twisted iron, and horticultural wreckage. The Russian officers' resort to which we were assigned had large, wood-paneled rooms with baths. It reminded me of the Presidio in San Francisco. Luxurious, considering!

In the afternoon, we toured the city and were given a briefing by a Swedish UN colonel. We then met at the city hall with Enver Kapba, vice premier minister of the so-called "Republic of Abkhazia." He was also chairman of the committee for refugees. He gave us a twenty-minute welcome, occasionally checking over his shoulder for the approval of three burly Russians, two of whom never took off their overcoats despite the ninety-degree weather.

The conference room was filled by *our* party, the Abkhazians, and the Russians. During the meeting, it was stated that the Russians would have to protect the border because 250,000 ethnic Georgians had been evicted from Abkhazia, with twenty thousand killed and four times that many wounded, injured, or sick, a very convenient excuse for Russian intervention. Abkhazia calling itself an independent republic made me think of Marin County, California, declaring itself independent and demanding international recognition. But what it really was, of course, was a blatant Russian land grab so that the two great resort cities of Sochi and Sukhumi could be reconnected, just like old times.

Next came the question-and-answer session, which was given by a woman from USAID named Denise. Getting right to the point, her best question was, "Who hands out the relief supplies if we set up here?"

The puppet vice premier responded, "We do!"

"Who's 'we'?" Denise fired back.

The vice premier shrugged. "The Republic of Abkhazia, of course."

Denise, blonde and thirty-five or so, looked skeptical. "Would you repeat that?" The vice premier repeated himself, and then a wonderful thing happened. All of our humanitarian group and other NGOs rose in unison and moved toward the door.

The vice premier was instantly bracketed by two of the burly Russians, as he shouted at the humanitarian group, "Please, please. I misunderstood what you ask. Stay, please. Be seated, please." As the humanitarian group returned to their seats, the visibly shaken vice premier heaved a sigh of relief and said, "Oh, thank you! Oh, thank you so very much!"

The rest of the meeting went very well. Our group, in its wisdom, had established its position of power—after all, we had what they wanted! That's how it works. As we left city hall, we noticed that the vice premier had been whisked away. No more Q & A for him, today! We were then taken to a Turkish restaurant where we had a loud and wet meal. The French guys had a separate table. The joke at dinner that night was, "Only a Turk can make money in this town."

The next morning at our military compound in Sukhumi, I buddied up with a thirty-five-year-old doctor from the Sudan named Ali Mootram Akra, who reminded me of former Seattle Seahawks quarterback Warren Moon. It started with Dr. Akra giving me some Advil to relieve a gimpy ankle. He spoke perfect English and had studied at Brown University and the John Hopkins School of Medicine but couldn't go home. He described Sudan as a place where Francis Ford Coppola should have filmed *Apocalypse Now*. He said that the rest of the world had no idea what a disaster this area was. I walked with him up the lush tropical pathway past the women's quarters and headed for the great Iron Gates, which had surly Abkhaz and Russian guards on duty. It was not hard to tell them apart, as the Abkhaz wore whites socks and were sloppy.

We showed our special visitors' passes to the guards, and Denise, who happened to be from Mill Valley, California, shouted at us, "Wait up!" She had been trying to make a social connection with my handsome Sudanese doctor friend, but he wasn't interested and we continued walking across the street to a kiosk to get some cigarettes. Looking back, we could see Denise approaching the gates. Two other members of our party had already appeared at the gates and then walked toward the harbor on the right. Denise was not far behind.

A German aid worker wearing sunglasses like mine was murdered during a UNHCR-sponsored humanitarian trip to Abkhazia.

Suddenly, we heard racing engines and the squeal of under-inflated tires. Two cars that looked like rusty old Pontiacs were coming right at us. A drag race? Without hesitation, Dr. Akra pushed me backward. I fell awkwardly over a crumbling wall and into a building, with the doctor on top of me. AK-47 rounds began ripping the air and splattered against the wall across the street. A white UN Land Rover turned around and was coming up fast. The guards from the gate were scrambling for cover. Denise was screaming and pointing down the street away from the gates, where the two guys were down and one was struggling to get up. Denise went for help. We went over to the victims. The shorter of the two, a Belgian, had a bullet hole in each shoulder. The second guy, a German, was crumpled up against the wall with blood splattered all around him. Dr. Akra attended to him and was shocked to see that the top of his head was missing. The missing three inches of skull was clinging to the wall by strands of flesh. But then, almost matter-of-factly, he took what looked to be a bloody divot and tried to gently pat it back in place. Just as matter-of-factly, he picked up a pair of dark, wraparound sunglasses and asked me, "Aren't these yours?"

I replied, "No, but by God, they sure could have been!" And I wondered if moments like these were common in the Sudan.

Denise was by the gate as the UN emergency people arrived in an ambulance. Dr. Akra went to work on the Belgian's shoulder wounds. He would return to Georgia with us the following afternoon. The dead German was boxed up, and it was decided to drop his body off at the German Embassy in Tbilisi when we got back. Although tragic, the killing didn't matter much to me personally, and I didn't have any reason to exploit the situation.

After recovering our senses, a bus picked up the fourteen of us still wanting to go south to Gali and the Inguri River Bridge, which marked the border between Abkhazia and Georgia. The ride to the Inguri River border was scenic but full of "cleansed" houses and wrecked facilities. On the way, we visited several rural hospitals and passed through the town of Ochamchire. Much to the delight of our party, the road sign to Ochamchire presented a natural opportunity for our leader in song, Burt Arbuckle, to break into *"Oh Chamchire—Ochi chyornye,"* and he sang the revised song with gusto.

At the river, we were able to walk across into Georgia on a collapsed automobile bridge. There were a lot of very young, blond soldiers standing around with cartridge belts draped over their shoulders and cigarettes hanging from their lips. You could sense their hostility and arrogance, but it was their immaturity that really scared me. You could see it in their eyes that they had recently taken the lives of others.

The only Russian we saw there was a general who looked like an Uzbek. We set up a picnic lunch and the general joined us. He was mildly friendly and enjoyed our gourmet tea. Orchards of orange trees spread as far as the eye could see, right to the foot of the snow-capped Caucasus Mountains—gorgeous *Georgian* real estate!

Later that evening, we had dinner back at the Officers' Club in Sukhumi, courtesy of the UNHCR. We sat on a long porch with the Black Sea making little slopping noises on the pebbled beach a few yards away. The three Frenchmen were with us but never got close, always sitting by themselves. I thought to myself, *What's with these guys?* They seemed smart and tough enough, but it was as if they wanted to remain invisible. I asked Denise, the woman who had trumped the Abkhaz vice premier, if they had a national inferiority complex after losing two wars. "Hell, no!" she replied. "The bastards think they're better than anyone else. They *do* have an old culture and a beautiful language, you know. But Frenchmen are lousy lovers. They have little dicks and no control…" Denise was on her eighth glass of something but kept on talking. Then, out of the blue, she said, "I was a cheerleader at Tamalpais High in Marin County before I went to UC Berkeley."

Astounded, I responded, "I was the *student body president* at Tamalpais before going to UC Berkeley!" She began to rub her neck and we made some more small talk until she asked me if I still had any of that Advil. Then she wanted to know if I gave backrubs, to which I replied, "Yeah, backrubs are my specialty—with or without the Advil."

She lit up a Turkish cigarette and asked, "Will you give me a rub *down*?"

"Or up?" I responded.

She smiled. "That's the best part of a workout, isn't it?"

"Depends on the workout."

"I need an adjustment right here," she said, pointing below her navel. "Are you also chiropractic?"

"The best," I replied.

"Where's your room? When I finish this cigarette, I want you to adjust me. Fix my old cheerleader zigzag. Isn't that what you guys say?"

I took a couple puffs off her long cigarette as we talked, and when we stood up I realized that it had been laced with hashish. "I like your cigarette," I told her.

"You'll like it better in a few minutes. You will!" she said emphatically.

We stopped at her room for a few supplies and continued on to my room. I shoved two beds in front of the double door that opened out into the balcony. A very yellow, crescent moon was low in the sky. The Black Sea was indigo. The sound of forties big band music came up from the lawn. Denise's clothing fell onto the floor. She was very hot. Her hips and pubic area bumped and shook. She couldn't wait! She was helping herself now, digging and groaning. It was as if she was saying to me, "Hurry up, buddy, or I go it alone." I did. She did. *We* did! Multiple. Endless. Crazy. A couple of show-offs. This wasn't about romance. This was about *anger*, hers and mine, and even though our issues were different, the game was the same. After such a day, the contrast in feelings was incredible. She kept saying, "Had enough? Do you want to give up?" She called it, "Fuck fighting." She was many years younger than I, and I wondered what I had missed by coming along a generation earlier.

"Can I wake you up for more?" she asked.

"Sure," I said. She didn't. Maybe it was better.

The next day began at eight o'clock when we took the motor coach back into Russia to the airport at Adler. The wounded Belgian had been doped up, and the dead German was brought up in a white UN recon car. The airport was jammed with vacationing Russians headed back to Moscow. Every time Denise and I made eye contact, she would rub her cheek and slyly stick her tongue out at me.

We sloshed onto our Georgian Airlines charter and, to nobody's surprise, Burt Arbuckle set up his suitcase table in the aisle and produced six bottles of vodka and brandy. He whistled the *"Marseillaise,"* which finally got a smile out of the Frenchmen. Soon we were all singing *"Oh Chichania,"* with dozens of dirty verses. As we landed, we were singing, *"On the road to Kutaisi, where Russian girls are greasy, and where the playing fishes fly. . ."*

We were a bit more subdued as we got off the plane, having had a chance to think about the last two days. People picking us up at the airport had heard about the shooting. The wire services had spun it around the world. The German ambassador claimed the box with the dead German. A May 10, 1995 dispatch reported that:

> A German humanitarian aid worker was shot and killed by unknown assassins outside the entrance to the UN Headquarters in Sukhumi, Abkhazia (Georgia). Gerhard Langer and a Belgian, who survived, were visiting Abkhazia to offer aid to this war-

ravaged provincial capital. Langer's purpose
for being there was obviously unappreciated.

The story failed to mention that Langer was blue-eyed and
wearing white Nike shoes. He looked like he could have been
my younger brother! Perhaps the assassination was a warning,
but a warning to whom? Or maybe all four of us were the targets and, thanks to Dr. Akra's quick thinking, they missed the
doctor and me.

Denise disappeared into the night. A week later she was
transferred by the USAID people to Almaty, Kazakhstan. I never
saw her again, but she will always be with me in bad times. She
was a gamer, a real pro. She asked hard questions.

Snapshot 15

"Dr. Advil"

A FEW YEARS after the assassination in Sukhumi, I was having an early dinner at Betsy's Guest House in Tbilisi. As I
entered the second-story dining room, the candles had already
been lit and the ten tables set. A window was open at one end
of the room, which bent the flickering flames in my direction.
I could hear cars climbing the hill in front of the hotel, tires
bobbling over the cobblestones. The only person there for the
seven o'clock seating was in the corner by the window. Betsy,
always a hands-on hostess, would typically hold court in the
TV room across the hall with cocktails until eight o'clock, and
then the guests would pour into the dining room. My usual
table was about as far away as you could get from the guest in
the corner, who was in his late thirties, handsome, and black.
I knew immediately that I should join him because that's what
we do at Betsy's. Betsy's is like a boarding house for the regulars and, anyhow, people might think I was avoiding him or
something.

"Do you mind if I join you?" we both asked simultaneously
and half rose from our chairs.

"I'll move," he answered, "it's too noisy here by the window."
My dinner partner was slender, with light coffee-brown skin
and a small mustache.

"Hey, don't I know you?" we again both said at the same time.

"You're the California guy on the UN-sponsored Sukhumi trip, right?"

I replied, "You're the 'Advil doctor,' *persona non grata* from the Sudan, who knocked me over the wall when the shooting began. I never really thanked you properly for saving my life!"

Dr. Akra replied, "Well, I never really thanked *you* for taking that NGO lady off my hands! She was getting pretty aggressive. So maybe we're even."

I always find it a happy moment when you run into someone like this on the road. We rattled on for an hour and a half and didn't even notice the room had filled with revelers from across the hall who were finally hungry. We didn't know any of them and they didn't need us anyway, or at least they didn't think they did.

If there was a message in our meeting, it was that we were *still* working the project, which was the rehabilitation of a once grand culture and region. We were both in it for the long haul.

By this time, Tbilisi was on its fourth U.S. ambassador. The pioneer NGOs were gone and the follow-up people, judging by their conversations, were just beginning to learn what Dr. Akra and I had learned years earlier. Their intentions and qualifications were good, but the institutional or corporate memory was not there. There was no continuity, and most of these new people had to learn from scratch. No wonder it takes so long to grow an infrastructure, especially when there is extensive dependence on foreign assistance.

We enjoyed sharing these and other perspectives and agreed to keep "marching uphill" before vowing to meet again in a couple of years. As we warmly shook hands and gave each other a mini hug, I couldn't help but ask him if he had played rugby when he was a student at Brown University.

"No," he replied, but he told me he did very well in soccer football, starting for the varsity for three years. He was their star "striker." I knew all along that there was a special quality about him. He had a winning attitude and, even though he wasn't a rugby player, I had sensed it. Then as we parted, he couldn't resist asking, "How was it? You know what I mean, with the NGO broad, I mean *lady,* that night? She wasn't really my type, too pushy."

I replied, "Mine either, and she was *no* lady!" Broad smiles appeared on our faces. This guy, this doctor, a political refugee from the Sudan, was a class act, a true citizen of the world. I don't even know whether he was a Muslim or not. It never came up.

Chapter 33

Happy Days in Dutch Flat
(My First World)

WHILE WRITING THIS MEMOIR, it became apparent to me that my activities overseas working for Bechtel may have appeared strange to others. But quite the contrary is true. I had not yet joined the intelligence agencies, although I talked to them on a regular basis. My first forty-five years were full of happy times. I met and married Marilyn at UC Berkeley when we were just twenty-two and twenty. By the time she was thirty, we had four children, born in four different U.S. cities, and a fifth born later in Tenby, Wales with the help of a midwife.

As I was a field construction engineer and project manager with Bechtel Corporation, we moved to a series of big projects, mainly pipelines, refineries, and steam power plants, approximately every year and a half. We were allowed to take one thousand pounds of personal effects for all of us. I was only one-seventh of this family, and out of necessity Marilyn was the commanding officer. The kids depended on each other for friendships, and I depended on Marilyn to be the road manager. She was a "brick." We had fun. People would stare at us when we descended on a restaurant. Moving was arduous but rewarding. All along, I promised to put down some roots in California when the kids were in their teens.

So after twenty years on the road, we bought a house in Marin County so that the kids could finish their education there. This was about the time I had my midlife crisis (burnout) and quit Bechtel. After a few stops along the way (stockbrokering and antiquing), I found my true calling in the intelligence business. At first, my travels to so many exotic and Third World countries were no big deal for Marilyn to understand, although she did notice my new ability to detach from the physical and emotional problems of home and family and focus on the job ahead. She always noticed my withdrawal, edginess, detachment, and "absent" eyes—my game face—before every trip, but seemed to accept my need to compartmentalize my activities. Much later, I began revealing some of these activities, especially during the course of writing this memoir. As far as other women, Marilyn mentioned after reading an early draft that she didn't feel any sense of anger or betrayal because our marriage was so solid and because she understood there was another life during wartime. But she also let me know, in no uncertain terms, that had she known of the dangerous and violent situations I frequently found myself in, she *never* would have let me go. Instinctively, that's why I didn't tell her.

Moving to upscale Marin County was not without its costs, especially when we had to deal with provincial society. At dinner parties, people invariably wanted to hear about my latest trip overseas. That could be a little tricky because of my garrulous nature, and I had to always be guarded about what I said. Of course, the CIA had warned me about this aspect of the work. They also realized it was one of my chief role-playing cover tricks, along with carrying way too much luggage, both unlikely characteristics of a covert operative, constantly reminding me that I would have no diplomatic immunity if anything went wrong. Eventually, I got permission to tell people that I was traveling overseas in large part to monitor the collapsing economy and infrastructure of the Soviet Union on behalf of the State Department.

Often when I got back from my travels, I would be called upon by our friends to entertain their friends. I think the hostesses would typically invite me there not to educate but as a curiosity to entertain. The women's interest quickly faded. The men, after trying to apply what they had read in *Newsweek* or *Time* to our conversation, would lose interest just as fast. I suspect that my lifestyle and hands-on, real-world experience was just too far removed from their worlds. It didn't help, of course, that Marilyn and I were nondrinkers, and we soon lost interest in attending these affairs.

We eventually took refuge in the Sierra Nevada Mountains. In the early sixties, while I was in Pembrokeshire, West Wales, I bought a house in Alta Dutch Flat, California, sight unseen. My father had phoned to tell me that Quartz Lodge, built in 1883, was for sale. It had eight bedrooms, a carriage house, and, best of all, was located on a beautiful round, wooded mountain lake, elevation 4,000 feet. Hot in the summer was 95 degrees, but cold in the winter was only 25 degrees. At first it was a summer home and later our primary home. The kids loved the scene. Each had his or her own bedroom. There was canoeing, fishing, and hiking. The house was full of early Western antiques and collectibles. Deer, bears, and an occasional mountain lion traversed our property regularly.

Both when we moved every year or so, and later when I was gone for three to six weeks at a time, Marilyn and I tried to spend quality time with our kids and to expose them to a range of experiences they couldn't get in the best suburban schools. All we really asked of the kids was that they finish college, and they all did, in spite of rock-and-roll distractions. Stephen, the "experimental" firstborn, survived the sixties and ended up with two M.A. degrees and a Ph.D., the latter from the University of Washington. He now works for the U.S. Geological Survey as Director of the Columbia River Research Laboratory, which conducts research on endangered fish and their aquatic habitats throughout the Western states. Corby graduated from Evergreen State College in Olympia, Washington, and is now a senior artist and computer-graphics designer at the NASA Jet Propulsion Lab in Pasadena; his artist concepts of the Mars missions have been seen worldwide. Shawn, mother of three, was a cheerleader at UC Berkeley and later a professional modern-jazz dancer; she earned her B.A. at "Cal" and is now a National Board certified teacher, specializing in early childhood education. Jamie, a high-school football star, played rugby at UC Berkeley, was house manager of the Sigma Phi fraternity, and is currently executive director of Alaska Public Broadcasting Inc. Late in my career, I actually got to play against him in Cal Memorial Stadium in a regular league game (which my team won). Tenby was born in Tenby, Wales; she graduated from UCLA, has three daughters, and works as a marketing associate for a national food-distribution company. All in all, I think we did a pretty good job as parents, but it was the kids' own special characters that shined through.

I began winding down my rugby playing days about the time I got heavily involved in the intelligence business. After a while, there was no need to take teams to Europe or the Soviet Union, and I took up competitive running. As it turned out, running was a huge asset for getting me innocently into places I might not otherwise have been able to get into and to see things I might not otherwise have been able to see. I also got into Master's (over thirty-five) track and field. I ran marathons, cross-country, and, on the track, the 400-meter hurdles and 3,000-meter steeple chase. At the end of my career, I made it to the Masters World Olympic Games twice. At six feet, my weight had dropped from 180 to 155.

To top everything off, Marilyn took up running ("to stay thin"), and within a couple of years was the second fastest middle distance runner in her age group in the U.S. (forty-five to fifty). She won four gold medals in the 800, 1,500, 5,000, and 10,000 meters on two 100-degree days at the Nationals in Wichita. She was gifted and, much to my surprise, this lovely and friendly lady had a hidden killer instinct on the track. It made me mad when she quit after a couple of years of success. I was jealous of her natural talent and spirit and that she could quit so easily after accomplishing her goals.

Of course, this is precisely what I couldn't do. I couldn't just compete or finish a competition and go home satisfied. This was just sport, but my need to get into stressful situations and engage in diplomatic and humanitarian aid only seemed to intensify. By the mid-nineties, much of my personal influence with Eduard Shevardnadze was beginning to fade because by this time, he was surrounded by his own people and, for better or worse, he was further isolated because of the 1995 assassination attempt. I was still interested in helping Georgia with humanitarian efforts, but it seemed the perfect time to slow down and let others carry on. But I couldn't seem to stop my compulsion to observe and report on all the hot spots in the region, to still be in the game. I just couldn't let go. I remained powerless to stop this urge, and so well into my sixties I was still going into dangerous situations on a regular basis.

Chapter 34

The Ultimate Betrayal
(A Shot in the Dark)

O N A LATE SUMMER AFTERNOON in 1993 while on a Sunday outing with friends, a CIA officer was reputably killed by a single bullet that smashed into his forehead, above his right eye. The victim was Fred Woodruff of Herndon, Virginia. A married father of three, Fred was a seasoned career CIA employee, temporarily assigned to the U.S. Embassy in Tbilisi. He was on loan to the State Department to serve as a security advisor to President Shevardnadze. Woodruff had been living at the Metechi Hotel for the past four months since being assigned to the embassy.

The case remains shrouded to this day. According to reports, Shevardnadze's chief security officer and bodyguard, Eldar Gugusladze, invited Woodruff and two women friends to join him for a drive into the Caucasus Mountains for a spectacular view of snow-capped Mount Kazbek, followed by a country meal with local friends. At the end of the day, the four headed back along the two-lane Georgian Military Highway toward the city. Woodruff was in the back seat of a two-door Russian Niva jeep with a friend, Marina Kapanadze, a thirty-year-old linguist who moonlighted as a waitress at the Metechi's tenth-floor cocktail lounge. The jeep, plainly marked as a government vehicle, had driven slowly past a rural roadblock security stop after a wave of recognition. A hundred yards down the road, Woodruff turned to glance through the rear window at the lone figure who had waved them through. Suddenly, he slumped over and, to Marina's horror, blood came gushing out of his head. Fred died on the country road before he could be helped, or so the reports said.

Fred had always been adventurous and frequently requested difficult assignments, but this time he was terribly unlucky. Or was he? I had left Tbilisi a week before the incident and was shocked to read of Fred's death. Marina was personable and I thought there was nothing unusual about these four going for an outing in the mountains. People got together and went sight-seeing all the time. I know I did.

I had met Fred on several occasions and passed along my personal observations on the vulnerability of the new president to almost any serious would-be assassin. I noticed during an earlier inspection that the men assigned to guard and protect the Georgian leader had a habit of looking the wrong way—watching their leader rather than the crowd from which an assassin might spring. My confidante Lou Jefferson had told me many times that, "If you watch the person you're protect-ing instead of those around him, you might have a chance to see him die—but that's about it." I told Fred an assassin could take the president out any time in a number of ways. I also showed him the main "contact" points on his office and, to stress the danger, told him that even *I* could toss a rugby ball into Shevardnadze's third-story window from the top of the building across a narrow side street. I had reported my concerns for the president's safety to our embassy, as well. Ironically, two years later this same street would be the scene of an assassination at-tempt against Shevardnadze when a car bomb was detonated.

Fred was a friendly guy and at the time of his death not on any kind of spy agenda that I knew of. Our country was officially trying to help Georgia get on its feet, realizing that Georgia desperately needed the leadership of her native son, Eduard Shevardnadze. Additionally, private individuals such as George Shultz, James Baker, and George Bush were all supporters of this new Central Asian democracy, with its constitution patterned after ours. Fred understood the broad array of enemies Shevardnadze had acquired, including Gamsakhurdia's separatists, North Ossetians, Chechens, *Mafiya,* and, at the top of the list, the Russians.

Shortly after Fred was killed, assistant secretary of state and Soviet expert Strobe Talbot hastily announced that it was "okay" for Woodruff to be in Georgia because there was a presidential and congressional "finding" that officially sanctioned it. This unfortunate public statement was killed almost immediately, but the cat was already out of the bag—*Georgia had been cleared for covert activities*. Now everybody would want to know what was going on there. CIA Director at the time, James Woolsey, flew in for a memorial service and to escort Woodruff's body home. Shevardnadze had gladly accepted the aid of U.S. security specialists and was personally embarrassed and depressed that his own security team had been violated. People in the intelligence community were appalled at the ineptness and carelessness of President Clinton and the State Department, which placed all of us at an increased danger level.

As an independent contractor, I was often disappointed by the lack of support for my operations, especially during the Clinton administration. I would be told that, "Your area—Central Asia—is not exactly at the top of the administration's priority list, but we want you to continue as best you can. We need you there and highly value your role in that area and the info you collect, as well as your perspective." Bottom line—I personally paid for a lot of the government's business. I didn't hesitate, nor do I have any regrets about this aspect of my activities. I just knew the job had to be done. But, in retrospect, this lack of focus on that part of the world, and the all too often inattention and follow-up to my reports, proved costly in terms of American lives and intelligence failures.

A couple years after Woodruff's death, at an informal meeting in California, James Woolsey and I were talking shop. After hearing my complaints about the lack of attention by the administration regarding Central Asia and the Caucasus, he joked—as he'd joked with others—"I hear you! Remember the guy who crashed his small plane onto the White House lawn? That was me trying to get an appointment to see President Clinton!" Woolsey had resigned as Director of Central Intelligence after less than two years.

Fred Woodruff's alleged shooter, twenty-one-year-old Anzor Sharmaidze, was rounded up and confessed to the crime, only to later recant at trial, claiming his confession had been coerced. The presiding judge, Jemal Leonidze, with twelve years on the bench, based his evaluation on the statements of several witnesses, including Marina Kapanadze, as well as the ballistics evidence. Leonidze stated, "It was a simple case. But then you can never be sure."

From my first hearing of the circumstances of Fred's death to the sentencing of Sharmaidze for his chance killing, the case seemed to pose more questions than answers. As a longtime shooting enthusiast, I was troubled by the marksmanship of the twenty-one-year-old peasant-militia man and considered this well-placed bullet a long shot, maybe one in five hundred, or more likely, one in five *thousand*—a hole in one. Perhaps robbery was a motive, or this could have been a grudge shooting, but there was always the possibility that Marina was working for the KGB, who didn't like the CIA apparently meddling in Russia's backyard. And there were many other possibilities that I don't think even got proper consideration. The legal proceedings were all too quick and neat for me.

Several months earlier, I had passed through Moscow and spent several hours in the office of the *New York Times* with Moscow bureau chief Steve Erlanger. I had correctly represented myself as a coordinator of an NGO health organization working in Georgia dispensing much-needed supplies and wanted to check on several people I was working with. Things were slow that day and, as a courtesy to me, they got on the computer and followed up on a lot of leads. Among other things, I learned that Woodruff had recently traveled in Central Asia and had briefly been involved in the counter-narcotics section of the CIA which, in and of itself, meant nothing out of the ordinary at the time.

However, a few months after Woodruff's death, "super spy" Aldrich Ames was arrested and I began picking up on coincidences that seemed to link the two in close proximity around the time of Fred's death. I learned that Ames had visited Tbilisi shortly before Woodruff was killed on August 8, 1993, and quietly passed on to my higher-ups my observation about a possible overlap of responsibilities and areas of influence.

Ames had ostensibly come to Georgia because it was a major transport route for heroin, hashish, cocaine, and opium from Asia to Europe via Turkey, Bulgaria, and Rumania. It's possible that he sold traffickers information on drug operations that he had gathered during his most recent posting at the agency's counter-narcotics center. Perhaps Woodruff *told* Ames about some Georgian officials' involvement in drug dealing and, perceiving possible exposure, Ames put the spotlight on the potential whistle-blower and the local *Mafiya* did the dirty deed. My guess—and that's all it really is—was that Ames had been tipped off that Woodruff was hot on his trail and might be fully aware of what Ames was doing. These conclusions were all speculation, but the dots were there and I felt the need to expedite things by connecting a few of them to attract interest from a not-always-alert operation.

But what *actually* happened on that fateful picnic may never be known or only exist in secret files. I, for one, will never believe Fred's death was any "chance killing." One thing is certain—both the Georgian and American governments wanted to put the suspicions to rest, and they put a spin on it that was probably, under the circumstances, helpful in eventually nailing Ames. As for Ames, he will never tell all he knows because this is how he bargains to avoid execution as one of the two or three worst traitors of all times.

At any rate, when Mr. Ames was arrested on February 20, 1994, he was accused of working for Moscow for the past nine years and, in doing so, had betrayed at least ten of our important foreign operatives, all of whom were executed by the KGB in the basement of Lubyanka. Up until that time, Ames had fingered only foreign operatives, and this would have been his first fellow countryman. How Ames, a genuine scumbag, got away with it all is another story and is well documented. But for now, Woodruff's "star" hangs on a wall in Langley, Virginia, "one of the few" killed in the line of duty.

For my part, as an independent contractor I would not have been on Ames' shit list, although he had access to the identity of all but the most sensitive operatives. Likewise, CIA "supertraitor" Harold J. Nicholson betrayed the names of all the new operatives trained in the two years prior to his capture in 1996 and, again, I didn't qualify. However, I *was* asked to stay out of Moscow specifically, and Russia in general, until further notice because the "office" wasn't sure what "they" thought I knew. Fortunately, new air services had been developed and the necessity of going to Central Asia via Russia was greatly diminished for me.

Those of us close to the incident had plenty of time to discuss and speculate about it, but my job was to report what I actually saw. That is the role of the foreign observer. Overseas human intelligence is perhaps 15 percent of the CIA budget and 3 percent of the overall national intelligence operation. None of this money is set aside specifically for my speculations. The dot-connecting is the job of the policymakers and analysts in the home office. That's the nature of the business. Compartmentalization is essential. Our enemies are particularly adept at keeping secrets in the family—small cells, no written documents, etc. We *try* to do the same, but a bureaucracy is a bureaucracy, and in our land of many freedoms, covert activities frequently become public too soon to be effective, but not too soon to be politically embarrassing to our leaders and deadly dangerous to the men and women in the field.

A natural result of this compartmentalization is that I usually don't know what higher-ups think about my presentations other than "That's interesting, go on" or "Thank you, keep in touch." There is rarely instant gratification for me, and if I needed it, I would probably be in another line of work. Often having little to go on, the intelligence can be flat out wrong and, as a result, the agency publicly humiliated. So "tight mouth, no talk" is the rule. Ironically, a disciplined group of agency people can be quite boring, particularly young ones in the presence of their superiors.

However, I always figure that as an independent contractor and an older guy, I can offer a few *opinions*. When I do, I get a collage of reactions that run the gamut from increased rate of breathing, sighs, and squirming to averted eyes, hands over mouths, and shrug-of-shoulder moments. Best of all is the furious note-taking on ubiquitous small pieces of paper, and I always wonder what it was I just said.

After debriefing, one of my favorite case officers would take me by the elbow and say, "Let's you and I go for a little walk in the woods. I want to hear what that little bird you often refer to on your shoulder has to say." Of course, it is not company policy to go any further into two-way conversation on most matters. I am not *supposed* to know what happens next, and I do understand that. It affects the raw nature of the product, and besides, you can't tell strangers what you don't know, and I want *them* to understand that, too. The less you know, the safer you are.

I have found out, however, with the patience I developed in my later years, that if I keep an eye on the "big screen," at some point in time the answers to most of my questions will slide by my brain like messages on a ticker tape, often in the shower or while I'm jogging. Connecting the dots is mainly for the bosses, but even children can connect the dots in their coloring books and come up with the correct picture, if they have the right dots. You work with what you've got.

I will never know if what I came up with about Aldrich Ames, my speculations about Chernobyl, or, later, for that matter, notorious British traitor John Cairncross, were useful dots that helped my superiors come up with the correct picture. What I *do* know is that the right people got the right information not long after my reports. So, knowing that company policy has severe limits on feedback, I must allay my personal frustration and rely on my *own* self-gratification, if you will.

Chapter 35

Vladivostok and Ulan Bator
(On Being First)

A s a child I loved being first in things, no matter what. It
was sort of a game I played to amuse myself. Later, as an
adult, I especially wanted to be first with anything concern-
ing the old Soviet Union or the New Russia which followed
the breakup. I pride myself on having taken the first American
rugby team to northern Europe, then to eastern Europe and,
not long after, to the Soviet Union as well.

I got a kick out of the fact that I was the first to wear Western style wraparound Porsche Carrera sunglasses and white
Nike running shoes when I jogged my daily five or six miles
on hills and through narrow streets from Moscow to Tashkent.
Generally, people were either surprised or amused, or both,
to see me, because at that time the Soviet people ran only in
parks, the countryside, at sporting clubs, or in actual competition. I purposely avoided busy streets while jogging because on
two different occasions I witnessed drive-by shootings. I especially remember during the early nineties when the Republic
of Georgia was going through its post-Soviet Union civil wars,
with its curfews, blockades, and roving "Georgian cowboys,"
how bullets would sometimes splatter all around me.

On one occasion in Tbilisi, while jogging beside the Kura
River—which flows from Turkey through Georgia to the

Caspian Sea—I ran under a lovely mosaic-tiled overpass. As I did, two passing cars fired fully automatic AK-47 rounds, which ricocheted off the walls and ceiling. When I felt the wind of one bullet crease the top of my head, I hit the ground and then leaped up, turned around, and ran in the opposite direction until a mile and two overpasses were behind me, whereupon the incident was repeated. Although President Shevardnadze had dismissed this sort of thing as only so much "hooliganism," I decided I had had enough running in public for a while.

As a result of incidents like these, to this day I am nervously aware of cars that slow down near me or pull alongside while I'm jogging. I never stop. I immediately look for an alternate route. Even at my home in California's High Sierras, I get pretty defensive if a car slows down behind me. Two of my former associates were murdered while at home on leave. The stage we dance on is worldwide.

But, whether it involved athletics or going to remote places in the old Soviet Union, I was always looking for "firsts." That's why, when I heard in 1992 that Aeroflot had started flying from San Francisco directly over the North Pole, I waited a few months before flying to Magadan, Siberia. From there I flew to Khabarovsk, a drab Soviet outpost three hundred miles inland from the Sea of Okhotsk, opposite the southern end of Sakhalin Island. Khabarovsk was named after a Cossack explorer who conquered the Amur region in the seventeenth century. The city was founded as a military settlement in 1858 by Count Muraviev-Amurski, governor general of East Siberia, who did much to advance Russian interests in the region. Russia's second favorite river after the "Little Mother Volga" is the "Little Father Amur." Until the completion of the railroad to Vladivostok in 1897, the town was just a trading and military post on the Amur. By 1992, although built on little more than swampy forest, Khabarovsk was a major industrial center of over half a million people.

On this particular visit, I was representing Interperspective Corporation and looking for new areas where tourism might take hold. I found Khabarovsk depressing as I looked across the border into China and wondered if it had been worth the trip. It was the middle of the afternoon and there was nobody on the promenade alongside the cliff by the river except for three drunken Russian women in their thirties, cavorting, dancing, and play-fighting near a low wall overlooking the river. Empty vodka bottles were perched on the wall. A large boom box blared garish Western music as the women laughed and swore, shouting for me to join them. In the distance, a dozen very tall smokestacks poured toxic smoke—black, brown, and yellow—pluming sideways in the wind.

I had heard through the diplomatic grapevine, with an intelligence slant, that there would soon be a direct flight from Khabarovsk to the then still closed city of Vladivostok six hundred miles to the south on the Sea of Japan just north of Korea, and that I might be able to get a seat. An Intourist employee at my hotel had even asked me if I would be interested. I was glad I had come after all.

I had been told over the years that if ever I had an opportunity to get into Vladivostok I should take it because, as a naval base and military center, that secret city had been closed for years, even to most Russians. Now, suddenly, just as the Soviet Union was beginning to show cracks in its seventy-year-old iron façade, that opportunity seemed to arrive. I asked around and was told that I might be able to get a ticket at a particular desk in the hotel. They asked me a ton of background questions and seemed to already know the answers to many of them. Somewhat frustrated that I didn't get anywhere with the Intourist people that day, I flew on to the Siberian capital of Irkutsk. It would be six months before I got back to Khabarovsk.

On that next trip to Khabarovsk, I again decided to look into going to Vladivostok. When I got to the hotel, I found one of the same Intourist women at the desk, but this time she had a complete change of attitude. She asked me the same questions I'd been asked before. Then, without giving me any kind of run-around, she said there was a daily flight—down in the morning and back in the afternoon—and asked if I wanted to go, which, of course, I did. Without requesting it, she issued me a special visa. I couldn't help but think, "They *want* me to go!" I soon realized I was probably the first American civilian these people at the desk had processed into Vladivostok and they were as excited by the whole exercise as I was. They realized, as did I, that something important was happening. Times had changed. Things were opening up. For me, it was quite a feeling.

The next morning, I got up and went out to a surprisingly clean and decent military airport. Air service was always better in the Soviet Union when the military was involved and, as many of the generals were away, there were still empty seats. The plane took off almost as soon as I sat down. The flight took about two hours. We flew fairly low over the forests and lakes and it reminded me of New Brunswick, Canada. Both the pilot and copilot wore holstered pistols, and we landed at a busy, well-laid-out military airport with a small civilian facility, about a half-hour from Vladivostok. Military and technical personnel were everywhere. Rows of fighter planes, ammunition depots, and long runways for the big payload planes made it clear that I was on an active military base. It looked clean and there was a feeling of efficiency that told me this was a place of consider-able importance.

Walking through a building that would pass for a small-town terminal in the United States, I saw lots of cars but no taxis. It had been raining and the forest around us smelled good. I started asking around in Russian for a taxi. A couple of bearded Russians in their early forties heard me. They were astounded to see a lone American with a backpack looking for a taxi in Vladivostok. They seemed absolutely dumbfounded when I told them I was from California. They started talking about the scientific programs at UC Berkeley and were visibly impressed when I told them I was a graduate. They wanted to know where I was going, and I told them I just wanted to go into town and have breakfast at the Intourist hotel as I was flying out again late that afternoon. This brought on lots of animated conversation, some of it understandably cautious, considering the situation. The two Russians said they would take me into town and one of them even asked me to stay overnight, saying he would show me around. I got the feeling that they had never seen an American before, and I accepted their offer of a ride.

When I got to the Intourist hotel, I was told I could have a room and they asked for my passport. When the counter personnel saw it was an American passport, they looked shocked. They passed it around and looked at it. One of them held it out in front of him like it was hot metal. I was told that it was the first American passport they had seen in Vladivostok. They copied it and looked at it some more. They were friendly, but awkward. I think I was more comfortable than they were. We all laughed. When a slight pause ensued, I asked if there was a problem and they said no, because they had instructions that tourists might be coming in now. They had even heard talk of a sister-city relationship with San Diego and a U.S. Navy vessel visiting, but they had never actually seen an American before. In fact, I was not only the first American they had seen, but the first foreign civilian to appear in their memory, and one of them had been there since 1943. Another "first" for me! Although I got a real rush from the thought, I didn't try to explain to them my schoolboy idiosyncrasy. Surprised though they appeared to be, they were anything but hostile. They welcomed me with hugs and kisses.

Shortly after I registered, the fellows I had met at the airport picked me up and drove me around. The harbor reminded me of a compacted Vancouver, British Columbia, although the air was heavily polluted. When we got out of the car amidst a large group of people, I *knew* I was not in Vancouver because there was the same old thick smell of a Russian crowd—aging perspiration, damp cloth, garlic, cabbage, and wet lettuce. As we continued to drive around the city, I saw shipyards and a heavy military presence. I had studied old photos and satellite images and thought I knew what to expect—a very modern and efficient city and military base. But now that I could smell the garlic, I could see that, in sharp contrast to the airport, what was once an active and up-to-date harbor and base (the "arsenal of the east" of the Soviet Union) was beginning to look like a World War II surplus junkyard. There were a few ships. Everything looked broken and scavenged. Cranes were idle. Electric wires dangled. Sidewalks buckled. Buildings hadn't been painted for years. Cars were stripped to the chassis. It was a ghost town. These were the things satellites didn't show. The Soviets had run out of money! Only the military personnel looked as if they had any sense of purpose at all. Vladivostok was a long way from the Kremlin and very vulnerable at the end of the Cold War.

Every now and then we passed a park. In spite of obvious neglect, Vladivostok had a certain charm to it. It was filled with quaint wooden structures, some of them quite handsome, and ships with barnacled hulls. When I managed to get away from the military aspects of the city, there was an almost Victorian feel to the place. But heavy industrial equipment and entrances to tunnels were everywhere. In spite of this, I never got a sense of any great activity or production. Signs of rust were everywhere in the harbor.

My two acquaintances and I stopped for lunch in a small, crummy restaurant where my "guides" drank vodka shots and laughed a lot. I had come to assume that they were there to keep an eye on me, but they seemed like good guys and I liked them. They even talked me into ordering bear steak—my first taste of bear meat. A lesser "first," but a "first" nonetheless. It was coarse and tough and although I had to chew hard to get it down, the flavor was okay. The Russians loved it and added lots of onions.

As we drove around the area, I noticed that although there were quite a few Japanese cars, there were no Asians or even Eurasians in sight. Only Russians. Russians everywhere and, despite the diversity of the Soviet Union, that was all. Even though as early as 1992 a lot of Chinese and Japanese were exploring the former Soviet Union, they were everywhere *except* Vladivostok.

Another thing that struck me as we drove around the following morning was that although it was a weekday, there were an awful lot of drunks on the streets. This was not unusual in most northern Russian cities, but I was surprised to see it in an obvious military center that had long been totally restricted. Like rusting machinery, I saw this as another sign of the end of the Soviet Union. Generals used to rank above doctors and scientists when it came to pay, but now there was no money to pay anybody. Soldiers who had been absent without leave were not treated harshly. Now, due to the sheer magnitude of the defections, the government had lost authority over the military. False pride had been replaced by disillusionment. You could feel it everywhere in Vladivostok. The unhappy military just walked away without fear. Riding around on the ground brought insights no technical intelligence could furnish.

When in the course of a conversation my driver, Vladimir, learned that I had mixed feelings about having eaten bear meat the day before, he drove me to a place about ten miles out of town that he said served the very best. It may have been the "very best," but, again, I thought it was too tough and I can't really say I liked it. As we talked, I mentioned that a friend of mine had asked if I could find out what happened to the American B-25 bomber from one of the World War II Tokyo raids that had gone down near Vladivostok. Vladimir told me that although the Soviets finally let the pilot and crew return to the States, nobody knew what happened to the plane itself. Vladimir, who said he was an airplane buff, told me there was an air museum in Vladivostok that I couldn't get into but that he would check it out for me. Before I left Vladivostok, he informed me that the plane in question had run out of gas and landed safely and fairly intact near Vladivostok, and that the Russians had then turned it around and used it in the war against Germany. So it had flown over the Pacific to hit Japan and had ended up in the fight against Germany. A good story.

It really was an extraordinary visit. Almost every time I was introduced to someone, I was told that I was the first American they had ever seen. Vladivostok has been open to tourism for a number of years now. But knowing that I was probably the first American *civilian* fed into my need to be first. Big deal, huh?

After Vladivostok, I flew back to Khabarovsk and on to Irkutsk, the capital of Siberia, which was founded in 1652 as a caravan trade link through Siberia to the east. Irkutsk still retained its frontier style, filled with picturesque log buildings and an oddly Polish flavor left over from the Polish POWs who had been held there during World War I. Irkutsk's principal attraction is Lake Baikal, the world's largest fresh water lake. Located fifty miles and ninety minutes out of town, Lake Baikal holds 20 percent of the world's fresh water supply and is an incredible 390 miles long, twenty to forty miles wide, and in places five thousand feet deep. The Russian Orient Express travels along many miles of the southern shore of this unique and pristine treasure of nature, and my soul was touched every time I saw it.

A long, long, *long* way from Moscow, and with needs different from those of Moscow and western Russia, Irkutsk could one day perhaps become the capital of a new Siberian Republic. The general decline of the Soviet Union affected Irkutsk less than other regions because there wasn't a whole lot going on there in the first place. Their problems were regional and Moscow didn't seem to care that much, so I didn't notice a lot of change during the 1980s, except that a good Intourist hotel had been built on the river. *Glasnost* and *perestroika* were hardly issues in Irkutsk.

During my trips there, I always checked on the decline and fall of the local outdoor dance pavilion down by the river, crumbling from shoddy workmanship and bitter Siberian winters. The Russians tried to buy off the "little man" all across the Soviet Union with dance facilities and children's amusement parks, virtually all of which became early victims of the national economic crisis. I had a particularly strong memory from the Soviet days of the Irkutsk pavilion with its sagging strings of multicolored lights, inundated by running kids, their austerely dressed parents doing a Slavic version of Siberian rock and roll. The music groups were awful. Bad music and bad dancers reeling in the midnight sun. Lots of cigarettes and vodka. Like the music, I was the stranger, the intruder. But as bizarre as the whole scene in the eerie light was, I could use it as a way to measure progress. The decline of this symbolic tool for the maintenance of Soviet power represented the ultimate failure of a broken system. People were seeing the world in a new light, and at all levels there was change in the wind. Already in 1992 the pavilion was abandoned, covered by the weeds of only a few years. The awkward drumbeat had stopped. The squealing guitar was gone. I was saddened by the empty scene but, nevertheless, glad that I had been there to witness the first glimmer of change, as rustic as it was.

Some tourists were passing through Irkutsk at the time, and they told me I might be able to get into Ulan Bator in Outer Mongolia. Feeling a little cocky after getting into the forbidden port city of Vladivostok, I decided to try to get into Mongolia's capital. This was great! My dance program was always open, not only to "firsts," but to opportunities to test the inefficiency and corruption of the disintegrating Soviet Union. Security checks were already sloppy at borders everywhere and, as a result, I could slip through borders and in and out of factories, government buildings, and universities more easily. If and when I was stopped, I would act surprised and then ask, "Is this the sports club?" (Or the library, or concert hall.) "Oh, I'm sorry." The further I was from Moscow, the worse it got.

I was told I would need a "very special" visa to get to Ulan Bator. "Very special" turned out to be fifty dollars, American, put into the hands of a guy who looked like the "wrong guy" but was obviously the *right* person when it came to getting into Ulan Bator. I flew Aeroflot into Outer Mongolia. We landed in Ulan Bator, at that time a sort of "city of the dead" on a god-forsaken plain in the middle of an abysmal nowhere. No wonder the Mongols went to Europe. Ulan Bator had absolutely no personality for me in the sense that we think of cities as having personalities, so when my hotel manager offered to take me to dinner in a "yurt" outside the city, one of those round-domed sort of tent places where they entertained Russians, I jumped at the opportunity.

When I arrived at the yurt, we found thirty Russian bureaucrats and tourists pouring down hot food and vodka, drowning out the music with their revelry. The "house" drink was *kumis*, made of fermented mare's milk. Also available and very popular was 150-proof vodka. I can hardly think of anything worse than watching thirty Russians getting drunk in a yurt in Outer Mongolia. They just zoned out and got ever more stupid. The first hour was generally okay, but then they began to fall off chairs and slide under tables. No shame. No problem. When "Ivan" got drunk, I moved out of my regular body into another space and insulated (not isolated) myself from the fray. Naturally, it was not a time to learn *anything* from them. Of course, *they* couldn't learn anything from *me,* either.

Eventually, under luminescent moonlight, we drove back over the Mongolian plain to Ulan Bator. Chinese were everywhere, and everyone seemed to be suspicious of everyone else. They *all* seemed suspicious of me. It was depressing. I wanted to leave after the first few hours and, although I hate to say it, I don't think I'd ever want to return to "Yurt City," even though the economy would eventually pick up considerably.

Unlike Vladivostok, I *wasn't* the first American in Ulan Bator, but I was definitely a new experience for most of the people there. For them, I was definitely a "first." And, like Vladivostok, I didn't get the feeling that I was being watched too closely, except out of curiosity. But when I returned to Irkutsk, I found myself being followed everywhere, always at a distance, by "hard guys" with dogs in jeeps.

I went out for a walk my first evening back. As always, the town was picturesque, with only a few two- and three-story modern buildings, dirt and cobbled streets, and no streetlights. It was very late summer, and small bands of boys roamed the streets looking for piles of windswept white thistles to turn into sparklers with a toss of a match. A jeep with my "watchers" and their dogs tracked me the whole time. They were always just around the corner or peering from side streets. They didn't want to take me in, and when I tried to bum a ride with them, they kept their distance. Finally I realized I was lost. Tired and frustrated, I had wandered around in circles looking for a recognizable landmark or building in the dark. After an hour or so, a plane flew low overhead. Earlier, I had noticed planes flying low over my hotel on the river as they approached the airport. I followed the noise, and twenty minutes later I found the river about a quarter mile from the hotel. My after-dinner stroll had lasted three hours. I was tired and irritated.

When I reached the lobby and plopped down for a moment's rest, almost immediately the two jeep men rushed into the lobby but didn't notice me at first and woke up the desk

clerk. I was sitting in a chair next to the kiosk that sold cigarettes and newspapers and pretended to be reading the local
paper. They were asking questions about the foreigner (me). I
got up and walked over to them and said in my very best Russian, "You have a beautiful city. It reminds me of my hometown
in California. Would you care for a cigarette?" They awkwardly
accepted the cigarettes. I lit them and said, "Good night, gentlemen," while muttering under my breath, "You *assholes!*"

It was one-thirty in the morning, and when I got to my
room I noticed my bags had been sloppily searched. So what?
I hadn't disappeared, just gotten lost. Disappearing was my
greatest fear when I sometimes lost my way. I had obviously
stirred more than curiosity in at least some quarters. Maybe the
jeep men were just trying to figure out what I saw as a connection between Vladivostok and Ulan Bator. It would have been
too simple for them to believe that I was simply seeking "firsts."
Of course, they would have been correct in that belief. There
were always things to see and smell and, above all, report on.

Chapter 36

Chechnya
(A Hero's Release)

IHAD DONE RECONNAISSANCE WORK in 1994 during the First Chechen War and saw some of the most brutal violence and ethnic cleansing of all the local wars I covered. And so after the First Chechen War, I vowed to myself that I would never return. But when the Second Chechen War broke out in 1999, I realized it was only a matter of time until I would find myself back there.

I had visited Grozny, the capital of Chechnya, twice before the latest hostilities broke out, and I noted it was a pleasant but uninspiring farm town with some petrochemical facilities, similar to the California Central Valley town of Bakersfield. When violence turned into downright war, I volunteered to look into Grozny on my next trip to Georgia.

Chechnya had been declared off limits to our embassy people and I had not realized how bad things had become. For some unexplained reason, Mirian, my regular companion on such trips, was not available to go north to Grozny, approximately a hundred and twenty miles from Tbilisi. Mirian recommended a neighbor, Adzul, who was an ethnic Chechen married to a Russian lady and lived in the suburbs of Tbilisi. He had a decent beige-colored Lada sedan and spoke some English.

The road was good, but as we approached the city of 300,000, we encountered several roadblocks manned by surly, rough, unshaven, heavily armed Chechens. They looked like Christmas trees with guns, grenades, ammo belts, and knives hanging all over them. As we neared the city, we noticed a lot of chopper activity and low-flying Russian military planes. Eventually we heard artillery fire that could only be Russian. Fearing that his Lada might be commandeered by either side, Adzul parked in an area he knew just off the main two-lane highway. He agreed to stay put until I returned, and I reminded him that so far I had only given him gas money. He would get the balance when he delivered me safely to Betsy's in Tbilisi.

It was a good idea to follow the main road walking into town, no detours. It would enable me to find Adzul later, even at night. I had gotten lost before by taking shortcuts or going cross-country. It's a terribly helpless feeling in hostile areas. It was obvious Adzul didn't want to be seen with me. He probably figured I might be taken for a journalist and it was open season on journalists. Several had been killed recently and another was kidnapped and being held for $50,000 ransom. Both sides—the Russians and the Chechens—hated the media because of the distortion and spin they printed. Occasionally, I had spoken to various media people, but I soon stopped that practice due to the misquotes and articles they wrote out of context. A lot of them were political opportunists, lazy or chicken, or both. I tried to avoid them whenever possible.

I left Adzul and walked several miles into the civic center and downtown commercial area. I was amazed at the extent of the damage so early in this conflict, and eventually the city was virtually destroyed. I spent a few hours assessing the damage to the infrastructure, but by the middle of the afternoon regular incoming artillery rounds suggested it was time for me to leave. During a particularly noisy period, I holed up in the entrance hallway of a heavily damaged three-story, state-owned apartment building. The apparently random shelling of the city stopped being random in my case, for at least one round, when a mortar shell landed on the top of my refuge. Instinctively I looked up to see if I was in danger. The direct hit was three stories above me, but the building shook and I was showered with a cloud of ancient dust and swirling granules of ceiling plaster. I caught one tiny jagged bit of plaster in my right eye, where it was to stay embedded for the next three days. Until I understood this bit of sand better, I tried not to rub my eye to get rid of this barbed intruder. A piece of broken mirror was my doctor and it said "don't touch." Continually lubricating it with water provided some relief, and I could still see with both eyes. I could hear the kind of small arms fire involved in street fighting maybe half a mile away and approaching. Several big rubber-tired armored vehicles hurried past heading downtown toward the shooting. I also heard the ominous "clonking" sound of small mortar rounds being fired. I didn't know who was doing what to whom, so I left my hallway refuge and went out the back of the building. I was aware that this was often a bad move because it was standard practice in organized combat to simulate a frontal approach and then bag the bad guys as they bailed out the back door. One thing I pretty well knew for sure was that what was happening was not textbook or organized. So I went out the back door anyway. As I cleared the yard and parking area, I glanced back at the apartment building. The top floor was ablaze and a plume of black petroleum-based smoke curled into the sky. Four or five armed nondescript Chechens were scrambling out the same door I had just exited. They ran from some danger, danger they saw and I didn't. But I took the hint and as the evening darkness surrounded me, I found my highway and headed straight arrow for a rendezvous with the beige Lada, water, and my kit with pain-killers.

At first, I did scout's pace (one-hundred-yard run, one-hundred-yard walk), just to clear the area. I passed several fresh corpses along the way and, sadly, beside a wrecked light blue government transport truck lay the driver. The middle of his body was soaked red. He moved enough to catch my attention. He wasn't dead yet but he was going to be soon. I hated moments like these, but my training came to my assistance. During basic training, my mentor's first voice said, "He is not your problem. This is not your war. You can't do anything for this guy. Your duty is first to your family, your country, your God!" But I couldn't just abandon him, so I told him in Russian that I was an American and I would get help for him. I knew I was lying, but the only gift I could give him was the faint hope that someone would find him. A dark feeling swept through me. I was almost overcome. I allowed it into my consciousness. If the Russians found this young man, dead or alive, they might mutilate him and hang him up for public view. I should put him out of their reach. I was unarmed. I was not a doctor. I was not his god! That lie was the best I could do. I repeated, "I'll send some guys to pick you up." He squeezed my hand. I squeezed his.

As I left the downtown area and was passing through older, single-story houses, I realized I was brandishing my small white cloth flag with a red cross on it. I was not hiding. After all, I was a humanitarian guy and that was my armor—I was a neutral. Much to my surprise, I had burst into song to prove it. Years earlier I sang in a college *a cappella* group and I even had a year with the San Francisco opera chorus as a spear-carrying tenor. Tenors who get up close to B-sharp were at a premium, but the lure of playing football for the Cal Bears took over. I could always sing, but football had a short player life. My wife thought I sounded like "a poor man's Robert Goulet," but what did she know? Goulet was a baritone. So, there I was in Chechnya, singing at the top of my voice. I started with *Onward Christian Soldiers* then *Ave Maria* but dropped both immediately, realizing I was in a Muslim city. *Pagliacci* and the *Barber of Seville* fit my mood. As I passed by houses with blown-out doors and windows, I saw inquiring faces peering out to see what kind of nutcase was out there. I had to fake most of the words. I thought if Sid Caesar could do it, so can I. I got and gave some thumbs up and waves. At one point, two guys, probably ethnic Georgian (Georgians are all singers and will sing at the drop of a Mars bar), swaying with alcohol and arms locked, stood in front of their rubble-strewn doorway and motioned me to join them. They sounded pretty good and I was tempted. My "angel" had taken my mind and body out of danger and the crest of a wave of terror and indecision. Somehow the singing had given me a release and I was able to avoid the immobilizing effect of too much adrenaline and survive again, not through intellect but through instinct.

Forty-five minutes later when I found Adzul, it was almost dark. Even worse, Adzul was stumbling drunk and showed no sympathy for my dying Chechen story by saying, "He was a fool to be downtown in a government vehicle. You see why I parked here." I suggested if we saw any Chechens headed that way to ask them to look for the truck driver. Adzul said, "Okay, sure." As he spoke, we heard two short Kalashnikov bursts from the direction I had just come. Adzul looked at me and shrugged.

A few minutes later, a captured Russian recon vehicle pulled up and stopped. Four armed Chechens jumped out and confronted us. For a moment, I forgot my eye problem. Adzul talked the talk and produced a quart of Smirnov #150 from the beige Lada. The bottle went back and forth until empty. They thought I was strange not to participate in mourning their fallen compatriot in the blue truck. "Oh, him. We saw him. He was almost gone. His guts were hanging out. Petrov gave him a hero's release." They all nodded. "No one could help him. He is in the trunk of our vehicle. We will see that those vile Russians don't dance on his grave." I felt okay again. I was off the hook—my hook—and lucky to know it. I marveled at the way my conscience had manifested and sought redemption. The

Chechens drove off boisterously. I heard the word "American" a couple of times.

I drove Adzul about ten miles farther up the highway and parked behind an abandoned warehouse to get a little sleep and sobering rest. He had come through for me. It was cold, maybe 40 degrees F, so we elected to roll up the car windows. That was fine with Adzul, although I became the unfortunate victim of the foul fumes from his alcohol breath. Likewise, I was the victim of some of his careless hygienic practices. But I didn't want to be cold and go into shock from my "wound." My sensory memory bank has stored those odors forever in my subconscious and they are with me even now as I write.

Back in Tbilisi, the embassy had a roster of competent local Georgian doctors. Good eye guys were available, and my Chechen foreign body was removed. By the time I returned home to California ten days later, however, a viral infection had started. Eight years and three failed corneal transplants later, my right eye was removed and replaced with a prosthesis, complete with a tiny American flag to mark the top, which hides just under the open eyelid. Quite a souvenir of Chechnya.

Happily, my handlers decided we knew all we needed to know about this particular war and so ended my Chechen excursions. When people ask me about Chechnya, I usually reply, "We know all we need to know about what's going on there—it's a disaster and a real quagmire!"

Chapter 37

Business Administration 1B
(The "Mafiya")

I T WAS THE SECOND WEEK in October, 1997, and I had been on my paper route for five weeks, covering all eight republics. I had planned my itinerary so that I would spend my last ten days in Georgia. I had an appointment in Tbilisi with Eduard Shevardnadze to let him know that I would be winding down my trips to Georgia and to ask if he had any messages or special concerns for me to convey to George Shultz. I also wanted to attend the first revival of the Georgian Harvest Festival, which is called "*Tbilisoba.*" It is very much like one of our state or county fairs and features Greco-Roman wrestling, a dozen dance companies, and various ethnic groups playing all kinds of music, including rock and roll. Plenty of Girl Scout cookies, barbecue, and shish kabob. The whole city of a million and a half was involved, with an estimated 200,000 actually attending.

It was typical of Shevardnadze to restart this Georgian tradition that would help unite his people. From a vantage point above the grounds I watched as he left his car and plunged alone like a fearless ship into the parting friendly sea of his people, leaving in his wake excited cries of "He's here! He's here!"

For two days I mingled with the crowd at the festival. I watched people spend money, laugh, drink, and eat. There were lots of very young children and pregnant women (an important economic indicator). People were dressed up for the occasion. Most of them seemed glad to see each other—old friends and survivors out in the sun, out of hiding, finding new hope in their renaissance. The Russian communist cloud of repression had finally lifted. It was an awakening from a darker age. I was grateful just to be there.

Later that week, I spent about an hour with Shevardnadze and told him what I had seen and felt at the fair. His face softened and, for a moment, his thoughts seemed adrift. As I was leaving, he took my hands in his and said, "Thank you again for visiting with me. I want you to know that you seem to come here at the right time—the right time for me, that is. I understand that you might write a book. Here is *my* book. I have autographed it, but I give it to you *quid pro quo* so that I might obtain a copy of *your* book, and," he chuckled, "I hope it is shorter than George Shultz's book."

I responded, "It's a deal."

He smiled and said, "You and I are about the same age, so don't wait too long as I'm also anxious to see how you explain this *Interperspective Corporation* that is on your business card." He started to laugh. Gela Charkviani also laughed. Shevardnadze gave me a big hug—uncharacteristic for him—and I joined in their laughter. What a great moment. What great men they are. They knew who I was—sure they knew. But it was okay. They *needed* me.

I went back to Betsy's and changed from my diplomat's blue suit into Aeroflot clothes and waited for Mirian to take me to the airport. I was ready to go home. The fair was closing down and people were jamming the Metro stations to return to the suburbs (cars were still a luxury). As Mirian and I reached the divided motorway leading to the airport on the outskirts of the city, a motorized column of about fifteen military vehicles passed us going in the same direction. I rolled down the car window and snapped a few photos to finish the film which contained my Shevardnadze pictures. A few minutes later, one of the big, rubber-tired scout vehicles wheeled around and came back in our direction, forcing us to the side of the road. We rolled down the windows. Mirian said, "Stay in the car! I will deal with this." Two poorly dressed and very drunk Georgian "soldiers" approached our car—one on each side. I asked Mirian if he wanted my passport or visa. He replied, "No, these trashes probably can't read."

Mirian was cool and talking in Georgian. The guy on my side demanded my camera and when I said *"Nyet!"* the barrel of an AK-47 came through the window and pointed at my head. By the tone of the conversation, I didn't think Mirian was doing very well. These guys were scruffy and surly, but I had been through this sort of thing dozens of times before with "my man" Mirian. He would clear it up!

Then, the guy on my side, who reeked of Georgian wine, pushed his AK-47 into my ear. It hurt! Suddenly, he clicked something on the AK-47, turned from the car, fired six shots into the field next to us, and then returned the AK-47 to my ear. Now the barrel was *hot* and in my ear. I really wanted to get out and "kick ass," and I knew that I could, but that little inner voice that is one of my companions said, "Give him your film." So, just like in the movies, I opened my camera, pulled out the film, and pushed it through the window.

Mirian began shouting and jumped out of the car, telling them that I was a personal friend of President Shevardnadze and that they had destroyed the president's picture. He demanded their IDs, made notes, and told them to get out of his sight. In a rare moment of anger, he kicked the guy from my side with a sweeping, sidewinding soccer crippler on the knee, picked up his AK-47 and put it in our trunk. The man was writhing on the ground and his leg looked awful. Mirian crossly said, "Let's go! Why didn't you wait before dumping the film? I almost had matters settled. Don't you trust me?" He was hurt that I didn't have confidence in him, and maybe a little upset that I might be leaving for good.

I responded, "Mirian, that stinking little shitface had his AK-47 in my ear twice for Christ's sake, and it didn't sound like you were winning your conversation. You couldn't see the AK-47 in my ear."

"That guy is 'shitface'?" Mirian smiled. "And now he has a newly broken leg." I smiled back. Mirian continued, "Why do you think you understand a conversation when you don't know the language, the words, and, oh, what is 'shitface'? What does it mean? This is new one for me. I know 'shit' and I know 'face' and now, I guess I know 'shitface.' So, let's go to the airport."

Betsy and Professor Rondeli had come to see me off. Mirian told them what had happened. Alex said he would report it to the "right" people. Rondeli recognized that I might have been premature by several seconds in "peeling out the film," as he put it. But, with an AK-47 in my ear and the guy out of control, I didn't feel I had any options.

We all hugged and Mirian, as usual, helped me through baggage control. Back in the early days, the guy at the scales would always hit me for seventy-five dollars of overweight or I would miss the flight. I would give Mirian the seventy-five dollars and tell him he could keep everything over twenty-five dollars. I just didn't want to deal with it. Mirian and I had a kind of departure routine—almost a father-and-son sort of thing. I always made sure he knew I loved him by saying so. It meant a lot to both of us.

Although I was glad to get on the plane, I was pissed that an almost perfect trip had been messed up by my own carelessness. It was definitely okay to take pictures of old military equipment, but it was *not* okay—didn't make sense—to take pictures of a drunken asshole anywhere in the world. And to make matters worse, I had lost my cool even though it did turn out all right. I mulled over the question of whether I had panicked or made a good instinctive decision when I gave up my film. Mirian had suggested that I was not patient, "as usual." I rationalized that the scene was not "as usual." But at least I got to fly first-class to Moscow on a new Georgian Airlines Tupolev Tu-154. After 1995, competition had made travel inside the former Soviet Union better. I sat in one of two big swivel armchairs by the window.

After an hour, I decided to see if the toilet was as good as the rest of the first-class cabin. I had already approved of the flight attendant, who looked like Kirstie Alley, and I recognized the young man seated next to me as someone I had seen from time to time attending business conferences at the Metechi Hotel. When I stood up, the young man asked in good English if I would mind if he had a cigarette while I was up. I said, "Sure, go ahead."

When I returned to my seat, I said a few words and resumed my reading of a paperback copy of *Patriot Games* by Tom Clancy. I noticed that my seatmate was about six-foot-five and 240 or so pounds. He was dressed in Oxford gray flannel slacks, a two-tone hound's-tooth sports jacket, a button-down blue shirt, stockbroker-style loafers with those fringie things, and Argyle socks. I thought if I didn't know better, this guy could have been a rugby player from Dartmouth or Brown and second row in the scrum. So I asked him if he had ever played rugby, and he lit up the way all rugby players do when they identify themselves to another rugby player. He introduced himself as "Dado," and we proceeded to talk rugby all the way to the airport outside Moscow. He had made the Georgian National team just before the breakup of the Soviet Union and had always regretted not being able to test his skills by playing in international competition.

The cockpit door opened and, as we were about to leave the plane, I couldn't find my passport! The Russian immigration official at the top of the stairs told me I was entering another country, Russia, and *must* produce my passport, something new to me. Vnukovo Airport was previously an internal Soviet airport but now handled the new former Soviet republics as "foreign." Although new passport regulations were in effect after the Soviet breakup, they had never been enforced by the Russians due to sloppy security. Before I even had a chance to panic, I felt the stairs shake as Dado came bounding back up. Speaking with authority, Dado showed some kind of identification to the immigration officer and told me to follow him. The immigration guy saluted both of us. Dado helped me with my three bags. He stopped for ten minutes in an office, and when he came out said, "Follow me. Don't stop and don't look back!" We went through several buildings and a VIP lounge before emerging through a VIP pickup door. We climbed into a Volvo of a friend of Dado's named "Gia" and screeched out of the airport. It was dark now, and the airport was thirty-five miles from the city's center. We were in a forest and, as many times as I had been to Moscow, I couldn't tell if we were heading for the city or not. Gia turned on some Moscow music.

After about a mile, the exit road became two lanes—a *good* two-lane road, but no passing. Ahead of us was a slow-moving caravan of cars. As cars passed the slow-moving leader, we moved up until we were directly behind an old sedan. Gia weaved his headlights from side to side, but we couldn't figure out what was happening. Finally, after several minutes, Gia saw a chance to pass and, as we did, we were able to understand the situation. Both back seat doors were wedged open by a rough pine coffin. A homemade Russian flag was attached to the coffin and several people were huddled by it. At least three people were jammed into the front seat.

Dado and Gia discussed the situation in Russian, not realizing that I spoke Russian, too. They decided the coffin must contain a soldier who had just come back on a "Black Tulip" (war dead transport) flight from Chechnya—a hero's return with full Russian military honors. Yep, that's all he gets. Gia had seen other families who had come to pick up their sons, but it was a ghoulish sight for me. In my case, my contract clearly stated that if I "went down" over there, I was to be cremated and sent home in a box by UPS.

As Gia and Dado talked, Gia said, shaking his head slightly in my direction, "By the way, who is this guy?"

Dado replied (probably for Gia's benefit), "I don't know yet, but I intend to find out."

I leaned forward, peering out intently to see if we were actually headed for Moscow. It's moments like these when your fears *can* run away with your judgment. I had been on various "shit lists" in Russia for at least fifteen years and had actually been advised not to stay over in Moscow on this particular trip. And yet here I was—in this Volvo with Gia and Dado. Gia was changing the music and, with an hour to go assuming we were headed toward Moscow, I decided to talk to them. I said I was an economics consultant and business development representative for several big American companies. They were interested and, in English, Dado said, "We are in business."

I asked, "Do you market your products?"

"Yes, of course," Dado replied. "That's the whole idea. To sell. We have gas stations. We are, like you say, an integrated operation."

"How many gas stations does your company have?" I asked.

"Ninety," Dado replied.

"How many gas stations are there in Moscow?" I wondered out loud.

Dado smiled. *"Ninety."*

"Nice going! What's your secret?"

"Well," Dado said, his smile growing larger, "you might call it Economics 1A."

"I doubt it!" I fired back. (I could think of a better name.)

"We—my company is ten key guys—buy tankers and train-loads of oil and sell it. I personally take—you say 'take home'—about two hundred thousand to three hundred thousand dollars a month."

"Holy shit!" I exclaimed. Dado laughed. (They *love* American slang!) I asked, "Do you reinvest in Russia?"

Dado's laugh went back to a smile. "Yes, of course. We have operating expenses, but, and I will tell you this privately, I move as much cash as I can to banks in Cyprus."

"Hah! Economics 1A! Don't you get a little help from your friends?" I inquired.

"Isn't that a Beatles song?" Dado asked, showing off his knowledge of the West. Then he said, "I must also tell you I have a very good insurance company."

"Insurance company? Why insurance?" I asked him.

"Because they insure, like you say—*make sure*—everything goes smoothly and I am successful."

"Oh," I said, the light dawning. "I'm beginning to get it. You mean you work with a 'facilitator' company."

Dado said, "You are a nice guy, but it's okay for you to say '*Mafiya*,' because that's what a lot of people call it."

All I could think to say was, "Okay."

He laughed and continued, "Let me explain to you how it works for me. I am only one young guy but I have good ideas and good timing, and I have a very good business if the central authorities co-operate. They—the 'board of directors'—like my ideas. They like my style. They trust me, and I make them a lot of money."

"What's the tariff?" I asked.

Dado replied, "Ten percent."

"Do they sit on you with audits?"

"No. We avoid a lot of paper, always."

"What if you screw up?" I wondered.

Dado confessed, "I have. We dropped two hundred thousand dollars last March. I wasn't paying attention. The market went down suddenly. Somebody was playing games."

"What happened?"

"No problem," Dado explained. "They understand that business is not always perfect."

"Are you afraid of them?"

"Oh, no. We need each other. Anyhow, the mayor of Moscow and the chief of police are on the board of directors. They all wear blue suits and have big cars and two or three homes, but they really are helpful. The government is useless." I couldn't help but think that the government might be useless but they had the mayor and the police chief. Dado continued, "You can't operate without an 'insurance company.' The banks are good to me when I need cash to buy a trainload of oil. They say 'How much do you want and for how long?' It's always short-term and quick rollover. They are truly my friends."

"How about rough stuff?" I wanted to know.

"What is rough stuff?" Dado asked.

"Are you safe?" I continued.

"How do you mean 'safe'?"

"From competition or criminals," I clarified.

"There *is* no competition. Criminals stay away from me. They know who my 'insurance company' is. But if you mean violence to my family, I have four children and carry a special radio. If I call for help, twenty heavily armed men will arrive within ten minutes no matter where I am. A spotter gunship will be there in fifteen minutes. It really works. I had to push the button a couple of times already."

I observed, "You are very open about this. I am a stranger."

"No, you're not," Dado replied. "You are okay. I know you are a friend to Georgia." My mind went *Ooops!*

The car pulled up at the American Embassy and I said, "You can let me out here. I'll get my passport problem straightened out."

Dado was adamant. "We will wait here until you say to go." I returned a couple of minutes later. It was the Sunday of a three-day U.S. holiday and the embassy service units were closed. I was worried about checking into the Intourist hotel without my passport. I had been there recently but knew it could get sticky. You really need a passport. It's your ID. Dado then said, "Let's go."

At the hotel, Dado jumped out of the car carrying my two heaviest bags. He pushed through a wall of security guys onto the main floor with all its hookers, hoods, and Kansas farmer-type guests. He pulled the head receptionist aside and showed his plastic "insurance company" card and said he would personally vouch for me until Tuesday. Then, when we couldn't find any porters, he helped me take my bags up to the sixteenth floor. Could he be gay? I asked myself. No, I thought. Couldn't be! Anyhow, I don't attract gays anymore like I did when I was younger. He interrupted my thoughts with, "I'll call you in the morning."

It was midnight when I finally dropped off to sleep. I was irritated with myself for having lost my passport. Your passport can be your only friend at times. About two-thirty in the morning, I woke up suddenly and pulled down my wardrobe bag. I unzipped it and reached into the inside breast pocket of my navy-blue suit. There it was! My passport! Still there from my visit to Shevardnadze's office. I had my best friend and security blanket back. I slept well the rest of the night.

Dado called in the morning and asked me to lunch. When I said I was busy, he said, "How about dinner?"

I said, "Okay, I'll be ready at six."

"Good," he responded cheerfully. "Do you want to play racquet ball at my club?"

"No, thanks," I answered.

"Do you want girls for dining? You know, nice ones, who speak English?"

"No, thanks," I replied. "I'm pretty tired and, actually, I'd rather hear more about you."

At six o'clock, my phone rang and Dado said, "*Allo*, look out your window." I looked down sixteen floors and could see Dado standing by a giant BMW. The headlights flashed, and from his cell phone he asked, "Are you sure about the girls?" I told him I was sure.

A few minutes later I joined him. He was dressed better than I, but not like some of the nouveau riche Russian guys who looked like 1925 Chicago gangsters. I climbed into his beautiful new car, noting the pride in his eyes as I did. We drove off in the direction of Sheremetyevo Airport. About halfway there, we turned off the boulevard. Dado was talking with someone on his cell phone. It was dark and getting darker. We were passing through a warehouse and commercial district that was pretty well shut down, and the usual comments came to me from the little bird on my shoulder: "What the fuck are you doing here? You don't know this guy. You haven't even run an ID check on him. You're in *his* backyard now."

The BMW pulled up in front of what looked like a small factory warehouse, with several cars parked on the sidewalk. Dado smiled and said, "I think you will like this place after five weeks of travel." It was only seven in the evening—early for Moscow—as we passed through two swinging doors into a bar/restaurant/night club that was sort of a combination of Santa Fe, Albuquerque, and El Paso. The place was jumping! For a moment, I lost my sense of where I was. There was Grand Ole Opry music and a banjo player. A dozen or more hostesses in "Daisy Mae" outfits hustled food and adult beverages. Now I knew how Russians must have felt when they got off the plane in "La La Land" (Los Angeles). Surprise and cultural shock were tightly linked in my mind, and I began to laugh.

Dado watched me with amusement. I laughed until my eyes were wet and asked, "Are these guys Americans or foreigners?"

Looking proud of himself, Dado answered, "Yes, maybe some, but mostly these are young Russians like me who like the West."

I told him, "My favorite movie is *Butch Cassidy and the Sundance Kid.*"

Dado's laugh grew. He was obviously elated, as he said, "Mine, too!"

Dado ordered giant cheeseburgers and salad. He had a couple of beers and at times looked very American—almost Ivy League. He invited a couple of very attractive girls to join us—"just to talk." One was a chemist and the other an anesthesiologist, both in their late twenties. For a moment I considered it. But I was tired. Too tired even for a furtive moment of male fantasy. At that instant, a very large dish of vanilla ice cream with sliced bananas and chocolate sauce was put in front of me.

Although embarrassed, I told Dado of finding my passport. We chatted about our families. He asked me to stay at his dacha the next time I was in Moscow, and I invited him to California. I mused to myself, "I should hit Dado up for a job. He could use a guy like me, with my qualifications. Hell, I had even taken Business Administration 1B." They were all very nice to me. I promised to return in a few months and told Dado I would call him and we would do something special. Later, he left me at the entrance to my Intourist hotel. It had been a great "travel day" for me.

Dado helped me out of a tight spot in Moscow. Not long after, a Moscow paper called his death the "assassination of the week."

During the next couple of days, I shared what I had learned with my agency contacts in Moscow. I worked off my two-hundred-item checklist that I had developed during my Bechtel days. There's less room for error if you break information down this way. It was like a form set in my brain, and I was constantly dropping observations into its slots for later analysis. As a result, my memory was nearly photographic, which proved most helpful because I didn't keep notes or, early on, make recordings or take pictures. Only after the Soviet breakup did "Tourist Jim" become comfortable taking pictures, and not always even then.

After I got back to the States, an associate called me aside and asked if I knew a "Dado Bonjornadze" and, if so, how well? I related some of the details of my Moscow stay and talked about how he had really bailed me out when I misplaced my passport. I concluded by saying how warm and friendly he had been, and that I had come to feel very close to him. After listening intently to me, the man said, "I'm sorry to tell you, but Dado is dead. He was murdered outside a restaurant in the Moscow suburbs. There were two women with him at the time. One of them survived. Dado had your business card in his wallet and his 'insurance company' contacted the U.S. Embassy regarding you. They seemed to know that you were a regular visitor over there. However, they didn't seem to be able to make sense out of the file they must have on you, or how to connect you to Dado, except that you both played rugby and supported Georgian development. Is there anything *else* I should know? I thought you were low profile in Moscow, just passing through. Jesus, James, you almost made 'Murder of the Month'!"

I replied, "Yeah, okay, yeah." I was really floored by the news. A Moscow paper called it "the assassination of the week" and downgraded Dado as some sort of gypsy and, worse yet, "a Georgian."

My associate broke into my thoughts with, "And oh, yeah, the word is for you to stay out of Russia—or at least

Moscow—till this settles. Can you do your paper route without going through Moscow?"

"Sure," I replied. "Several ways. Direct to Tbilisi through Frankfort or Istanbul. British Airways and Lufthansa are both good, and now I can also connect from Beijing, Khabarovsk, and Irkutsk by Aeroflot."

We were both silent for a minute, but I had a sinking feeling and wanted to talk. I said, "You know, it's a joke in a way, but people who know me over there don't really like to see me coming." We were both silent for another minute. I continued, "They get nervous because bad things frequently seem to happen before, during, and after my visits. Maybe it's due to the fact that I often travel in May and October because of the weather, and those are also the months with the most violent history. It makes me look smart for being there at those bad times, but, believe me, it's mostly luck or coincidence." Then I asked, "Am I a suspect in the assassination?"

My associate replied, "You were at first. But the right people talked and you're probably in the clear now. But wait until we have a more positive picture. The 'insurance company' was pissed and embarrassed about losing a big producer."

I volunteered, "For what it's worth, I, for one, thought Dado was a straight up guy. He didn't *have* to be dirty."

"Sure! Right!" my associate exclaimed sarcastically. Actually, nobody had said bad things about him. Apparently he was brilliant and his opposition wanted him out of the game. You know, like stupid cheap shots on quarterback Joe Montana.

I bypassed Moscow on my next two trips, but found it necessary to pass through ten months later. Even then, I was advised to "stay indoors." It was a tough time. If I were to make a memorial list of the people I've known who have gone down in the storm that is the reconstruction of Reagan's Evil Empire, Dado would certainly be in my top ten.

Chapter 38

Alexander
(For the Record)

I WALKED QUICKLY through the quiet Tbilisi streets. The city had begun to fit itself comfortably around me, and I moved almost as if by reflex. I was on my way to a meeting with Alexander Khaindrava, a shadowy figure who had worked for, and been hunted by, the KGB. Alexander's story, in and of itself, embodied much of the recent history of the Soviet Union, as well as the worlds of Central Asia and the Transcaucasus, especially the new Republic of Georgia.

Blocked momentarily by a whining old peasant woman with a face like an eroded rock formation, I thrust a few crumpled bills into her hand. With watery blue eyes as wide as a cat's on seeing a small rodent break from cover, she grunted and sniffed noisily and turned away. Then, suddenly, the old woman turned back and gave me a look that told me that although she didn't like me, she desperately needed me. She communicated fear like a living, moving virus. *Was she a sign, a warning?* I wondered. Probably not, although I had spent so much time in Central Asia I had begun to believe in signs. Certainly, the old peasant woman seemed *sad*. On the other hand, much of today's world is sad, and confusing. I reflected for a moment that I had seen more beggars and down-and-outers on my last visit to San Francisco than I had seen in the much bigger and much poorer city of

Beggars in the Cold War's aftermath spread sadness like a virus.

Tbilisi. But I cut myself short, remembering Georgia's very high suicide rate. Maybe I, too, was a little depressed. Nevertheless, I had a rendezvous with living history and had to keep moving.

As I looked around this city I had come to love, a city that reminded me of parts of Paris and parts of northern Greece with a little extra added, it dawned on me that today, instead of "Yankee go home," the walls of the world told people like me that we were now merely surplus to the requirements of a New World Order. And unwritten—but very real—signs from the Clinton administration told us that America's on-the-ground intelligence operatives were destined for a slave ship full of bitter, displaced, and betrayed people—a factory making the wrong goods for the wrong age. To some of its practitioners, the intelligence business remained what it had always been: dim, certain, and eternal. For others, the Cold War had been like a college fraternity, but with that fraternity now closing down, their numbers were decreasing daily. I swore silently, thinking of how the "new boys" were always talking about "Russian economics," while the "old boys" asked, *"Is* there Russian economics?" *Damn it! Both* groups felt like misplaced persons lost among the political chatterers in Clinton's Washington.

I stopped, angry with myself for feeling almost maudlin. I jogged in place for a moment, trying to shake off the depth of my near total world-weariness. I shook my head vigorously, trying to cut off the depression even as it threatened to grow within me like a nightmarish weed in a speeded-up film sequence—flowering hideously into a place I did not want my mind to go. I wondered, *Do I even want to meet with Alexander, at least today?*

As I walked down Rustaveli Boulevard, leaves rattled and scraped like tin on the sidewalk around me. The smell of gasoline was sharp in the air. Small noises scratched on my nerves like fingernails on a blackboard. The breeze blowing down from the Caucasus Mountains was at first warm, then cool on my face. Snow-capped Mount Kazbek was a golden cone capping the range ridge fifty miles to the north. Still, I was drained. The place I inhabited inside myself felt empty and, for the moment at least, I didn't seem to have the ability or the will to replenish it. I was reminded of the many wounded men I had seen over the years who I knew were just waiting to die, rather than to recover. But I had to get on to the meeting with Alexander. Alexander! My mind reeled as if I had been awakened from a drunken stupor.

I had first met Khaindrava on a plane flying out of Abkhazia in 1992, where he had actually been fighting the rebels. He was seventy-two at the time, and I could still smell the blood on him and see the high-voltage sparks in his eyes reflecting a glorious personal triumph. Alexander had been fighting the rebels partly out of frustration over the dismal fact that too many young Georgians had refused to go and fight, and partly because he strongly believed in the unity of the new Georgian Republic. But he also boasted on the plane of killing two Russians and two Chechens, and I suspected there was a part of him that was out to settle old scores. I knew how he felt. Shevardnadze had called for all able-bodied men. "Am I not able-bodied?" Alexander had asked.

On the plane, Alexander's forceful personality had generated a strong magnetic field that drew people to him. The names of the great and good, the bad and not-so-beautiful, their deeds and misdeeds, had flown out of Alexander like missiles aimed at less knowledgeable minds. He had been a prisoner of the Japanese in Shanghai throughout World War II and then had become an agent of the KGB in China until 1949 when the Communists took power. After the communist takeover, Alexander worked for a time in a Shanghai brewery and married his first wife, who happened to be an American. He had joked with me on the plane that not only was his first wife American, but all of his early girlfriends were American, too! We talked about how he had lived one floor above Shevardnadze during the 1950s in Tbilisi and how he had closely followed the Georgian leader's career as he rose from being general secretary of Georgia's Communist Party to eventually becoming foreign minister of the entire Soviet Union.

My pace quickened as I reminded myself that I *must* get Alexander, who by now was pushing eighty, to talk about Shevardnadze. And then, almost instinctively, I looked back to see if the old peasant woman with the face like an eroded rock formation was still there. She wasn't. When I finally reached Alexander's apartment building, I made my way through the dingy foyer, past the casual litter of humanity that lounged and slumped around me, and climbed up to Alexander's rooms on the seventh floor. Alexander met me at the door and, after glancing up and down the hallway, locked us in. We reminisced a bit about our plane ride out of Abkhazia in 1992. When we sat down, I turned on my tape recorder and asked, "Did your American wife want you to become an American?"

Alexander nodded. His heavy, imposing head moved slowly, reminding me of an aging but very dignified donkey, a donkey that could still kick. He stopped nodding and thought a few more moments about my question before responding, "My American wife, she wanted to get me a visa. Gave me books. Talked and talked and talked. But I couldn't go."

"Were you a Communist?" I asked.

"I was then, yes. But that was years ago, before I saw the corruption of the very soul that communism carries with it."

"When you were a Japanese prisoner in Shanghai, they tortured you, didn't they?"

Alexander's reaction to my question seemed almost palpable in the air around us, like the scent of gasoline, something flammable. He stood up and sat down, stood up and sat down again, before finally responding, his voice low but the words etched with grit and meaning. "They did...yes." Alexander paused and stared at me. He continued, "Beatings. Electric wires. Water. Cigarette burns. All the usual. Sometimes...quite often...a little worse."

"A little worse?" I asked with a quiver in my voice.

"Yes." Alexander's eyes flickered, as if he were viewing a high-speed series of still pictures projected on a screen. He concluded, "They were very brutal, but I do not think about it much now."

"Did you have any religious beliefs at the time?" I questioned.

"Oh, yes, I was always religious. I was Communist, of course, but, yes, I was always Georgian Orthodox."

"I guess *everybody* from the Soviet Union was a Communist in those days. But at some time you did renounce communism?"

"Yeah, sure," Alexander chuckled, "but, inside myself—only inside myself. It was dangerous otherwise. When I eventually got back here to Tbilisi, the KGB immediately went over my biography and wanted to know about my being a Japanese prisoner. When I told them that I had been a political prisoner as well, they shouted, 'What? Political prisoner? What is that? Political prisoner?' Hah! In fact, I learned English from my cellmates, American marines who were captured at Wake Island. They were great guys."

"But didn't you work for the KGB after the war?" I asked him.

Alexander laughed out loud. "Yes, yes, but they didn't know what to make of me. They didn't want to arrest me because they didn't want a record of whatever it was they wanted to do to me."

"Why was that?" I asked.

"Some kind of rivalry within KGB and other security services. It was always like that. They would try to eat each other up before they ate you guys up."

"But who did they think you were?"

"Well, after the Soviet Union broke up, one of them told me that back then they thought I was a Japanese spy, and then they thought I was an American spy."

"You *did* have an American wife," I pointed out.

"I did, yes! And they *knew* that I had worked for them—KGB—at one time, but they thought that maybe I had been—what do you say—'doubled'?"

"But you hadn't."

Alexander smiled, and then said quietly, "Well, if I had, I probably wouldn't talk about it." I thought, *Good point,* as I adjusted the microphone.

"Okay, so we're back to the fifties and you're here in Tbilisi, and although you've got them puzzled, they're not going to lock you up. So what did you do?"

"Well, I studied languages. Then I began teaching English at the Polytechnic Institute, and the KGB came back to me and asked me to be their man in the Polytechnic. So I was appointed head of the interpreting services for the International Congresses."

"And you were working for the KGB or, at least, had the KGB connection?"

He gave me a look that said, *Foolish question,* before replying, "Oh, certainly!"

"What about the Intourist people?" I asked. "Some of *them* were KGB, weren't they?"

Alexander shrugged, and then laughed out loud. *"All* of them were KGB."

I had to laugh with him. "I knew that. They were everywhere, weren't they?"

"Oh, yes," Alexander snorted. He repeated his dignified donkey nod before raising his head slowly until his eyes were level with mine, adding, "Absolutely. They had all my interpreters reporting to them."

"I guess your interpreters were in a position to hear many things," I murmured.

For a moment, Alexander nervously squirmed in his seat. He rubbed his nose with his thumb and forefinger before responding, "Yes, and the KGB wanted to know *everything*. They never stopped asking, but I had no choice. It was very tiring. I remember one of them, a man in charge of this sort of thing, asked me to get his niece into the Polytechnic Institute, which I did."

"Did that make things better for you?'

With a small jerk of his great wonderful head, Alexander replied, "He did seem to be very grateful one night when he told me, 'Alex, you can say anything.' Well, I did talk to him some, but afterwards I checked to see if the table we were sitting at was wired."

"Was it?" I asked.

"I don't think so, but, then, with KGB you never know, and there was no improvement in the way I was treated."

I asked him, "Now that the Soviet Union is gone, is the KGB still active as an arm of Russia, or even here in Georgia?"

"In Russia, yes. But those here in Georgia, well, they work for Georgia. Some of them are good boys. But anyway, even after I did that favor for the KGB chief, they kept checking me out, and checking me out, and checking me out."

"But you *were* working for them, weren't you?" I asked bluntly.

At the age of seventy-two, Alexander Khaindrava volunteered for the Georgian Army.

Alexander studied my face before answering, "Yes, I was working for them. But they kept checking me. Finally, I just quit the job and they appointed someone to fill it who didn't know anything about anything that didn't have to do with KGB, and everything got bad. They didn't do a good job of interpreting any more. Even though they were interpreters, that was no longer as important as spying for the KGB. They were no longer...professional."

"Didn't they have to be good interpreters in order to be good spies?"

"Yes, of course. Actually, it was all very stupid. But then many things were stupid in those days."

I agreed, asking, "Shevardnadze was rising in the Communist Party of Georgia back then, wasn't he?"

"Oh, yes," Alexander replied. "He became general secretary."

"Okay, so how did Shevardnadze get to Moscow, become Soviet foreign minister, and help to shut down the Cold War?"

The skin on Alexander's face seemed to be moving in more than one direction and, as if to emphasize the insistence of his thoughts, his words came chopping out in a fast stream. "Shevardnadze! Hah! Shevardnadze! Yes! Back when the Politburo was still supreme Soviet power and Abkhazia was trying to break off from Georgia, the leader of Abkhazia was called to the Politburo and told by Suslov who was the ideologist..."

I interjected, "You mean, the man who set the 'party line'?"

"Yes, for Brezhnev and the rest." He continued, "Suslov was known as the 'Gray Cardinal.'"

I said, "In other words, Suslov told them if what they were doing was *politically correct?*" I thought to myself, *So that's where "PC" comes from!*

Alexander's head shrugged with his shoulders. "Yes, something like that. Very much like that. But anyway, Suslov and one other Politburo member told the Abkhazian not to worry about the Georgians, to tell the Georgians where to get off."

"That was certainly direct," I opined.

"Yes, well, that was pretty much what was said. Somehow Shevardnadze got it on tape, and when he was called to Moscow by Brezhnev and Brezhnev asked him what was going on in Abkhazia, Shevardnadze put the tape recorder down on the table and played the tape. When it was finished, Brezhnev asked him if he would play it for the Politburo. When Shevardnadze said he would, Brezhnev said, 'Good, but don't mention Suslov, only the other fellow.'"

"What happened next?" I asked.

Alexander explained, "The 'other fellow' was kicked out of the Politburo and Shevardnadze was awarded the 'Order of Lenin' for bravery and, oh, 'manly behavior'—something like that. At least that's the way the papers put it—'manly behavior.' Anyway, Gorbachev was party secretary in Stavropol at the time, and he and Shevardnadze began to meet to talk things over—that sort of thing. Shevardnadze, of course, was party secretary here in Georgia, and Gorbachev had seen that Shevardnadze never took bribes."

I was fascinated, and pondered, "That impressed Gorbachev? The fact that Shevardnadze took no bribes?"

"Oh, yes, of course," he responded immediately.

I had to smile, "I guess it *was* unusual."

Alexander returned my smile. *"Very* unusual. And Gorbachev *was* impressed! Shevardnadze even tried to totally *eliminate* bribe-taking in Georgia. That was too much, but he, himself, would not take bribes and, as I said, Gorbachev was impressed."

"So then, when Gorbachev came to power in the early eighties, he asked Shevardnadze to come to Moscow and Shevardnadze became his foreign minister? Is that right?"

"Yes, but not right away," Alexander clarified. "Gorbachev sent him on some diplomatic missions while Shevardnadze was still first secretary in Georgia, and he saw that Shevardnadze was good at that sort of thing."

Feeling I was on to something, I reiterated, "Gorbachev learned that Shevardnadze not only didn't take bribes, but he was also good at diplomacy."

"Exactly," Alexander responded. *"Then* Shevardnadze became soviet foreign minister."

"They made a good team, didn't they?" I commented.

Alexander leaned forward, looking right into my eyes and, emphasizing his words with his hands, replied, "Yes, they did, but not just because Shevardnadze did not take bribes or was a good diplomat..." His voice trailed off.

"What do you mean?" I asked.

The wrinkles in Alexander's face wrestled to control his emotions. It was quite a sight. He appeared to be having trouble confronting his own thoughts. His words came out softly and slowly. "You see, I have great admiration for Shevardnadze. Great admiration." His voice grew stronger. "You must understand, the thing about Shevardnadze for me is that he's a *brave* person—a very brave person. He showed that in Abkhazia when he went right to the front lines. He did not worry about bullets or bombs or anything. He showed that he is not only a leader, but a *brave* leader. His bravery—that is crucial."

"You had some recent army service in Abkhazia yourself, didn't you? Tell me about it."

Alexander explained, "Well, I saw all these young fellows who wouldn't go, who wouldn't fight, so I got up and said if they won't go, I'll go."

Right then, it struck me. I had said exactly the same thing to my kids thirty years ago when discussing Vietnam. Indeed, if it weren't for that conversation around the kitchen table, I probably wouldn't be here in Georgia interviewing Alexander in the first place.

Alexander sighed deeply before going on. "And then, you know, they said on the TV that there was this seventy-year-old man going off to fight. I hope it shamed some of the younger ones."

"Do you think it did?" I asked.

Alexander's features darkened. "I don't know. Maybe. But then, of course, Shevardnadze made my nephew minister of state for Abkhazia, and they would only let me do border things and such for a while. But after that, my nephew told them to let me go to war because I kept after him, and I went up to the fighting and had shell concussion twice. I even got caught in two ambushes and shot two Russians and two Chechens."

"The Russians are fighting the Chechens to keep Chechnya in Russia, aren't they?"

Alexander replied, "Of course, and they are fierce fighters, those Chechens, but what I say is let the Russians and the Chechens shoot each other, not Georgians."

"The Chechens *are* standing up to Russia."

"Yes, and I admire them for that. But the thing is, when it comes to Russians in Abkhazia, well, most Abkhazians, their real origin is Georgian. Nothing to do with miserable Chechens *or* Russians."

"Were there many Russians in Abkhazia, fighting Georgians?"

His face showing pain, Alexander responded by booming out the single word, "Yes!"

"What did they do?" I asked.

"They were pilots. Tank people. The big guns—all Russians. My nephew was on the helicopter with Shevardnadze when they—the Russians—tried to force him down with a downdraft from another helicopter."

"You're saying the Russians tried to force down Shevardnadze's helicopter?"

"Oh, yes. Very bad business. But the Russians always like to make trouble here. They've been doing it for centuries. Long before the Communists. Probably long after the Communists."

I nodded. "So, it's nothing new."

"No, no, of course not. Abkhazia is part of Georgia, but the Abkhazians are fundamentalist Muslims, like the Chechens, and that creates complications that the Russians like to play on and add to and make more of..."

A little confused, I said, "The Chechens are revolting against the Russians, aren't they?"

"Yes, yes, that is right." Alexander swallowed, a soft, guttural sound, before continuing, "The Russians have—how would you say—let the 'gin' out of the bottle, maybe? If the Russians could push the Abkhazians away from Georgia, then the Chechens think, why shouldn't they and the Abkhazians leave Russia and, together, form a Muslim republic across the northern slope of the Caucasus?"

I paused, contemplating the implications of such an arrangement. "But the Russians have something else in mind for Abkhazia..." I interjected.

"Yes, yes. They love the warm water of the Black Sea and skiing in the mountains. Abkhazia's Sukhumi, a lovely old Black Sea city, is like Sochi to them, a place to relax and get warm. And then, of course, the Russian gangsters are already there, in Abkhazia, selling everything wherever they can sell it, to Armenia, wherever. But..."

I interrupted, "It's a fine place."

"It is. All of them—the Russians, the gangster Russians, the Chechens—they like the weather there, the mountains..."

"It's a resort," I agreed. "One of the finest pieces of real estate in the world."

"A resort, yes. And, of course, they, the Russians, have this very secret laboratory on the coast where it is said they can make earthquakes."

"Is that verified?" I asked.

"No, no, but that uprising in Armenia was preceded by an earthquake, and I think the Russians *wanted* that uprising."

"You don't think…" I began.

"I don't know," Alexander replied, "but with the Russians, anything is possible. They have been doing experiments along that line."

I continued, "There are Armenians in Abkhazia, aren't there?"

"Oh, yes, they have been there since Lenin gave part of Armenia to Turkey and they ran from the Turks, and now they join the Russians to try and get Abkhazia away from Georgia and they are very violent. But now that it looks like Abkhazia will remain Georgian, they are leaving for Russia."

"For Russia?" I mused.

"Yes, or Armenia. Even they understand that Russia, not so good."

That made me laugh. "*'Not so good.'* Isn't that an understatement?"

Alexander returned my laugh as he responded, although his laugh was more like a gargle arising from his stomach. "Yes, you know your Mr. Reagan was right. The Russian Soviet Union *was* the 'Empire of Evil.'"

"You liked Reagan?" I asked.

Alexander's eyes glittered. "I did, yes. The thing about Reagan is, he was right!"

"About the 'Evil Empire'?" I asked.

"Absolutely," Alexander responded, "and everybody knew it. He spoke the truth. The truth has great power. And you people in the West should understand that, today, it would be best for you—for the world—if Russia was never strong again and not give them money…"

"They ran out of money, didn't they?" I said.

"Yes, and it would be better for the world, now, if they *stayed* out of money."

"Do Georgians dislike Russians?" I asked.

"Yes. Well, not all Russians, but yes. Of course, the Russian men don't like Georgian men because when Russian women see a Russian man and a Georgian man, they always go to the Georgian man."

"The Russians *tried* to put some heavy industry here in Georgia, didn't they?"

"Stalin did, yes, when the Germans took the Ukraine, but Georgia is not the place for heavy industry."

"Tourists?" I inquired.

Alexander smiled. "Tourists, yes, of course. And agriculture. Maybe the high-tech stuff. We are highly educated, you know."

Of course I knew. "Tbilisi is a good town to look at. Like Greece and Italy. Very civilized. Tbilisi should attract artists, painters, poets…"

Showing emotion, Alexander murmured, "People of the soul."

"That's very good," I agreed. "People of the soul."

Alexander smiled. "Did you know that we have a very big movie studio right here in the middle of Tbilisi?" he asked. "Lots of ground around it."

"You mean a movie lot?"

"That's it, yes. A movie lot."

I thought about that and offered, "One thing that bothers me is that Georgia is an orphan."

Alexander looked puzzled and a little emotional as he asked, "What do you mean?"

I continued, "Armenia has its ties with America and Russia. Azerbaijan has its ties with places like Turkey. There are a lot of Slavs and Eastern Europeans in America. But Georgia is like an orphan to most Americans. Most Americans don't even know where Georgia and the Caucasus are. It has no comparable diaspora."

Alexander jokingly replied, "Well, people must *like* it here, I guess." And then, turning serious, he continued, "We *do* have American friends, like you, don't we?"

It was now my turn to show emotion. "Absolutely. I have become like a missionary, and Georgia is my mission."

"You are our friend," Alexander said softly.

With my eyes welling up, I agreed. "I am, indeed, your friend, Georgia's friend."

I stared into Alexander's eyes, hoping that the man knew just how deeply I believed the words he had just uttered. The intimacy I felt in those eyes was compelling, and I felt complimented that Alexander had trusted me enough to tell me his story.

Chapter 39

Networking
(Playing Chess)

D URING LATE SPRING of 1999, Rusico Gorgiladze, President
Shevardnadze's special advisor and my close friend, spent
the better part of five days in California. She stayed with my
family at our mountain home, and she and Marilyn hit it off.
Forty years old, Rusico was from West Georgia near the Black
Sea, the same region where Eduard Shevardnadze grew up—
Guria Province. Together, we had arranged for her to lecture
at UC Berkeley and at Stanford, where she also had a meeting
with Dr. Condoleezza Rice (who was Stanford's chancellor at
the time), and Charles Palm (who I had first met in 1997, while
helping the Hoover Institution with its project of copying the
Georgian Communist Party papers). As a high-ranking government official, Rusico traveled on a diplomatic passport and represented Georgia at various diplomatic meetings, the UN, and
elsewhere. A fellow for a year at Harvard's Kennedy School of
Government, she was involved in improving the foreign image
of Georgia. Additionally, she conducted lectures on conflict
resolution and related subjects.

I had known Rusico for five years and had traveled with her
for days at a time in Georgia as well as in the United States.
A trained psychologist, she dressed well, didn't drink, and
liked "clean" dirty jokes. You couldn't take a bad picture of her.

Like many women in the former Soviet Union, she had only recently quit smoking. Rusico could be very feminine in a European type of way, or she could be tough as nails. The change was often instantaneous and for reasons I hadn't registered. Yet she was a thoughtful and friendly woman whose flashing black eyes reminded me of Lena Horne's, and she knew all the words to "Chattanooga Choo Choo." I was able to help her in many ways, and she was a lot of fun and very interesting to be with.

When you work in the former Soviet Union, you must assume that there are a lot of KGB types around, whatever you're doing. *They* quite naturally assume the same about you. It would never occur to them that the United States would want to know how they were doing now that they were "independent," or who their friends are, or what their plans for the next ten years might be. Their logic is that anyone who hangs around places like Dushanbe, Ashgabat, and Baku must be on *somebody's* secret payroll, because why else leave the comforts of the United States? It rarely matters to them what your true reasons for being there might be, because, for the most part, they don't believe they have anything we could possibly want. Basically, they're right. Their people have a hard time looking beyond the immediate future, and are instead focused on having electric power twenty-four hours a day, heat when the winter comes, some new clothes, *any* kind of automobile, and education for their children. Who can blame them? Of course, they have the wonderful cultural traditions that sustained them through seventy years of occupation, but with few exceptions (Alex Rondeli being a huge one), most of them are caught up in the daily struggle for survival.

By this late date, I didn't think my intelligence background or general activities were a secret anymore, and people showed me courtesy by not bringing it up. Indeed, many of the people I dealt with didn't *want* to know my background, and, if they were aware of its darker side, they no longer cared, especially since what I was currently doing was in their best interests. Also, by knowing me, they believed they might get a few advantages through "insider" knowledge and perhaps make a buck out of it.

But, lest I get too secure in this line of thinking, my years of training and experience would surprise me and kick in on occasion. This happened during my five days with Rusico. We toured California's Napa Valley, inspected Kaiser Permanente in Oakland, had lunch in Yosemite Valley, and visited Monterey during the first four days. We laughed as we read maps, sang "Sentimental Journey," and saw some of California's most famous and beautiful sights. On the fifth and final day, we found ourselves heading to Marin County's Mount Tamalpais for a few hours among the redwoods at Muir Woods National Monument. I was to put Rusico on a plane for Boston shortly.

In 1999, I helped arranged a trip to California for Rusico Gorgiladze.

During eighty hours together of uninterrupted chatter on dozens of subjects, I had never directed the conversation toward what I might *want* to know. Never! Too risky! Not only might I tip her off that I was looking, but any information I might get from her could be contaminated by the process. Besides, I had learned in rugby that you never force things. You go with the flow and if it's meant to be, the ball will bounce up into your hands for a painless score. But you must always be in position and on alert.

I also suspected that Rusico had hoped to learn more about *me,* either as a personal goal or at the request of someone higher up. So, like a Mark Twain barefoot country boy, I pretended to make little circles in the dust with my big toe. Some call it "spinning," but I prefer to call it "swirling," and that's what I did with Rusico when she questioned me. We stopped to pay at the entrance to Muir Woods. "Let me pay for this, Jim," Rusico offered. "You have been very good to me."

"Okay," I replied and took her five dollars.

As we drove into the park, I was only half listening when she started in with, "Jim, I want to thank you for this wonderful week. I know it's been very expensive. Do you have to pay for it all or can you charge it to your expense account?"

I thought to myself, *Whoops! What expense account?* Usually I'm ready with a consistent and reasonably plausible answer, and I replied, "As you know, I'm a private consultant and wear a lot of hats. I'm also semiretired and, as you might have guessed, I'm financially well off. But my central purpose" (I cursed myself for using the word *central)* "is to write an adventure novel about the Caucasus." I thought to myself, *Give her hors d'oeuvres, not a club sandwich.*

We walked among the giant trees. I just kept chattering as she mentioned places I had been that I had never mentioned to her—places that, with my compartmentalized approach, I *wouldn't* mention to her, indeed, *couldn't* mention to her.

Finally, I said, "Well, you know the Caucasus is just a part of the big picture, and, as you know, I've seen almost all of the old Soviet Union—except Tajikistan" (I left her some bait). Then I added, "You are the Princess of West Georgia, and I've always found you an exciting person to be with."

She thought about that and said, "Jim, I never knew you had feelings that way. I think you're great!"

"You know," I volunteered, "there are people who probably think I'm some sort of intelligence observer because of the way I travel, but that's just the way it may look. I *will* say that from time to time, I've been contacted by the intelligence community after one of my trips. But they usually just want to know my impressions of the state of an economy or the morale of the people in a given area, things they can't find out with their technical intelligence. I give them, well, you know, 'man on the street' sorts of things."

I kept up this line of fluff until she seemed off target enough to let it go. And then, in one of my impulsive "attack, don't defend" moments, I asked, "If, on your return, you were asked by your superiors what the highlights of your trip to California were, what would you say?"

Rusico replied, "Well, of course, my presentation at UC Berkeley, and then going to the Hoover Institution and George Shultz's office. Oh, and meeting with Condoleezza Rice."

I said, "Okay, give me five more."

"Yes, all right. Yosemite Falls, the dining room at the Ahwahnee Hotel, eating dinner at Clint Eastwood's Mission Ranch, visiting Francis Ford Coppola's winery in Napa Valley, and, of course, Carmel."

I replied, "Good. That's just what I do when I travel. Hit the good places, the places I want to experience and remember. I particularly like sharing such things with a real princess."

Rusico asked, "Jim, what does 'hit' the good places mean? Why 'hit'?"

I thought to myself, *We're moving on.* I explained, "'Hit' means a brief visit, like 'hit the restroom.'"

"Oh, I think I understand."

Muir Woods was dripping with fog, and for a few moments Rusico looked like Alice in Wonderland. Later, at the airport, she bought several large color posters and, pointing to an aerial view of San Francisco Bay looking west from Berkeley, said, "This is my favorite." It depicted a sunny day in the East Bay, with a blanket of fog lying so deep over San Francisco that all you could see were the towers of the Golden Gate Bridge and the peak of the Transamerica pyramid building.

I couldn't help imagining symbolism in the photograph. But my cover was still in place.

Scout's Honor

SITTING IN A FASHIONABLE RESTAURANT in Palo Alto, California, in the late fall, I wondered if the annual Big Game between my alma mater, the California Bears, and their rival, the Stanford Trees (they will always be the "Indians" to me), would become a mud bowl. The first rainstorm of the season had brought flooding, mudslides, and many accidents to the Peninsula area. Nevertheless, fashionable and prosperous-looking working people were noisily enjoying their fashionable meals.

A little while later, as I sat in the corner facing the main entrance, I was joined by two of my Pants Factory associates. Sitting opposite me with tight-lipped faces, they seemed surprised and perhaps disappointed with my comments regarding some "recruitment" problems they were having. "Look," I said, "I have no problem approaching strangers or people I've just recently met about almost anything. But I *am* really bothered by requests to recruit people I've known for many years who have become friends—real friends—even though I'm one of the 'good guys' with a good cause." My lunch mates glanced at each other, but before they could say anything, I continued, "Yeah, sure, you've probably always had a good idea what I'm all about. But, you see, I really *do* get into my act. Virtually everything I say and do is on the up and up, and when I put on my 'hat,' I get up close and personal. I give of myself—I give and I get just like I would in any friendship, and once I gain somebody's confidence, it is not something I can easily betray. It goes against my very being."

This ability to be just who I am is one of my chief assets as an independent contractor, and the discretion it allows me is a luxury I suspect few of my full-time agency counterparts could afford. As I tried to explain my thoughts on the subject, I wondered if my colleagues even halfway understood what I was talking about. Still, I tried. "I have no problem hiring assets in the field—paying bribes, big tips, or specially targeted project dollars—if they are cold-calls or people who have already been 'turned.' But I *do* have a problem setting the hook on a long-time, personal connection. Let somebody else do that. I don't even want to know the details of how or even *whether* someone has turned."

As I was spouting off, I realized that "compartmentalization" was a *mantra* to the official intelligence agencies, and, for the most part, I'm glad I didn't have to deal with most of its constraints. But I also realized that this was an advantage they had that I didn't, because *they* didn't have to make as many choices that could have a negative impact on people they knew. I realized that, in most cases, my superiors didn't *want* me to know that somebody had turned, which was fine with me because to know would only hurt my effectiveness, and the turnee's.

From the street, I could hear the clashing pep bands and the raucous sounds of the Cal and Stanford fight songs, but that didn't distract me from the point I was trying to make. I continued, "It's one thing to cold-call an adversary, but an offer to 'turn' a friend could result in a bullet in the back of his head if things go wrong, and it's simply out of my range and I just won't do it"

I wasn't articulate enough to say it, but another reason I'm so dead set against this sort of thing is because I would be asking a close person—a *friend* perhaps—to abandon his principles and to give away his very soul, the one thing we all share in common. But I did manage to make my point obliquely. "Hey, I know a lot of guys whose pathology allows them to betray confidences, break promises, and take advantage of good people just for the sport of it, but I am *not* one of those guys."

Much of my sense of honor began in the 1930s on the Berkeley playground where I learned that "Scout's Honor," or a promise made, was sacred, particularly for this little Methodist boy who would never let an American flag touch the ground. I already knew the Golden Rule and the Ten Commandments almost as soon as I could read, and I had my mother's bar of soap in my mouth on more than one occasion. On the job, when *my* code of ethics allowed and when circumstances dictated, I mostly dealt with people who bought my story because of how I packaged it. My adversaries usually assumed more than they should have! I could *feel* it when they finally thought they "had my number." Oddly enough, that was the moment I had theirs and I would discreetly set the hook.

Sometimes, though not often, I would be there when they tried to call my hand, only to discover that it was *they* who had been had, a frequently explosive moment. Arrogance was a problem for Central Asians, especially those who had worked with the Soviets, and ignorance compounds arrogance. They had been brainwashed into regarding European and American intellect and resolve as being inferior to their own. Who's to say, but our styles sure are different. One thing we all understood was that *they* had a cultural capacity for being cruel. We all have it, I suppose, but my enemies' evil was more readily available to them. I had to always assume I meant *nothing* to these people. This was a difficult aspect of the game to accept, but you had to accept it if you wanted to play in their league.

So, lest I sounded too soft, I reminded my colleagues, "It's all hardball, and you'd better know it in the first few days. Social and humanitarian issues are nonissues when you're facing live fire and wish to continue breathing!" My lunch mates, seemingly startled by my sudden about-face, snapped to attention as I concluded, "The *mission* is the thing, and any friendship fallout that develops is just frosting on the cake. For that possible outcome, mutual respect can be a worthwhile and sustaining byproduct. But, of course, you can never be entirely certain your 'friends' share your feelings."

Understandably, my much younger associates seemed to be getting lost in my dissertation and, but for my record of "combat" in the field, might well have thought I was too old for their line of work. But then the thirty-year-old brought me full around when he said, "Thanks for sharing your thoughts with us today. We all thought you were an old World War II, right-wing dinosaur with no conscience. It's great to find a professional like you, a real role model sort of thing. It's fascinating to see how *hard* being soft can be." And then, "Aha!" It was at that exact moment I knew I got them, or wait a minute, did they just get me? *C'est la guerre!* (Such is war!)

Chapter 40

The Third Man Theme
(And Then There Were Five)

FROM THE EARLY 1950s on, I was in and out of London frequently and even lived there for a while. This gave me a perspective on the growth and changes that happened there as the city tried to recover from the carnage of World War II. As a result of Hitler, the entire country of Great Britain had been bombed and rationed into virtual national poverty. The middle class, which was never extensive, disappeared altogether, and the country was gravely lacking in leadership due to the monstrous casualties among the officer corps. There was a period of time after World War II when the dark specter of communism almost took over. Traditional class warfare was a natural stimulant to the socialization of industry and of health and welfare. It all happened quickly in the vacuum created by the end of the war, and it was no accident that communism, long in the womb and without a strong developing middle class to combat it, was about to sink Britannia beneath a "red tide" generated from Moscow. For me, watching the changes that happened to London over the past fifty years served as a model and personal metaphor of sorts for what would or could happen to similarly affected nations throughout the world. The struggle is essentially the same, as are the solutions.

The terrible depression immediately following World War II caused many people to sell off their cherished antiques and heirlooms in order to survive. As a result, antique markets such as Camden Passage, Bermondsey Market, Portabello Road, and Burlington Arcade flourished when foreigners, particularly American tourists, began to arrive in large numbers. All over Britain, small shops and Saturday night markets sprouted up. England was old and *loaded!* Every house had its share of antiques and other valuables, and much of this found its way to the export market. I picked up a lot of goodies through the years, and I still like to make the rounds of my favorite shops, especially in London's West End, Chelsea, and Kensington Church Street areas, when passing through on my way to Eastern Europe. Through the years, I made friends because I was a regular, a knowledgeable dealer who owned a shop. In fact, the business card I used for my antique shop in the 1980s listed a branch office in London in addition to my main office in San Francisco. All the more reason to be traveling overseas as much as I did.

One of my favorite shops was 31 Holland Street, just off Kensington Church. The sign read, "Constance Stobo—English Lusterware, Staffordshire Animals—18th Century and 19th Century Pottery." This shop was only two blocks from my regular hotels, the Gore Hotel and Kensington Palace, the latter being directly across from the palace of the same name, and the scene of Princess Diana's floral outcry. It was incredible; I was there to see it.

When in London, I often made friendly small-talk calls on "Connie," who was several years my senior. She was born in Aberystwith on the far west coast of Wales overlooking the Irish Sea. She had attended college there and worked summer jobs in nearby Tenby, Wales, which was where my family and I lived while I worked on an oil refinery for Bechtel. I collected early pottery, and Connie always put nice things aside for me to look at during my next visit.

It was during one such visit in the late 1980s that I mentioned in passing I had been traveling east a lot and had spent much of my time touring the USSR with my rugby team as well as antiquing. Sybil, a longtime friend of Connie's who assisted in her shop, had listened and volunteered that Connie might have something of interest to share with me. So, after some more small talk, I volunteered that I was with the U.S. Foreign Service. They had already guessed as much. Thinking there would be much more to say, I excused myself with the statement that I would stop by in five weeks to pick up my latest purchase and to hear the rest of the story.

Five weeks later to the day, I knocked on the always locked door and was given a warm hug by Connie and a businesslike handshake from Sybil. We huddled by the small coal fireplace (my "Lord Nelson" was already packed in bubble wrap) and sipped tea while sampling delicate pastries. Connie and Sybil exchanged affirming glances and nods, and I thought I heard the trace of suppressed giggles.

Connie finally passed me a large magazine-size envelope full of thick, rough, brown paper and motioned me to look at it. I slid the contents out onto a low brass tray table in front of the small flickering fire. I responded instantly to a hardback book with a red paper cover, titled *Philby: The Long Road to Moscow*. Along with the book were several packets of letters bound with shipper's cord. Connie finally dumped a number of photos and snapshots across the table. At the time, Connie was seventy-five and stately. She reminded me of a cultured, slender version of Barbara Bush with a similar sharp wit, and at first I didn't recognize the gorgeous young woman in the bathing suit sunning herself on the beach of Majorca, drink and cigarette in hand. However, the book title hinted to me that the handsome young man in many of the photos was Kim Philby. I recovered enough to say, "I'd recognize the lady from Aberystwith anywhere and you have hardly changed, but who's the clownish schoolboy fellow leering at you?"

We all laughed with relief—it was out now. Connie, who is referred to in the book as "The Shadowy Civil Servant," had been Philby's main girlfriend for four years during the early fifties, or was she his mistress? Either way, I call her, "Philby's Cover Girl."

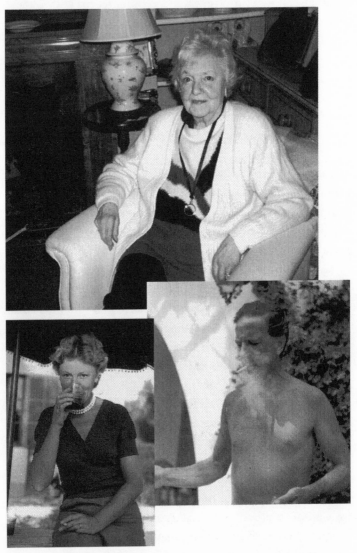

An antique dealer in London shared an intriguing spy story from the past.

Philby, a son of the British establishment, had a thirty-year career in his country's Secret Service, all the while being a dedicated communist agent who penetrated his country's Secret Service so effectively that, in 1944, he became the director of its Counter-Soviet Department. John Le Carre called this "a feat of duplicity unequalled in the annals of espionage. He was the link man between the British Service and the American Central Intelligence Agency from which position he was able to betray every important secret of Western intelligence."

We chatted for a while, mostly on the light side. Connie had lived with Philby, traveled with him, partied with him, drank with him, and slept with him. After the tea had shifted to claret and port, Connie was in a spirit of fond remembrance and volunteered that "he drank way too much" but that this had probably obscured the fact that she may have been less than a sophisticated lover. At first to her surprise and disappointment, but later to her silent relief, Philby eventually moved on to a job in Beirut for the London Observer and on to a new girlfriend.

Connie was not involved with Philby when the revelation of the notorious KGB spy ring of Guy Burgess, Donald McLean, and Kim Philby resulted in the calamitous crisis that devastated international relations with Britain. That is well covered elsewhere. Eventually, a fourth "super spy" was added, Anthony Blunt, whom Connie met at the Courthold Gallery. TV really ran with *that*, especially since he was a friend of the Queen and had, unbelievably, been knighted (later to be de-knighted). Although Connie was interrogated when it all hit the fan, she was cleared within a short period of time. But it had been a painful experience for her.

More recently, the British Intelligence Service MI-5 had been at Connie's door as a follow-up to a perfectly innocent visit by Russian ex-patriot Svetlana Alliluyeva, Stalin's unsupportive daughter. "I didn't have the slightest idea who she was," Connie explained. "She was nice enough and we shared our interest in porcelain, but she was low-budget cheap! It was only after her third visit that MI-5 came forward. They thought that maybe I might have new news about my old associates." Connie was astounded—forty years ago? Were they joking? All she could remember was that Philby's old friends were brilliant, snobby, elitist, and liked to drink. It was only later that she learned they were active Communists. As it turned out, she also learned that several were homosexual, bisexual, or nonsexual, in addition to being traitors.

But there was still something else on Connie's mind. She had read about the case of the "Third Man Theme" (Philby), followed not long after by the headlines, "And then there were four—'The Fourth Man Theme'" (Blunt). Clearly, without saying so, she wanted me to know—and whomever I worked for to know—that she thought there was still *another*—"Number Five!" I wondered why she thought this way and so I asked her. She explained that she had met and mixed with Philby's friends on and off in various venues. But on a number of occasions, she motored to places with him and was left in the car or at a local pub while he disappeared, sometimes for an hour or so, and sometimes longer. She remembered this because she had felt used, often ran out of cigarettes, and had gotten cold and hungry. In her gut, she just *knew* there were more people involved. I said, "Wow, that's fascinating!" I offered to see if any of my friends in high places would be interested and promised to get back to her. I thanked her for her trust in me as well as for the tea and shortbreads, my favorite.

Pass on the word I did, and, much to no one's surprise, not long thereafter, John Cairncross came forward and admitted he was the missing link in the "notorious" spy ring. He had been recruited along with the others at Cambridge University in the 1930s and, as a KGB agent, had passed British military intelligence about Germany to the Russians. After graduation, he served in a number of government offices, most notably the

Signal Intelligence Agency and the Secret Intelligence Service. Since "coming out" and working on his memoirs, Cairncross died in 1996 at the age of eighty-two. The pardoned Blunt had died in 1983, and the other three, who served an ignoble exile in Russia, died in that country.

With Cairncross exposed, Connie had felt a subtle sense of relief. The vague feeling of hiding an unknown secret had left her. Her hugs were now warmer and long lasting. We occasionally dined at the San Lorenzo Restaurant on Beauchamps Street near Harrods when I had time. We never really talked about Philby again for she was too lively and didn't need to anymore. When Sybil was there, I would get a long and intense handshake or, should I say, handhold and a long, emphatic wink—which I have yet to decipher.

Connie closed her shop and retired to her comfortable flat in Chelsea. The last time I saw her was in 2000 when I was passing through on my way to Georgia. We had dinner together, and as I was leaving her apartment, she told me not to write or bother to see her anymore but that she would always remember our hugs and friendship. She hesitated as if not sure it was right to say but did anyway, "It's a pity we did not meet at some other time or place—like when we were younger, perhaps on the wide, sandy summer beach near Aberystwith or at a rugby 'do' after a game in Swansea." As her voice trailed off, her glistening eyes told me to leave and not to look back. Standing near the black wrought-iron fence at the entrance to Connie's flat, I tried to wave down a cab in the late-night drizzling rain and had a moment of déjà vu. I had heard that same line somewhere before in my travels. *Who? Where?* I thought to myself. *Oh, yeah, Helena, that Russian KGB broad on the train. That's it.* She, too, had said 'Don't write' and I had known what she meant, but *what* a difference between the two!

A taxi with its headlights flicking on and off veered toward the curb where I was standing. The amber vacancy light went off and the door swung open. "Jump in, Gov-ner. How about the Gore Hotel? That's where I picked you up, right?" As we sped off, "Alfie" (that's what I call London cab drivers, all twelve thousand of them) finished telling me about his recent trip to Las Vegas and Disneyland with his three kids. As I got out, Alfie couldn't help but say, "When you get back, you tell Bill Clinton to keep his eye on the donut, not the hole! Ha, ha, ha. See ya next time, mate."

Through the years, London cab drivers provided me with some of my best insights into the fields of economic and political development. They always have interesting comments and are a living demonstration of the emergence of a broad middle class so necessary for the development of Third World countries. I have also gained much of my optimism from watching the Brits for fifty years. They truly endure. Although Britannia no longer rules the waves and their empire has all but disappeared, the British soul will live on forever.

Chapter 41

Weaving Spiders
(The Club)

THE BOHEMIAN CLUB of San Francisco occupies a special place in my heart. Because of my itinerant lifestyle, it has been a source of refuge and inspiration for me for the last forty-one years, a sort of home base of friendship, outlasted only by my wonderful marriage of fifty-eight years and my participation in sports, particularly rugby, for forty-five years. As a men's social club, the Bohemian Club is very different from most of its counterparts. Founded in 1872, its San Francisco headquarters is a three-story, red-brick building laced with ivy that, structurally at least, survived the 1906 fire and earthquake. The Club originated as a place for writers, singers, poets, and the like to meet and exchange thoughts and good cheer (Jack London was one of its early members). Creating entertainment for members and friends is a vital part of the Club's activities and, indeed, its very reason for being. Each year, the Club puts on original plays, light operas, and other productions, using its own members, who are nearly professional in caliber.

Because I have moved twenty-seven times since I was born in 1929, the Club has been an anchor for me. The Club is *not*, as often portrayed, just a rich man's club, although many of its members are successful in their communities. In fact, it may be one of the only clubs in the country that you can't buy your way into. Although some members are among the rich and powerful, a significant percentage are musicians, writers, actors, struggling schoolteachers, clergy, sailors, and soldiers who belong—indeed are *sought*—because of their diverse talents and dedication to keeping the Club active through their participation. Those who are exceptionally talented are usually accepted for membership quickly, while financiers and industrialists might wait twenty years to get in.

I gained early membership in the Club as a contributing member when I joined the chorus. I had been singing in choirs and choruses ever since that warm spring afternoon in Berkeley when I was seven years old and the mournful strains of the "Volga Boatman" had drawn me to the open window of my elementary school.

At the Bohemian Grove, James Baker and I were just two rugby players.

Despite rumors to the contrary, the Club is not political, and, although a number of celebrities are members or guests of members, no autographs, cameras, tape recorders, cell phones, or doing business of any kind is allowed. Our slogan is: *"Weaving Spiders Come Not Here!"* So, it is with some embarrassment that I write the following confession of a "weaving spider."

In August of 1997, during the Club's Bohemian Grove summer encampment on the Russian River at Monte Rio, California, I happened to be there a day earlier than usual and listened to an interesting talk by the "Lakeside Speaker," Ervin Duggan of National Public Radio. Later, during lunch over adult beverages, we were able to get the low-down on some very serious issues at National Public Radio—e.g., does Jim Lehrer wear a wig? do Elizabeth Farnsworth and Margaret Warner have good bodies? (they're always sitting down), and so forth.

Near the end of the lunch, a friend of mine, Bill Jaeger, whom I had known for several years, called me over to meet with two men sitting at his table—John Raisin, Director of the Hoover Institution, and Herbert Hoover III. Both were Club members. After some chitchat, Hoover said he had heard that I traveled extensively in the former Soviet Union and wondered if I knew that, shortly after the end of the Cold War, he had negotiated to copy the Russian Communist Party papers in Moscow. They consisted of approximately one hundred million papers. This was a move to preserve a record of what had taken place during the seventy dark years of Soviet rule, not only for the libraries of the world but for the Russian people themselves so that they, too, would know what really happened—before the shredders erased it all. This was brilliant, and I told him so. I also told Hoover that not only was I amazed that they were able to do this, but that they had even thought of it. Then I asked, "What can I do for you guys?"

Hoover responded, "Are you going to Georgia soon?"

"Yes," I said.

"Do you know people in the government, like Shevardnadze?" Hoover asked.

"Yes," I replied. "I know most of them. The good ones at least. There's a lot of turnover."

Hoover looked thoughtful. "When are you going again?"

"In about two weeks," I replied.

"Do you suppose you could ask the 'good ones' if we could talk to them about *their* Party papers?"

I was puzzled for a moment and then said, "I thought you guys had already done that."

Hoover explained, "In Russia, yes, but not in Georgia. Georgia is very important, not only strategically, but it's also the birthplace of Stalin and Beria of 'Evil Empire' fame, as well as Eduard Shevardnadze." And, coincidentally Gorbachev, only five hundred miles north of the Georgian border at Stavropol. It must be the climate, or southern exposure.

"Yes," I agreed. "It's fascinating that these three were born within a few hundred miles of each other and none of them are Russian. Before *these* guys came along, what made Georgia famous was having the most people over a hundred years old. I've often thought that Shevardnadze must feel a need to atone for the evil of the other two—two of the greatest mass killers in history, two of the greatest proponents of atheism, from Christian Georgia. Sure, I'll help you, but isn't this talk we're having against Club rules?"

Hoover looked surprised and asked, "What do you mean?"

I clarified, "Aren't we 'weaving spiders,' doing a little networking?"

Hoover answered, "Hell, yes, and this is only the beginning."

I was glad to meet Hoover and excited about what they wanted me to accomplish during my next trip to Georgia. But we were both a bit cagey—like two cats circling each other with words. Hoover assured me that he was talking about an aboveboard business arrangement with the Georgians, but would not say how much the Hoover Institution would offer. However, he sketched out the general approach that had proven successful in Moscow. The basic requirements were as follows:

1. The documents would be *only* Communist Party papers.
2. Copying would be done in Tbilisi.
3. Only *copies* would leave Georgia.
4. Copyrights would be set up and royalties charged.
5. Internet access would be established.
6. Document preparation would be directed toward research and schools.

As I stood there discussing this new adventure, I marveled at how the world works. The barbecue lunch was over, and the twenty or so club members in attendance were listening to one of their brothers play his guitar and sing some old Burl Ives songs of the African Veldt. All the while, two of their number were discussing how to "capture" the Communist Party's papers in Stalin's backyard! Such thoughts would have been outrageous seven years ago and were even now, for that matter. Nevertheless, cards and promises of phone calls were clandestinely exchanged.

The next morning, while walking down the river road toward the great outdoor dining area that seats one thousand in a cathedral-like grove of redwoods, I ran into Bill Jaeger who was returning from breakfast. We greeted each other, and I said, "Thanks for yesterday's good food and music and, by the way, thanks for the intro to Herbert Hoover. We may have something going there and I'll keep you posted. Anyhow, I want you to know that, as of now, you are in the loop."

Jaeger laughed. "Oh, Jesus, Jim, I don't know if I *want* to be in the loop. How 'bout just *getting* looped?"

"Sorry, Bill, it's too late," I replied, before adding, "I've got to get one thing straight. Why did Hoover nab me at the party yesterday? You didn't even know I was going to be there."

Bill explained, "Well, we were just standing around tippling a couple of drinks when the subject of travel in the USSR came up, and I said, 'You ought to meet Jim Waste over there—he travels a lot in Central Asia as a public health consultant.'" Then, turning serious for a second, he said, "That's all. Nothing else, if you know what I mean. If there *is* anything else, Jim, it's his nickel."

We both laughed, cutting the tension, and Jaeger said, "Well, Mr. Phantom, if I'm in the loop, I guess I should also mention that I met a guy at a cocktail party at Piedmont Camp after our lunch yesterday who's the Hoover Institution's librarian. His name is Charles Palm."

I was startled. "You're kidding! That's the next guy I'm supposed to meet."

Jaeger chuckled. "He's staying here tonight."

Charles Palm had *organized* the copying of the Russian Communist Party papers, and I tracked him down that night to discuss the Georgian project at length. Three weeks later, I arrived in Tbilisi and spent a couple of days sounding out a few "old Georgian friends" regarding the delicacy of this matter. They agreed that the Russians had set the precedent.

Shevardnadze happened to be in Iran until midweek, so I set up a preliminary meeting with Gela Charkviani. Their offices were right next door to each other, and Gela was always ready to listen to the latest gossip on former secretaries of state George Shultz and James Baker. Gela's father, incidentally, had been Communist Party secretary in Georgia for fourteen years—while Stalin was still in the saddle. Gela remembered seeing Stalin at social events when he was a young boy.

I decided to bounce the Hoover deal off Gela first and let him take it from there. I've found that it works well to make others look good whenever you can, and Gela had always been there for me. Gela's eyes widened when I told him of the Hoover proposal and, with his Ezio Pinza-like voice, said in perfect English, "Are you pulling my leg? You walk in here after all these years and want to buy the Communist Party archives, which are probably rotting in storage?"

Caught off guard, I thought to myself, *Maybe I'm moving too fast.* I gave him a few more facts and waited for a response.

He sat quietly for a moment and then proclaimed, "It's a deal!"

I was shocked, mainly because I didn't think it would be so easy. And then, of course, I realized he wouldn't have the authority to make a decision like that. He was having fun with me, as usual. Gela's English was better than my Russian, so he always had the edge on me in the humor department.

Before I could comment, he rushed to make it clear that, speaking for himself, he would welcome the opportunity to let the world's scholars evaluate Georgia's role in the "great experiment." There had been some rumors about his father's political philosophy and ethics when Gela was young, and he particularly liked the idea that his father's name would finally be publicly cleared. Gela had researched his father's "work history" and found that his father was "clean," which meant that he had not been involved in "dirty deals"—the curse of Party membership.

I volunteered that, as far as I knew, Shevardnadze was "clean," to which Gela jumped in and said, "This is one of the reasons he and I work so well together. We don't have, as you say, 'skeletons in the closet.' I will arrange a meeting for you when he gets back."

Several days later, Gela called me in for a late-afternoon appointment with Shevardnadze. I reviewed the Hoover plan with the Georgian president, and his first comment was in the form of a statement: "This matter must be handled publicly and through the Parliament. We will use the front door only. These records belong to the people, and the public must be considered at all stages."

He glanced at Gela and asked, "Gela, aren't there a lot of Stalin and Beria documents stored somewhere? Maybe even down in the basement getting wet? Perhaps we should look into getting things like that preserved for our children. The Stalin birthplace at Gori has very little money coming in from tourists. Maybe we can get Mr. Hoover interested in *this* situation."

Before I left, I explained how I happened to be the messenger. I had suggested to George Shultz that he might be the best person to discuss the Hoover proposal with Shevardnadze, and he proposed that I handle the initial discussion. Shultz said that he would not feel comfortable approaching his friend Shevardnadze on a matter of such personal significance. He didn't want to take advantage of their friendship and thought we should approach Georgia through more formal channels. On hearing this, Shevardnadze told me through Gela that George Shultz was a "real classical act." I didn't correct the usage.

Also of great interest to Shevardnadze was the fact that George Shultz had remarried. Shultz's wife, O'Bie, had passed away and this saddened the Georgian leader, especially since his wife, Nanuli, and O'Bie had gotten along so well. Shevardnadze worries about his "good friends" and he wanted to know what Shultz's new wife was like and whether she was good for him. "Younger?"

I replied that her name was Charlotte Mailliard Swig. "She's very attractive, smart, and a devoted public servant. And the answer is yes, she's younger." Sixty-three at the time, to George's seventy-six.

He smiled. "I know George likes to sing." The moment was right and I opened a file folder containing wedding photos and articles from San Francisco newspapers. Shevardnadze looked through the file and, beaming ear to ear, nodded his head in approval. "Grace Cathedral—a church wedding—good! Say 'hello' for me."

After that meeting, George Shultz wrote a letter on behalf of Hoover, and Rusico Gorgiladze visited Charles Palm at Stanford. The necessary arrangements were made, and the recording of the official history of the Georgian Communist Party was undertaken.

Snapshot 17

Many Wet Eyes

E VERY SUMMER, several thousand men of the Bohemian Club get together for "Scout Camp" in a seven-hundred-acre redwood grove on the Russian River, seventy-five miles north of San Francisco. Guests come in from all over the world for two weeks of "Low and High Jinks," botanical talks, and lectures by Heads of State and celebrities who have included the likes of Jimmy Carter, Anwar Sadat, George H. W. Bush, Merv Griffin, and Clint Eastwood. No pictures are allowed. No autographs can be solicited. No tape recordings. Everything is off the record.

Like the Club itself, the Bohemian Grove encampment is private but democratic, and you're just as likely to run into a schoolteacher as the president of a computer company, as long as they're willing and able to participate. The purpose of the camp is to have fun and to share who you are with others. The medium to accomplish this is the original entertainment that the campers create, including plays, musicals, and storytelling. Everybody takes part on some level, even if it's only Henry Kissinger carrying a spear or George Shultz in drag. It's all great fun rather than some right-wing conspiracy, as some of the media would have you believe.

When major programs are presented, and also as a warm-up for plays, as many as two thousand members will gather on log benches in the outdoor theater, accompanied by a brass band, to sing traditional American camp songs such as "In the Good Old Summer Time," "My Darling Clementine," and "I've Been Working on the Railroad." If your alma mater is played, you rise and sing along, and, surprisingly, the number of members having attended UC Berkeley—a public school—outnumber all others, including Stanford, ten to one. As the singing gets louder, those who were in the Air Force rise to sing "Into the Wild Blue Yonder," and when the band begins "Anchors Aweigh," another group gets to their feet. Then comes "As the Caissons Go Rolling Along," followed, as always, by the "Marine Corps Hymn." *Those* few who rise are the envy of the rest.

The time spent together in the redwood forest is about as close to a Boy Scout Jamboree as one can get as a grown-up, and although women are invited to a few of the entertainment programs at other times, the summer camp is off limits to them. Men have an indirect way of communicating, usually by doing things together, and I'm not sure how many women understand the male camaraderie thing, anyhow.

It's always a great experience, but I particularly remember a warm Saturday in August of 1972 when my friend Gordon Knapp, a former Assistant Secretary of the U.S. Air Force, asked me to sit with him and his guest from the Pentagon, four-star general Bill Evans, at the "Low Jinks" show. We were all in jeans and khakis and a little loggy from a heavy camp dinner. Before the evening program began, the crowd warmed itself up with song, as is the custom. When the singing started, the general's eyes brightened. He was just a guy without his stars here, and he told us that the music reminded him of his childhood in Northern Michigan. He looked at all the men around him who had come together for good fellowship and sort of shook his head in wonderment. Not disbelief, but wonderment. He nudged Gordon and me, as if to say, "Look, I'm singing and I know the words!"

Then there was a drum roll and everybody rose to sing "The Star Spangled Banner" with both reverence and passion. When we got to the "rockets' red glare," I glanced at the general, who had tears running down his face. Finishing with "the land of the free, and the home of the brave," Gordon leaned against him as if to provide support. As we sat down, the general hooked his arms through ours and wouldn't let go for several minutes. Finally, he said, "Thank you for having me here. I needed this. I haven't heard the national anthem sung like that for a long time. In the sixties, patriotism became politically incorrect and I worried that if these songs were no longer sung, who would carry the torch? They must be sung. By singing them, we come together with those who have gone before us. They evoke the times and places that we *must* remember if we are to continue to be the United States of America." It was at that moment I knew how he got those four stars!

Chapter 42

Bohemian Knights
(It Was Meant to Be)

I WAS IN A HURRY because I had made a last-minute decision to go to the Bohemian Club in San Francisco for an evening of fellowship and in-house entertainment. As I sped across the Oakland-San Francisco Bay Bridge on a late afternoon in October 1999, I marveled at the gleaming white "City of Oz" heroically profiled against the azure blue Pacific sky before me. No matter how you approached San Francisco—the City—the view was always spectacular. I loved the place despite the fact that I couldn't stand to live there.

The City had five thousand whores during the Gold Rush days and probably has five thousand whores today. English may soon become its second language. Hippies got their name here, and radio saw its beginnings. So many aspects about the place make it unique, like people jumping off the Golden Gate Bridge (more than one thousand), Alcatraz, San Quentin, and a predominantly gay Board of Supervisors. Sodom and Gomorrah or Paradise—depending upon your persuasion. Above all, San Francisco is a city of choices.

I drove up one of the hills toward the Club, where only a *few* knew what I did on my many trips to Eastern Europe and Central Asia. I was running through my latest "story" or "cover" in my head and was only half listening to a weekly conservative talk show host named Michael Savage. I shared his rage over what was happening in America and his insights were often surprisingly profound, but he seemed to self-destruct in that rage just often enough to dampen his message. The fact that he never worried about being "politically correct" was refreshing to me, and he certainly was on the right track. Even so, his words were merely background music for my thoughts.

I knew my next field trip might be my last, and I was finally taking my best friend, my wife Marilyn, with me. Travel conditions in once forbidden parts of the world were better now, and airlines, hotels and, perhaps most importantly, toilets were vastly improved. And, of course, my involvement in what might be politely called "dangerous foreign affairs" had diminished. Life-threatening situations were now fewer, and the possibility of being taken hostage on my paper route had decreased. Although Marilyn was well traveled otherwise, she had never accompanied me on the paper route because I was vulnerable there, and with her along, it would have been that much worse. Fortunately, she had not pressed to go until now.

As I approached the Bohemian Club, I decided to park at the old Trader Vic's parking lot directly across the street from the Club. By the time I crossed Taylor Street at six o'clock, which is only two blocks away from Union Square, the shopping hub of the City, there were already a half-dozen hookers and assorted transvestites wandering the neighborhood. The panhandler on the corner of Post and Taylor had been there for twelve years. I staked him out one day and watched him take in over $150 tax-free in two hours. For a moment, I wondered how he was able to keep control of that spot for so long and whether or not he, too, had a good "insurance company." There is still no doubt in my mind that there are more homeless on the streets of fashionable and prosperous San Francisco than in any comparable city in Central Asia.

The Club's doorman is one of the few people in the United States who still calls me "Mr. Waste," and he greeted me warmly.

I quickly learned that I had arrived on a very special night featuring a Congressional Medal of Honor program. As usual, I had not read my mail and was pleasantly surprised. The Club was jammed with members and guests, and although the average age of a member is fifty-three, I noticed that *this* crowd was in their sixties, seventies, and eighties. Spirits were high. It was a special gathering of a club within a club—the Knights of War! These were members who had served and fought in World War II, Korea, and Vietnam, and they were now dying off fast. During World War II, in particular, combat deaths averaged fifteen hundred per week for four years. These guys had come home and, for the most part, never talked much about it again.

There were six hundred veterans attending dinner that night, along with a few sons and grandsons. The youngsters must have been thinking, "What a load of bullshit—these guys with bad feet and pot bellies. What do *they* know?" There was quite a bit of bad language being bandied about, but this was a men's club and these were old soldiers and sailors. The banquet band played music from the forties and fifties, and promptly at 8:30 p.m. everybody moved into the Club's theater for the show. Admiral Stockdale introduced the host for the evening, Major General Patrick Brady, a Medal of Honor winner from the Vietnam War. Brady had successfully completed three thousand helicopter evacuation flights carrying five thousand casualties and had three helicopters shot out from under him in one day alone. A five-minute movie clip telling his story was shown. Not bad for a start. But that was only the beginning.

Ten more Medal of Honor winners were waiting backstage—four from the Army, three from the Navy, two from the Marines, and one from the Air Force. As each of their stories was told and shown on film (sometimes footage of the actual event, other times realistically recreated from combat footage), the honoree would come forward to a standing ovation and be seated on the stage while the other stories were told.

Brady's story was typical. There was no doubt that these men all qualified for the Medal. Their stories were difficult to believe—truly way above and beyond the call of duty. Only 170 recipients of the Congressional Medal of Honor were still alive, and eleven of them were with us that night. Virtually *all* had been wounded, and I couldn't help but remember the movie *Sergeant York* with Gary Cooper I had seen as a young boy. York had single-handedly shot sixty-seven Germans and captured 150 more in World War I. These guys in front of me were in the same league. They, too, had *been* there. I sat in awe of these men. The audience murmured in amazement.

During a short break, the band played "Sentimental Journey." The guy sitting on one side of me had been shot down in a World War II B-17 raid on the Rumanian Ploesti oil fields and then escaped from a POW camp. The guy on the other side of me was Hal Hyde, one of the American soldiers you see in those films showing Americans and Russians meeting in an Austrian field when Germany was almost beaten. It was the fastest hour and a half I had ever spent.

As Brady concluded the program, he spoke for himself and the ten guests on the stage who, incidentally, looked remarkably well considering their escapades of half a century ago, although Admiral Stockdale and one other limped noticeably. In the films, they had all been young and fit, but they still looked good. Brady looked at his fellow Medal of Honor winners and said, "I know that for each one of us up here who has been so honored, there were hundreds—no *thousands*—who were equally heroic, the difference being in our case someone saw us and reported what they saw. So, with that knowledge, we know that here in this theater tonight are many such men, and *we* salute *you*, our brothers in arms!"

The eleven Knights of History stood and saluted the audience, and the audience returned the salute. The band played "God Bless America." Everybody knew the words. Everybody had wet eyes. It was their night. Our night. My night. It was all the reward I'll ever need. I finally made it! I really *belonged* in this crowd and had probably seen a lot more action than most of them because of my twenty-five years of foreign service. Although I was honored to be among any of these guys in the audience, it occurred to me that I had finally made it as a member of the Greatest Generation. All along, it was the fact that I missed serving like my friends, the ones who were on the Tamalpais High honor roll that had haunted me all these years, and now that I finally realized the source of my compulsion to stay in the danger game, it was over. I could let it go, and I did.

Still choked with emotion, I made my way through the lingering crowd and headed up the stairs away from the theater. I was almost to the front entrance of the building when the clerk at the reception counter handed me a note that said, "Call the office." I did. Eight important people had been assassinated in the Caucasus. I would have to leave the next day, but without Marilyn. Marilyn's trip to the Caucasus would have to wait.

Although I was to make two more trips, I knew I could stay home now. And to think I went to the Club that night quite by chance. If I hadn't, I might still be blindly hung up on my obsession. Life works in strange and wonderful ways, but it does work if you're patient.

Chapter 43

End of an Era
(Chivalry Is Not Dead)

THIRTY-SIX HOURS after my emotional evening with the Medal of Honor winners at the Bohemian Club, I was on the airport tarmac in Yerevan, Armenia, en route to Tbilisi, Georgia. To the south, snow-capped Mount Ararat rose majestically out of the flat charcoal-gray Turkish plain. Symbolically, the afternoon light divided the mountain in half—dark on the East side and glowing gold and red on the West side. For a moment, I felt a tingling rush pulse through me and then it was gone. I could hear myself saying aloud, *Thank you, God, for protecting me through the years and finally revealing to me why and how I was needed.*

Although I was only fifty-five minutes from Tbilisi, I was told there would be a four-hour delay, so I left the British Airways jet for a stroll around the new airport. An hour later, I was a prisoner in the airport manager's office being interrogated by four KGB types, backed by a half-dozen heavily armed and bearded professional soldiers. Fortunately, I was *in*bound rather than *out*bound because forty-eight hours earlier, assassins had killed Armenia's Prime Minister Vazgen Sarkisyan, Speaker Karen Demirchyan, both vice speakers, three MPs, and another minister as they sat during a meeting of Parliament. Understandably, the government officials were nervous.

A view of Mount Ararat confirmed my sense of closure.

Although I thought the *real* reasons for the incident were ignored by the press, the shootings had been captured on film and broadcast throughout the world. United States representatives had been in the area during the weeks before, and I suspected the ever watchful Russian Bear foresaw something in the works that might forever deny them a possible future grab of the Azerbaijani oil fields on the Caspian Sea, or so their paranoiac reasoning went. I figured the Russian long-range plan was to eventually get control of Nagorno-Karabakh—still controlled by Azerbaijan but largely populated by Armenians—to be able to use it as a springboard into Baku. But their puppet government in Armenia was wavering under U.S. influence. My mind raced as I thought about potential consequences. I'm not a conspiracy analyst, but there had to be a political reason for this.

After several tense hours of questioning, I was able to convince them that I was on my way to Georgia and that Armenia was an unscheduled stop. Finally, they released me and I boarded a clean British Airways Airbus and resumed my trip to Tbilisi.

To the west I saw the last light of day somewhere over the Black Sea and forty-five minutes later felt the cabin tilt forward as we began our descent toward Tbilisi. Off to the left jutted the snow-capped peak of Mount Elbrus, Europe's highest mountain at 18,500 feet, glowing rose pink in the sunset's afterglow. The Caucasus Range, now a faint gray-blue silhouette, hovered barely discernible but still dominated the horizon. Finally, we saw the freckled amber lights of Tbilisi.

After landing, we coasted down the sloping runway and stopped four hundred yards away from the new airport building, which was a great improvement over its cattle-loading predecessor. Although British, Swiss, and Turkish airlines brought in the money customers, they still had to park away from the terminal, forcing the passengers to ride on standing-only buses. Only Georgian airlines were allowed to park at the gate, a leftover from the old Soviet mentality.

We had landed at ten o'clock at night, and although the Georgians went through customs quickly, it was one-thirty in the morning before the last foreign visitor had paid his twenty dollars to obtain a seven-day visitor's visa (even though he might be staying for two weeks). A week later, I would have to extend my visa for another seven days at the Immigration Office in town, another unnecessary inconvenience to deal with although it could have been done at the airport. Of course, the three visa windows were manned by only one official and, not having a "DIP" (diplomatic pass), I was near the end of the line. With all the languages being spoken around me, two words stood out—"Stupid" and "Moron!" One person shouted "Bureaubrassholes"—a new one for me!

By one-thirty in the morning, all of the taxis and junkers had given up, and I had to bribe the lone customs official to take me to Betsy's in Tbilisi twenty miles away. My pounding on the steel security door with a loose cobblestone produced a blurry-eyed night clerk who let me in. While he carried my overfilled bags to my favorite room on the second (getaway) floor, I glanced into the kitchen. I looked forward to hanging out with the Georgian family who prepared the home-cooked meals I had enjoyed so often, and talking rugby to Gogi, their 270-pound son. I was glad to be there. I unpacked and crashed from my forty-five-hour trip. It was three in the morning.

At seven-thirty, I heard the garbage man pick up at Betsy's. The links on a steel chain would drag against a brake cylinder and sound like a San Francisco cable car. The clanging sound of the driver's shovel scraping garbage into the truck woke me up most mornings at Betsy's. I didn't mind. It was part of the scene. It was only the first of a cacophony of sounds that made up the daily rhythm of life at Betsy's.

Not long after, I heard a dog barking in the backyard somewhere between the orange and apple trees, and two other dogs on the street right in front of me seemed to answer. I was particularly conscious of these Third World dogs because I had recently been bitten by a suspected rabid dog in Georgia and been forced to take the necessary shots. I guess because of this, I got a sort of bizarre satisfaction out of watching the two in front of me have back-door sex.

There had been a time during the civil war and the transition years when marauding packs of homeless, mangy dogs ganged up in parks and went on raids along the boulevard. Foreign public health officials declared that thirty-six rabies deaths in Georgia in one year was a disaster when compared to two or three deaths per year in all of the U.S. Who am I to disagree? I may have been one of the last bitten as the packs were finally hunted down.

Ironically, the same week I was bitten in Georgia, my wife was attacked by a pit bull and bitten five times on her leg while jogging less than a mile from our home in the Sierras. Marilyn had always sweetly pointed out that dogs bite me because I have "bad karma" (eleven bites in thirty years). I would maintain that dogs bite joggers on general principle, especially those who wear dark glasses. Nonetheless, Marilyn has beautiful karma and still was bitten five times! But *she* didn't have to get the shots. Thinking about it all made me wonder where "safe" is.

My thoughts of canine carnage were soon interrupted by what were probably my favorite sounds at Betsy's, when I heard the husky contralto voice of the ice-cream woman shouting *"Nakini!"* (ice cream!), along with the clinking of coins as she made change. Never without her smock or scarf, and most common during the warm months from May to November, the ubiquitous ice-cream woman trudged up and down the hills in her

I consider ice-cream sales an indicator of trickle-up recovery.

Georgian version of Birkenstocks with a large cardboard box slung over her shoulder by a thick rope. I would hear her from far away, then closer, then under my window, and finally fading away. One night a London banker friend and I did a cost study during a rooftop dinner and concluded that this wretched semi-toothless creature was making two hundred dollars a month, which was nearly equal to the government-financed salary of Alex Rondeli, Chairman of the Political Science Department at Tbilisi State University, with whom we were dining. For me, ice cream was one of the first indicators of what I call a "trickle up" recovery. It ranked right up there with Marlboro cigarettes and Mars Bars.

As I was reflecting on these different sounds that morning and how different they were from the chaotic first days of independence, I became distracted by the coarse shouting of a fifty-ish Georgian husband angry with his wife. From my courtyard window, I had frequently seen the drunk and abusive husband push and slap her around, possibly because she ran a day school for children and undoubtedly brought in more money than he did. This was one time too many! In the interests of international relations, I gave him the first five minutes "gratis" and then opened my window, knowing he would look up and see me from his garden below. I proceeded to heroically expose my aging weightlifter's body and, copying his brutish tone, called him an "asshole" and every other crude thing I could think of. This caught his attention. He replied by giving me "the arm," the Georgian version of "Up yours!" and by making reference to the Muslim insult of using their fingers as toilet paper. I thrust my hands through the bars on the window and pumped my fists up and down. Shocked, the abuser stepped back, trying to see me better through the fruit trees, which I did not permit. Instead, I turned to a nonexistent companion and shouted in Russian, "Get me a *bomba* (petrel bomb) and I will make that asshole into shish kabob!" With a flourish, I stuffed a paper towel into the top of my Evian bottle and made a show of lighting it in the open window with my Flamo lighter. The abuser ran into his house and slammed the door.

Twenty minutes later the police arrived, and he rushed out and pointed at my window. Moments later, there was an almost apologetic knock on my door. I answered in my blue diplomat's suit as I was now on my way to a State reception at the Parliament building. I spoke to the police in my most polished Russian and, brandishing my passport, proceeded downstairs. Hotel guests peeked through doors ajar, and with great deliberation I climbed into the back seat of a BMW driven by "my man" Mirian. Mirian showed concern, but I put a finger to my lips. Before we drove away, Mirian told the police I was the "ambassador from California" and winked at me in the rearview mirror.

Juvenile as it may seem, I take great satisfaction from moments like these. I guess it's just my style. Betsy's house staff heard about the "terrorist bomber" who frightened the abuser they hated so much, and for the rest of the visit I was treated with noticeably more respect.

Several days after "Bomba Day," I received a flat cake box. Inside was a giant two-layer chocolate torte. Squirted artistically on top was a Molotov cocktail bottle with a flaming fuse and half a dozen first-grade-style American flags, all in bright colors with a simple note saying, "Thank you, *Meester*." It was signed "Mrs. Nino Chavchavadze, your neighbor."

That was nearly a decade ago. By 2002, the shops along Rustaveli Prospect where I finally walked with Marilyn on her long-awaited trip were beginning to look like a poor-man's Rodeo Drive. My favorite potholes were conspicuous by their absence. The lawn in front of the Parliament building was being watered by sprinklers. Students carried little backpacks. The abuser was in jail for embezzlement and was missed by nobody. Most of Betsy's "originals" had moved on to other places. The technical people and the "follow-uppers" were replacing the more colorful "pioneers."

In recent years, Georgia has been in the news under less than favorable circumstances. In 2005, President Bush visited Tbilisi and spoke before a crowd of 50,000 people, even larger than when Ray Charles sang "Georgia on my Mind" a decade earlier. An unexploded grenade was found less than a hundred feet from where President Bush had been standing.

In the summer of 2008, war broke out between Georgia and Russia. The Russian Bear had never really been in hibernation, and decided to invade the Georgian province of South Ossetia from its bases in the Russian province of North Ossetia, claiming they were provoked into defending themselves by the mighty Georgian army of 6,500 troops. The invasion went so well that the Russians rolled farther south across the border into Georgia, passing through Gori—Stalin's birthplace—to within a few miles of Tbilisi.

Over a thousand died in this adventure, which also resulted in extraordinary loss of property. As is their imperial practice, the Russians decided to stay put until extreme international pressure was brought to bear. They then begrudgingly pulled most of their troops out of Georgia proper, though "checkpoints" remained and "buffer zones" were established around Abkhazia and South Ossetia.

Russia has recognized the independence of Abkhazia and South Ossetia. The rest of the UN—along with the European Union, NATO, and most of the rest of the world—recognize these regions as an integral part of Georgia. In January, 2009, Russia announced plans to build a Black Sea naval base in Sukhumi, the capital of Abkhazia. Having caused the breakaway of "independent Abkhazia" and having out-waited the protests, the Russians have virtually annexed the northwest corner of Georgia.

I wasn't surprised by these developments; it just took a while. The Russian Bear is still a Black Bear. This is how they operate their imperial game. They start a fire and arrive to put it out, then stay on without an invitation. How can it be acceptable that the 2014 winter Olympics will take place in Sochi, a stone's throw from this international outrage?

Russia notwithstanding, the spadework is done and Georgia is beginning to look like a First World rather than a Third World country. It's the young people who are making it happen—for them, communism was someone else's nightmare, not theirs. They realize that communism was a fundamentally flawed system that discouraged workers' natural proprietary interests. With no individual stake in the future of their country, the economy had been pegged in such a way that people often found it unprofitable to work, thus threatening the very foundation of social order. Sure, it will take another twenty years to evolve a reasonable infrastructure, but the young Georgians are beginning to buy into the universal truth that to succeed, they *have* to have a personal stake in the future, and that this is something that only freedom—both economic and political—can provide. Secure in this knowledge, their potential can only be limited by the power of their imagination.

The last I heard of Betsy, she was still living in Tbilisi and running an interior- and garden-design business called American Design. She was a great friend and colorful lady, a living testimonial to "hanging in there." A true female entrepreneur in a Byzantine and very chauvinistic society, Betsy succeeded in Tbilisi in spite of her inherent honesty, and made it on her own in spite of the odds. I had thought the Guest House was very risky, but she ignored the risks and made it a huge success. Betsy is a great role model for Georgians unfamiliar with free enterprise.

Gela Charkviani and I once had a good laugh over the fact that Betsy, an American, was now a successful capitalist in Tbilisi, whereas she had once been a lobbyist for a government workers' union. Recalling that his father was First Secretary of Georgia's Communist Party under Stalin, Gela pointed out to me the irony that as a little boy he used to sit on the formidable dictator's knee. Now, however, he was more concerned about whether he'd be able to play jazz on the piano at the Bohemian Club if he and Shevardnadze visited California.

On Sunday, November 23, 2003, Eduard Shevardnadze was forced to resign the presidency of Georgia. What was viewed as widespread corruption in the parliamentary elections became unacceptable to a young and largely Western-educated opposition. And so, rather than use the military to suppress the insurgency, Shevardnadze simply stepped down to a chorus of cheers from the thousands of peaceful protestors who had gathered outside the Parliament building.

I wasn't surprised by the outcome of this "revolution of flowers," because I had gotten to know the character of the Georgian people as well as their leader. In the end, Shevardnadze's charisma and brilliance could not overcome the institutional deficits caused by the Russians when they crippled the Georgian infrastructure with their sudden and near total withdrawal. Nor could the struggling Georgian economy, wracked by years of civil war and thousands of refugees, compensate for the loss of the vast Soviet marketplace. *Nobody* could have surmounted these problems or the Georgian *traditions* of patronage and nepotism, but Shevardnadze got them off to a good start. He had given them hope but, unfortunately, couldn't deliver the process.

Key Georgians met with the president, and he agreed it was time for a change. It was democracy at work, and he once joked that "It's better to be right than to be president." But isn't it interesting that the Russian foreign minister, Igor Ivanov, was there to help negotiate his resignation? The more things change, the more they stay the same.

I was with Eduard Shevardnadze during some of his darkest hours. I will always remember him telling me on his seventy-second birthday that he was "wiser" than I because he was a year older. I chuckled while reading in the newspaper that when asked by an unimaginative reporter where he would go after he resigned, he replied (with a twinkle), "I am going home to write my memoirs." Knowing him, I wouldn't be surprised if he'd added, "Maybe I'll take up golf."

Wow! How far we have come—that is, those of us capable of growing. When I can no longer go to Georgia, I will often rejoice that I was there at the beginning and able to help. Sometimes it seems as though having been involved in this Third World country with a First World culture was like participating in a Gilbert and Sullivan production!

I miss the hot summer nights on Betsy's rooftop and will always remember the thump-like explosion we heard from up there back in August 1995 as it echoed against the hills, the plume of black smoke that followed, and how everyone's eyes widened when we realized it was the Parliament building. We knew that Shevardnadze was supposed to be signing the country's first constitution that night, and we had all rushed toward the smoke. It was the second major attempt on Shevardnadze's life; he survived that night, and survived a third attempt in 1998, but I was proud to share that moment at Betsy's with my friends because, like Shevardnadze himself, we had all run "toward the fire" and not "away from the flame."

Chapter 44

Rings on a Tree
(The Power of Perspective)

OVER THE YEARS, I've given a lot of thought to how governments, cultures, families, and we as individuals evolve
over time. I covered a lot of mileage in the service of my country and inadvertently developed a perspective or overview
of things that separated me from the fly-over congressional
"experts" and the quick turnover of the State Department professionals.

It turns out that my choice of "Interperspective" (international perspective) as the name of my company was more
appropriate than I had expected. My views on where matters
stood were more often based on the continuity of the situation than any one particular incident. By checking my paper
route several times a year, over a number of years, I would notice *change*—improvement or deterioration, or lack thereof.
It was the comparisons from visit to visit that taught me the
most and for which there is no substitute. You can't measure
growth, movement, the weather, or the stock market in a few
days. Without trends, conclusions are only temporary.

I have spent much of my life living near a redwood forest
in Northern California and from an early age was impressed
by the cross-sections of fallen tree stumps with their hundreds
of rings—some wide, some narrow—with each ring reflecting

the environmental conditions of annual growth. Local nature museums displayed little colored markers denoting locations on a stump coinciding with historic events such as the signing of the Magna Carta, Columbus' voyage to America, and when gold was discovered at Sutter's Mill. I often wondered what I would hear if only those rings could talk.

Then one day while jogging (my own personal form of meditation), it came to me that cultures and people are like forests and trees. Each culture, each person, has many "rings" of different composition recording unique events during their lives. Old cultures have many rings, and newer cultures have fewer rings. China has a 5,000-year recorded history, the Near East 5,000 years, and Europe 2,500 years. However, sub-Saharan Africa has only a 200-year recorded history, and they did not have a single manufactured brick wall before 1800.

The number and composition of rings in a given culture contribute substantially to that culture's behavior, frequently more often than do logic or intellect. It is a subconscious phenomenon with very real consequences. For instance, a culture's beliefs in myths, superstitions, and religion, along with its prevailing attitudes toward such concepts as generosity, fair play and revenge, can—and often do—muddy up and confuse territorial disputes that might otherwise be fairly clear and manageable.

For forty-five years, I competed in serious sports on a local, national, and international level. After the first ten years, my body seemed to acquire a memory for what it needed to succeed, and I learned to listen to those needs and to accommodate them. Business courses taught me the importance of corporate history and institutional memory, which are merely facets of a broader business culture. I am particularly interested in the various cultures of Native Americans, or "Indians" as they used to be called. In their case, as is still the case in many parts of the world today, much of their culture and many of their traditions have been passed down from generation to generation, largely unwritten, making it easier for revisionist manipulation.

Expectations vary greatly from culture to culture and even between the sexes. In his groundbreaking book *Men Are From Mars, Women Are From Venus*, Dr. John Gray points out that men and women have different cultures and that their inability to recognize this in each other is often the source of conflict. The differences between men and women are a lot more than physical or intellectual. Sometimes a great event such as a death in a family, inheriting a fortune, or a 9/11 can instantly change outlooks and attitudes without social persuasions or influences of any kind.

My experiences in Central Asia, especially Azerbaijan, Uzbekistan, and Tajikistan, as well as in the Caucasian enclaves of Nagorno-Karabakh, Abkhazia, and Chechnya, continually demonstrated for me that the root causes of the current deadly conflicts in these places are the *same kind* of root causes for the continuous unresolved difficulties in the Balkans, Indonesia, Palestine, and Israel or, for that matter, Watts, California, Cincinnati, Ohio, and East St. Louis, Illinois. I call these root causes "root rings," and they are thorny circles that record painful events or conflicts that damaged tribal institutions or cultures in the past and which are still unresolved.

When humans suffer pain, they express themselves— "Ouch!"—and that helps to relieve the pain. However, unexpressed pain converts directly to anger and is stored away. In time, we may lose sight of the original cause of the pain which, now buried and invisible, manifests itself in random, unexplained hostility and venting, and which will continue to do so until properly expressed. The significance of this residual, subterranean force is often misunderstood, poorly defined, or just seems unrealistic and unacceptable, and, as a result, the significance becomes lost. After passing through a prism of distorted cultural memory, such root causes frequently result in violence when a contemporary incident taps into the suppressed, unexpressed anger, and, like the legendary Hatfields and McCoys, old conflicts take on a new life of their own.

Yet, no behavior need be locked in forever, and this is the great hope for the future. But first the "root rings" must be recognized, isolated and acknowledged, and there must be appropriate empathy on the part of those *outside* the afflicted culture for there to be true understanding. As my children of the sixties say, "You gotta know where they're coming from!" However, the mere identification of the "root rings," as important as it is, may not be sufficient to resolve conflict. It is only the beginning of a process. A psychoanalyst helps a patient find and relieve his pain, but it is the patient who has to confront the underlying sickness. Only then can he begin to heal. This process applies to nations as well, and understanding that culture can be both static and fluid at the same time is key.

By this time, the reader may have noticed a touch of "natural piety" in this book, an acknowledgement of—and a respect for—the existence of a natural order to all things. Maybe a touch of the mystic creeps in. So it should come as no surprise that I believe in magic. This is so because I have *seen* the work of my own "Merlins" firsthand. International relations are an art, not a science. When George Shultz, Ronald Reagan's secretary of state at the time, sang "Georgia on My Mind" to Soviet foreign minister Eduard Shevardnadze *in Russian*, the then-British prime minister Margaret Thatcher described it as the most effective act of individual statesmanship she had ever seen. Why? Because such simple acts, moments—gestures of goodwill—helped break down decades of mistrust and misunderstanding. Ronald Reagan, James Baker, and George Bush performed similar magic. These great "Merlins" had demonstrated the previously inexpressible: that they all shared a common goal—the universal need for peace—as well as the common knowledge that further conflict was unthinkable.

When Ronald Reagan called the Soviet Union the "Evil Empire" and challenged it to "Tear down this wall!" results were achieved that military force could never have accomplished—core institutional change without bloodshed! These were the Golden Rings! Truth is the ultimate power and, like it or not, even bitter opponents can be set up to recognize this fact if the right kind of magic is used. So, finding the true "root ring" causes—the trouble rings in the evolution of a culture—and making adversaries aware of the real causes of disputes is essential. Sometimes it seems impossible. But I have watched a number of very successful people in action. It can be done. The truly great ones deal in the world of *truth*. They deal with the causes of problems more than the effects. They recognize that most issues are usually the symptoms of sickness and not the sickness itself. The cultural key is recognized, acknowledged, and dealt with.

They say "It takes one to know one." The ultimate magic is that honest men recognize this quality in each other and that, acting in good faith, they can do magical business without any tricks.

Epilogue

THROUGHOUT THIS COUNTRY'S HISTORY, when military engagements were over, the participants would go home to public recognition of their achievements and national gratitude for their sacrifices. The big exception, of course, was the Vietnam War. But even Vietnam veterans have their "wall of honor" nobly situated on the Washington Mall and, for the most part, they have finally been accepted back into society. Intelligence people generally receive no recognition at all or are treated with disdain approaching that received by the returning Vietnam veterans. There *is* no public wall of honor for intelligence people, just a small memorial inside a windowless building in Langley, Virginia. Intelligence people are forever hidden behind a "wall of secrecy." It's tough work with little thanks, and yet I kept doing it.

At first, my trips were sporadic and I only traveled when duty called. But then my obsessive-compulsive tendencies got the best of me and I became addicted to the game. I needed to go, like it or not. Some used to say about my forty-five years of playing rugby after college that I was a perennial sophomore, that I would never grow up. Well, as a matter of fact, I grew up real early! I just couldn't show my growing pains until very recently.

In the fall of 2007, Marilyn and I took a nine-day cruise, weaving through hundreds of low-lying barrier islands along the Atlantic coast from Charleston, South Carolina, to Jacksonville, Florida. The trip was a Christmas gift from our five adult children.

The weather was ideally cool, clear, and dry. We enjoyed seeing the history of a world we had only read about: the unique Southern architecture, strange trees dripping beards of Spanish moss, Fort Sumter, and the Citadel. Best of all was the courtesy of the South, where strangers greeted us with "Sir" and "Ma'am" and "Where y'all from?"

It so happened that Veterans Day occurred on our sixth day out. After dinner that night, a celebration of remembrance was held in the upper-deck lounge. Popcorn and root-beer floats were served as Lori, our tour guide, gave an interesting, twenty-minute history of the U.S. Coast Guard along the southeast coast. At the conclusion, the forty-year-old Lori asked if there were any veterans in the crowd of mostly senior citizens. To her surprise and the amusement of everyone in the lounge, virtually all the men and several of the women stood up. You would never have guessed by looking at these folks that they were once our nation's protectors. My wife nudged me hard, several times, and gestured that I should stand. She whispered, "You're as qualified a veteran as these guys are." So, reluctantly, I rose and joined the others.

At Lori's suggestion, the standees stated the war they participated in, the branch of service, some of the battles they were in, and the ships they were on. WWII, Korea, and Vietnam were represented most; a woman from Desert Storm even spoke. I felt anxious as the standees delivered their often dramatic comments, greeted by respectful "oohs" and "ahs" and appreciative laughter. My years of service to my country had been essentially secret, even to my family. I wasn't used to talking about it in public.

Even after my epiphany at the Bohemian Club, I'd never considered myself to be part of the military, though I'd often worked closely with them and had been told that my final equivalent rank was a GS-15 or bird colonel. As I stood among the veterans, I recalled journalist P.J. O'Rourke's reaction to the demolition of the Berlin Wall. "It really was a war, wasn't it?" Yes, the Cold War *was* a war, and it was *my* war.

It had been a lonely war for me but, on this Veterans Day, I finally accepted that my twenty-five years of service truly qualified me as a veteran, and I could say so to the world. In a single moment, the questioning, silent whisper of my inner voice of self-doubt and guilt finally went silent. It was an immediate and unconditional release.

Heads turned my way as I said, "My name is Jim Waste. I was a covert intelligence officer for the CIA in the former Soviet Union and in Central Asia. I made thirty-five trips to my mission area during and after the Cold War. That was, and still is, my war—the Cold War."

I suddenly felt loose, light, and warm, a sort of orgasmic release. Marilyn took my hand as I started to sit down. Something was finally over and she knew it. Then, my otherwise soft-spoken wife said in a loud voice, "He was a spy!"

For the last few days of our voyage, I noticed (not imagined) gentle smiles, subtle head nods, and half winks from my peers. It was all I needed.

I have learned that if you have core values and good character, you can win consistently. I've known a lot of winners and treasure their acceptance of me. I feel good about what I've done, but I'm *not* quitting yet. There's a world of things I still can do. Baker and Shultz are still going, as is Shevardnadze. So I have my role models. There are still great games going on out there, and I might yet "die with my boots on" rather than playing dominoes at the Bohemian Club.

I've made sure to tell everyone I've had a great life and that I love them. But after being bitten by a suspected rabid dog on the right butt cheek, I realized that I was mortal and have accepted that fact. I also realize that I may have become somewhat limited by this new knowledge of my own mortality and that I will have to make allowances for this new weakness.

The reality is that you may have to play a perfect game to stay alive in the intelligence business, and at my age I worry when I forget the odd detail once in a while like someone's license plate number or a word in Russian. I no longer enjoy jumping off anything higher than four feet, but I still get in my three miles of running each day and work out with weights three times a week. I still know what it takes to do the job.

Few native-born Americans appreciate the U.S. Constitution and the freedoms we have as much as I do. I've been to the "other side" and feel lucky to have this perspective. When I cross the Golden Gate Bridge, and follow 19th Avenue through Golden Gate Park, I always marvel at the beauty of this place I call home.

Twice on the trip to the airport, I pass by military cemeteries with their flags flying forever at half mast and thousands of tablets gleaming white in the afternoon light. They had done their best. I'm still trying.

Author's Note

I WOULD LIKE TO THANK the many friends who helped me in big and little ways to write this memoir. Louis Jefferson and "Captain" Jack Ringwalt, my close associates in Interperspective Corporation, were key to encouraging me to record for posterity my deeds and perspectives. Sadly, both are no longer with us. Lou was close to my age and served in the U.S. Army in World War II. His book *The John Foster Dulles Book of Humor* (St. Martin's Press) describes his encounters with Eisenhower, Nixon, Nikita Khrushchev, and many other dignitaries of the time while serving as Dulles' security officer.

For most of this memoir I had no notes at all. I didn't keep them for obvious reasons. I made a number of tapes on my return from trips after 1991, and I started carefully taking pictures, also after 1991. The pictures were helpful to Lou and Jack. Lou, more than anyone, encouraged me to get my story on the page—in ballpoint pen. He then worked hard to read my scrawlings, transcribing them into the rough manuscript. I am forever indebted to him for his friendship, inspiration and overview, and professional journalistic talents. Because of Lou, I leave this legacy.

"Captain" Jack Ringwalt is a different story, a surrogate son in many ways. Early on I realized that he was one of the very few people I could fully trust. It was my hope that Jack could one day accompany me on one of my missions, but health issues made that impossible for him. Like Lou, Jack thought my activities were interesting and entertaining and encouraged me to write them down. Between the two of them, I just thought I had a captive audience.

Jack grew up in Omaha, coincidentally where my mother was born. He married Janice Yen, whose father, Hai-chiu Yen, was personal secretary to Chiang Chin-kuo, the son of Chiang Kai-shek and successor to his father as president of Taiwan. Jack and Janice's daughter Denise ("DeeDee") is now nine years old.

When, after several years of writing the book, the project slowed due to the mass of material, computer failures, and battle fatigue by Lou and me, Jack came off the bench and revitalized the project. The fourth quarter as well as the overtime is all Jack. He proved to be not only a good editor on details and organization, but perceptive as to the song I was trying to sing. He could hear my voice—a voice that I was not always aware of along the way. I had read some letters and articles he had written and was impressed. Jack had a lot of talents and one we discovered was that he was a writer—a good one. I enjoyed working with him as a partner in the final stages. His dedication and loyalty were surpassed only by his tremendous courage as he fought his own battle with advanced pancreatic cancer. Unfortunately, Jack lost his battle in July of 2006 at the age of fifty-one, and his legacy surely must include that he edited the entire final manuscript of this book during the final months of his life. His commitment to finish the job was humbling.

I especially want to thank my wife, Marilyn, and my five children for allowing me the freedom to do my thing, to find my way, to follow my destiny. Had they known the dangers involved, I might have been prevailed upon to find another way to go. Ironically, had *I* foreseen the dangers involved, I might have chosen some other way.

Many, many thanks to those who read the early pages in development and for their thoughtful comments, which were very important to this neophyte writer. I particularly want to thank my sons, Dr. Stephen Waste, Corby Waste, and Jamie Waste, and my daughters, Shawn Hacker and Tenby Wright. I am also indebted (in alphabetical order) to James Baker, Maria Barlet, George Bazgadze, Patrick Brady, Kent Brown, Victoria Brucher-Hutchison, Gela Charkviani, Chuck Clemmons, William Courtney, Nancy Ann Coyne, Paul Davies, Chris DiGuigine, Joe Dwyer, Clint Eastwood, Steve Erlanger, Ward Flad, James Garrison, Rusudan Gorgiladze, Bobby Hacker, Betsy Haskell, Warren Heiman, Gerald Hill, Herbert Hoover III, Harold Hyde, William Isacoff, Bill Jaeger, Steve Johnson, Uri Karasnakov, Michael Kelley, Alexander Khaindrava, Gordon Knapp, Stuart Kuhn, Pekka Liemola, Gerry Marmion, Merle McQueen, Bob Medearis, Ned Meister, Mirian Meskhi, Tammy Mirabella, Abdurahim Muhidov, Stanley Music Harry Neuwirth, Pat Newsom, Charles Palm, Richard Pohle, Constantine Rizhinashvili, Alexander Rondeli, Sergei Rosonovski, Rush Sands, Raymond Donald Schmitz, Bob Setrakian, Janet Shields, George Shultz, Harry Scott, Maya Sharashidze, Janis Shelhorn, Pat Skees, Rod Stark, George Vukasin, Austin Walsh, Bill Wan, David Ward, Bill Waste, Catherine "Trinkie" Watson, Eric Wente, Kelly Wright, Mike Yancey, and Bob Yates, as well as the Bechtel Corporation, the Reagan Library, the staff at Betsy's Guest House, the members of my BATS rugby teams, and many more at home and abroad.

Special thanks to Dr. Eleanor Siperstein and her daughter, Dr. Laurie Siperstein-Cook, who helped translate my cryptic faxes into something readable for Jack to work with. In addition, their research skills proved invaluable.

Many thanks to Alice B. Acheson, whom I met at Book Passage in Corte Madera, for her encouragement and marketing suggestions, and especially for hooking me up with manuscript consultant Lydia Bird. Addressing Lydia's insightful questions, comments, and criticisms enabled us to produce the final manuscript. I was also impressed to learn that Lydia was an adventurer, having covered some 40,000 ocean miles, including a singlehanded passage from the U.S. to Greece on a 42-foot sailboat. Plus she had visited Georgia at the same time I was working there, while living in Bulgaria with her husband, a State Department reporting officer. She understood my mission—"Takes one to know one."

I also want to thank Tom and Sarah Fugate—my new friends and neighbors near my High Sierra home—whose assistance in jump-starting the final production of *Don't Shoot* assured my getting across the finish line after things had bogged down. Appreciation as well to graphic designer Daphne Phillips, who did a great job on maps and photographs in long-distance teamwork with Lydia and Tom, and to book designer Anton Khodakovsky, who created *Don't Shoot's* striking cover from as far away as Moscow.

Lastly, my thanks to Jean Headley Darmody ("Clean Jean the Typing Queen" of Headley Office Services) for her expertise in typing, computerizing, proofreading, and polishing the final manuscript with Jack Ringwalt. Her contribution to the successful completion of this project can hardly be overstated.

Thank you *all* for your time and support.

I spend very little time in D.C. or in offices. I'm not a Beltway boy or politician. I'm a citizen soldier, a foot soldier, a reporter of events—my events—and I have written almost purely from memory. There is no spin intended in these pages. The truth is easy to write about. It's easy to remember and, for the most part, comfortable to review.

This book does not include any classified or secret material. The manuscript was reviewed by the CIA; that review does not constitute CIA authentication of information, nor does it imply CIA endorsement of my views. Some dates are approximate. Some names, places, and organizations have been changed to protect those involved. The various corporations and institutions I worked with—including the Hoover Institution, Kaiser Permanente, Bechtel Corporation, the Bohemian Club, and the Georgian Foundation—are in no way involved in the intelligence business, unlike Interperspective Corporation.

As I stumble and wander through the chapters of this book, not heroically but intuitively playing it by ear, I notice my naiveté was one of my strengths. I didn't know that I couldn't or shouldn't do something. Often I literally didn't know what to be afraid of. I wonder now why I got in so deep, but it doesn't matter any more. I made it and I have no regrets. Would I do it again? Yes, but next time I could do it better.

JAMES WASTE was born in Berkeley, California, a third-generation Californian. He played football and rugby at UC Berkeley, graduating with a degree in business administration.

During his twenty-year career with the Bechtel Corporation, Waste worked as a field construction engineer and project manager on major power plants, refineries, and pipelines in the United States and abroad. Later, while pursuing a more leisurely livelihood as a dealer in high-end antiques, he was recruited by the CIA to help evaluate the physical collapse of the Soviet infrastructure, which led to three decades as a covert operative in a fast-changing world.

James Waste and his wife Marilyn raised five children, and live in California's Sierra Nevada mountains.

Made in the USA
Lexington, KY
05 February 2010